SOCIAL ECONOMY OF DEVELOPMENT IN

India

Thank you for choosing a SAGE product!
If you have any comment, observation or feedback,
I would like to personally hear from you.
Please write to me at **contactceo@sagepub.in**

Vivek Mehra, Managing Director and CEO, SAGE India.

Bulk Sales

SAGE India offers special discounts
for purchase of books in bulk.
We also make available special imprints
and excerpts from our books on demand.

For orders and enquiries, write to us at

Marketing Department
SAGE Publications India Pvt Ltd
B1/I-1, Mohan Cooperative Industrial Area
Mathura Road, Post Bag 7
New Delhi 110044, India

E-mail us at **marketing@sagepub.in**

Get to know more about SAGE

Be invited to SAGE events, get on our mailing list.
Write today to **marketing@sagepub.in**

This book is also available as an e-book.

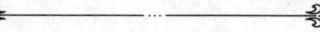

SOCIAL ECONOMY
OF DEVELOPMENT IN
India

K. S. CHALAM

Los Angeles | London | New Delhi
Singapore | Washington DC | Melbourne

Copyright © K.S. Chalam, 2017

First published in 2017 by

SAGE Publications India Pvt Ltd
B1/I-1 Mohan Cooperative Industrial Area
Mathura Road, New Delhi 110 044, India
www.sagepub.in

SAGE Publications Inc
2455 Teller Road
Thousand Oaks, California 91320, USA

SAGE Publications Ltd
1 Oliver's Yard, 55 City Road
London EC1Y 1SP, United Kingdom

SAGE Publications Asia-Pacific Pte Ltd
3 Church Street
#10-04 Samsung Hub
Singapore 049483

Published by Vivek Mehra for SAGE Publications India Pvt Ltd, typeset in 10.5/13 pt Palatino by Zaza Eunice, Hosur, Tamil Nadu, India and printed at Chaman Enterprises, New Delhi.

Library of Congress Cataloging-in-Publication Data

Name: Chalam, K. S., author.
Title: Social economy of development in India / K. S. Chalam.
Description: Thousand Oaks, California : SAGE, [2016] | Includes
  bibliographical references and index.
Identifiers: LCCN 2016026480 | ISBN 9789385985119 (hardback : alk. paper)
Subjects: LCSH: Economic development—Social aspects—India. | Welfare
  economics—India. | India—Social conditions. | India—Economic conditions.
Classification: LCC HC435.3 .C54 2016 | DDC 338.954—dc23 LC record
available at https://lccn.loc.gov/2016026480

ISBN: 978-93-859-8511-9 (HB)

SAGE Team: Supriya Das and Alekha Chandra Jena

Contents

List of Tables

List of Abbreviations

ACB	Anti-Corruption Bureau
ACR	Annual Confidential Record
AICTE	All India Council of Technical Education
AP	Andhra Pradesh
ASCE	American Society of Civil Engineers
AYUSH	Ayurveda, Yoga and Naturopathy, Unani, Siddha and Homeopathy
BALCO	Bharat Aluminium Company
BCCI	Board of Control for Cricket in India
BIFR	Board of Industrial and Financial Reconstruction
BJP	Bharatiya Janata Party
BOP	Balance of Payments
BPL	Below Poverty Line
BPO	Business Process Outsourcing
BSP	Bahujan Samaj Party
CACP	Commission for Agricultural Costs and Prices
CAD	Capital Account Deficit
CAG	Comptroller and Auditor General
CBI	Central Bureau of Investigation
CDI	Caste-related Development Index
CID	Caste-based Index of Discrimination
CII	Confederation of Indian Industry
CMOP	Caste Mode of Production
CPC	Communist Party of China
CPI	Corruption Perception Index
CRBI	Crime Records Bureau of India
CSDS	Centre for the Study of Developing Societies
CSIR	Council for Scientific and Industrial Research

CSO	Central Statistical Office
CSR	Corporate Social Responsibility
CUD	Cow Urine Distillate
CVC	Central Vigilance Commission
DMK	Dravida Munnetra Kazhagam
DRDO	Defense Research and Development Organisation
DST	Department of Science and Technology
ED	Enforcement Directorate
EU	European Union
EVR	Erode Venkata Ramasamy
FA	Faculty of Arts Intermediate
FAO	Food and Agriculture Organization
FAPSIA	Federation of Andhra Pradesh Small Industries Association
FAR	Floor Area Ratio
FDI	Foreign Direct Investment
FEMA	Foreign Exchange Management Act
FICCI	Federation of Indian Chamber of Commerce and Industry
FII	Federation of Indian Industry
GAIL	Gas Authority of India Limited
GATS	General Agreement on Trade in Services
GCF	Gross Capital Formation
GCFA	Gross Capital Formation in Agriculture
GDP	Gross Domestic Product
GEM	Gender Empowerment Measure
GM	Genetically Modified
GMR	Grandhi Mohan Rao
GNH	Gross National Happiness
GSDP	Gross State Domestic Product
GVK	Gunupati Venkata Krishna Reddy
HCA	Historic Cost Accounting
HCU	Hyderabad Central University
HDI	Human Development Index
HPI	Human Poverty Index
HRD	Human Resource Development
HYV	High Yielding Variety

IAS	Indian Administrative Service
ICAR	Indian Council of Agricultural Research
ICMR	Indian Council of Medical Research
ICRISAT	International Crop Research Institute for Semi-Arid Tropics
ICS	Indian Civil Service
ICSSR	Indian Council of Social Science Research
ICT	Information and Communication Technology
IIM	Indian Institute of Management
IIT	Indian Institute of Technology
ILO	International Labour Organisation
IMF	International Monetary Fund
IOC	Indian Oil Corporation
IPCC	Intergovernmental Panel on Climate Change
IPKF	Indian Peace Keeping Force
IPL	Indian Premier League
IPR	Intellectual Property Right
IPS	Indian Police Service
IR8	A semi dwarf rice variety of Indian Rice Research Institute
IRRI	Indian Rice Research Institute
IT	Information Technology
JNU	Jawaharlal Nehru University
KCR	Kalvakunta Chandra Sekhar Rao
KVS	Kendriya Vidyalaya Sanghatan
LDC	Least Developed Countries
LIDCAP	Leather Industry Development Corporation
LPG	Liberalisation, Privatisation and Globalisation
MCCs	Multi-Caste Corporations
MCI	Medical Council of India
MCP	Male Chauvinist Pig
MDG	Millennium Development Goal
MFN	Most Favored Nation
MIT	Massachusetts Institute of Technology
MNC	Multi-National Corporation
MOP	Market-Oriented Party
MOU	Memorandum of Understanding

MP	Member of Parliament
MSME	Micro, Small and Medium Enterprise
MSP	Minimum Support Price
MTF	Modified Therapeutic Food
NA	Native American
NAC	National Accreditation Council
NCTC	National Counter Terrorism Centre
ND	New Democracy
NDA	National Democratic Alliance
NEET	National Eligibility and Entrance Test
NFHS	National Family Health Survey
NFSB	National Food Security Bill
NGO	Non-Government Organisation
NIN	National Institute of Nutrition
NREGP	National Rural Employment Guarantee Programme
NRF	National Renewal Fund
NSP	Net Selling Price
NSS	National Sample Survey
NSSO	National Sample Survey Organisation
NTR	Nandamuri Taraka Rama Rao
OAE	Own Account Enterprises
OBC	Other Backward Classes
OECD	Organisation for Economic Cooperation and Development
OTC	Over the Counter
PCR	Protection of Civil Rights
PDSVA	Petróleos de Venezuela, S.A. (Petroleum of Venezuela)
PF	Provident Fund
PG	Postgraduate
PGMIER	Post Graduate Institute of Medical Education and Research
PHC	Physically Handicapped
PI	Public Intellectual
PIL	Public Interest Litigation
PM	Prime Minister

PMK	Pattali Makkal Katchi
PMO	Prime Minister Office
PMRY	Prime Minister Rozgar Yojana
PPO	Political Process Outsourcing
PPP	Public Private Partnership
PRSP	Poverty Reduction Strategy Paper
PSE	Public Sector Enterprise
PUCL	People's Union for Civil Liberties
PUSA	PL 480 of United States of America
QCC	Quality Control Circles
RBI	Reserve Bank of India
R&D	Research and Development
RDA	Recommended Dietary Allowance
RPI	Republican Part of India
RTE	Right to Education
RTF	Right to Food
RTI	Right to Information
RUSA	Rashtriya Uchchatar Shiksha Yojana
SARC	South Asia Regional Cooperation
SC	Scheduled Caste
SDG	Special Drawing Rights
SDP	State Domestic Product
SEBI	Securities and Exchange Board of India
SEZ	Special Economic Zone
SIR	Special Investment Regions
SK	Safai Karmachari
SOP	Sales-Oriented Party
SP	Samajwadi Party
SRSP	Social Responsibility Support Programme
ST	Scheduled Tribe
TBP	Tungabhadra Project Board
TI	Transparency International
TINA	There Is No Alternative
TNCs	Trans-National Corporations
TQM	Total Quality Management
TSP	Tribal Sub-Plan
UBS	Union Bank of Switzerland

UDHR   Universal Declaration of Human Rights
UGC   University Grant Commission
UNCTAD   United Nations Conference on Trade and
            Development
UNDP   United Nations Development Programme
UNICEF   United Nations Children's Emergency Fund
UPSC   Union Public Service Commission
USAID   United States Agency for International
            Development
VIP   Very Important Person
VSL   Value of Statistical Life
VSNL   Videsh Sanchar Nigam Limited
VSP   Visakhapatnam Steel Plant
YSR   Yuvajana Shramika Rythu
WTO   World Trade Organization

Preface

The social economy expounded by pre-Marxian scholar J. C. L. Simonde de Sismondi, developed by Tawney, Hobson, Schumacher and others, is currently being pursued to understand the harsh realities of neocolonialism and its consequences. The echoes of some of the issues, scrutinised by the subject, have found their resonance in welfare economics. Social economics was concerned about the abuse of labour, of competition on the excess of production, etc., as it affirmed its disbelief in laissez-faire. The ideas of social economists have found their way in the discussions of scholars who are humanistic in their approach to development, as against those whose ideas are responsible for the devastation and degradation of ecology and human values.

I had an opportunity to teach history of economic thought to a few batches of PG students in the Department of Economics, Andhra University. I developed love for the subject and used to discuss topics from the standard textbooks of Charles Gide and Charles Rist, Alexander Grey, Joseph Schumpeter and so on, but the topic on Sismondi was kept for the final session of the academic year. Though we used to teach Adam Smith, David Ricardo and Karl Marx for months together, the topics related to non-English thinkers were given unenthusiastic treatment. The writings of J. C. L. Simonde de Sismondi (father figure of social economics), Saint-Simon along with Lord Lauderdale and several other thinkers were lumped together as bourgeois socialists. When we look back on the subject now, it appears to me that the ideas of these thinkers deserved more reflection to appreciate the typical problems of India. It is under this background I chanced to read articles on social economics in professional journals and came across Mark A. Lutz publications on the subject. I was convinced of the need for resurrection of the framework of subject in the context of unique conditions of India.

My books *Readings in Political Economy* and *Economic Reforms and Social Exclusion* have received good response from students and scholars, but I found something missing to appreciate the social institutions in India. Keeping the current discourse on socio-economic concerns within the modified agenda of the state, I have started expressing my ideas through articles, lectures, etc., at different forums. The response was very encouraging and some friends suggested that I bring out a book on the subject. Thus, it is a half-done response to the demand, though I have plans to produce a serious study based on my experiences and academic reflection. I am still of the view that, given the resources, the work(s) is my long-cherished dream. This is only a preliminary upshot brought out with an idea to get feedback from readers on the issues involved. The book is planned to address the socio-economic issues that are generally relegated as super structure disputes with a bearing on the base. There seems to be no appreciation of the dichotomies involved and their intensification under liberalisation, if an honest attempt is not made to resolve them. These are typical conditions evolved over a period based on the geography, history and culture of the subcontinent that need not be a replica of the West or some other region.

I have selected some writings of my columns for the present work from *The Hans India*, English daily, *Janata*, *Mainstream* and *South India Journal of Social Sciences*, and some material that I presented as addresses at different seminars and conferences. The material is reorganised for the book. I am grateful to Ramachandra Murthy, Tankasala Ashok, Laxmaiah of *The Hans India*, G. G. Parikh of *Janata*, Sumit Chakravarty of *Mainstream*, Ravela Somayya, Amar Singh, D. Raja, Rahgavachari, Madhava Rao, Chandu, Chinna Rao, Rekha Saraswat, our colleagues and a host of readers who have been encouraging me to travel in the direction of my preferred path. I have extensively drawn examples from Andhra Pradesh due to my field experience with this state. I know the strengths and weaknesses of some of my notions and the enormous intellectual inputs necessary to convince people on a subject of this nature. Yet, I feel that it should be placed before the public in whatever way it is possible so that others can perfect it further, as age is an important factor in such an initiative. I express my appreciation and gratitude to the Editorial team of SAGE Publications for meticulously going through my manuscript and suggesting improvements. I am grateful to everyone who has given me their time and energy, particularly my family members, in the completion of this book. I am not associated with any organisation on a regular basis and, therefore, the views do not reflect either my present institution or the institutions where I worked in the past.

—**K. S. Chalam**

Vicharena nasti kim chid ahetutah
(Nothing happens without cause and reason)
—**A Buddhist adage**

1
Introduction

Social economy, as a study of the dynamics of socio-economic parameters in a traditionally fragmented society, is re-emerging in the context of globalisation. It is discrete to the study of civil society or third-sector activities in advanced countries as expressed by some perverse scholars. It is much wider in its scope and content and is distinctively appropriate as an approach to study a country like India. Economists are under the impression that the subject, namely the third sector, is concerned with issues that are not within the domain of the market and social scientists consider it as an interdisciplinary area. However, the third sector has never been autonomous, but rather has become an adjunct of the dominant market players, who in some countries have been alleged of using it to sidetrack the radical crusade against the ugly designs of corporate capitalism. Like the selling costs of a firm that drive customers towards its brand, some civil society activities in several countries are suspected of being used by market players with a hidden economic agenda. Some transactions of the third sector can no doubt be examined like any other firm or organisation and subjected to critical scrutiny. Nevertheless, by no means can it be equated with a subject matter that is much broader and sublime in its outlook and insight suitable to any study of Third World economies (that are also ex-colonies of the West). The newly independent economies along with the recently liberated societies are said to be enjoying the freedom to pursue their own policies appropriate to their conditions. The intrusion of neocolonial powers in the garb of aid and advice through the so-called third sector makes the recipients dependent. In fact, India has refused to get aid from some countries on the plea that the amount given is so small and its propaganda so great.

Scholars of social economy look to India for the kind of inspiration that Gandhi,[1] Schumacher[2] and others have provided as a continuation of the traditions of Sismondi,[3] Tawney,[4] Hobson[5] and Marx.[6] The two-hundred-year-old legacy of the subject is found to be getting marginalised under the weight of neoclassical and certain radical theories. Some of the issues pursued by scholars of the social economy have found their echo in welfare economics. But it does not explain the creation of surplus value as exploitation of labour discussed by Sismondi, the father figure of the subject. In fact, classical economists such as Ricardo,[7] Malthus[8] and James Mill,[9] who were contemporaries of Sismondi, opposed humanitarian relief because of their understanding that welfare measures for the poor led to an increase in the population. Such an approach is quite different from that of the Catholic faith and Pope Leo XIII's solution to the conflict between labour and capital. The social economics of Sismondi and his followers was concerned about the abuse of labour, of competition, on the excess of production. The underconsumption theories of Sismondi have helped in identifying sectors with overproduction and business cycles that the world economy has encountered in the past and are now being experienced everywhere. Social economists have no faith in laissez-faire and strongly support the State being responsible for making policies to maintain public works, welfare and social order in society. Interestingly, the ideas of social economists have found their way into the discussions of scholars who are humanistic in their approach to development, as against those whose ideas are responsible for the devastation and degradation of ecology and human values.

The nature of social economics includes the idea of common goods and a social dimension of economic analysis with a limited role for the market. Sismondi considered economics as the management of the national fortune for the happiness of all as against economics defined as the science of wealth. The discipline has endured several upheavals in order to address the needs of the people and is undergoing further transformations to concede emerging concerns in the 21st century like rights as entitlements. The scope is widening.

Mainstream economics has helped in solving the problems of poverty, inequality, wants and diseases under certain assumptions of a class society. Indian economists including B. R. Ambedkar,[10] Ram Manohar Lohia[11] and a few others have used such concepts and found that a caste-based economy and society needs something more than what is given in the textbooks to comprehensively address the issues. Both Lohia and Ambedkar, and to some extent Jawaharlal Nehru,[12] thought that socialism would address some of the peculiarities of India either before or after independence. Ambedkar, trained in the USA, and Lohia, educated in Germany in the discipline of economics, were disillusioned with the progress achieved after independence. They found that a majority of the socially deprived and economically marginalised castes have remained without any change in their living conditions. They have pursued different strategies to achieve their goals. It is not out of place to note that Schumacher, influenced by Gandhian ideas, was a close acquaintance of Lohia in Germany. Interestingly, no one seems to have evaluated these scholars who have substantially contributed to social economics in India. At the same time, mainstream economists have failed to address the typical problems of caste. Some ideologues recognised the problem and equated it with class. However, it has not enhanced our understanding of the social economy of castes, leave alone untouchability and discrimination. Amartya Sen,[13,14] Jagadish Bhagwati,[15] Pranab Bardhan[16] and Akerlof[17] looked at caste as a social institution within a market paradigm. They analysed caste as a social institution but did not develop any specific model to address the core issue of discrimination and human dignity associated with it. Jawaharlal Nehru considered the economic fragment of equality and introduced socialist measures that in due course benefitted the entrenched castes. Further, India has discrete categories such as Adivasis (tribals), minorities and artisan castes that have remained outside development models.

The Constitution of India under Article 15(4) speaks about the "socially and educationally backward classes of citizens and the scheduled castes and scheduled tribes."[18] Though constitutional and statutory commissions have been appointed to study and make recommendations for the amelioration of the socially deprived, the judiciary, particularly a section of the elite and their allies, scuttled the attempts with an alibi of equality before the law.

There are scholarly studies on caste and other social institutions of India, mostly undertaken by Western social anthropologists in the beginning, some of them later became Indologists followed by Indian scholars.[19] Several scholars like Berraman have conceptualised caste as institutional inequality.[20] There are practically hundreds of studies available on the Indian caste system that would make any attempt to present a summary seem trivial. Yet, the general approach of many of them is almost the same: purity and pollution ideas of the Brahmins on the one extreme and untouchables on the other, as representatives of the binary, as if there are no other castes in between. The fact of the matter is that caste as an institution varies from region to region and its spread is sporadic over a period of time. Even the recent scientific discoveries on the genetic origin of caste are reduced to a discourse on upper castes and lower castes.[21]

The mid-term appraisal of the Tenth Five-year Plan and the preamble of 'inclusive growth' to the Eleventh and Twelfth Plans is a testimony of the existence of divides and despairs in India even after 60 years of independence. The iniquitous nature is predominantly prevalent among certain castes and groups, well recorded in government document, thereby bringing out the need to adopt a different approach to understand and evaluate the unique social system in India.

The survival of caste as a sub-system or as an autonomous structure of exploitation supported by its own base even after globalisation is a riddle that needs to be addressed by scholars. The market has not provided any answers to this problem and is alleged to have been a conduit for strengthening the already existing social inequalities in India. The property rights constructed and justified through legal processes and with the help of neoclassical theories did not look at the traditions that constrained (restricted) property ownership to certain castes. In fact, the traditions have facilitated certain dominant groups to reinforce social networks at the international level to emerge as global players. In order to facade the sinister design, some actors of the third sector are encouraged under the market paradigm to show that all-is-well-that-ends-well with the socially marginalised groups. However, empirical data has exposed the ruse of this model.

Several dichotomies are present in the Indian socio-economic situation that seems to have failed to explain the existing inequities in development. The approach of obtaining knowledge through sense experience in the European context seems to be inadequate for getting a better knowledge about social phenomena. Does there exist any alternative to advancing our understanding of the social being who is subjected to the tyranny of social discrimination that restricts his/her freedom? Do the narratives and the discursive explanations of individual victims describe the reality in India? Is the approach of social economics appropriate to study Indian conditions? How does the family as a strong institution reinforce or debilitate the existing situation?

We try to address some of these questions in the following chapters.

CIRCULATION OF FAMILIES UNDER CAPITALIST PATRONAGE

Certain traditional practices do tend to surface even in modern social relations because of their being quite strongly internalised by people. The family as an institution is one of the strongest foundations of Indian society and is seen to be re-emerging in some of our contemporary socio-economic and political organisations. Though we lament the younger generation's disregard to family norms and values due to their exposure to the Western ways of thinking and practices, it survives in other forms. For instance, most marriage advertisements and innovative business practices introduced by the media clearly show that most youngsters oblige family stances on caste. The family is the strong base upon which the caste or ethnic or *gotra* superstructure appears to have been built. Even those who wear an ultra-modern attitude on their sleeves, verify sub-castes before dating a colleague in IT hubs. The media is full of allegations and counter-allegations of political families opposing one another in public domain and united in private affairs.

The definition of the Hindu undivided family adopted by the Income Tax Department (India) for purposes of property, income, etc., is referred to as coparceners to fix up the legal share in a complicated description. The common understanding of a family as a group of parents and children living together can be taken as a working definition since the meaning keeps on changing with the prevalent culture, era and other considerations. It is alleged that individuals and their families that attend to a dominant leader should come under the notion of a family for political patronage (after the recent political nominations of RTI commissioners in Andhra Pradesh). However, we must recognise that the Hindu or the Indian character is based on the advisory of the founding fathers of the varna system. We are of the view that a structure (paradigm) that was designed for a group of small settlers has outlived its purpose due to its user-friendly dynamism. It appears to have been designed for and by the *saptarishis* (seven sages). The Indian family is somehow linked to the traditions of the saptarishis. Even if the dominant *shudras* and some non-*kshatriyas* became rulers, they were later linked to the saptarishis through their gotras, a bygone purported practice of the *dvija* clan(s). It is also mentioned by the law-givers that such practices shall keep on changing in different *yugas* (ages). Therefore, the original seven rishis—Vasista, Bhardwaja, Jama dagni, Gautama, Atri, Viswamitra and Agatsya—form the routes of the family trees which everyone, including the Hindu *Dalits* and *shudras*, is supposed to follow in their rituals even today. Therefore, the number conferred with this status seems to have increased several folds with the availability of modern gadgets such as computers, the Internet, etc. One can find one's own gotra on the internet, thanks to the Hindu social net.[22]

The public relations exercise done by Western experts for Narendra Modi (ex-CM of Gujarat during his campaign for the prime minister election) brought out a pioneering clue that the British crown has its roots in Gujarat to give a fillip to his stature as a prime ministerial candidate. In fact, the West is now looking for its roots in India due to the enormous hard work done by our IT professionals as part of their leisure time activity (social networks) under the guidance of their shrewd elders. Is it a new consciousness? No. It began during the rule of the East India Company, when William Jones, looking at the Bengal *bhadralok*, declared at the Asiatic Society lecture (1783) that they were all his long lost kin and blood relations in terms of language, colour and other parameters (see Trautman T. R.).[23] Therefore, there has always been a family link between the West and the East. Strangely, it is the native Indians who have been forced to continually change their faith and masters, losing their roots and history. However, some intellectuals are also trying to build their links with the West through language and religion and the emerging Dalit capitalists are embracing the West if they have not already converted to their faith under the same scheme. This is a very interesting dimension of 21st century global capitalism.[24]

Thus, family bonds and their preservation are some of the pious duties of every Indian irrespective of his/her faith in any organised religion due to the traditions of the country where he/she belongs. As members of a traditional society, Indians value the family. It is also not difficult to maintain it, unlike the

West where the family is an aggregate irrespective of social class (either Malinowski or Morgan–Engels). The Indian family is the basic unit for caste solidarity with ritual sanctions and family antiquity in terms of the gotra. However, there is only a small, about 5–10 per cent of the population, which is offered this facility. Therefore, it has never created problems and people are seen lavishly sporting family names/titles after their proper names to indicate their ancestry (only for illustration and not with any ill will, George Fernandez, Christ Reddy, Mastan Choudary, etc.). Some of them have emerged as big players with business empires perhaps capitalising on this advantage.

The family name as a status symbol has not been widely used by certain Dalit castes particularly in the recent phenomenon of Pydi, Jangam, Mala, Madiga, etc. upsurge in Andhra Pradesh, while everyone has started copying Sarma, Varma, Sastry, etc.; in North India, one can notice even in institutions like JNU, names such as Vikram Harijan, Ravi Kushwaha, Prem Jhatav and Ram Julaha (mostly ascribed to signify the caste of the person and not chosen by themselves). There seems to be no relief for some who have converted to other faiths in search of a different identity, as noted previously, and the caste titles haunt them. In fact, a new dimension of social dynamics is evolving, particularly among the caste-based reservation communities (mainly among the scheduled castes [SCs]). As the number of places reserved in the public sector (including education, employment, etc.) is limited to the proportion of the caste in the total population, it is restricted to a few among them and is not an open-ended affair. Thus, one finds that out of 17 million jobs in the public sphere, reservation is limited to just 2.72 million (at 16 per cent) for SCs. Out of an SC population of 200 million, it is a small fraction of 1.36 per cent and the proportion maybe similar for the OBCs. It is not even unguent cream. The proportion of OBCs, Muslims and *Adivasis* is also slowly increasing. Naturally there emerges intense competition among the relevant eligible families only and in terms of numbers, they are under great stress. Since family and caste are interrelated, each reinforces the other.

AFFIRMATIVE ACTION

A cursory look at the history of affirmative action after independence clearly shows that there the trend has been towards the accretion of benefits by a few. Given the present scheme of selection, it is alleged that a few families appropriate them. This is not a typical phenomenon of reservations alone, as the Indian ethos, irrespective of the caste, is family based. Such a trend among the upper castes has not created any tensions since their number is small and open ended with the availability of expanding opportunities in a growing private sector. But, the restricted number has set in motion a rat race among the Dalits and the benefits seem to have been cornered by a few families among the reserved castes. But, the bulk of the Dalits in rural areas and in urban *bastis* (slums) are untouched by any scheme and are happy with the Antyodaya Anna Yojana, NREGA, etc., that keep them alive and do not motivate them to raise any demands. It has emerged as an identity dispute with every non-dvija caste opting for a reservation tag as had happened during the British Raj. Behind this, the spirit of the family is present to satisfy the norm of some representation to the Dalits. The left and progressive groups are not an exception to the family menace (with apologies to Rohit, the Dalit scholar who committed suicide remarked on this phenomenon in his suicide note).

The intelligent and shrewd intellectual class of a particular ideology is now theorizing that if the Dalits can make use of globalisation and create 100 billionaire families, it would be easy to resolve the problems of their community. Various experts have produced reports and dozens of papers including edit page articles with half-truth and fabricated data of own-account enterprises in 2005 to present a rosy picture.[25] They cite the information to manufacture a story of the favourable impact of globalisation on the weaker sections, saying that there are 43 per cent OBC and 9 per cent Dalit enterprises today. Interestingly, they seem to not have reported that a majority of these sections do not have their own premises, their enterprises include boot polish bunks, vegetable vending, etc., and their total asset value is not equal to one day earnings of some top business houses (e.g., as in the recent share market boom). The scholars appear to be unfamiliar with the history of the artisan guilds, freeholds of lands, etc. that were under the jajmani system and that were slowly appropriated by the so-called big business families with the connivance of the company officials. In other words, the theory seems to be in consonance with the notion of circulation of Hindu families that is adequate to make them viable within the system (as is practised in upper castes where the number is very few). In fact, the spirit of Dalit activism, it is alleged, has already gone into the family mode quite long ago. It is strange that those who eulogise Dalit capitalists as a solution to the vexed problem have not produced any evidence/indication that the emerging capitalists are called as capitalists without the caste stigma (or from different backgrounds). Alternatively, the system, as in the past, is being recreated as a residual mechanism of the *panchama* in a different garb.

A detailed analysis of enrolments in higher educational institutions and job seekers in the organised sector for instance, clearly indicate that they all belong to particular family backgrounds. Some of them may be comparable in terms of quality, merit and etiquette with that of the elite. The OBCs, Muslims and other marginalised groups who are offered quotas in jobs also experience similar family phenomena of capturing opportunities. However, they form a small fraction of the whole and do not convey the complete story which actually needs sound and empathetic indigenous thought to comprehend it. There has been no significant changes in the lives of the poor post globalisation and more so for those who missed the opportunity a few years ago and have, therefore, remained in the rural areas and urban bastis stereotyping the past. In states like Andhra Pradesh, separate corporations for Brahmins, Kapus, non-reserved groups, etc. have been created and it has been alleged that, like the job of a temple priest, the benefits have been cornered by few families. Does social economy then help to comprehend the typical characters of India?

HOW DOES THE SOCIAL ECONOMY
ADDRESS INDIAN DISPUTES?

While addressing some of the previously mentioned unique questions that the Indian development model encounters, the social economy does also look at the social dimension of common good. Social economics, as distinguished from asocial matters like the concept of social exclusion, is found to cover a remarkably wide range of social and economic problems. Even in the practical context of identifying 'the excluded' in France, René Lenoir, a French Government official, spoke of the following as constituting the 'excluded'—a tenth—of the French population: mentally and physically handicapped, suicidal people, aged invalids, abused children, substance abusers, delinquents, single parents, multi-problem households, marginal and asocial persons, and other social 'misfits'.[26] But, the nature of social economics is not confined only to issues of excluded groups but are a consequence of neoliberal development models pursued in some of the advanced countries. The common good is understood here as the shared interest of the members of the society, narrowly practised as extended families in India. These, in sociological terms are popularly called castes and communities. Since the family is a strong unit of social bonds in India, any development policy as previously noted should not be confined to a few privileged groups. This phenomenon is both a conflict and an engagement with the concept of liberty of classical writers. Therefore, the social economy, as explained by Sismondi and elaborated by later day scholars, as an image of shared humanity that should encompass caste, creed, gender, region and other narrow considerations shall remain as the heart of the issues that can encounter Indian particularities. Neoclassical models of development that have been sincerely implemented under different names in India have not addressed these issues. In fact they have strengthened the divisions and despairs and created a wide gulf between nature and man. Therefore, social economics that is concerned about the shared interests of human beings for balanced development is considered here as an evocative approach for scrutinising developmental issues in India in the pages that follow.

NOTES AND REFERENCES

1. Mohandas Karamchand Gandhi called as the Father of the Nation, led a bloodless revolution against the British to acquire India's freedom. His *Experiments with Truth* and his writings in the *Harijan* journal are known to have influenced thinkers around the world.

2. Schumacher, *Small Is Beautiful: Economics As If People Mattered* (London: Blond and Briggs, 1973).

3. J. C. L. Sismondi, *New Principles of Political Economy* (London: Transaction Publishers, 1991).

4. R. H. Tawney, *The Acquisitive Society* (New York: Harcourt Brace Jovanovich, 1948).

5. J. A. Hobson, *Imperialism: A Study* (Ann Arbor, MI: University of Michigan, 1965).

6. Karl Marx, *Das Capital*, Vol. 1–3 (Moscow: Progressive Publishers, 1965).

7. David Ricardo, *Principles of Political Economy and Taxation* (London: J. Murray, 1817).

8. T. R. Malthus, *Principles of Political Economy Considered with a View to Their Practical Application* (London: J. Murray, 1820).

9. J. S. Mill, *Principles of Political Economy with Some of Their Applications to Social Philosophy*, Vol. 1 and 2 (New York: D. Appleton and Co., 1891).

10. B. R. Ambedkar, *Dr Babasaheb Ambedkar Writings and Speeches*, Vol. 17, ed., Vasant Moon (Mumbai: Government of Maharashtra, 2000).

11. Ram Manohar Lohia, *Collected Works of Ram Manohar Lohia*, Vol. 9, ed. Mastram Kapoor (New Delhi: Anamika, 2010).

12. Jawaharlal Nehru, *The Essential Writings of Jawaharlal Nehru*, ed. S. Gopal and Uma Iyengar (New Delhi: Oxford University Press, 2003).

13. Amartya Sen, *On Ethics and Economics* (New Delhi: Oxford University Press, 1987).

14. Amartya Sen, *Inequality Re-examined* (New Delhi: Oxford University Press, 1995).

15. Jagdish Bhagwati, "The Case for Free Trade," *Scientific Americana* (Nov, 1993).

16. Pranab Bardhan, *Political Economy of Development in India* (New Delhi: Oxford University Press, 1999).

17. George Akerlof, "The Economics of Caste and of the Rat Race and other Woeful Tales," *The Quarterly Journal of Economics*, Vol. 90, No. 4 (1976).

18. Constitution of India under Article 15(4).

19. Surinder S. Jodhka, *Studies in India's Caste System* (New Delhi: SAGE Publications, 2013).

20. G. D. Berreman, *Caste and other Inequities* (Meerut: Folklore Institute, 1979).

21. www.livescience/genetic study reveals the genetic origin of Indian caste system, accessed 1 November 2014.

22. Hindus including the so-called untouchables crave for a gotra at the time of marriage and during various rituals in contemporary India. It has become an identity now in the USA among the immigrants and has reached murky proportions such that a few academics who have settled there have called it a sickening situation (in 2013).

23. T. R. Trautman, *Aryans and British India* (New Delhi: Yoda Press, 1993).

24. There are instances where a European or Indian scholar has been measured as a critique of the capitalist system merely to settle and capture the imagination of the weaker sections. Later, they have come out in their true colours when corporate capitalism supported them due to their alien background. There are some groups and NGOs working for the MNCs and MCCs (multi caste corporations) reinterpreting even a renaissance leader like Joti Rao Phuley as a messiah of the masses who carried the message of Jesus. (See articles in *The Forward Press* bilingual journal and articles published in it.)

25. Chandra Bhan Prasad and others, "Rethinking Inequality: Dalits in Uttar Pradesh in the Market Reform Era," *Economic and Political Weekly*, Vol. 45, (28 August 2010).

26. René Lenoir, *Les Exclus: Un Francais sur Dix* (Paris: Editions du Seuil, 1974 [1989]), cited in Amartya Sen, *Social Exclusion: Concept application and Scrutiny* (Manila: Asian Development bank, 2000).

2

Concept of Social Economy: Past and Present

The journey of economics or political economy began from Great Britain during the 18th century. Considered as one of the outcomes of the age of enlightenment in Europe, it equipped several thinkers to reflect on contemporary society, sowing the seeds for intellectual debates to be more productive in the centuries that followed. Adam Smith was Professor of Philosophy at Glasgow and author of *Theory of Moral Sentiments* before initiating his magnum opus, *An Enquiry into the Nature and Causes of Wealth of Nations*. This book by Smith gave the scope, layout and content of a subject that was in a nascent stage. However, the Tory government consulted him to formulate some of the policies of the time. While the issues relating to production, exchange, value and distribution were not fully developed then, intellectuals of the classical period following Smith, such as Ricardo, Malthus, Marx and several others, participated in the debates that contributed to the emergence of a discipline later. Alfred Marshall was the first professor of Economics at Cambridge, who took upon himself the task of assimilating and disciplining the material that had been generated in the previous centuries into a discipline called economics. Thus, political economy became economics and emerged as one of the earliest social sciences to be taught in the university structures. We must keep in mind here that this discipline is part of the Anglo-Saxon tradition and does not recognise the cultures and academic traditions of others.

Social sciences, including economics, were introduced by the East India Company as part of university education programmes in 1857, modelled on the London University. Scholars have been working on studies to find out as to what extent the knowledge base of the British was responsible in guiding modernisation or orientalism in India.[1] Civil servants, barristers and teachers subjected the modernisation project of the British to a lot of scrutiny, most of them having been trained at Cambridge or Oxford University. Naturally, the teachers thereby followed the syllabus and the methods of teaching used in the British universities, including subjects like economics, with little change. The same textbooks that were used in England were also adopted here. It is a fact that the syllabus or course structures followed in the UK were also used here for a long period, until the hegemony of the American school of thought entered India in the 1960s. In other words, economics as a discipline offered in the Indian university system, both at the undergraduate and postgraduate levels, seems to have followed the same thrust as has been observed in English-speaking countries.

The economics fraternity was a very small group as late as in 1908, when there were only 16 professional economists in the whole of England. The subject gained popularity due to the rigor and indomitable intellectual spirit associated with the training offered by committed scholar teachers in universities. It has become one of the leading academic disciplines, not only in social sciences but also in the entire system of higher education in the world today. No social science discourse or government policy can be complete without economics and economists. Therefore, the problems, opportunities and threats of the discipline in India are the same as that in the West.

Ever since the subject surfaced as a strong academic pro-gramme with practical and policy orientations, it has found itself in several controversies and challenges. It appears that the discipline has had to take a shock or a jolt at the end of every hundred years. It started with *The Wealth of Nations* in 1776, challenging the mercantilist and physiocratic orthodoxy, by enriching with theories of the classical school further elabo-rated by Marx and the Marxists. By 1876, there seemed to be another thrust in the form of the marginal revolution and its mathematical orientation that led to the development of the neoclassical school of thought. Economics became a full-blos-somed flower in the hands of Marshall, Pigou and others, and had diversified into special and different orientations in order to address issues of an emerging new society in the Soviet Union. This was the period that saw intense debates about the content and intent of economics, leading to the launch of some schools of thinking based on ideological orientation and meth-odological convictions in different parts of the world, particu-larly in the USA. By 1970, economics had not only become an independent discipline but had also started claiming status as a science due to its capacity to predict and explain the exact nature of economic phenomenon with the help of mathemat-ics and statistics. It is alleged by rival disciplines that econom-ics has acquired arrogance and has started drifting away from other sister disciplines with whom it had travelled for two hundred years.

Social economics, as explained in the previous chapter, was initiated as an intellectual parallel to the mainstream disci-pline. Scholar teachers such as Sismondi, Hobson and others were disappointed with the overemphasis given to material-istic exposition rather than humanistic elements in the content of economics. Social economists were deeply concerned about the sustainability of development within the broad framework of social ethics and environmental limitations.

Social economics was defined by Sismondi as, "The man-agement of the national fortune for the happiness of all." The subject goes beyond laissez-faire and anticipates the distribution of private property among all. The subject owes its origin to the writings and reflection of Sismondi (1773–1842) who witnessed and experienced perhaps the most momentous tensions in human history, namely the American Revolution, the French Revolution, the Napoleonic wars and the 1848 crisis. The situation today, after the end of the Cold War, the Jasmine Revolution, Cuba–US relations, the return of orthodoxy with the support of neo-imperialism, the ascendency of quantitative methods in socio-economic issues, etc., recreates more or less the period in which Sismondi lived. It is not just a duplication but also a shadow of the critical period that makes social economics relevant now. Political economy for Sismondi:

> [I]s not founded solely on numbers, it is rather an assemblage of moral observations which cannot be submitted to calculation and which continuously change the facts. The Mathematician who wants to constantly make abstractions is bound to suppress haphazardly essential variables in each of his equations.[2]

He has further argued that nations can grow wealthy even in the absence of a foreign trade surplus.[3] This is exactly the opposite of the official view of the development strategy advocated and implemented in India since 1991.

Globalisation and international support in the form of new institutions such as the World Bank, IMF, WTO and sponsored research did not allow the dissent to be heard within the precincts of academic institutions. The hegemony continued until the 2008 economic crisis. The present challenge seems to have surfaced much faster than the previous episodes of crises in the discipline. It is in a deep debacle now, due to several contributing factors and internal contradictions of alienation. The abrupt paradigm shift (in the discipline) took place not due to continued experiments with ideas and theories, but due to a historical opportunity in the form of the fall of the Berlin wall and the end of another form of social experiment in the Soviet Bloc. Economics that has generally remained neutral to ideological orientations with a broad framework that accommodates different viewpoints suddenly became opportunistic to capture the situation with total commitment to a one-sided view. In the process, it joined hands with programmes that have been internally unstable and externally hegemonistic, such as management, public policy, etc. Further, "the over reliance on mathematical modelling and its subsequent attitude towards other social sciences left many disillusioned and dropped from the field of pursuing further." This statement by a former student who left an important economics school in the West speaks about the present-day situation in the field of economics.

The market and the State are projected as binary institutions, with the success of either of these two institutions depending upon the breakdown of the other. They are both, however, extrapolated as if mutually exclusive and autonomous. But, K. S. Chalam in one of his studies explains how the state in India is caste biased with the market dominated by the dvijas after the 1991 reforms.[4] Mainstream economists, however, have not cared to look at the social background of the billionaires who amassed wealth using state power. It is easy to depict the state as an inefficient supplier of public goods and an institution that helps promote capitalism. Is this a universal phenomenon at all times and in all regions? Buchanan and Tullock,[5] J. Bhagwati[6] and others have theoretically demonstrated how the rent-seeking nature of bureaucrats and pressure groups lead to reductions in net social welfare. This formulation based on the experiences of a settler country such as the USA or a few post-colonial nations does not examine social institutional structures and the class or caste background of the bureaucrats who are termed as rent seekers along with their links with colonial masters (past and present). The weak argumentative power of the left or social democrats after the fall of the Berlin wall helped the Washington Consensus Group to demolish Marxian, New Left and even humanistic traditions of economics under the guidance of imperialist institutions and their associates.

The crisis in mainstream economics that we are discussing here should remain a needless exercise, to evaluate and certify a system that it is supposed to deliberate, had the discipline remained neutral not becoming a part of the system experiencing the present crisis. The impact of the American and European economic disasters on India is all-pervasive now (2015), since the Indian economy is closely linked in terms of foreign trade that is well beyond the size of its GDP. Policymakers and experts are now in a quandary in terms of explaining and justifying their pre-reform formulations and promises. In this context, social economics has emerged as an important alternative paradigm to assess the situation. It is considered a more relevant approach in an economy like India that was forced to accept liberalisation for socio-political reasons in 1991 rather than the economic justification given by some experts.

ECONOMIC DEVELOPMENT AND SOCIAL JUSTICE

Social economics as a branch of economics is concerned about development with a difference. The subject considers economic development as a process through which both quantitative and qualitative factors such as institutions, organisations and culture keep on influencing policies of a country. It is different from growth, which relies purely on quantitative expansions of economic variables at the aggregate level such as the GDP or per capita income. We see quite regularly in the Indian media that the economy is growing at a particular rate to indicate the health of the economy and not necessarily the people. Economic development, or simply development and its impact on the lives of the people, is more important today vis-à-vis the measures used by economists which are being increasingly discredited because of their concerns more with quantitative issues rather than human existence. The political economy approach (of the Chicago school) to development has reduced the delicate social and human passions and sentiments to a subordinate position and insignificant levels of analysis in the dialectical process of development.[7] Reason, as Amartya Sen, pointed out has never constituted as an instrument of justice in India. The trickle-down theory of growth with justice, etc., seems to have failed to produce tangible results.

Realising the limitations of the measures of development, like the GDP, the UNDP initiated a concept to measure human development two decades ago with intellectual support from scholars from the subcontinent, Amartya Sen and Mahboob Ul Haq. This concept is being used in place of the GDP, to get a better understanding of the status of development of people that takes care of the health, education and income of the people as a composite index. Disillusioned with some of the developments in economics, a group of scholars started examining the ethical dimensions of growth about a century ago in France, on the same lines as Sismondi. They developed the notion of social economy as one that studied the ethical and social causes and consequences of the economic behaviour of institutions, organisations, theories and policies. However, it was not popularised in India although civil society activities have increased several fold here since 1990. Some of the theories failed to explain the so-called development that brought about changes in the forces of production or the capacity of the factors that were involved in the processes of growth. Have these developments really influenced the relations among different groups of people, were the relations of production made to change, or have they remained static?

In a country like India, with several dimensions and divergences, the social economy rather than measures such as the GDP, Human Development Index (HDI) or per capita income could be considered more useful to learn about the impact of economic growth. It is also necessary to understand whether the basic structure of the economy and society, as laid down in the Constitution, has been protected or has eroded. It may be too ambitious to anticipate such a broad framework to be used by economists trained in neoclassical traditions either in India or abroad as the hegemony of English is significant as per scholars like Sen (see footnotes of *Idea of Justice*).[8] We need to explore whether development or growth in a country could really resolve the already existing contradictions or widen them.

It is possible to examine the process without using the established terminology, within the notion of social economy as it is concerned with the ethical dimensions of development. In fact, the concept is being mischievously used to explain the expansion of the voluntary sector or the non-market segment of the economic activities of cooperatives, NGOs, foundations, agencies, etc. and has not been extended to examine the disparities and despairs that growth has created. The hedonistic West has absorbed the so-called otherworldly India and transformed it as a materialistic nation by sponsoring spiritual activities and contributing to the popularisation of our culture in English and other European languages. What else is needed to record the positive contribution of growth? Conversely, the aim of a social economy is stated to serve society without profit, autonomously manage the economy with democratic decision-making and give primacy to persons rather than capital and the redistribution of profits. It reminds us about the broad principles of state policy enunciated in our Constitution. In fact, the apex court has interpreted some of these to give protection to the poor who are affected by the mad rush for sizeable gains in the economy, with complete disregard to the welfare of the destitute. In other words, courts are occasionally using the principles of social economy although our basic constitutional morality encompasses these values.

Interestingly, neither the USA nor the UK is interested in the notion of social economy, though some Scottish scholars think about it. The importance of the social economy in countries such as Cuba, Argentina, Venezuela and a few others is slowly increasing, giving way to an alternative theory of development. It seems India and some Indian experts are not interested in the same, though we boast of Gandhian principles that broadly correspond to the same. The overindulgence of some of our policy-makers in the Western market model (not even Chinese market socialism) of development has affected the structure and nature of our society and economy.

It is noticed that the country is heading towards a 'Dutch disease', a concept coined by some economists based on the experience of the Netherlands, a developed country. Netherlands, Holland and the Dutch have relied on abundant natural resource-rich gas deposits for economic development. The exploitation of this natural resource has improved the balance of trade and the contraction in the agriculture and manufacturing sectors due to the resource export boom has been more than compensated for by increased incomes in the resource sector. It is further characterised by high capital intensity that has displaced labour, and the increase in employment in the mining sector has failed to compensate the workers who lost their jobs in agriculture and industrial sectors. This phenomenon was experienced also by Nigeria, Mexico and others, though not by Indonesia. Scholars such as Krugman,[9] Yajuroyamada[10] and others have argued that if some key manufacturers, having strategic complementarities with others, are obliterated by the natural boom like mining exports (maybe even IT services), the economy may not only get back to its former development position but might even be trapped in a low-level equilibrium.

The recent legal tangles in the area of mining and other natural resources appear to give us an early warning to redesign our policies and to not get trapped like the Dutch. One can look at the emergence of a new class of extortionists with strong political and bureaucratic connections during the reform period, unlike the lumpen proletariat who could be absorbed in any growing sector. It is reported that the power relations of the new class has enabled them to distort state policies, control governments to grab resources and even gain legal rights over public properties. They are emerging as partners in the development of the rich and not of the common man. The present model of growth and the measures to estimate their contribution to development are least bothered about how the growth has taken place, including the wealth created by the extortionists. The notion of social economy as an approach of study seems to be of some use in countries like India, at least to record and protect the hapless victims of growth.

THE LOGIC OF SELF-INTEREST AND ITS VICTIMS

The paradigm of neoclassical economists as against that of the social economists has definite core values. But, a one-sided debate on development has enabled several states, including India, to adopt libertarian policies in the name of reducing poverty and accelerating economic growth. In the history of ideas, 'self' and 'self-interest' are considered central to human progress. Anthropologists and philosophers have deliberated how savages became civilised through encounters with nature and circumstances in the long journey of humankind. But human beings, who once lived in groups, became independent and again shackled, ultimately to fight against artificial conditions to become free. In this evolution, she/he has accumulated unimaginable depths of knowledge and experience to be used to either restrain or remain unfree.

It was during the Age of Enlightenment that a strong cultural and intellectual foundation was laid to free humankind from superstitions. There were intense scholarly debates by schoolmen (scholastics) on every important event, giving birth to disciplinary knowledge. David Hume, William Petty, Anne Robert Jacques Turgot and François Quesnay, to name a few leaders of the era, contributed to human sciences before Adam Smith published his *The Wealth of Nations* in 1776, a few years before the French and American Revolutions. It was David Hume and Adam Smith who set the fundamentals for a libertarian ideology. Interestingly, Marx also had his moorings in Smith.

The present issue of how self-interest is responsible for the development of a capitalist system has evoked debate that has become one-sided due to the hegemony of the Bretton Woods's institutions and a stoic silence from its opponents after the fall of the Berlin Wall. This has enabled several nations, including India, to adopt libertarian policies in the name of reducing poverty and accelerating economic growth. Though the rudiments of liberalisation, privatisation and globalisation (LPG) were present in the early 1980s, the loud declaration was, however, made in 1991. This has unleashed the sleeping giant to leap forward and created billionaires from India who found their names listed in the Fortune 500. Yet, several socio-economic internal contradictions, including inequalities, have widened.

Though the metaphysical deliberations about the self and its liberation from temporal attractions were deeply imbedded in different societies, elucidation of the concept as self-interest during the Enlightenment period seems to have been baked in pure materialistic course of demeanour. Adam Smith was given credit for using the concept to usher in a new era in Europe, using gifts of enlightenment. It is necessary to keep in mind the historical conditions and the uncivilised exploitation of colonies by the East India (mercantilists) company under the protection of the State that made Smith react. He was compelled to appeal to the self-interest of every individual as an author of *Theory of Moral Sentiments* for the possibility of enhancing the happiness of enlightened individuals and society. He explained how spontaneous realisation by every individual to truck, barter and exchange one thing for another as a part of pure self-interest would benefit everyone with daily bread. He further discussed the topic with illustrations showing how it would work as an 'invisible hand', as a self-regulating mechanism, that would bring good to society. The concept of the division of labour and how it is limited by the extent of market are broadly related to laissez-faire. The basic elements of capitalist development, thus, revolved around the notion of self-interest. However, the role of the State to moderate disharmony of interests as advocated by Smith was capriciously kept aside.

The metaphor 'invisible hand' of Smith, like the base-superstructure of Marx, created warring groups to continue with their intellectual cudgels. The application of these ideas to contemporary situations by policy-makers to find practical solutions has created more problems than resolutions. In fact, Nozick,[11] author of *Anarchy, State and Utopia*, took the philosophical debate to a newer height. He has argued that it was within the principle of liberty and justice when a basketball champion like Chamberlain was given 25 cents each by a million people to earn an income of $250,000, which was more than the average income of individuals, irrespective of how it would upset the distributional aspects of a society. This justification countenanced businesses to bring Indian Premier League (IPL) to India. It is further argued that if individual talents or resources are kept idle, they are a waste; and if they are traded in the market, they become wealth. What is the harm if individual players are bought and sold like commodities depending upon their demand, as has been asked by some Indian experts? This is possible only in a post-modern society where everything is commoditised for the market. It is in the same context that the neoclassical economists have developed models of optimisation of welfare. Pareto, the libertarian, developed the thesis of welfare optimisation within the given system that operated under the spell of the invisible hand. Amartya Sen responded to this by saying, "[A] society in which some people lead lives of great luxury while others live in acute misery can still be Pareto optimal if the agony of the deprived cannot be reduced without cutting into the ecslasy of the affluent." Indians have learnt about the economic and political process of IPL through Justice Mudgal and Justice Lodha Committees reports.

The theories of the libertarians have contributed towards the expansion of globalisation within the parameters of liberty and equality without qualifying the context, historical significance and identity of each nation. India, along with some other Third World countries, was attracted towards a neosis around the 1980s that eventually became a national policy in 1991. During the last two decades, irrespective of the political party in power, they have sincerely adhered to the agenda of making self-interest the catalyst of economic development with a quantum jump of wealth of cronies and, thus, the GDP. This has enabled a dozen out of 1.2 billion people to own all most all that was created during the period.

This accomplishment was attributed to the play of the principles of the invisible hand and self-interest in every walk of life, be it income, scams, corruption, rapes, moral turpitude, demeanour of the nation, etc. No one can take the credit or blame for the growth or decadence, except the preceptors of self-interest as a virtue. Unfortunately, the exuberance has started dwindling and the drubbings are so pervasive that the preceptors of self-interest in the West were swallowed long ago. The behemoth in India in the early part of its operation devoured in the form of Hawala and Jain diary, and is now eating into the vitals of our civilisation.[12] Now, in times of acute depredation, does the Buddhist precept of seeking refuge in society (*sangham*) that the social economists adhere to provide any metaphysical solace?

DOES GROUP INTEREST PROMOTE SOCIAL GOOD?

It is widely discussed in India that around 30 leaders belonging to different political parties of the country were united as spectators of a spectre of a business game. It is called the IPL and was sponsored by the Board of Control for Cricket in India (BCCI), the champion of Indian cricket. It is an example of how groups are joining together irrespective of the so-called political party that they belong to. The total value of the cricket business was around $3 billion in 2012 (₹150–200 billion). The benevolent government has given tax exemptions on the revenue earned. Interestingly, most of the political parties including the opposition that ripped into the ruling coalition recently on the issue of different 'gates' in Parliament have remained quiet on the issue of match fixing and spot fixing. Thus, the IPL has emerged as a symbol of group interest. The fixing drama that unfolded for about a week continued till the Parliament session ended as there were no issues to feed the media that have cunningly avoided asking questions as to why we need IPL.[13]

It is reported that the BCCI Chairman (Narayanaswami Srinivasan), who was at that time alleged to be the one who involved in the match/spot fixing through his son-in-law, is not new to such operations. He is alleged to have been involved in the India Cements land acquisition and related frauds in Andhra Pradesh. There may be such characters in the IPL/BCCI who might be maintaining a low profile, or it is the media playing mischief by highlighting those who are not with the media houses and down playing others who are the kith and kin or business partners, as is well-known as the 'press fixing' drama in India quite for some time now. As someone has rightly remarked, it is through the manipulation of the three M's, that is, money, mafia and media, by which the present system operates.

The economic benefits of operations such as the IPL/casinos/gambling, etc. are being discussed by experts in terms of how earnings from the same can be legalised and the state could gain by imposing taxes on such operations. There have been informed discussions in a section of the print media as to how the processes in Las Vegas, USA, could be copied to curb mafia activities and at the same time economically gain from them. It is estimated that the betting trade in India is about ₹3 trillion and the government would get around ₹200 billion as tax revenue from the same. Thus, we have very brilliant ideas on how to make the so-called illegal activities legitimate deeds through legislative action. Perhaps, there may already be a ready-made private bill to be introduced in the Parliament soon to make such activities legal. The experts are trying to convince us that it is all part of the game and nothing to be worried about the its wicked dimension. However, the matter of the fact is that the operations of Hawala, match fixing, the real estate boom, etc. are only the process of transforming the black money into white and legitimate. How can they be curbed? The kind of innovations introduced by our indigenous businesses is so vast and deep, it is quite possible that they will find some other routes to avoid taxes and accumulate wealth. Further, there are some political leaders from traditional business communities involved in many of the operations, indicating how deeply the system is entrapped. It appears that the black money drama of the political parties was actually a ploy to alert their counterparts to transfer the money to other tax havens and then redeploy the same in India as foreign direct investments (FDI). It is known to our financial experts that the RBI has recorded around 2010 that the lending for real estate through financial institutions reached ₹16 trillion, appearing to be an indicator how money transactions worth 10 times that of the white transactions had already invested in the economy to create buoyancy. The IPL was allegedly to be used as another source. Therefore, the group interest of IPL leaders is only a part of what has been happening in the country for centuries. There is a definite record of such happenings during the British rule in India in the form of speeches of Edmund Burke indicting the East India Company officers in the British Parliament.

The group is pursuing their interest in a democratic country that guarantees individual freedom to take up any profession or occupation, trade or business, guaranteed under Article 19(g). If you ask any legal luminary or public Intellectual, they might support the activities of the BCCI/IPL and could add that they are serving the nation by providing entertainment if not sports to the interested public. So what is the harm or problem if they follow their group or private interests? In this context, two schools of thought, namely 'social choice' and 'public choice', have addressed some of the issues relating to private interests and 'the calculus of consent' in a state to make decisions on policy, which are worth mentioning here.

Perhaps some economists and management experts might be ready with theoretical formulations to substantiate why we need IPLs and how they help create wealth. Economists have long been arguing that any individual activity that does not involve the loss of welfare to others can be promoted. The libertarian scholars cite Pareto optimality, saying that it is impossible to make some one better off without making somebody else worse off, to formulate policies of welfare and development. This principle advanced by the Italian scholar Pareto, who was said to be close to Mussolini, the fascist leader, is parroted by every scholar to substantiate activities like the IPL, as they do not disturb this optimality and promote individual liberty.

Another group of scholars claim that no voting rule that satisfies a decisive, consensus, non-dictatorship and independence is possible given social choice (Arrow's impossibility) under the Pareto conditionality. Buchanan, who developed a similar public choice theory, has also examined rent-seeking actions of bureaucrats while formulating public policies.[14] World Bank economists have used arguments to annihilate 'State' authority on the ground that public choice decisions do not necessarily promote welfare. "Politics", Buchanan said, "is a process with which individuals, with separate potentially differing interests and values, interact for the purpose of serving individually valued benefits of cooperative effort." Thus, he was critical about American politicians and bureaucrats as rent-seekers (an activity through which companies gained through lobbying without any benefits to society) but very appreciative of the institutions promoting liberty. We are citing these theories (mostly technical) here as it is under their brilliant indulgence that most government policies are formulated everywhere in the so-called free world including India.

The private interests of the IPL group or some other activity such as using the tonnes of smashed ganja (cannabis resin) of the Customs and Excise Department profitably, to create wealth, etc. are issues that need to be debated. Both ganja and IPL, with all kinds of support structures, provide entertainment and simultaneously create wealth and so why should we not promote them? Are we not deriving revenue by sponsoring IMFL?

The libertarians had a strong foundation in positive economics that did not speak about normative issues, as a value-based economics was a 'dreadful thing to accept' (John Richard Hicks). One might still question this cynical proposition by saying that policy-makers are not chumps to accept plans that involve public morality. But, we had in India proposals from

some economists like making corruption a legal activity with
the market forces deciding the worth. Now the IPL is in force.
However, the issue raised here appears to be simple and silly,
as they are, in fact, concerns that are being confronted by the
common man every day. We do not have competent people
to counter the elegant arguments of experts to outwit them so
that scarce resources are used for the benefit of the deprived
or for the social good (clean air, water, etc.). The civil society,
public intellectuals, media, etc. have a role to play here rather
than leaving it to the 'paid intellectuals' to think, reflect and
formulate policies on our behalf. One may not possess the
abstract reasoning of mathematics, a language and not an ideology, to hoodwink common man. But the active involvement
of the common man in public reasoning as well as participation in alternative exercises would definitely provide solutions
to TINA (there is no alternative). In fact, some of the theories
seem to be commissioned or arranged for window dressing of
corrupt practices used in the transactions of wily operators.

There is, in fact, a long tradition in the social sciences to
counter the arguments formulated by the libertarians from the
time of Hume. Sismondi, Marx, Ruskin, Hobson, Schumacher
in the past, and Rawls and Amartya Sen to some extent in the
contemporary world are articulating resolutions to respond to
these challenges. Sen has resolved the impossibility riddle of
decision-making through the process of interpersonal compar-
isons. Addressing the problems of the rights and liberties of
the minorities and weaker sections in terms of social goods that
satisfy their basic needs, capabilities and information broad-
ening he has said: "[A] state can be Pareto optimal and still
be sickeningly inequitable."[15] We may also consider here how
policy-makers in India have proscribed the concept of a public
good (common good that provides utility to every one without rivalry) in their quest for creating wealth by auctioning
even natural resources such as rivers, mines, aquifers, coastal
zones, etc. Interestingly, policy-makers have used select theories like the one stated previously that have fascist tendencies
with Western values of market significance. The institutional

structures of other societies that have promoted welfare for the people have no relevance in their formulations and are covetously been annihilated if found to survive.

The IPL episode is only a small chunk of a large mass of rapacious aggrandisement of a select group belonging to traditional business groups who care less for human values except garnering money. The group interest in the form of IPL so far has not shown any proclivity towards helping the disadvantaged. Further, they keep on inventing institutions that facilitate exploitation, corruption and distribution of the spoils. Fascinatingly, they are the ones who use liberty as a value to exploit for their own or group benefit with a minimalist state needed to ensure the enforcement of contracts and nothing else. Even Aristotle's *Nicomachean Ethics* that defines human good as happiness acquired through the virtue of justice seems to be not in the reckoning. Further, the ideals of a welfare state were buried few decades ago by the narcissist scholars to shun their conscience.

LIBERTY AND THE GUN CULTURE

Liberty, equality and fraternity, the three noble values that humankind had authenticated to eternity originated in the French Revolution. It was on 26 August 1789 that the National Constituent Assembly of France had adopted them as part of the Rights of Man and Citizen. It had a profound influence on the course of history in different parts of the world, particularly after the end of colonialism.

The Constituent Assembly of India also adopted justice and the three values as part of its Preamble to the Constitution on 26 November 1949. We could entice evoke the basics here to re-examine the concept of liberty in the context of a recent debate on the contours of liberty. The notion of liberty is being used by libertarians to argue against the proposed confiscation of guns in the USA by calling it an infringement of liberty (after the Newton, Connecticut, school incident in December 2012).

The debate and its contents could have large repercussions on the contours of policy in several countries. In fact, the three values are inseparable and it is difficult to think about one without visualising the remaining two. The present United States of America as a colony of the European nations won its independence in 1776, and the people of France presented the Statue of Liberty to the USA in 1886 as a mark of respect.

Hence, the notion of liberty, which the Americans and their friends the world over eulogise in terms of the freedoms they enjoy, including the 'gun culture'. Some Indian libertarians, who would like to emulate American values, should recognise the costs involved in sustaining the system. The history of the world became curious with the verve bestowed by the French Revolution and the Enlightenment in Europe. The nations that were engaged in free trade and colonial plunder made school-men reflect on the human condition and the future of civilisation. Adam Smith expanded the concept of liberty to restrict the functions of the state to a few activities. Under the same paradigm, J. S. Mill explained the boundaries of liberty from a utilitarian perspective in his *On Liberty*.[16] The issue of liberty was intensely debated during the 1980s under the aegis of the World Bank; it is being repeated now in the context of the Sandy Hook Elementary School shootout (December 2012) where 27 children were killed. Barack Obama is seen deeply moved by the incident and seems to consider reforms to contain the menace. Protagonists argue that any control over the right to possess and keep arms is a step to curtail liberty as guaranteed in the US Constitution. But, the so-called universal right to bear arms in the USA is related to the Second Amendment in the 18th century when there was no professional army. Therefore, an amendment was made to create an armed citizenry as "a well-regulated militia, being necessary to the security of a Free State, the right of the people to keep and bear arms, shall not be infringed."

Unfortunately, the background and the circumstances under which the provision was made have not been reflected while deliberating on the issue of liberty to hold arms. The primary function of a firearm is protection. The argument is that if everyone is armed, any kind of massacre would not take place. Some of them are citing examples when there was no armed militia/police to protect the people, to a period when the USA had emerged as a super power to abrogate the status of the universal police. Further, it speaks very lowly about the competence of the American law and order machinery and the state itself. Yet, the USA has 54 guns per 1,000 population, one of the highest in the world (while 156.5 million applications are pending). The incident and the sympathetic arguments in favour of holding a gun seem to be justified in the paradigm of a market hegemony.

The social contract theory appeared during the same period as that of the liberty principle. It was debated by the free marketers how individual liberties were to be subsumed to get protection under the State or even for the survival of democracy. Philosophers and scholars such as Robert Nozick, Milton Friedman and others (mostly of Jewish origin) argued for uncompromising priority to be given to libertarian rights irrespective of the consequences. But Karl Popper, one of the chief philosophers of the 20th century, agreed that society was a voluntary association of free individuals respecting each other's rights and needs to be governed by the framework of protection given by the State.[17] Amartya Sen has addressed the issues raised by these scholars in his *Development as Freedom* to explain that any expansion of freedom is both a primary end and also the principal means of development. In this context, he draws our attention to Marx's insistence that rights cannot really precede the institution of a State. Sen joins ranks with John Rawls on the 'priority of liberty' and has stated that, "[A person's] liberty should get just the same kind of importance (no more) as of other types of personal advantages—incomes, utilities and so on—have."[18] Also, liberty and rights may have political significance and it is possible to address them under procedural transgression.

The paradigm of liberty seems to have originated in the Judaic conception of 'sin' and dignity by birth, with a colonial mindset of 'Whiteman's burden of modernizing' the non-whites. Similar opinions are being expressed by a section of the upper caste Hindus after the NDA-II came to power in Delhi. Scholars like Upendra Baxi have opined that the invocation of rights as part of the Universal Declaration of Human Rights (UDHR) is essentially Western. The UNDHR declaration has also some subtle arrogance to convey that they alone can liberate our minds and souls and in the process give us development, which is problematic in a post-colonial society. Unfortunately, most of the economists are pretending to be ignorant of these developments.

The social institutions in the Third World, including the common property resources, family norms and values, etc. are useless as per the libertarians and are devoid of any merit for harnessing economic growth. Therefore, liberty as a value is necessary to strengthen the free market mechanism and property rights need to be promoted to exploit the resources for our own benefit. There are plenty of examples as to how the Apex Court in India has helped to validate the unauthorised and appropriated public properties as the legitimate property of a few who were in power. No doubt, there are one or two cases of public litigation where public interest is upheld. But they constitute only a few examples. The way the wealth and property are concentrated in the hands of a few with legal backing reflects the evil.

Therefore, one can think of the lack of freedom and deprivation even in advanced countries in the form of health care, sanitary arrangements, clean water, functional education, gainful employment, social security, etc. have led to movements like Occupy Wall Street recently. Are the previously stated issues really worthless to be considered as rights so that priority can be given to liberty while its consequences can be forgotten? How can we think of giving priority to liberty in terms of bearing a gun that leads to unintended consequences like killing hapless children? Has human civilisation not demonstrated the intrinsic worth of kindnesses against animal brutality to reinforce the thin line between the two? Does group interest carry any value to promote the common good? Some of these questions have been abundantly answered by Indian freedom fighters, Gandhiji in particular, in their quest for independence from the colonial masters. They did not expect that the present native rulers would use the language of the colonial era in free India to help clear the way for aliens again to arrive in India in a new garb and pride.

END OF THE INTELLECTUAL TRADITION IN INDIA

It is quite often seen in public discourses that references are made with allusion to a particular intellectual in support of an argument. Intellectual activity is generally not considered as a profession and is not defined as someone doing a particular kind of job. It is by tradition the actions of those who use their intellect to produce useful and purposeful ideas that is called intellectual. She/he is differentiated from a philosopher, and there is no need for a person to first qualify as a philosopher to become an intellectual or vice versa. Intellectuals are respected in all traditions and in different periods of human history. It may be due to the fact that they conceal their desires, emotions and obsessions in the pursuit of justice, rights and values. Their output consists of concepts, notions, viewpoints, etc., including of fellow intellectuals, to make them relevant to the larger good of society. The intellectual is different from those who use their intelligence, a cognitive activity or knowledge that is mentally demanding for a career. That is why chess players, engineers, scientists (social, natural and physical) and a host of others who are knowledge workers are not considered as intellectuals unless they turn out to be 'public intellectuals' who defend rational ideas. There is a sudden dearth of intellectuals for defending the exploited and the marginalised in the manner in which the elegant arguments are popularised by the adversaries in the 21st century India.

Western scholars of the history of ideas qualify intellectual traditions as human thoughts in written form which have influenced the course of human destiny. This definition seems to have a bias towards the West that had a tradition of written comments but is not as ancient as the Asian, African or other civilisations. Edward Said first questioned the debate on the prejudices in the history of ideas and the origin of the Western civilisation in 1978.[19] The credit for the so-called post-discourses in the academic world should go to Said who challenged the Anglo-Saxon hegemony. Though a section of Indians does claim ancestry to most of the ideas and innovations, they never raised such questions. In fact, recent research in Indian history brings forth evidence that shows how some of our experts or pundits have joined the bandwagon of Anglo-Saxons claiming that they were all from the same stock of people.

Amartya Sen in his work, *The Argumentative Indian*,[20] has established the unique Indian identity. He presents the Indian intellectual tradition as devoid of *babas*, corporate gurus, etc. (popularly made out as the Indian tradition), with distinctive characters. It is strange that none of our publicists, who are very popular in the international circuits for their beautiful English, have ever presented to the world that Socrates was only Greek Uddalaka Aruni of *Chandogya Upanishad* or Satyakam Jabali in popularising the intellectual discovery of 'dialectics'. In other words, by owning and internalising the descent of popular Western materialist cultures as popular values, some of our contemporary activists have defeated our claim to the unique intellectual tradition. However, although we may not claim a Voltaire, Paine or Marx in the modern period, we definitely did have a great intellectual tradition as good and maybe even as prodigious as the Western one in all respects. Those who claim that they are the sole inheritors of this tradition project only the idealist part of it and never bother to assert that we have a rich rational and materialistic tradition that is more ancient than any of the modernist trends. Even the true nature of the *Shatdarsanas* and the pre-Vedic contributions are not publicly discussed to link them with indigenous influences on the so-called falsifiable science and technology.

This may be due to excessive dependence on the Anglo-Saxon model of academic deliberations and a complete neglect of original practices as well as the modernisation and upgradation of ancient traditions. This was due, to some extent, to the low social background of the leaders of those schools of thought. It is perverted to such an extent that it is no more possible to reappraise it due to the hegemony of the traditional scholarship and religious fundamentalism in public discourse under the organised control of a few. This has almost sealed one of the oldest intellectual initiatives. But, there seems to be renewed interest in pre-colonial Africa after Said, Amin and other scholars have been fighting against the Anglo-Saxon supremacy amongst intellectuals. A characterisation called 'Timbuktu' a myth in Africa, has been challenged by indigenous thinkers through the resurrection of the city in Mali, West Africa, as a world heritage site, to defeat such malice from the West. We do not have such practices, but instead create myths and legends to uphold the hegemony of a social group. Strangely, the cultural leaders are now willing to compromise and accommodate the Western market in India to sustain as their lackeys.

There was some hope when the European intellectual tradition of enquiry was introduced in the form of English education in India. But it seems to be fast disappearing, in the name of globalisation and the almost total surrender to the dominant commercial values of the West in the form of the commodification of culture. If there are some independent thinkers and scholars concerned about indigenous traditions, they are under the tutelage of religious groups or NGOs who dictate their agenda.

Academic independence has been inspiring some young scholars and activists who could turn out to be organic intellectuals in due course of time if they are provided with intellectual guidance as in the case of JNU scholar Kanhaiya Kumar and others. The emergence of an intellectual group as a class of experts, consultants, specialists, creative writers, etc., to serve the interests of corporates or the market, cannot fill up the space of an intellectual who has intensity of feeling for the poor and the oppressed. Some of the enlightened sections are now being targeted and branded as anti-national by a section of Brahminical Hindus as if the Hindu group is given the status of a nation in our Constitution.

The advent of a few thinkers and activists as an autonomous group from below is not accorded the status of an intellectual due to their caste background and is denounced as mediocre by the peer groups of the 'other'. Therefore, some of them are migrating to other areas and countries. We do not have a tradition of social sciences and it was introduced and encouraged mainly by the colonial system of education. Social sciences or social studies teaching and research have produced some of our best leaders and intellectuals, who have done tremendous service to the nation in the 19th and 20th centuries.

The domination of the American business culture in the form of academic programmes including management or MBA has completely swallowed the social sciences. The best brains, even after completing their IIT training, do end up pursuing it. Some informal training in psychology and related disciplines has led to a spurt of personality development trainers. Historians have become tourist guides. In the past, the tradition was of teachers entering the public domain on behalf of people. Some of them are now becoming entrepreneurs and running coaching centres, while a few have become consultants to politicians to provide advice to run governments. Regretfully, none of these experts is aware of the traditions of social economics as articulated by leaders such as Mahatma Gandhi, M. N. Roy, Ram Manohar Lohia and B. R. Ambedkar, to name a few.

The creation of temporary intellectuals by the media is momentary, like the daily newspaper that becomes waste paper the very next day. Thus, the roads to development or the spontaneous blooming of an intellectual are almost closed. The end of intellectual tradition in India is imminent. But it is only with the presence of an intellectual that the identity of a nation or a public cause is possible. There is a tendency among experts to follow a particular ideology, not due to its intellectual appeal but simply because of its economic significance. This is happening perhaps according to the designs of the corporate market economy.

THE IDEOLOGICAL CRISIS IN DELHI

Intellectual decadence or design seems to have entered the policy-making machinery. There was a break with the past and a different menu with sound ideological support drawn from the mercantilists down to Jagadish Bhagwati,[21] Williamson[22] and a host of others was formulated. It was just not an economic reform; it was a paradigm shift. The ideology of a free market based on monetary and fiscal policies as prescribed in the neoclassical macroeconomic models was adopted. It was promised that a sincere attempt would be made to follow the 'ten commandments' of the Washington Consensus. It included divestment, FDI, trade liberalisation, property rights, etc. that would liberate poor countries from the scourge of underdevelopment and poverty. We have sincerely implemented almost all of the prescriptions for more than two decades. Countries such as Argentina, Sub-Saharan Africa, and South-East Asia have followed this package lobbied through the World Bank, IMF, etc. Yet, the South-East Asian financial crisis occurred in 1997, followed by the Argentina tragedy in 2001, and several other negative experiences followed.

The Nobel laureate Joseph Stiglitz has pointed out the limitations of the free market package in the Third World economies with underdeveloped and highly imperfect markets. He wanted democratisation of globalisation. This did not change the heart of our advisers. In fact, some of our Indian-born foreign citizens have suggested that the imperfections in the market could be tided over through more liberalisation. On the other hand, the development experience of some of our far eastern neighbours like Japan suggest that they have given importance to the so-called low productive sectors such as agriculture, textiles, etc. to provide social stability as the foundation for economic development in as early as the 18th century. It sounds like Gandhian as enunciated by J. C. Kumarappa who said that a theoretically self-sufficient village economy with values of human dignity was possible. Giving the example of a monkey as a predator and a tiger as a parasitic, both being self-centred animals with no sense of duty, Kumarappa elucidated how how humans have a feeling of the right to consume and produce more than required to create surplus.[23]

The experience of Germany, according to some scholars, is quite contrary to the English and American experience. While the Germans emphasised technology-based production and creation of surplus, the English relied solely on trade and comparative advantage. There are several such examples from history and contemporary experiences that can be emulated, provided we follow our own policies based on our culture and resources.

There are very few instances in history where the state is found to have damaged developmental institutions, and it appears that the government is slowly convinced of the constructive role that the public sector of the Nehruvian era can play. Yet, we need to develop an ideology that combines community, market, state and institutions rooted in our culture to deal with poverty and underdevelopment at our own speed rather than depending upon a borrowed promptitude. A few of the policy advisers use monetary mechanisms to accelerate growth. It seems they have not looked at Milton Friedman, the doyen of monetary policy who said:

> Imagine that the US Federal Reserve sends out a helicopter for a cash rainfall upon US consumers.... It is easy to picture US consumer showing no reluctance in picking up the bank notes and spending them, and to an important extent, on imported goods too. The Feds' helicopter payloads thus find their way in to otherwise half-empty container returning to Asia, finally ending up as official reserves in the coffers of Asian central banks, which are forever content with

holding barren pieces of paper in exchange for the products shipped to the United States.[24]

India, like many least developed countries (LDCs), is fond of the barren paper supremacy (dollars), and should learn from the example and formulate policies that 'decouple' the sputtering US financial locomotive. Social economics as an alternative framework seems to have the promise to address some of the shortcomings of the present development policies in India.

It is proved by data sets that there is direct correlation between our reserves and the share market. The share market swelled seven times higher than the reserves in 1991 and now stands at a staggering capitalisation of ₹66.34387 trillion when the reserves were only ₹13.61013 trillion in 2010–11. It is strange how the financial scams and Gali frauds (Gali Janardhana Reddy of Karnataka)[25] have taken place (under the Foreign Exchange Management Act [FEMA] regime) despite regulators such as the Securities and Exchange Board of India (SEBI) and RBI. The financial advisers in the North Block seem to have the formidable task now of converting the resources as durable assets that educe well-being for all and not necessarily to transfer public assets to private individuals.

PUBLIC PROPERTY FOR PRIVATE USE

Social economy is concerned about common properties and their conservation for the use of future generations. But the present day economists and policy-makers call for their effective use now and in larger quantities saying that it would create wealth, with least regard for public good or bad. The difference between public property and private property is that the former offers benefits to society as a whole while the latter profits individuals. Common properties, generally referred to as public property, are local resource such as grass, wood, weeds, fish, etc. controlled and utilised by small communities and traditional castes. Common property resources have been depleted throughout the world with the advent of the colonial terms of trade based on the market and are being studied to provide sustainability, not only to resources but also to the communities that depend upon them.

Public property is defined (Prevention of Damage to Public Property Act 1984) as,

> [A]ny property either immovable or movable (including machinery) which is owned by or in the possession of or under the control of, Central government, any State government or any local authority or any corporation, or public company, or any institution undertaken by the Central government.

It is declared so through a Gazette notification. Though it is a legal definition, it conveys the meaning of public property as one that belongs to the people of the country and the beneficiaries or the inheritors are the public and not private individuals.

It is said that the colonial system changed the characters of most of our public resources after the introduction of its methods of exploitation. Scholars like Madhav Gadgil[26] and others have recorded how common property resources in regions like the West coast (Uttara Kannada) have undergone radical transformation; that might give us a clue as to how public properties have moved into the hands of individuals.

However, the anthropological approach to the study of common property resources has certain limitations to enable an understanding of the complexity of the transfer of public properties as private possessions. The analysis of the reassignment or alienation of land and other resources such as mines, state-owned machinery, etc. could be better understood through class analysis. One can use either a Marxian, or a non-Marxian or a Weberian class to understand the dynamics of how properties in countries like India change hands. Class in the Indian context, both as an economic and a social category, can be a useful tool to scrutinise the process of transformation (as of now) of flaccid resources under the control of the state into vibrant wealth-creators in the hands of select few individuals. It does explain how the ruling classes use their political power in the democratic drama of decision-making for getting public resources either for themselves or for their cronies. It is neither a new phenomenon nor limited to Andhra Pradesh or Karnataka alone. It has long been present in our history and while it was once confined to a few it has spread to many groups after liberalisation.

There are several connected issues in the process of the transformation of public property into private property within the legal structures of the country. It appears that people have misunderstood Jairam Ramesh[27] when he raised the issue of public toilets in rather discreet language. The Constitution has given scope for certain freedoms to establish institutions and own properties that are exempt from taxes under Article 27. The makers of the Constitution may have thought that, given the plurality of the country, each group would work in the larger interests of the public if given this freedom. The aim of the provision as per the founding fathers of the Constitution may have been to disallow individuals or a cluster of them to form interest groups in order to amass properties mostly from the public and convert them as fiefdoms to benefit a few individuals or their companions. The crux of the problem is that huge public properties and wealth have been accumulated in the hands of a few individuals without much use for the groups for which they were intended for or to the people of the country in general.

We have learnt from media reports how the controversial Swami Nityananda[28] bribed another *swami* to acquire ₹15 billion worth of property. People talk of such incidents if they are known public figures, but there are millions of such cases (all denominations) that elude the public realm. We have millions of registered public trusts or organisations not only to avoid taxes but even to conceal their ill-gotten money. People who talk of corruption do not touch this issue as some of them come under this category and most of their frauds do ultimately turn up here.

It is in this perspective that the data furnished by the Census 2011 on places of worship, schools, toilets, etc. is really revealing. It is reported that places of worship of all religions numbered 2,398,650 in 2001 and became 3,013,140 in 2011. These numbers are directly proportional to the increases in GDP. The more interesting aspect of it is that there are more places of worship in West Bengal than any other state except the (vast) Uttar Pradesh (UP). Andhra Pradesh comes at sixth place (fifth in population size). It is also reported that the number of schools, colleges and hospitals put together stand at 2,789,732, that is, about 300,000 less than the number of places of worship. Most public institutions, including schools, hospitals, places of worship, etc., are generally built using public resources. This may be one of the reasons why a political party that declares allegiance to chauvinistic ideology got into power and the business community cleverly uses this resource to convert public property into private possession. Public properties worth several times more than the official GDP figures are under the control of this group. Interestingly, World Bank economists do not talk about the market value of the hidden wealth and its public use. The notion of crony capitalism does not absolve them as it is only an extension of capitalism in a different guise. The propaganda machine as usual talks about virtues and values to make way for their cronies to amass wealth excluding others.

Strangely, once it becomes institutionalised, the property thus obtained converts into the personal privilege of a few. There are priests who are underpaid, discriminated, starved and humiliated in places where there is no public glare, while the rich establishments enjoy the luxuries of life.[29] Unfortunately, because of our increasing intolerance of issues of faith, the real predicament of control, regulation and order and, above all, the public cause never surfaces in public discourse. Is it not helpful for public institutions that control trillions of rupees worth of public property to develop a code of ethics to contain fraud and prevent these from becoming private assets?

The nature of Indian development during the last two decades is an example of a dichotomy. It is noticed that self-interest and group interests are both limited to traditional communities and castes. Others are either not aware of it or articulate about the advantages it can have for the community. Interestingly, capitalist development has not decimated religious fundamentalism as in the Western secular world. In fact, it has strengthened beliefs in faith, widened caste deprivations and justified socio-economic inequalities in elegant philosophical and theoretical elucidations.

The evolution of social economics and classical and neoclassical theories seems to have grown as analogous to each other in their worldview of development. The neoclassicists and their disciples as cult followers have vulgarised the notion of self-interest as individual gain/benefit that ensues out of accumulation of wealth with contempt for fellow humans and society. Social economics on the other hand look at the social benefit not only from a utilitarian point of view, but also in relation to the use of resources by the future generations. The subject looks at the evolution of society and tries to answer challenges of not only the present but also in terms of the future needs, as it respects human dignity and considers all human beings are born free and equal. Lord Buddha considered the personal needs of the Bikkhus to be minimum and held discourses to keep needs and wants under control considering the genuine needs of other living organisms. The same principle was expounded and related to the modern times by Gandhiji, Schumacher and others. At the same time, the Buddhist philosophy in its emphasis on continuous change as *anitya* has been very much concerned about the developmental needs of modern man without compromising on the competing demands of the present and the future, and seems to be an ontological answer to some of the ugly consequences of globalisation.

Thus, social economy as a branch of economics is an original thought that could make scholars examine issues beyond textbook rhetoric. This could be considered as an appropriate approach to understand the unique problems of India with intrinsic benefit.

NOTES AND REFERENCES

1. K. S. Chalam, *Modernisation and Dalit Education: Ambedkar's Vision* (New Delhi: Rawat Publications, 2008).
2. J. C. L. S. Sismondi, *De la Richesse Commerciale*, trans. Sismondi (J. J. Paschoud, 1803), 104–6; *New Principles of Political Economy*, trans. R. Hyse (London: Transaction Publishers, 1991), 2.
3. K. S. Chalam, *Economic Reforms and Social Exclusion* (New Delhi: SAGE Publications, 2011).
4. Chalam, *Economic Reforms and Social Exclusion*.
5. J. M. Buchanan and G. Tullock, *The Calculus of Consent: Logical Foundations of Constitutional Democracy* (Ann Arbor: University of Michigan Press, 1962).
6. J. Bhagwati, "The Capital Myth," *Foreign Affairs* 77 (May–June 1998).
7. K. S. Chalam, ed., *Readings in Political Economy* (Hyderabad: Orient Longman, 1999).
8. Amartya Sen, *The Idea of Justice* (New Delhi: Oxford University Press, 2009), footnote page 50. Sen was critical about the European enlightenment project to make society better off through reason. But we in India take pride in the enlightenment project after the brutal suppression of the Lokayata tradition in the ancient period and conveniently and cunningly use it to showcase India against the Europeans.
9. P. Krugman, *International Economics: Theory and Policy* (New York: Harper Collins, 2003).
10. Yujiro Hayami and Yoshihisa G, *Development Economics* (New Delhi: Oxford University Press, 2012).
11. R. Nozick, *Anarchy, State and Utopia* (New York: Basic Books, 1974).
12. The Hawala Jain Dairy case is a popular media disclosure as to how the architect of the economic reforms got involved in the episode.
13. The IPL drama in the months of September–October 2013 has shown how some individuals like Srinivasan due to his background was treated despite of the fact that he was the culprit of the scam was exonerated by the Courts and the state and public. The Opposition Parties raising the issue of the Coalgate involving the PMO held up the Parliamentary session of the monsoon session in 2013. It is estimated that an amount of more than 1.75 trillion, higher than the 2G fraud is implicated in this.
14. Buchanan and Tullock, *The Calculus of Consent*.
15. A. Sen "On the Foundation of Welfare Economics: Utility Capability Rationality and Reason," in *Ethics, Rationality and Economic Behaviour*, ed. F. Farina, F. Hahn and S. Vannucci (Oxford: Clarendon Press, 1976), 53.
16. J. S. Mill, *On Liberty*, eBook (Australia: The University of Adelaide, 2015).
17. Karl Popper, *The Open Society and Its Enemies* (London: George Routledge and Sons Ltd, 1947).
18. Sen, *The Idea of Justice*.
19. Edward Said, *Orientalism* (New York: Vintage Books, 1978).

20. A. Sen, *The Argumentative Indian* (UK: Penguin, 2006).

21. Jagdish Bhagwati, Professor of Economics and Law at Columbia University, is a devote advocate of free trade and adviser to Narendra Modi. He is a Gujarati-born scholar.

22. Williamson Oliver E, Professor of Economics at California University at Berkeley, is a Nobel laureate in 2009 and coined the term Washington Consensus.

23. J. C. Kumarappa, *Gandhian Economics* (Varanasi: Sarvaseva Sangh Prakashan, 1951).

24. Milton Friedman Quotes, www.goodreads.com, accessed on 10 Aug, 2015.

25. Gali Janardhanareddy was a cabinet minister in the Bharatiya Janata Party (BJP) government in Karnataka. The Central Bureau of Investigation (CBI) booked him for his involvement in illegal mining and changing the state boundary with Andhra Pradesh and he was sent to jail and later released on bail. He has presented a diamond crown worth millions of rupees to the Lord Balaji of Tirupati.

26. Madhav Gadgil, see his 'Madhav Gadgil Homepage'.

27. Jairam Ramesh, Union Minister for Rural Development advocated the construction of latrines in rural areas by referring to the data on schools and stated that we have more places of worship than schools and latrines, and this became controversial due to the reactions from a section of intellectuals.

28. Nityananda is a god-man from Bangalore who was in trouble because of his escapades with women devotees.

29. The world came to know about several trillion rupees worth of gold, precious stones, etc. stashed in Ananta Padma Nabha Swamy temple in Travancore (Trivandrum) in Kerala last year which is now being hushed up. There are temples such as Lord Venkateswara, Vaishnodevi and several Hindu temples and Muslim, Sikh, Jain, Christian and other minority places of worship that seem to have trillions rupees worth of properties accessible only to a select few. The judiciary, bureaucracy and the legislative bodies of the government dare not touch the issues as the aggressive postures of the faith merchants harm their election prospects. In fact, all of them, it is alleged, collude and promote the fortunes of religions in the name of secularism and socialism. Sadly, the Marxist rhetoric has no takers as they do not have a concrete programme of action to combat fundamentalism. In fact, the accumulation of religious properties has taken place through the process of primitive accumulation in the past (by starving the poor) in India, but such religious accumulations had been productively used for development of the people in countries such as China, Japan, etc.

3

Economic Liberalisation and Social Development

The liberalisation of economic policy in India is said to be founded on the notion of the efficiency of the 'invisible hand' of Adam Smith. Neoclassical economists have advanced theories and empirical results to show that the welfare state has failed everywhere and the idea of common good is a fallacy. Therefore, some of them have argued that the self-interest of the individual needs to be endorsed to stimulate growth in a less developed country like India. It is under this backdrop that most economic frauds during the last few years in the country are exposed in the world of business enterprises. There are, however, instances of other realms where such occurrences have been manifested such as the BCCI/IPL, Coalgate, etc.[1] We have inherited different kinds of business organisations through the colonial legacy among which the joint-stock companies or business corporations, etc. are prominent. The Managing Agency System introduced by the British to run some businesses through Indian agents like the tea gardens, etc. have been abolished and are only part of history now. The kind of business organisations that conquered commerce and trade are a very important unit of analysis for understanding the resilience of capitalism in the 21st century. The Indian model of development is unique as it has allowed the traditions to survive without annihilating social institutions that came in its way of modernisation. In this context, the triumph of world capitalism declared by experts as final for lack of any alternative (TINA), particularly after the Soviet and Chinese experiences need critical reflection, as they are our immediate neighbours. We discuss some of the typical case studies here.

The efficiency and the democratic space provided by the business corporation is eulogised by management gurus as the most sustainable model that is beyond disparagement. In fact, we have dozens of treatises and memoirs by great innovators and entrepreneurs who became icons overnight after the 1991 economic policy. They have all used the public/private corporation as a tool to accumulate capital and run businesses. It has been claimed that the company/corporation as a registered business organisation is within the values of any democracy and at the same time enjoys the freedom to do what is good for the company or corporation. This is one of the most important innovations adopted by the capitalist system to compete and outwit a demoralised totalitarian Soviet model.

Economic liberalisation in the form of industrial and business easing is not an end in itself; it also has an impact on society as well as on social institutions. Social development is generally understood as a process through which groups, institutions, social relations, etc., having both economic and social implications, are kept at the centre of any analysis. The economic factors that are unleashed to bring about growth also affect social practices and the culture of saving, investment, etc., not only as per the assumptions of experts but in relation to our traditions. They, therefore, need to be studied and reorganised as per our needs and agenda.

Though the modern capitalist system is far ahead of what its critiques hypothesised during 19th century, the fact that intellectual and media support during the current phase has disguised most of its failures is now discernible. The money that was invested to outsource the intellectual discourse on capitalism seems to have failed to endure the system from its moral and intellectual collapse in the form of the 2008 recession and its aftermath. We have today episodes of economic breakdown everywhere. There is a serious upshot in the ethical dimension of business ventures due to the unscrupulous practices paraded as optimal outcomes. This has no doubt enhanced the economic status of some individuals and groups. But, all of them have lost the moral bearing that the accomplishments are within the norms of civilised and commonly agreed behaviour. It is here that one can find that the erstwhile socialist countries were more upright during the periods of collapse than the kind of decadence we witness in the liberal societies now. The moral consequence of the recent happenings is so serious that the threats on human survival are imminent. The naked display of extreme voracity increasingly internalised by some persons and groups is so dreadful that might ultimately annul the distinction between a human and an animal. It is in this context, that we examine how the corporation has been used as a tool in this process.

The Fabians and Labour Party functionaries in Great Britain promoted the advancement of the corporation as a business organisation during the early part of the last century. Economists such as A. C. Pigou[2] and J. M. Keynes[3] wanted to use the corporation as a tool for successful nationalisation of basic industries in the course of the gradual transition to a socialist economy. The kind of public corporation that they perceived was an institution that would avoid political control over public utilities and at the same time would enjoy autonomy to take prudent decisions in the day-to-day functioning of the business. Though England had pioneered the concept in an ideological backdrop, the corporation has emerged differently in diverse economies. Thus, the kind of corporation like the BBC in England is different from those in France, Japan, USA and others.

A corporation is a legal entity with a set of objectives to run public utilities in the beginning and which has been slowly adopted by business enterprises. In fact, the Tennessee Valley Authority is an example of a legal entity created through a legislative process to operate the irrigation project in the USA.

The basic legal characteristics of the business corporation include legal personality, limited liability, transferable shares, delegated management under a board structure and investor ownership. These five characteristics respond to the economic exigencies of the large modern business enterprise. Thus, the Harvard scholars examining the essential elements of corporate law maintained that everywhere there must be, as necessity, provision for these five features. As mentioned in the Harvard University web page,

> To be sure, there are other forms of business enterprise that lack one or more of these characteristics. But the remarkable fact—and the fact that we wish to stress—is that, in market economies, almost all large-scale business firms adopt a legal form that possesses all five of the basic characteristics of the business corporation. Indeed, most small jointly-owned firms adopt this corporate form as well, although sometimes with deviations from one or more of the five basic characteristics to fit their special needs.

In virtually all economically important jurisdictions, there is a basic statute that provides for the formation of firms with all of these characteristics. As the above pattern suggests, these characteristics have strong complementary qualities to reduce costs of conducting business.

Economic liberalisation introduced in India in the 1980s was formalised in 1991 through the industrial policy of P. V. Narasimha Rao. It is reported to have unleashed animal spirits that are essential, as per experts, for economic growth. At the same time, it is the open-ended policy that has subjected the economic institutions to considered exposure to private interests to loot and corrupt. It is necessary to interrogate to what extent this has helped social development and liberated our traditional orthodoxy.

THE BUSINESS CORPORATION AS A FIEFDOM

The public corporation or private corporation in India was introduced through the Companies Act, 1956 and was reintroduced in 2012 with some modifications. The difference between the private limited and public limited companies is that the former needs seven members and the latter can be registered with a minimum of two members and with limited liability. The latest amendment to the act has provided for a one-man company/ corporation. There are other provisions such as voting rights, election of chairman, nomination of auditors, etc. But, there is also a provision through which the board can amend the articles and memorandums, making the provisions trivial. The interesting part of the functioning of the company or corporation is that it can allot its shares (Article 42) to any private party and call it a public offer and can allot shares to its directors and employees (read family members). The corporation can buy back its own shares when it grows strong through different means to make it a purely family affair. Thus, the capital marketisation through the corporations is one and half times that of our GDP, or ₹13,541,699 trillion, is under the control of a few families.

The foremost issue of the corporate world is that we have so far 1,289,229 registered companies including suit case companies. Interestingly, only 872,957 are in operation, with a majority of them in finance, banking, insurance, real estate and service sectors, with only 22 per cent registered as manufacturing firms. Does it convey the anarchy or a native grown pattern in our economic operations that reflects our society? It is difficult to convince some of our activist scholars that feudal characteristics prevail and sustain in an advanced capitalist system. But, India, according to R. S. Sarma[4] and others, had feudalism during 300–1200 AD. Sarma has qualified that his study "does not consider its impact on social and cultural life." There are scholars, who claim that India had a different kind of Asiatic mode of production that does not necessarily correspond to the European feudal category. However, it is relevant here to understand that feudalism as a form of governance or mode of production is related to land and the fief of a lord. The landlord under the fiefdom controls everything, exploits the workers and could develop an ideology based on faith or social bonding to keep them under his control. It seems that such characteristics of fiefdom have sneaked into our corporate world. This was manifested openly during the last few weeks when BCCI chairman openly accusing his detractors as a bias against the South. A popular weekly has made an observation on a much touted corporation and the promoter as having, "[M]issed a tricky by mechanically passing the baton on to each of the founders. The firm effectively closed the door outside talent which could have taken in to the next level of success" (Semi-capitalism in *Outlook*, 17 June 2013). There seems to be some kind of a bias against the South from the time of Satyam in the media as the episodes of billions of rupees of scams in other parts of the country are given tepid treatment till they overflow under their gravity, and not otherwise.

Thus, all the support structures and the ethos of liberalisation in India do not show any evidence of conflict with feudal institutions such as fiefdom, caste, the joint family, guilds, etc. to apply the tenets of corporate law. This interesting innovation warrants a critical reflection and debate on the Indian model of development.

CORRUPTION, BLACK MONEY AND THE ELITE

Most of the issues relating to black money are connected to corporate capitalism. It is known that state corporations do not get involved in the practice of bribing to get their products marketed while private corporations, among themselves or with state corporations and customers, do associate in giving discounts, margins, etc. to transfer some benefits to the customer. At the same time, this process helps syphon off public money for private use, defined as corruption, and stories of black money or money laundering in the country have been an issue of debate for quite some time. It is baffling for an economist who dabbles in macroeconomic growth models and provides every week some figures for the rate of growth. In fact, in the thick of the debate on black money, corruption and issues relating to democratic values, there were also voices from intellectuals who defended liberalisation, globalisation and all that. The debate on growth, equity and justice has been broadly divided into two camps from the beginning of the modern period. One group consists of the idealists and the other, the materialists. The idealists defended inequity and accumulation on the basis of the right to freedom, merit, inheritance of property, attributes of conduct, etc. The greatest proponent of inequality as a value was Frederick Hayek who attacked the concepts of equality and socialism as 'a road to serfdom'. This tradition, starting from Hayek and Milton Friedman down to the present defenders of globalisation, includes Jagadish Bhagwati.

We have a host of scholars and thinkers in different parts of the world, including Jawaharlal Nehru, B. R. Ambedkar, M. N. Roy, R. M. Lohia, Amartya Sen and Marxist scholars such as Prabhat Patnaik, P. K. Bardhan and Amiya Bagchi, who have been defending the concept of equality. The discussion was centred on intellectuals because there was a serious squabble between the Supreme Court Bench composed of Justice Sudarshan Reddy and Justice Surinder Singh Nijjar and noted economist Jagadish Bhagwati during the same week in the media in 2011–12.[5]

The issue of corruption and black money, money laundering, Swiss Bank accounts, etc. came into prominence due to the Supreme Court judgement delivered by these judges in 2011. The judges pointed out that the problem of corruption became serious because of the neoliberal policies that started in 1991. It is in this context that Jagadish Bhagwati has observed against parts of the judgement about the competence of the judges and even mentioned that the judges could learn from the former Chief Justice P. N. Bhagwati. Jagadish Bhagwati is a very reputed and respected scholar in economics and law, who might bring a Nobel Prize in the near future. His argument is that the reforms have reduced high-level corruption by reducing the interference of the state. He was a strong proponent of limited role of the state, and even argued for the withdrawal of the state from economic activities. He takes pride that he was instrumental in introducing economic reforms in India. In the third Professor Hiren Mukherjee Lecture delivered by him in the Parliament in 2010, he argued that the reforms brought rapid growth, and poverty was being reduced due to globalisation. He added that, "the common man derives his caffeine from these drinks (coke, Pepsi) while the well-off critics get theirs from the espresso and cappuccino coffee in the cafes." The second green revolution, he said, will take place with genetically modified crops like Bt brinjal, etc. These benefits are made possible by globalisation and the technical efficiency it has brought into India.

Bhagwati is almost of the same opinion as that of the Anna Hazare team,[6] that corruption at the lower level is pervasive and the middle classes is fed up with it. However, he has suggested a Western model of reducing corruption by way of funding political parties to fight elections. It is strange that economists like Jagadish Bhagwati, who live in the USA, should have used their expertise to reason out the problems of the current crisis in America rather than advising others. How is it that Fannie Mae and Fredie Mac, along with the Lehman Brothers, created a financial crisis in the USA that is still haunting the world? Is it not a fact that the USA and Europe (not Nordic countries), where the role of the State is minimised as per their advocacy, have experienced serious economic problems? The subprime catastrophe was created by the wicked, the selfish and the invisible market failure. They are all corporate frauds. It was the invisible foot of the 'State' as everyone knows, that ultimately rescued the US economy and society from disaster. It was the American state that declared an economic stimulus package with $168 billion in 2008 and $850 billion in 2009 to save the honour with taxpayers' money. Yet, the elite in India who subscribe to the ideology of the free market and free trade do not agree that the State has an important role to play, not only in regulating the market, but also in protecting the citizen from the self-interest and greed of the few. It seems that some of our elite critiques target the politician for corruption as if politics is differentiated from economic activity in India. Today we see the convergence of all political parties (except one or two) on economic policy in India. No one is so obtuse as to believe that there are no connections between them. It is proved beyond doubt that all political activity today is directed to get power to distribute and accumulate resources. Unless the State, as an arbitrator representing constitutional morality, is present, there will be chaos. It is the honesty and integrity of the scholar that makes him comprehend the realities to formulate genuine policies. It is with great regret that we have to cite here that civil society activists Bhushans who have testified that eight out of the 16 former Chief Justices of India were corrupt. It was reported that black money is internally stashed in some babas' ashrams. The people of Andhra Pradesh know the role played by Justice P. N. Bhagwati (brother of Jagadish Bhagwati) in the Puttaparti Sai Baba episode of unaccounted wealth. What we can learn from these elite idealist's elegant theories or whether we need honesty and sincerity of purpose to bring common good to the majority is a question to be answered by the critics of the 'State'.

Unfortunately, India is known for its several dichotomies, both in social life and in economic policies. Inequities and discrimination have been the foundation of private life while abstract ideas of equality and unity have remained the declared goals of the public being. As a result, several malpractices and abuses of power seem to have been espoused by many believers and are surviving with the grace of God. Therefore, the present malady is not a sudden outcome of the 21st century. It is perhaps deeply rooted in our ethos and can be edged out when it reaches intolerable proportions. This may be one of the reasons for the manifestation of corruption in a wider sense and is taken for granted by people if it is within tolerable limits. Or we may also premise that the poor, the vulnerable and the hapless are the victims of this menace waiting for an opportunity to react, may be violently, in due course as it has happened elsewhere! Confronting the problem with token struggles would ultimately benefit the wicked as it might have already happened in the case of the black money stashed in Swiss banks.

It was reported in 2006 that the Swiss banks had around $1.47 trillions of black money stashed by Indians which amounts to around ₹75 trillion in its present value (2012).[7] Politicians have been talking about it for the last almost one decade, sufficiently warning the hoarders to lift the money from there. Some of us anticipated in 2012 that one need not be surprised if the foreign banks would ultimately declare that the present value of the money deposited by the Indians might be around $100 billion, in future and is legal. There are already indications to that effect (see the White Paper on Black Money). It is not out of place to refer to the so-called soft scams in the financial markets. There are soft scams of the sophisticated type where the dvijas are involved and hard scams, it is alleged, are those where the shudras are involved in activities such as mining, real estate settlements, etc. Further, the amount of investments coming from the Indian satellite Mauritius is, according to some, another conduit of black money. Another significant indicator of transfers can be studied through the lending of banks to real estate that stood at around ₹17 trillion by the end of March 2010 as per the RBI. It is presumed by analysts that the boom in real estate is because of the facility of transfer of the illegal money which is three to four times more than the book value. This has also resulted in scams in the lendings of banks, the LIC, etc. Most commoners are not aware of what is happening in the share markets, the ICT body shopping business, etc. till a Ketan Parekh or Harshad Mehta emerges. But no one talks about these soft scams until the poor taxpayers' money is diverted to overcome the problem of NPAs later through a budget support or a sophisticated economic policy prescription. They just do not attract the attention of our politicians, whistle-blowers or business media.

The politicians who talk about black money seem to have not looked at internal conduits. These sources are made legal with the tacit approval of all the parties. Perhaps every political party, business house and public person is in this. It seems the intelligent, with the support of so-called consultants, are interpreting Articles 27, 29 and 30 of the Constitution to their advantage. Most of the institutes get a religious, minority, etc. tag to invoke the above provisions to avoid tax and to internally stock ill-gotten money. The Enforcement Directorate (ED) of the Income Tax Department has exposed only Baba Ramdev.[8] It seems the reforms attempted by the government to avoid the tricky issue under the Income Tax Act 1961 are kept in cold storage due to pressure from various sources. Interestingly, babas are exposed now as brands putting faith in the marketplace. There is an alleged nexus between dubious god men and corrupt practices. But, international agencies like the Transparency International (TI) may not capture this phenomenon unless they understand the social and cultural practices in India.

The TI, with branches in different parts of the world, seems to be honest, making all efforts to educate the people and governments about the menace of corruption. The main objective of estimating the Corruption Perception Index (CPI) is to "enhancing understanding of levels of corruption from one country to another." Therefore, it is a composite of various corruption indices made on a 0–10 scale. Statistically it is called as the sample mean of standardised sources such as the *World Competitiveness Report*, the *Wall Street Journal*, and the *Asian Intelligence* issue, etc. According to experts, it follows a nonparametric bootstrapping method. There is no single definition of corruption and each source uses its own concepts such as bribes, amounts paid as bribes, damage done due to corruption, etc. Experts have questioned this measure on the grounds that it is an opinion survey based on a questionable sample of different categories and aggregating the data to arrive at a figure with several standard errors. We can leave the technical questions of its limitations, which the TI itself underlines in its report. What is important is that it is a survey of opinions of business groups and entrepreneurs on corruption through a questionnaire to judge how doing business in a country is problematic. There are expert groups to crosscheck the information from various sources, including the World Bank which collects information on bribes paid in different countries. It appears that it is an attempt to understand the business environment in each country and gives possible clues about how to approach the system to build business or trade. The by-product of this is that the Third World countries are educated about corruption in their countries while the developed ones are just onlookers to sermonise the virtues of honesty.

Switzerland has emerged as one of the least corrupt countries in the world as per the TI score card. It is known throughout the world that the so-called black money or ill-gotten wealth is stacked in Swiss banks. Are these two things not contradictory? One might say that Switzerland is doing business in finance and it has nothing to do with the kind of money deposited or invested there. But, the Organisation for Economic Co-operation and Development (OECD) countries, particularly the neighbouring countries have complained that some of their citizens are stacking black money in Swiss banks through money laundering and causing internal problems. For instance, they have complained against the distinction used by Switzerland between tax evasion and tax fraud to conceal some of the illegal transactions. But, the OECD forced Switzerland to change the distinction and made the government to bring in a Money Laundering Act. Interestingly, Switzerland has not joined the European Union and it seems it is only a member of the OECD group, the developed countries economic organisation. Switzerland is a beautiful country and records the highest tourist visits of the world (some may visit for transactions more than once in a year).

In order to understand the moral righteousness of Switzerland emerging as the least corrupt country, let us look at its economic operations. The country is one of the first among the developed countries in the world with a GDP of $524 billion for a population of less than 8 million people. The per capita income is, therefore, the highest, approximately $37,666 (₹1,883,300) nearly 40 times that of India. The Union Bank of Switzerland (UBS) is one of the largest banks in the world and is in the news because most of our black money is reported to be stacked here. It has branches in 30 countries with 15,000 employees. In fact, one of the largest sources of income of the country comes from its financial sector which contributes about 12 per cent of its GDP. The banking sector in Switzerland employs around 140,000 people, the largest employer. There is no unemployment here. The total money invested or the liabilities of the country are nearly 260 per cent of its GDP. Another statistic is startling as one third of the worlds' outside investments are made only in Swiss banks. The data clearly show that the standard of living and the economy are sustained due to these financial operations (pharmaceuticals, watches, etc. are secondary). The issue is that these legal or illegal transactions are not taken into account in ranking Switzerland by the TI as the least corrupt country.

It is not only Switzerland, but the economic history of some of the advanced countries of the world indicate that they became rich through exploitation, primitive accumulation, extortion, illegal transactions, unequal exchange rates and other unethical practices. There appear to be some countries in the Nordic region such as Finland, Norway, Denmark, etc. who, for their non-corrupt practices following social democracy, figure in the TI list. We know very little about them as they are non-English-speaking countries. What emerges from this discussion is that the ranking of countries as least corrupt is only a biased view of the West without taking the real economic transactions of these countries into account. It is better to rely on each country's data on economic crimes, contextualised in terms of their history and culture, to rank countries as honest or backward. The TI data are expressions of advanced nations' perceptions about the Third World that may not necessarily be true compared to their economic history or present corporate culture.

THE ADVENT OF CRONY CAPITALISM IN INDIA

Capitalism is said to be an economic system based on merit and creation of opportunities that sustain it. But, critiques say it has relied on the extraction of surplus value from labour and the exploitation of resources probably by deceit. The notion of capitalism entered India with the British. There are now different varieties of capitalism in use in academic discussions. Classical economists including Adam Smith regarded capitalism as a natural form of economic organisation based upon human beings propensity to trade and barter in his/her own self-interest. The laissez-faire system of economic institutions, they said would achieve welfare for all. This was contested by Marx. He gave an elaborate analysis of the system in his magnum opus *Das Capital*. But, Marx did not explain directly what capitalism was. He has used a different method known as the mode of production to explain the different stages of socio-economic formations. It is found that Marx used the concept of the 'mode of production' 2,600 times in his works. Since the concept of capitalism is popularly known through the writings of Marx, it is better to know his formulation. It was his son-in-law, Edward Avelling, who in the abridged edition of *Capital* reduced the formula to M-C-M'.[9] It means that the capitalist goes to the market with his capital M and buys the labour C to produce and sell the commodity in the market at a price M'. The difference between M and M' is surplus value. Here, the capitalist and the labourer belonged to two different antagonistic classes. The dynamics of the capitalist system depended on the drive for surplus value including the expansion of production. The antagonistic contradictions of capitalism gave rise to class struggles between the working class and the bourgeoisie.

The development and resilience of capitalism in the 21st century (despite the prediction that it will disappear) has facilitated it to take different shapes and forms. It was in the year 1998 that the capitalist system underwent a terrible crisis in the East Asian economies. Scholars have started analysing it as a financial crisis and it was attributed to what is called 'cronyism' that prevailed in these economies. A few families and their cronies captured the state in these countries particularly in the Philippines, South Korea, Indonesia and Thailand. The cronies with the support of the bureaucracy got favours, such as permits, licenses to exploit natural resources, tax concessions, etc., to remain successful in business. It is necessary to link capitalism as discussed previously with cronyism as witnessed in East Asia to arrive at the concept of 'crony capitalism'. Interestingly, it did not talk about how international corporations were under the control of a few families living in the USA and the EU.

Crony capitalism takes place in the form of collusion, forming cartels, avoiding taxes or getting tax cuts and restricting others to enter the closely knitted networks of business. There seem to be four important conditions to accomplish crony capitalism, namely:

1. The presence of opportunistic capitalists, manipulating things in their favour, rather than depending upon free competition.
2. Crony intellectuals or experts to defend and eulogise the significance of capitalism as a viable system.
3. Pliable bureaucrats who would crawl when the minister says to bend the rules in favour of a few cronies.
4. A section of the media that survives on the spoils of the system and brazenly brings out distorted stories to influence public opinion in favour of crony capitalists.

Though many Indian activists have discerned the features of crony capitalism in India, they never realised that it was crony capitalism prevalent particularly during the last two decades after 1991. It is in this context that one can study how the 20th century experts looked at it. Among many scholars, Hobson[10] is one who has analysed the concept of imperialism as an oligarchy of a few capitalists (cronies) who spread it to other countries due to the problems of misdistribution of wealth in their own counties. It was Lenin[11] who had systematically studied the economies of the West in the early part of 20th century to present imperialism as the highest stage of capitalism. Lenin's explanation of Imperialism is relevant here to understand the concept of crony capitalism as he anticipated that such a thing would happen in the future. The characterisation of imperialism, particularly the emergence of finance capital through the operation of share markets, international financial institutions, etc., needs to be interpreted as crony capitalism as it was facilitated through the cronies and not due to free competition. We have witnessed the new phenomenon called insider trading, as in the case of Rajat Gupta, Occupy Wall Street, etc. They were all part of crony capitalism.

Crony capitalism is not new to India. Its genesis was weaved with the formation of the East India Company which comprised a few individuals who were closely related. It was the members of the company's families who were posted as officers to plunder India and take the booty back home as family income. After independence, the government realised that there was concentration of wealth in the hands of few. The Hazari Committee,[12] the Mahalanobis Committee,[13] the Monopolies Inquiry Commission,[14] etc. appointed by the government during 1965–69 brought out the fact that wealth was, in fact, concentrated in a few business houses. Some of it could also have been stashed in Swiss banks. The license-permit raj was manipulated by the cronies in their favour and did not allow others to enter various businesses. It is the same business houses and their extended families that have been involved in the so-called soft scams of share market, spectrum license, oil and gas, body shopping, etc. after liberalisation. The non-traditional business families who have just acquired political power seem to have manipulated it to secure natural resources, real estate, etc. in the name of permits and licenses for their cronies. The greatest advantage for crony capitalism to thrive in India is the primordial relations of castes. This has strengthened the operation of crony capitalism with emotional appeal to the castes in power. But, one should realise that the cronies are not going to benefit the entire caste, but only few families in the caste. This neophyte would facilitate the division of society to plunder without organised resistance, thereby helping to maintain orthodoxy even in the 21st century. The sooner we appreciate the folly of caste politics and corporate sponsored democracy to reinforce crony capitalism, the better for the country as a whole to realise the constitutional goals of socialism, secularism and democracy.

INEQUALITY WIDENED THROUGH TRADE

One of the important characters of crony capitalism is its reliance on trade and money. India has adopted a model based on foreign trade replacing its earlier model of import substitution after 1991.[15] The impact of trade on the economy and society are evaluated by the United Nations Conference on Trade and Development (UNCTAD) report on trade and development for 2012, a striking feature of which is that it is dedicated to 'policies for inclusive and balanced growth' and devotes a separate chapter on how international trade has widened inequalities in general, and in developing countries in particular. Those who are familiar with the liberalisation policies in India around the 1990s do remember how vigorously some economists had championed free trade. Interestingly, neither its supporters nor its admirers have ever looked at the experiences in our neighbouring South East and Far East. In fact, we have had better historical and traditional contacts with these countries than with the colonial Anglo-Saxons. But, for reasons better known to the elite of the political and bureaucratic executive, we have continued to follow the prescriptions of the West. It has given an impression that globalisation means contacts with a dozen countries, mostly English-speaking, and the cultural goods packaged and popularised through the media. Unfortunately, we know very little about Japan, Korea and other countries whose manufacturing goods are used every day. Strangely, the younger generation are not aware that the development models used in Germany, and being broadly pursued in Japan, are different from those of the Anglo-Saxons (though the Saxons are from ancient German descent, Germany as a nation is not put in that league). Ram Manohar Lohia had emphasised on this idea in his writings about half a century ago.

Frederick List, the German economist, had underscored the infant industry argument for protection without contradicting Ricardo's comparative cost advantage theory with his emphasis on long-term market failure. Latin American scholars adopted a technical method to elucidate the import substitution theory for developing countries. The issue is that Germany has never followed the Anglo-Saxon approaches of development as they did not boast of any colonies to rely upon for their domestic development. They used nationalism and developed science and technology of their own and contributed 2.5 times more scientific discoveries than England. Similarly, Japan, another giant in industrial development, used State support for the expansion of education and infrastructure with little rent-seeking activities by the bureaucrats. Both the nations, isolated during the Second World War (due to parochialism) have re-emerged as the most advanced countries with independent models of development. Scholars like Yujiro Hayami say that corruption in Japan has entered only the political executive, as demonstrated by the Tanaka episode of the Lockheed aircraft bribery, and it seems such persons shun public appearances due to the value system of 'public shame', unlike public elation of the corrupt in public life in India.

Against this background, the UNCTAD 2102 report has implications for India. It is reported that the merchandise trade of the world declined from 5.5 per cent in 2011 to 3.5 per cent in 2012. The growth rate declined sharply from 4.1 per cent in 2010 to 2.7 per cent in 2012, mostly due to the growth rates of developing countries and that of China (with developed countries confined to less than 2.5 per cent). Financial frauds and weak demand in developed countries have lowered exports from developing countries, including India. Except gold, all mineral exports have declined during the period. The report analyses the Kuznets curve indicating that in the beginning inequalities increase and after some time, with increases in productivity, disparities decline, seems to have not happened in case of India. On the contrary, Dani Rodrik and Alberto Alesina have proved that inequalities in primary income hamper growth. It is supported by historical data that the share of wages in the national income of the UK, the USA and Japan was around 60 per cent for a long period to sustain growth.[16]

This went against the rhetoric that the liberalisation of labour laws to reduce wage rigidities in the Third World would affect development. After a review of the theories, the report comes to the conclusion that,

> [T]these alternative views, by challenging the conventional wisdom that rising inequality is the normal result of development within market economies, may contribute to a new understanding of the functioning of a market economy, and can lead to a paradigm shift towards a pattern of economic development that is both more equitable and more efficient.[17]

The report notes that trade between the advanced and the developing countries has caused inequalities in the latter. The estimates of the proportion of the top quintile share of income to the bottom quintile show that inequalities are higher in developing countries than in developed countries like the UK. It is supported by the Gini ratios (measure of inequality) ranging from 35 per cent in the USA to 50 per cent in Malaysia, and India coming in between at 32.5 per cent.

The report notes that inequalities in the distribution of personal income are generally more pronounced in developing countries than in the developed or transition economies. As in developed countries, in the developing countries too, the income gap narrowed during the first three decades after the Second World War, but between 1980 and 2000 there was a general increase in inequality. The observations of the report on FDI are mixed. The prescriptions proposed by UNCTAD are radical and go against the fundamentalist ideas of the neo-liberals: "Since the turn of the millennium, trends in income distribution have diverged among developing regions. Greater taxation of wealth and inheritance is a potential source of public revenue that can be tapped in many developed and developing countries to reduce inequality of both income and wealth distribution and enlarge the government's fiscal space." For example, taxes on real estate, large landholdings, luxury durable goods and financial assets are normally easier to collect than taxes on personal income, and can represent an important source of revenue in countries that have high inequality of income and wealth distribution. In resource-rich developing countries, incomes from exploitation of natural resources and gains resulting from rising international commodity prices are another important source of public revenue. "By appropriating their fair share of commodity rents, especially in the oil and mining sectors, governments in such developing countries can ensure that their natural resource wealth benefits the entire population and not just a few domestic and foreign actors."[18] It is hoped that the prospective governments of the future will take this advice in earnest.

The Foreign Exchange Management Act, 1999 freed all transactions that were once regulated, giving capital flows an automatic route. It was thought that we would have an advantage in getting more FDIs as well as in takeovers outside so that the health and vigour of the economy could be doubled. It is difficult to judge whether it was a good decision or a manipulated push in view of the current crisis. In fact, IMF experts have studied the trends of various countries and have come to the conclusion that a capital account deficit (CAD) between 1.5 and 2.5 per cent of GDP is sustainable. We had such comfort zones in the early part of our liberalisation scene. But now it has become a big worry as the rate has reached the highest level at 6.7 per cent of GDP during 2012–13 (survey) due to fall in invisibles. Even the much pampered IT services did not come to the rescue and, in fact, they are also undergoing a crisis. The sign of a strain on the balance of payments (BOP) was designated when the moderate growth in net services coupled with lower net inflows under income account resulted in decline in net invisibles in 2012.

Some experts might say that opportunities are being created abroad and jobs are being provided to natives. But, this is not reflected in the inflows. The continuous weakening of the rupee has not lifted our exports as expected since our goods would be expensive abroad. Gold is physically demanded in Asia while it is a piece of speculation in the West. In fact, all of them are cumulatively affecting our domestic economy and prices. The common man is made to pay in real terms by foregoing his opportunities of wealth, health, education and the future of progeny. The sooner we realise this and reformulate our policies, the better.

In a globalised world, there are chain reactions in international trade, particularly when the dominance of the US dollar as a medium of international exchange is deliberately allowed to continue. Further, money is not printed now; it is electronically created, enhancing the so-called 'fictitious capital' without much growth in the real economy. It was believed that the mathematical modelling done by management experts would solve some of the problems of a huge set of equations and calculations with the help of computer software; however, it ended up in the 2008 catastrophe. Therefore, the crisis is imminent despite the 'quantitative easing' and other techniques used by Ben Bernanke in the USA and copied in India. The problems of effective demand that economists have been discussing for quite some time appear to be due to the high living standards that the West adopted without much contribution to physical production. The artificial demand created could sustain the economy through colonial (neocolonial) plunder that seems to have been converted into the illusion of expanding service sector with the support of artificially created so-called 'fictious capital' (as enunciated by Marx). The moment the Third World countries started imitating them, the system started crumbling. The sooner we realise the folly and resort to our original hard-earned experiences with mixed economic models or social democracy, the better it would be to at least avoid immediate distress. Nevertheless, it does not mean that the crisis will not recur once again.

THE EUROPEAN CRISIS AND INDIA

India and the South East Asia have been persuaded by experts and agencies to adopt European models of development to shy away from underdevelopment. In fact, this so-called 'white man's burden to modernise' the rest has become the greatest burden for the rest of the world today as it did not go well with them. In fact, Third World scholars and thinkers such as Edward Said and Samir Amin have raised the issue of euro-centrism in history, culture and political economy. Economists, on the other hand, have developed theories of export-led growth or import substitution strategies of development for developing countries. The euphoria of the Washington Consensus that guided globalisation seems to have slowed down due to the failure of market-supported theories in most of the countries where gloom prevails now.

It is in this context we need to look at the European economic crisis, the political turmoil in this region and its broad implications for India. Dr Manmohan Singh as PM, during his visit to G20 and Rio, strategically appealed to the West to invest in India's infrastructure projects as it was searching for investment destinations. Interestingly, he seemed to have realised that the solutions to our economic setbacks were to be sought within. The USA is not an isolated newfound land any more. It is an extension of Europe (if we cut the Atlantic in the map between the two continents). All European nations are represented in the USA, but the population data does not speak about them and only lists Asians, Hispanics, African Americans and undocumented immigrants. The OECD and European Union are economic blocs of the Anglo-Saxon or occidental nations that have colonies in the Third World, including India. The desire to continue with the past hegemony and lifestyles based on plunder appears to be haunting them unconsciously through the policies and strategies recommended by them to the Third World. The nations that have seriously taken their advice are now in jitters despite their sovereign entity. It is due to the fact that their economies have been deeply engaged with them and the contagion is suspected to be imminent. The European crisis has been discussed wherever there has been an economic slowdown in recent months, and particularly with reference to Greece, Spain, Portugal, etc. The economic crisis in Greece, once seriously talked about as a failed nation in the media, has suddenly disappeared ever since the right-wing New Democracy has taken the reins of power. The Tsipra left government in 2015 was forced to accept the EU prudent measures that affect the living standards of workers in Greece.

The political economy of Greece is an interesting case study to understand some contemporary issues. Two political parties, namely the PASOK socialist party and ND, the New Democracy, dominated the political atlas of Greece, with the former being a left-oriented party and the latter a right-wing group. There are several formations such as the Euro communists and others playing second fiddle in the coalitions. Both the left- and right-wing parties that came to power have expanded the public sector with public debt with the support of interest groups. Public debt reached $481 billion, one and a half times of its GDP of $302 billion in 2010. This resulted in a fiscal deficit of 15 per cent of GDP and forced the country to approach the IMF for a loan. The IMF has granted loans on very stringent conditionalities that embarrassed the political establishment. It seems that was the beginning of the crisis. Interestingly, two of the Greek innovations—democracy and tragedy—are being performed live.

The crux of the crisis was that the European states borrowed mostly from European banks at an exorbitant rate of interest of 18 per cent. Out of $2.84 trillion capital of the European Central Bank, $637 billion were given as loans to Portugal, Ireland, Greece and Spain. The problem of Spain is not public debt but private debt, since its fiscal deficit reached a peak at 8.9 per cent of GDP in 2011. The private debt of Spain was alleged to be linked with real estate bubble that around would be 90 per cent of its GDP. The implications of the Greece profligacy, according to some scholars, were that it promoted rampant corruption. The popular Vatopedi land scam during the period when the New Democracy was in power showcases how public properties were converted into private estates. The socialist party was also not free from this. As in India, where the Parliamentary committee appointed to enquire into the allegations failed to reach any conclusion except for naming five ministers who were involved in the land scam. The unemployment rate ranged between 16 to 19 per cent during the last few years that led to riots and the emergence of a new movement called 'I don't pay tax'. The rate of growth of the economy dropped to less than 0.5 per cent and to negative rates for the last few years. This has troubled the lenders, including the financial institutions of the USA that have large networks in the world. More than 50 per cent of the world's GDP is from the USA and the EU.

Interestingly, out of 500 billionaires of the world (*Forbes* 2014), 425 originate in the USA and the exclusive share of Greece is 12, including the world's richest person John Paul DeJoria. The billionaires are reported to have accumulated their wealth through banking, oil and gas, pharmacy and real estate. One may notice that banking, real estate and related fields such as cement and concrete mixture are the sectors in which Greece has been deeply engaged, both within and outside the country. It is conjectural to say that the money must have gone into the pockets of the super-rich with political connections. We learnt that it ended up as a political game as the Alexis Tsipras government resigned and got re-elected within months in succession in the year 2015. There is some debate in India about the fallout of the European crisis. It appears that India had very little connection apparently through trade. Our trade balance with Europe has been negative, except for 2011. It is strange that a country that boasts of high foreign exchange reserves and an overall positive balance of around

$55,719 million in 2011–12 and a positive trade balance with the European Union is behaving mysteriously in the face of the European crisis. What could be the reason? It is known that 60 per cent of the global currency reserves are in US dollars. India is an open economy now and amenable to all kinds of investments including the toxic derivatives through the share and money markets route. It is perilous in view of the fact that the market capitalisation in India, as per SEBI data by the end of December 2011, was ₹105 trillion.

It means that the value of the capitalisation is one and half times that of our GDP. We do not know how the channels are operating in manipulating the markets despite our sincere watchdog, the RBI. Those who are in policy-making with intimate connections with the markets and international agencies alone would know about the future of the Indian economy and, maybe, politics in the months to come.

GDP GROWTH AND THE POOR

Economic liberalisation in 1991 was justified by elite experts on the grounds that it would bring development much faster than before. The Supreme Court, in one of its references to the Planning Commission, has asked it to explain what poverty line is. The figures submitted by the Planning Commission raised several issues, including what was GDP, why poverty levels and the rate of growth of GDP in India are moving in opposite directions, etc. Social economists are concerned about the adverse consequences of changes in economic policies in terms of how it would affect the levels of poverty, the mortality rate, employment, etc.

The GDP, as a measure of economic performance, has been used and is being estimated by the Central Statistical Organization (CSO) in India. National income is not calculated on the basis of actual data on various sectors of the economy, as we do not have perfect information on all transactions of the economy. They are approximate figures estimated by the

CSO. There was debate in the media when the base year was changed after Narendra Modi came to power and the rates were seen differently. The validity of figures in measuring the welfare of the people was questioned. In fact, French President Sarkozy appointed a committee, consisting of Amartya Sen, Joseph Stiglitz and Jean Paul Fitoussi, in 2008 to point out the limitations of the GDP. The committee in its report pointed out the weaknesses of the GDP in terms of its failure to measure well-being and good health, and the amount of enjoyment one got from goods and services, state of environment, etc. It is exactly in this context that the issues of reductions in poverty through policies prescribed by the funding agencies were discussed.

The Planning Commission's submission to the Supreme Court, that a per capita per day expenditure norm of ₹32 and ₹26 for urban and rural areas, respectively, to determine those who are below the poverty line, needs to be examined in the backdrop of the players who were involved in the estimates. The concept of poverty was originally developed by Charles Booth, a British sociologist, in 1889, and was later taken over by statisticians. The first estimate of poverty was attempted by V. M. Dandekar and Neelakanth Rath in India on the basis of a concept developed by Food and Agriculture Organization (FAO) statistician Professor Sukhatme. It is assumed that people doing hard work need a minimum of 2,400 calories and others need 1,800 calories to sustain. Later, these figures were converted to the nutritional value of each item of food to arrive at the above figures. For instance 100 grams of cereals were estimated to give 345 calories, oil 900 calories, milk 92 calories, etc. The price of each unit was obtained to express it as food expenditure. The Planning Commission seems to have adopted it to define the poverty line as "per capita monthly expenditure of ₹49 for the rural areas and ₹57 in urban areas at 1973–74 all-India prices." Successive groups of experts have used the same methodology by adjusting the values in terms of the existing prices or CPI. The existing poverty in understanding the incidence and growth of poverty in India in the above methods prompted V. K. R. V. Rao to comment that it is only an estimate of under nutrition and not poverty. The data on poverty presented in Table 3.1 show the levels of poverty in different states of India. It shows that liberalisation has hardly touched the SC and scheduled tribe (ST) categories.

But, the clout of the so-called technical economists is so strong in the government that they have continued with the same concept. The NSSO (National Sample Survey Organization) was made to carry on the same until the Professor Arjun Sengupta Committee provided alternative figures of poverty in 2007. The controversy on the figures of those below the poverty line arose because of the per day expenditure norm set by the committee as ₹20 and ₹15, respectively, for the urban and rural populations. This gave a startling figure of 77 per cent of the population as poor. Thereafter, N. C. Saxena, a committed bureaucrat, was appointed to estimate the number of poor by the Ministry of Rural Development and he came out with a figure of 50 per cent poor on average at the all-India level.[19]

There are several alternative estimates available where the figure is found to be above 50 per cent. Interestingly, economists who have an understanding of the Indian society have very little participation and technical persons have assumed a greater role in determining the number. But all of them have assumed calorie intake of an animal existence for human beings for estimating the poverty line. They do not seem to have considered genetic disposition, location, age, social norms, self-respect, childhood diseases such as measles and other parameters that really matter in a socio-economic category like poverty. There seem to be serious ideological differences in the estimation and compilation of the figures on poverty in India. It is reported that, "across social groups the proportion of workers in casual employment in agricultural and allied activities was quite significant for SCs/STs compared to others."[20] It is interesting to observe that the quantitative figures and the conclusions drawn are found diverse in case of Aravind Panagariya and others who subscribe to the official view of the World Bank.

Table 3.1

Percentage of Population Below Poverty Line by Social Groups in States

	2004–05 and 2009–10								
	2004–05						2009–10		
	Rural	Rural	Rural	Urban	Urban	Urban	2009–10	2009–10	2009–10
States	SC	ST	OBC	SC	ST	OBC	SC	ST	Others
Andhra Pradesh	15.5	30.5	9.5	39.9	50.0	28.9	25.7	40.2	20.4
Assam	27.7	14.1	18.8	8.6	4.8	8.6	36.9	32.0	42.1
Bihar	64.0	53.3	37.8	67.2	57.2	41.4	68.1	64.4	50.8
Chhattisgarh	32.7	54.7	33.9	52.0	41.0	52.7	67.6	66.8	45.4
Delhi	0.0	0.0	0.0	35.8	9.4	18.3	–	–	–
Gujarat	21.8	34.7	19.1	16.8	21.4	22.9	19.2	48.6	19.2
Haryana	26.8	0.0	13.9	33.4	4.6	22.5	33.6	49.6	11.8
Himachal Pradesh	19.6	14.9	9.1	5.6	2.4	10.1	14.4	22.0	5.7
J & K	5.2	8.8	10.0	13.7	0.0	4.8	8.5	3.1	8.3
Jharkhand	57.9	54.2	40.2	47.2	45.1	19.1	44.1	51.2	33.6
Karnataka	31.9	23.5	20.9	50.6	58.3	39.1	35.6	20.3	23.7
Kerala	21.6	44.3	13.7	32.5	19.2	24.3	27.7	24.4	10.0
Madhya Pradesh	42.8	58.6	29.6	67.3	44.7	55.5	42.4	61.9	32.4

(Continued)

Table 3.1
(Continued)

States	2004–05						2009–10		
	Rural SC	Rural ST	Rural OBC	Urban SC	Urban ST	Urban OBC	2009–10 SC	2009–10 ST	2009–10 Others
Maharashtra	44.8	56.6	23.9	43.2	40.4	35.6	37.6	51.7	23.4
Orissa	50.2	75.6	36.9	72.6	61.8	50.2	47.1	66.0	25.1
Punjab	14.6	30.7	10.6	16.1	2.1	8.4	27.2	16.1	4.3
Rajasthan	28.7	32.6	13.1	52.1	24.1	35.6	38.6	35.9	19.5
Tamil Nadu	31.2	32.1	19.8	40.2	32.5	20.9	31.2	11.5	18.1
Uttar Pradesh	44.8	32.4	32.9	44.9	37.4	46.6	53.6	49.8	33.7
Uttarakhand	54.2	43.2	44.8	65.7	64.4	46.5	20.0	20.0	11.5
West Bengal	29.5	42.4	18.3	28.5	25.7	10.4	31.5	32.9	27.1
All India	36.8	47.3	26.7	39.9	33.3	31.4	42.2	47.3	28.0

Sources: 1. Planning Commission, Government of India. 2. Ministry of Rural Development, Government of India 2009.

If one looks at the Poverty Reduction Strategy Papers (PRSPs) of the World Bank, including recommendations made by policy-makers to implement economic reforms in the way they wanted, we will know the ideological dichotomies. It was expected in the 1990s that India would be able to achieve rapid economic growth that would reduce poverty more rapidly than before. To substantiate their argument, some of the policy-makers would always like to provide data that should be reflecting the decline in poverty. But, in one of our studies we have found that the rate of decline in poverty before reforms was a little better (more than 1 per cent per year) than the rate after reforms (around 1 per cent). A decline in the availability of cereals could not be reconciled with poverty figures.[21]

The rate of growth of GDP was publicly discussed by a chosen few to support their argument that reforms have brought fabulous gifts to the people. Some political economists have been questioning the efficacy of the growth rate and have given alternative measures such as the HDI, the HPI, etc. They argue that growth does not automatically reduce poverty, unless the profile of growth is distributive and egalitarian. In a recent study on Argentina by the United Nations Development Programme (UNDP), it was proved that reductions in inequality, measured by the Gini coefficients, have positively contributed to reduction of poverty. This has not happened in India. The story of poverty and unemployment in India is quite different from that of other countries.

In India there are structural inequalities in the name of caste, region, language, religion and other such typical categorisations. Poverty reduction or alleviation programmes need to address these divides as the Eleventh Plan has rightly recognised but failed to address them effectively. The Supreme Court has played its role as per the Constitution. Article 47 in the Directive Principles of State Policy enjoins upon the state "to raise the level of nutrition and the standard of living and to improve public health." Therefore, the Planning Commission, as a policymaking body of the government, has the responsibility to respond to the queries of the apex court with reasonable figures on poverty, with scientific analysis to prove its legitimate existence and not otherwise!

THE STRUCTURE OF ECONOMIC SURVEY MIMIC EUROPEAN MODEL

The official version of the development process is published in the economic surveys. India has been following a structure of presenting a White Paper in the form of economic surveys before the presentation of the annual budget. The economic survey contains details of the policies introduced, appraisals of performance including growth rates and the broad philosophy or commitment of the government. Issuing a White Paper on important subjects is a part of the democratic process of a country. Churchill called it an important tool of participatory form of democracy that involves a dialogue. It is essential that Members of Parliament (MPs) and the public participate in the discussion once the document is available for comment. We started an alternative survey in 1992–93 as a part of dialogue containing the people's perspective as very few were participating in the discussions about the state of the economy.

The document on the state of the economy is an authentic account of the economy and the public has every right to question the statements made in the report if they find that they are contrary to what they experience or observe in practice. As a matter of fact, the budget, being a constitutional obligation, is only an estimate of future revenues and expenditures, whereas the economic survey recounts the performance of the past year. And people should raise issues about the progress achieved or underachieved as per the previous year's policy statements. But, we often observe that public debates are organised on the budget, mostly in relation to direct and indirect tax proposals (income tax, customs, etc.) but hardly do they address the performance of various sectors and the direct or indirect burden passed on to the citizen due to the failure of policies or governance. Are the citizens not responsible to question and elicit clarification from government? The structure of the survey has undergone a metamorphosis. The survey for 1957–58 contained a very brief state-of-the-art account having only six chapters in 38 pages, including tables. In the year 2015, the size has increased 10 times, with 13 chapters and 424 pages. It is a textbook on the Indian economy. The original survey carried the spirit of government without any theoretical discussion or policy speculation. The government of the times knew that the courage of conviction of the leaders, most of them freedom fighters, could challenge even a statesman like Nehru.

It seems the ruling elite of the past were also responsive and accountable to the people for the policies committed in the survey. Therefore, the size and structure was carefully planned. Following the public private partnership (PPP) philosophy of successive governments after 1991, its structure underwent a sea change. The 2012–13 survey has shown that the GDP growth rate at constant prices is 5 per cent compared to 6.2 per cent in 2011–12. This is largely due to deceleration in the growth of the agricultural sector at 1.9 per cent, almost half of the previous year (3.6 per cent). Even the manufacturing sector has come down to 1.9 per cent, while it was already low at 2.7 per cent. The fiscal deficit was 5.1 per cent of GDP in 2012–13 and better than in 2010–11 when it was 6.5 per cent.

The striking revelation in the survey is about,

[How] two-way external sector transactions (gross current account plus gross capital account flows) have raised from 30.6 per cent of GDP in 1990–91 to about 108 per cent of 2011–12. Therefore, while the globalization of Indian economy has helped raise growth, it has also meant greater vulnerability to external shocks.

This is dependent on development, and all other aspects in the report are only platitudes.

The 1957–58 survey cited economic outlook, food grains position and prices, industrial progress as well as the balance of payments as important components. The statistical tables provided data on private imports and the type of goods imported. The 1974–75 survey had added a new chapter on industry and infrastructure to indicate the importance of the sector for the economy. But 1991–92 was a watershed year in the history of independent India since reforms were initiated to shed the Hindu inertia and to usher in rapid growth. The so-called socialist mode of industrial policy built over a period of time was given a decent burial. It was mentioned in the economic survey of 1991–92 that the abolition of industrial licensing, deregulation of public sector, removal of investment control, etc. were initiated. The chapter on the balance of payments clearly described the reasons for taking up the New Economic Policy. The adjustment strategy of the government consisted of exchange rate adjustments, fiscal corrections, structural reforms and mobilisation of 'exceptional' (emphasis added) financing from the IMF, etc. The 1992–93 survey found a positive outlook indicating that "we must protect the weak and help the poor to ensure peace and prevent mischief." It was also mentioned that LPG would bring the "most prosperous future for our people." Have we achieved this? The economic surveys that were presented in the Parliament show that strong and economically volatile reforms were brought in during 1998–99. Disinvestments in PSEs such as VSNL, GAIL, IOC, etc. to reduce their shares to 26 per cent of the investment were introduced. It was also during this period that reforms in the capital market were launched with the Companies (amendment) Ordinance promulgation on 31 October 1998. Again, it was amended in 1999 to facilitate the 'buy back' of shares by companies and the revision of SEBI rules facilitating equity funds in government-dated securities, both the in primary and secondary markets, etc.

Interestingly, a new concept of 'sweat equity', consisting of equity shares of a company to be given to directors and employees at a discount or for consideration other than cash, was introduced. In other words, the economy was capitalised and the scope for many more scams was made possible. The same viewpoint is replicated in the present survey. Thus, the ordinary politicians of 'Nandi' category who are not cognizant of such sophisticated operations are restricted to earning only millions, while those who have access to capital markets and a tradition of knowledge have become billionaires overnight. The official surveys subtend such information, but they need to be analysed in a broad framework of political or social economy to scrutinise who the beneficiaries are.

SMALL, MICRO ENTERPRISES AT CROSSROADS

It is reported that around 80,000 small-scale units have been closed down in one of our most advanced states, Gujarat, over the last 17 years. Yet, the rate of growth of the economy or the per capita income of the state has not declined. It may be due to the fact that Gujarat has one of the highest flows of foreign direct investment and is the home state of billionaire industrialist Mukesh Ambani and his associates. Therefore, we do not find much effect of the closure of small and micro-units on the development of the economy at a micro level. But, definitely, it is reflected in growing unemployment and social unrest in the state. In fact, our small-scale and cottage industries were an eyesore for the East India Company to establish its factories here to transfer the wares from India to Britain and Europe. The recent unrest in the form of demand for reservations for the Patels by Hardik Patel seems to have some connection with this unrest apart from the hidden agenda of the ruling party's ideology

The small-scale sector has lost its pre-eminence after the advent of the modern industry through the European colonisers. It is also reported that the FAPSIA of Andhra Pradesh, which claims that the state has 161,000 small units with a job potential of about 3.7 million, is in crisis due to the tepid treatment given to the sector by the government. In other words, small and micro-enterprises seem to be in trouble due to the fact that the state governments, primarily responsible for it, are not paying adequate attention to it. The role of the small-scale, cottage and village industries is very significant as they contribute the maximum employment, next only to agriculture. Realising this, P. C. Mahalanobis and Jawaharlal Nehru paid special attention to the sector during the Second Plan period. It obtained significance when a separate department, and later a separate ministry, were established at the Centre. It is reported that a majority of the entrepreneurs under this category belong to the artisan castes who are either from other backward classes (OBCs) or the SCs.

The industrial policies drafted by the government in 1956 and 1970 have given special treatment to this sector by reserving certain products. In fact, the 1970 Industrial Licensing Policy drafted after an evaluation of the policies that were responsible for concentration of wealth and emergence of monopoly powers, clearly defined the core sector and the relicensed sector (where investments were less than ₹10 million). The 1991 Industrial Policy was responsible for the liberalisation of the economy by removing all kinds of restrictions, made an open invitation to foreign investments and reserved some products for the small-scale sector. The list of products was clipped from 821 in 1999 to 506 in 2005 and stands at 350 around 2014. Restrictions on imports of some products seem to have been lifted indirectly. Now the small-scale sector has to compete with others in the market to survive. We are aware of our artisan guilds, the cottage industries, textiles and other artisans' products as part of history. They have survived despite neglect by the colonial rulers. Small-scale and cottage industries have played a dominant role in our exports as they constituted around 40 to 45 per cent of the total exports. As per 2011 figures, this sector contributed 73.217 million jobs in 31.152 million units. Interestingly, they turned out a value of ₹1,095,758 trillion with an investment of ₹773,487 trillion (with low capital-output ratio). This was unique as it contributed around 45 per cent of the total industrial output that constituted 9 per cent of the GDP. The problem with the government is that the Central government (Union List 7 and 52) makes policies and the state governments are supposed to implement them. The nomenclature of the small sector has undergone changes several times. The Micro, Small and Medium Enterprises Development Act, 2006 will guide it hereafter. The objective of the Act is to facilitate, promote and enhance competitiveness of the MSMEs. The enterprise is also defined as any industrial undertaking or business concern or any other establishment engaged in the manufacture of goods as per the 1951 Act or engaged in providing or rendering of any service or services. Any economic activity can be taken up, particularly the growing service sector that can be brought under the tax net under this broad definition. The micro-enterprise is one whose investment is less than ₹500,000; small enterprise is one with less than ₹2.5 million; and medium is one that invests between ₹50 to 100 million.

A new dimension is added here where the limits for the service sector are enhanced to ₹1 million, ₹20 to 100 million and ₹0 to 100 million, respectively. The act has added the concept of cluster development, importance to preferential procurement policy, Micro and Small Enterprises Facilitation Council, etc. In the recent budget, the government declared a special procurement policy for scheduled caste and scheduled tribe entrepreneurs to the extent of 4.5 per cent of the total government orders from 350 identified items. The above information relating to the contribution of the sector to the Indian economy gives a rosy picture at the aggregate. But, several problems are encountered by the small and micro-enterprises in terms of their size and competitiveness. Further, up to 24 per cent equity participation is permitted in the small-scale sector.

Therefore, it is difficult to establish who these entrepreneurs are. This will smudge the real investor who can be a big operator but smuggled in here to take advantage of incentives offered to micro units and the advantages of being small or of starting a subsidiary unit. The clubbing of village, cottage and agro-based rural industries as part of the MSME seems to have misplaced the special focus needed for some of them though it could help some individual entrepreneurs to take advantage of advanced technical knowledge and market networks, etc. Even the cluster approach, identified as a strategy, might help only three sectors, namely information technology, pharmaceuticals with an advantage of the IPR regime, and auto components. It is reported that some of the small units suffer from scarcity of skills, lack of incentives, lobbying, international patronage and flow of technology, etc. that make them vulnerable.

However, the MSME is a very big constituent of our economy with around 6,000 products in its reservoir that can come to the rescue of the poor, unorganised and scattered cohorts with modest care and concern from the state. They need only protection from ambitious and perfidious big fish. The social economy of India is reflected in the nature of products and in the method of organisation of production, reflecting the traditions of families, artisan guilds, panchayats, etc. They are all thrown out in the open for survival without creating alternative infrastructures or institutions. As a result, urban slums are mushrooming with displaced artisans.

There are several studies on the caste background of entrepreneurs in India with reference to the MSME. Ashwini Deshpande and Smriti Sharma in their study on caste and gender of small businesses in India have empirically proven that SC–ST ownership in the MSME declined during 2001–07, and that they are underrepresented compared to their share in population. The OBCs are a little different but not better than the others.[22]

AUTOMOBILES AND LIBERALISATION

The automobile is a gift of the Western civilisation to the world. It is now seen as the icon of liberalisation and privatisation that benefits a few. It has no doubt increased the speed of development and also the rate of exploitation of resources. Historians have established that the Indo-Aryans colonised India and other countries with the help of the horse in the past. Did they use the automobile for the so-called neocolonialism? Let us see how the automobile became a tool of economic growth.

Economists have developed models to show how the manufacturing sector, particularly the automobile (four wheeler, three wheeler, two wheeler, etc.) is responsible in utilising the underutilised labour resources for the development of many countries, particularly the labour surplus Third World countries.

One can find instructive articles by economists explaining how the automobile is the engine of growth. In fact, the American economy owes a great deal to the automobile industry for its present status, though Japan and Germany have also played an important role in this sector. Ford, General Motors, etc. are the pillars of the American economy. In fact, these corporate bodies decide everything in the USA and, consequently, in the world. The automobile industry in the USA is the largest in the world. Detroit city is the centre of numerous activities in this sector. Around four states in America entirely depend on the automobile sector. The unions here, the critiques say, benefit the Democratic Party. It is estimated that the total employment, both direct and indirect, constitutes around 9.1 million, and that includes 3.088 million truck drivers.

The average contribution of the automobile sector to the US economy is the highest, next only to the petroleum industry. It is estimated to be $292,000 per employee with the average compensation received by the worker in the industry at $69,500 per annum. This has changed the landscape of the USA. In other words, the whole economy and the society revolve round the automobile industry. This makes the American society the largest owner of cars in the world with 765 cars per 1,000 persons. (Western Europe is not different from the USA in this respect.) The Americans guzzle the world's highest amount of petrol at 18.6 million barrels per day. The amount of iron, aluminium, plastic, metals, etc. required to manufacture so many vehicles is anybody's guess. No wonder that they need Iraq, Libya, Afghanistan, etc. wherever there is fossil fuel. One of the reasons to introduce the liberalisation policy in India, according to our economists, was our balance of payments crisis in the mid-1991. The substantial value of our imports during the period consisted of crude oil. It is alleged that it was planned in such a way that licenses to manufacture cars, trucks and two wheelers were given liberally so that the demand for oil would increase to exert pressure on the government to go for a loan from the IMF.

It is common sense that when foreign reserves are scarce, more automobiles that consume oil would not be permitted. It seems some of our policy-makers were so intelligent that they must have anticipated it and would have laughed at people who made this observation! After liberalisation, the expansion of the automobile industry in India was made possible through de-licensing and by allowing 100 per cent FDI in this sector. This has revolutionised our economy, culture, way of living and thinking. The number of registered vehicles in the country has shown an increase from 300,000 per year in 1951 to 2.1 million in 1991 and to around 9 million by 2011. In Andhra Pradesh alone, there are around 7.218 million registered vehicles with half of them are in and around Hyderabad itself. Thus, India has emerged among the top 10 oil-consuming countries in the world. However, India is not America. It is geographically located in the southern hemisphere. It is a tropical country with semi-arid zones. The density of population is 368 persons per sq. km. Like most of the advanced countries that are located on the North, the density of population in the USA is 32 persons per sq. km.

The onset of winter provides good business to some drug stores while it remains an ordeal for many morning walkers in urban areas. It is difficult to go on a morning walk in any part of Hyderabad city now. It was not like this about a decade ago. It is a common sight that everyone carries a tissue even in social gatherings in Hyderabad. It is all due to heavy traffic and release of sulphur dioxide, carbon monoxide and other effluents by automobiles. This has become a regular feature not only in Hyderabad but in all parts of urban India. It has been studied by medical professionals that a 10-minute exposure to sulphur dioxide will result in changes in pulmonary function.

The incidence of pulmonary diseases has increased in the country several fold during the last few years. The indirect method of understanding the impact of fossil fuel pollution is attempted by arriving at the amount of drugs sold in the market. It is estimated that around ₹100 billion of drugs are sold over the counter (OTC) annually in India. This is only one aspect of the adverse effect of automobiles in India and there are several other issues such as traffic congestion, accidents, etc. Climatic conditions in Europe and the USA force them to depend upon some technology or machine that helps them to protect from severe winter. Automobile for them came as a boon, which they have tamed through stringent environmental regulations. We do not have such problems except in the extreme North. India as a tropical country cannot afford so much of automobile-related pollution except for public transport. There is no doubt that the sector has provided jobs to around 800,000 people and a business turnover of ₹1.65 trillion. It is estimated that around ₹850 billion were invested in the automobile sector with a capacity to produce 9 million vehicles per year by 2015. This makes it one of the largest manufacturing sectors in the world contributing 17 per cent of the excise income and around 5 per cent of GDP.

Apart from pollution, the automobile has changed the landscape of our countryside in terms of traffic jams in cities, diversion of scarce capital for infrastructure, etc. Coupled with the increase in urban population in our five metropolitan cities, including Hyderabad, no city in the country is looking good and comfortable compared to a decade earlier (with the few exceptions of VIP areas). The pollution load of Delhi with an automobile population of 10 million is around 500 metric tonnes of CO_2 per day and Hyderabad city has around 170 metric tonnes (old data) per day making people suffer ailments.

It is estimated by the Planning Commission that annually 80,000 people are killed in road accidents and it alone costs the national economy ₹550 billion. Therefore, it will never sustain a growth rate that would secure human happiness. Had the money been invested in a sector like agriculture where we have a comparative advantage due to biodiversity and cheap labour, the benefits would have been different. Is it not wise to devise our own policies that suit our conditions and culture rather than imitating other countries?

The blind imitation of the West of the northern hemisphere in habits and culture by the people in the southern hemisphere due to colonial aftermath made several cities crammed with flyovers, tall buildings, etc., perhaps designed to facilitate the automobiles. No metropolitan city in the post-liberalisation era looks decent with pollution levels having crossed danger-ous levels, not only due to the automobiles but also owing to the pressure on land for developing real estate. Assuming that some of them are getting their plans approved by the munici-pal or city agencies as per the norms, there is scope for misgiv-ings about the sanctity of such building plans. This would also indicate the amount of pressure put on the babus and political executives in getting orders passed favouring the powerful, leave aside the mafia. It is reported in the media that several million rupees of revenue is estimated to have been lost by the Greater Hyderabad city due to the failure to enumerate the number of constructions in the city.

Though scholars have not paid adequate attention to the medieval urban formations except Champakalakshmi and Irfan Habib, the Indus valley urban culture seems to have been recreated in the form of fort towns. According to one estimate, Agra had a population of 500,000–600,000 in the 16th century AD. Those who are familiar with the woes of urban dwellers during the monsoon season in Hyderabad, Mumbai, Noida and other cities in the country indicate that there is some muddled design in the original plan of cities. We can identify different factors that have contributed to this fall. But, the dissolution seems to be striking after the use of the European models for city or urban planning. The pressure of population and the rural out migration in search of work to urban areas are also responsible for this. But, European cities also experienced the same trends as in India in the past.

It appears that the designs of urban and metropolitan centres in Europe and North America were related to their geographical location. I am not an engineer to comment on the technical aspects of it. But, I think, the European cities do not have the problems of torrential rains. Monsoons are experienced in the West-Africa and Asia-Australia regions only. Europeans have a different kind of problem during winter. They have perhaps designed their cities, particularly the sewage and sanitary disposal systems, based on their meteorological conditions. The European scholars and teachers must have prepared textbooks based on their lived context-based experiences. It is likely that the same textbooks have been used in our civil engineering, public health engineering, environmental engineering, urban planning, etc. courses by default. Similarly, some of our bureaucrats are sent abroad to develop planning skills so that urban infrastructure plans can be implemented In India with ease. Yet, a majority of them seem to have failed to tackle the concerns of the common man during the monsoon when the sewage tanks and drinking water pipes break into one another and runoff with storm water on the main roads, displacing humans and even vehicles.

I have some experience with urban life in Delhi, Hyderabad, London, New York, Sydney, Warsaw and Mumbai. The care taken by the West for the easy flow of traffic is exemplary during winter. Those who are familiar with the 'salt *satyagraha*' may not know why the British were exporting ship loads of raw salt from India to the displeasure of the natives. The salt was not used for human consumption; it was used to clear their roads during winter. Now snow blowers, throwers and high velocity impellers replace salt. Engineers and technocrats have developed designs based on their existential conditions to make human life comfortable there. Though some of our engineers, particularly at the policy-making level, are very competent and are acquainted with our conditions, the supervisory staff at the junior engineer and below levels are alleged to be responsible for breakdowns.

If you have a chat with the junior staff, they would narrate a different story making the seniors and even bureaucrats responsible for the troubles. Otherwise, how could you appreciate lack of proviso on the sidewalks and pathways for runoff to sink or flow in the elegantly laid roads in cities? Why is the capacity of drains much lower than the quantity of storm water expected during the rainy season? How are the designs made or changed (the anarchy of frequent road cuts)? Is it not the duty of the engineering staff to inspect and supervise how the contractors execute the work as per designs or leave it to their caprice? Why has the Total Sanitation Campaign, devoid of any social ethos, failed? How far do the FAR, huge budgeted infrastructure projects based on European models solve our immediate depraved conditions of living?

It is in this context that one can look at the National Urban Sanitary Policy prepared by the Ministry of Urban Development and Poverty Alleviation for an insight into our planner's unimaginative ideas. The policy document has failed to address the poignant appeals of the Safai Karmachari (SK) Andolan that claims that even today millions of SKs carry night soil on their heads to clear the backyards in small towns and even in city agglomerations. If the SKs are not available in a city, the sewerage is allowed to pass into the dirty water drains that flow through slums or impecunious habitations to make the life of the inhabitants de-humanised. What kind of urban planning is this if we fail to address the basic prerequisites of humane living?

While economic liberalisation must have raised the aggregate incomes and rate of growth of GDP, it has definitely made India an adjunct of the USA or EU without the benefit of the quality of life that the latter enjoys. Also, social development in terms of human relations, leisure time activity, fresh air, free roads, crime free communities, preservation of ancient traditions, structures like monuments and diversity seem to have gone down in India. Liberalisation could have helped a few super rich families to find a place in the Fortune 500 group, but the common man (*aam aadmi*) and the socially deprived have been landed in precarious condition now. We may now have plans for smart cities, but how are we going to justify them without smart incomes for the poor? The social development that is anticipated in terms of increases in the HDI of the lower classes, changes in caste-class cleavages, improvements in the structure of the traditional society not based on primordial relations, etc. seem to have not been affected by such policies. What we have today in India is a model that considers and benefits a chosen few with born patronage.

NOTES AND REFERENCES

1. The British left several legacies in India including cricket as the most popular game among the elite in the sub-continent. The BCCI, board of cricket control, with its registered office in Chennai and the office bearers, the elite of the business and political community are responsible for organising national and international events. Keeping the popularity of the game and the business environment of infotainment, the BCCI and the cronies sought to convert it as a money spinning activity, have created another institution called Indian Premier League (IPL).

2. A. C. Pigou, *Economics of Welfare* (London: MacMillan, 1920).

3. J. M. Keynes, *The General Theory of Employment, Interest and Money*, revised (London: Mac Millan, 2007).

4. R. S. Sarma, *Feudalism in India* (New Delhi: Mac Milan, 1965).

5. Justice Sudarsana Reddy of Supreme Court was nominated by the Apex court to decide on a PIL case against corruption with Black money stashed in Swiss Banks in 2011–12.

6. Anna Hazare, a retired defence personnel, took to voluntary service in his place in Maharashtra. He carne into prominence through corporate media support on an issue called Lokpal to deal with corruption. After the new government came to power, no one knows his whereabouts.

7. K. S. Chalam, "Minimum Honesty Required to Curb Corruption" (*The Hans India*, daily June 2012).

8. Baba Ramdev is a god-man who popularised yoga on television and ultimately landed in the production and commodification of yoga and ayurveda worth billions of rupees, stationed at Haridwar, Uttar Pradesh.

9. Avelling Edward, *Student's Marx* (Calcutta: Academic Press, 1965).

10. Hobson, *Imperialism: A Study* (Ann Arbor: University of Michigan, 1965).

11. V. I. Lenin, *Imperialism: The Highest Stage of Capitalism*, originally published in 1917 (Progress Publishers, Moscow, 1965).

12. Government of India, *Hazari Committee on Industrial Planning and Licensing* (1968).

13. Government of India, *Mahalanobis Committee on Economic Power* (1964).
14. Government of India, *Submal Dutt Committee on Monopolies Enquiry* (1967).
15. UNCTAD, *Trade and Development Report 2012: Policies for Inclusive and Balanced Growth* (New York, Geneva: UNDP, 2012).
16. Alberto Alesina and Dani Rodrik, "Distributive Policies and Economic Growth," *The Quarterly Journal of Economics*, Vol. 109, No. 2 (1994): 465–90.
17. Ibid.
18. UNCTAD, *Trade and Development Report 2012*.
19. N. C. Saxena, *Report on Poverty* (Government of India, Delhi: Ministry of Rural Development, 2009).
20. R. R. Birdar, *Incidence of Poverty and Social Groups in India: Who Are the Poorest and Why?* (Bangalore: ISEC, 2012).
21. K. S. Chalam, "Political Economy of Dalit Poverty," *Poverty in South Asia 2003* (Kathmandu: SAAPE, 2003).
22. Ashwini Deshpande and Smriti Sharma, "Entrepreneurship or Survival? Caste and Gender of Small Business in India" (working paper 228, Delhi School of Economics, New Delhi, 2013).

4

Social Consequences of Economic Policies

The economic policies pursued by countries in the West have had the main objective of achieving a high standard of living. The newly industrialised or independent economies have aimed at several goals including poverty alleviation, reduction of inequalities, creation of employment, etc. The situation in India in the South Asian context is different. Several divides and discriminations are found to be predominant due to historical and traditional reasons. Caste, faith, region, language and other social factors either strain economic growth or dissipate development. Economists have used different approaches to understand the peculiarities of Third World countries such as the dualistic theory, the vicious circle of poverty, etc. But, some experts and advisors of the government, who have trained in the Western models, seem to have failed to understand the seriousness of the traditions of India and miscarried the policies to provide enduring development. Therefore, it is necessary to look at the social consequences and damages that the economic policies pursued in India have caused during the last few decades. The impacts of the policies followed in India after the 1980s are different and can be termed as post-modern in one sense and pre-modern in another sense with the revival of several traditional values, norms and institutions. This appears to be dichotomous and seemingly embarrassing for the political class due to the violent disorder in our social life during the last few months after 2015.

THE POLITICAL ECONOMY OF REFORMS AND REFORMERS

The background and the context of reforms in India can be termed as the Mandal and the Kamandal campaigns that created social disturbances in India during 1990. Therefore, it was alleged that, to digress the situation, the government had to officially declare the economic reforms agenda in July 1991. The major thrust and strategy for economic reforms were developed on the lines of the Washington Consensus and pushed through the politician-bureaucrat-corporate nexus. As a matter of fact, the major breakthrough for reforms was given, according to an estimate, by a dozen bureaucrats, who were on deputation to the World Bank and the IMF. It is reported that if some of them have failed to get sponsored, they have used the academic route to get study leave to pursue courses in business schools in Harvard, MIT, etc. Some of them do not have expertise in political economy or economics. They must have had brief stints as officers in departments that deal with economic matters and thereby claim to have the expertise for dealing with complex issues relating to the Indian economy. It worked well with the government that was convinced of the need for an LPG and followed the prescriptions given by international organisations. The shrewd civil servant simply dragged his feet on the dotted lines and pushed files. At the same time, there are several sincere officers who were concerned about the future of the poor and the country and looked at these developments with derision and opted out. There is an internal disparagement by a section of the officers who belong to a cadre like Economic service that was originally planned to manage economic issues was slowly disabled by the powerful lobby in bureaucracy and destroyed the cadre almost to extinction. Now economic policies are made or simply adapted by the few handpicked. Academicians who talk about the pros and cons of policies based on research inputs seem to have no place in the establishment. This is an interesting development that has substantially changed the direction of Indian bureaucracy.[1]

There are some studies on the politics of economic reforms along with treatises on the political economy of globalisation that point out the socio-economic background of the reformers. One important conclusion drawn by some of these studies is that a majority of the reformers come from elite families or have emerged as neo-elite with their exposure to elite institutions. They just do not have any empathy for the poor or any nationalist feelings in dealing with issues of national importance, except self-seeking careerism.[2] Economic reforms in India have reached a crucial stage and a few genuine policies are seemingly stuck due to the trust deficit in political parties. In fact, the political economist, as distinguished from a neoclassical economist, would anticipate such developments. After all, policies, particularly economic policies, are not made by advisers or bureaucrats. They are finally decided by the government in power through a parliamentary process. In other words, the State makes the decisions on the policy perspective that should be pursued in order to realise constitutional objectives. As we are in a republic, it is expected that the policies followed by the state should not contradict the principles laid down in the written Constitution, since the democratic state is a creature of the same Constitution. It appears that the policies adopted by different governments, both at the Centre and in the states, have given least consideration to these issues. Sometimes the matters have been dragged to the apex court and we know what happens there as the same elite constitute a majority in the judiciary. Thus, there appears to be a caucus in operation for the formulation and execution of economic policies.

The political economist or social economist must be in a position to understand what constitutes a State and its agency.

It is being debated that the Indian State is a caste–class State in terms of the composition of legislators. Therefore, it is expected that the policies pursued by the government reflect the aspirations of the class or castes in power rather than the people. The Constitution has given representation to the SCs and STs but their hundred and odd members alleged to have no voice in policy-making and so need not be considered as a part of democratic process. (The policy programmes of some political parties like the Bahujan Samaj Party (BSP) are discussed in the next chapter.) Thus, the economic reform agenda consisted of policies that would facilitate the easy flow of foreign investments, tax reforms to make it attractive to invest, a mining policy to exploit natural resources, liberating the money market to increase money circulation, reductions in unproductive subsidies in agriculture oil, etc. to limit fiscal deficit so as to get a rate of growth which is better than the Hindu rate of growth to generate more billionaires. The national economy is linked with international trade and is reported to have turned more growth and better rates than before. But, there were few hitches such as disallowing of FDI in retail trade that facilitate competitive prices to reach the consumer, divestments, etc. The Chicago-trained political economists have placed figures before us to show how it has reduced poverty levels. After 2015 with the NDA in power, the restrictions are removed and patriotism is extended beyond national boundaries to bring foreign investments and life styles.

THE CHANGE OF CLASS–CASTE NARRATIVES UNDER GLOBALISATION

Social scientists, particularly social economists, study the transformation of not only economic structures but also social relations that are interconnected. They have created different tools and concepts to describe their findings. One of the important socio-economic categories that have become popular is the concept of class, and, in the Indian context, caste. Schumpeter, one of the greatest intellectuals of the last century, in his *Imperialism and Social Classes* has said,

> Class is something more than an aggregation of class members. It is something else, and this something cannot be recognized in the behaviour of the individual class member. A class is aware of its identity as a whole, sublimates itself as such, has its own peculiar life and characteristic spirit.[3]

As there is no consensus among scholars on the core of class analysis or even on the definition of class, we use Schumpeter's definition.

Caste is the craftiest notion that has been haunting social process in India from time immemorial. This has been further complicated with new categories such as 'depressed classes', 'scheduled castes', 'backward (most) classes', 'scheduled tribes', etc. added during the British rule. In fact, there is no universally accepted term to describe all social categories as one, since some castes are listed as 'scheduled' in one state and 'backward' in some other states (dhobis, barbers, etc.). In the case of the untouchables and the Adivasis, there is no ambiguity as the criteria are uniform. The notion of 'depressed classes' was dismantled by the time the Constitution was drafted. Sociologists, particularly those who were trained in the West, had tried to formulate theories about caste. But sociologists like R. K. Mukherjee and others were critical about the theories of the dominant caste of M. N. Srinivas, who, according to them, brought confusion to divert the attention of scholars from class.

Class and caste have different characteristics. The former is a dynamic concept that keeps on changing with the mode of production (MOP) while caste has remained static for ages with some alterations at the top over a period of time without substantial change in the social ranks.[4] The study of castes became popular both in academic and political discourses after the Mandal Commission. It is strange that those who currently oppose or favour backward classes were silent for three decades after the Kaka Kalelkar Commission report in 1955. The commission had several conflicts of opinion among its members on the use of caste as a criterion of backwardness and cited the terms of reference of the commission, where it was asked to examine only 'classes and sections'. Thus, the confusion, as some activists think, is not a constitutional construct, but appears to be a bureaucratic meddle that seems to be triggering uninformed battles among different caste groups now.

It is difficult to understand the Indian socio-economic and, thus, political situation by using the dual categories of class and caste after globalisation as both are surviving in the USA and in other countries through the diaspora. The interaction between classes and castes is complicated due to the internalisation of some castes into class. The dvija castes and the bourgeoisie seem to be converging. This is mystified by some Western scholars due to their ignorance and lack of deep study, or may be due to the fake translations of certain transactions by the local elite or their nominees that they relied on. It seems this clash of opinions had prevailed during the 19th century when Marx was grasping and writing on India. Like his countryman Max Muller, Marx never visited India. The source material was so inaccurate that it made him coin the term 'Asiatic mode of production' to comprehend oriental societies with certain peculiarities that were absent in the Occident. Yet, the concept did not move the elite (Indian included) to change their approach to study classes and was responsible for the bloodiest turmoil in ideological debates. In fact, the intellectual limitations of some of the concepts led the Frankfurt school,[5] starting from Wittfogel to Adorno and several other postmodern scholars, to formulate different methods of discourses. The trauma created by Edward Said with his *Orientalism*[6] in academic circles gave a blow to the Indian literati caste, some using it for their own ends, and the message, being distracted, has not yet reached the target entity, the native Indians.

Now we can examine the contemporary situation in India after the official declaration of a capitalist mode of development about two decades ago. It was expected that caste differences and discrimination would disappear once economic opportunities were created. In fact, several scholars, such as Corbridge and Harris who tried to reinvent India, argued in favour of the continued relevance of class as a unit of analysis. There are an equally good numbers of scholars who contend that, without using the concept of caste, it is difficult to comprehend social and economic process in India. We list out some metaphysical and empirical dichotomies as preliminary first order issues that need to be addressed to proceed further to understand the significance of liberalisation in India (2011).[7]

The onslaught of globalisation and its deep penetration generally happens with the willing cooperation of State actors who know the consequences of liberating the economy from the social structures. It is strange that the so-called global opportunities benefited only a few upper and traditionally well-entrenched castes and did not spread across all eligible castes as originally publicised by the defenders of globalisation. Curiously, those who appear to oppose such policies for political reasons have actually strengthened it with the tactical idea of the Indian/Hindu way of liberalisation, industrialisation and modernisation. It has created a very innovative institution like the multi-caste corporations (MCCs) by bringing socially identical castes together to form business groups which are spread all around.The prospects for the development of crony capitalism have improved with the MCCs emerging as bridgeheads under globalisation. The ICT has facilitated the internationalisation of the petty bourgeoisie. This has not weakened the caste and has, on the contrary, improved its economic solidarity, widely differentiating the shudras as well. Realising the gaps and voids in the emerging complex situation, the global players have outsourced through their foundations, to develop academic ideas to counter the criticism. We have now formations like the Dalits or the OBC business conglomerates with credible scholars talking about the advantages of market economy. But, everyone knows that the weaker sections become very weak and remain subordinate to the dominant international bourgeoisie. The protagonists must have realised their folly by now after the recent Dalit bashing in Rohith issue, lynching by cow vigilantes and rape and victimisation of womenfolk during the mid-2016 in place of expected billions.

It has been established by some scholars that countries coming with FDIs are not interested in addressing the concerns of the ILO or the inequalities that are created through such investments, and are interested in only super profits (UNCTAD Report 2012). Further, it has helped develop consumerist elites, merchants and media; global bureaucrats and politicians and global professionals owning and controlling trans-national corporations (TNCs). The TNCs are class conscious and have an agenda to prove that socialist globalisation is a myth and also rubbish and the concept of caste as a stupid idea in a globalised world, perhaps under the influence of their upper caste–conscious advisors.

Yet, the UK Parliament passed a bill recently to restrain caste discrimination among people of Indianorigin. The spread of the evil among migrant workers across the globe with caste-based colonies even in the USA indicate the verve of caste under globalisation. It appears that such a trend might make slogans like 'workers of the world unite', the proletariat upsurge, etc. impracticable and the possibility of a class war a distant dream.

PREDOMINANCE OF THE MIDDLE CASTES

The notion of caste and class is so dominant that no intellectual discourse is comprehensive without referring to them in India. But, when we refer to the Hindus, Muslims, Christians, Jains, Parsis or Buddhists, we consider all of them as a homogenous group. This becomes problematic when we discuss critical issues such as communalism, casteism, secularism or political ideologies. People are lumped together and the good, bad and ugly are attributed to the whole community that they belong to or were born into. Therefore, when incidents such as terrorist activities or fundamentalist outbursts happen, we tend to attribute them to the religion or social group to which they subscribe or fit into. This is largely being followed in our media reports and the message is distorted or imperfectly communicated. In fact, everyone knows that we have economic or social groups within each category and, if communicated properly, we can reduce the pervasive damage. India, unlike other countries, is identified with the caste system while all others are signified by class categories. However, academics and activists have been using both the categories for understanding our socio-economic and political issues during the modern period. The role of the upper caste media honchos after globalisation can be termed as 'manufacturing of caste consent' to bring in a regime that benefits the *bhadralok* or dvija.

There are around nine theories of caste in India. Interestingly, there is ambiguity about the theories of class.[8] Though the term 'class' was used by Plato, the interpretations of Marx, Weber, Davis and Moore, Nicos Poulantzas, etc. have made it widespread in academic writing. The concept is being liberally used by laymen, experts and activists without sometimes knowing what is meant by class in Indian context. Are they referring to the works of Marx, Weber or others as each one of them has used it in a different framework? But the mainstream discourse appears to be related to Marxian classes as it was the Marxists and their critiques who brought the concept into public discourse in India.

Marx used class in the context of production relations within a particular MOP. Weber attributed different classes based on positive and negative privileges held by people in a market economy. Characteristics like quality, performance and possession were considered to determine the functional character of a class by Davis and Moore. It was perhaps the Greek-French scholar, Nicos Poulantzas,[9] who creatively elaborated the concept of 'classes in contemporary capitalism' by incorporating the advances made by Antonio Gramsci and others. As Poulantzas was working on the theme in 1975, when capitalism had reached its zenith, his contribution seems to be more relevant and up to date. Poulantzas advanced the concept of 'new petty bourgeoisie' based on three principles:

1. Classes cannot be defined outside of class struggle. Elaborating between class-in-itself and class for itself, Poulantzas said that classes exist as antagonistic and contradictory qualities of social relations.
2. Classes take objective positions in the social division of labour and are independent of their will. The reproduction of the actual positions occupied by the social classes (as bourgeoisie, proletariat, poor peasant or petty bourgeoisie) depends on the class contradictions and class struggle.
3. The social classes are structurally determined by the economic, political and ideological levels. Like Gramsci, Poulantzas gives importance to political and ideological factors as they are as important as the economic factors in MOP.

The traditional category of the petty-bourgeoisie comprising independent artisans, small shopkeepers, etc. has dwindled and been replaced by the 'new petty bourgeoisie consisting of white collar employees, technicians, supervisors, civil servants, etc'. Poulantazas brought in the idea of the functional relationship with capital as one of the criteria in determining the class position of a group. For instance, experts (including economists and social scientists) at all stages of the production process helped in legitimising the subordination of labour to capital by making it appear natural and by theorising that workers were incapable of organising production themselves. Even low-level clerks and secretaries shared the ideological positions of mental labour and, thus, belonged to the petty bourgeoisie and not the proletariat. The bourgeoisie was defined not only in terms of property ownership but also in terms of substantive dimensions, which characterised the social relations of production.

Thus, managers fulfilled the functions of capital and the heads of state apparatus in a capitalist State managed the State functions in the service of capital and, thus, came under the bourgeoisie. Poulantzas has discussed many other issues in the elaboration of classes in advanced capitalist systems that have substantially transformed from the time of Marx. Social scientists in the West have used his categories to arrive at the proportion of each class in various economies on the basis of secondary data. It has been found that the new petty bourgeoisie comprise 70 per cent of the economically active population in the USA.

Income is taken as the criterion in India to define classes. If the first 5 per cent of the rich and the 40 per cent below poverty line are set aside, the rest of 65 per cent may be the 'new petty bourgeoisie'. It is close to the proportion of people who have access to television and mobiles, two important factors that mould the new petty bourgeoisie. We know how disagreeable the petty bourgeoisie is. Interestingly, some of the traits of a middle class are reflected among the urban SC and OBCs. An attempt has been made by dvija experts to artificially create Dalit industrialists to counter the criticism against LPG.

The caste system based on the 'varna' is hierarchical/ritual-istic and the class system based on relations of production is economic. Given the present situation in India after 65 years of independent capitalist developments and links with the inter-national division of labour, the castes have gained vibrancy. It is possible to identify the castes that have benefitted from vari-ous policies and attained upward mobility. If we keep aside for the moment the dvijas, who are calling the shots at the Centre, the states are now increasingly captured by the shudras, while the fourth varna (panchamas) are outside the system.

There is internal differentiation within the shudras with the rise of the OBCs as the petty ruling caste. This is very complex to understand. The middle castes seem to have marginalised the economic agenda of emancipation. It is now confined to those who are the social proletariat or the SCs and the Adivasis who do not come under either class or caste (internal differentiation is low). Therefore, the traditional struggles look nonchalant and might soon become obsolete. The ruling castes are very clever in their manoeuvring in terms of bringing an OBC face to their agenda in recent 2014 elections. The emergence of the Modi factor is dividing the OBCs who have started emerging as the ruling castes, and this could get further polarised in the years to come if Hardik Patel and the Bihar elections are any indication as the two events in 2015 used caste narratives. It is noted that the followers of Lohia who formed the *Mahaghatbandan* in Bihar in the November 2015 elections used his vision of unity of the oppressed to get into power.

CASTE IN CAPITALIST DEVELOPMENT

The enthusiasm for research among young social scientists in India appears to be waning and those who are active are confined to the areas of received theory. Therefore, it is difficult to envisage innovative theories to capture emerging phenomena in our socio-economic life. It is possible to formulate a subject called 'grabbanomics' to capture the writings of scholars who justify unearned income as divine rents. In this context, we may acknowledge the work of a small group of young scholars such as Damodaran Harish,[10] Zacharias, Vakulabharanam and others[11] who are trying to understand the role of caste in the new economy of India, particularly with reference to the accumulation of capital by a select few. It is noted with great enthusiasm that a documentary produced by a newspaper, *Cobrapost*, revealed the Laxmanpur Bathe case where 58 Dalits were massacred and the accused evicted was a *kuladharma* belonging to the Thakur community of Bihar.[12]

When Damodaran Harish published his *India's New Capitalists: Caste, Business and Industry in a Modern Nation* in 2008, there was little reaction from academics and no discussion of how caste plays an important role in economic (capitalist) development. The rising new India is a nation that cares less for human values and is overwhelmed more by Western ideals, particularly business ethics. Yet, interestingly, it is still Bharat when it sincerely adopts the traditional values of caste and the related 'dharma'.

Economic development in India measured by the GDP is now entering into a new phase. Yet, some waver to call it capitalist development. What is the problem in calling it capitalist development when the whole edifice relies on foreign capital and internal and primitive accumulation? There are theories from the time of Adam Smith that capital is crucial in raising the productivity of labour through the expansion of the division of labour that fetches the 'wealth of nations'. Marx learnt classical economics from the English tradition, including Adam Smith, Ricardo and others, to elucidate his *Capital*. The previously mentioned Indian scholars have tried to combine Indian categories with Marxian classes to understand the new phenomenon that emerged since 1991.

The young scholars have produced enough empirical evidence that caste, and not necessarily class, has played an important role in India's development. The issue now is more about how to measure it and recognise it. Scholars, including Nobel laureates such as Arrow,[13] Becker,[14] Akerlof[15] and others, studied caste discrimination as an imperfect market condition. However, they considered caste as a race or class similar to some of our Indian analysts. They understood that discrimination based on caste or race would result in an increase in the cost of production with the given productivity in a competitive system, and would be harmful to the entrepreneur. However, they did not provide any microdata to support their arguments. In a different context, scholars such as Bowles,[16] Shapiro and Stiglitz[17] hypothesised the existence of an 'efficiency wage' as an incentive for workers to not cheat their employers and to remain loyal.

The attempt to understand this phenomenon has created some controversies, ideological splits, conspiracies, etc. on in the labour and left movements in India. The neo-Marxist explanations given by Samir Amin,[18] Gunter Frank[19] and other Latin American scholars have not been taken kindly in India, saying that the fundamental problem is surplus value and not how exchange and markets function (as theorised by them). Interestingly, economic development has failed to destroy caste in India and castes like the Burkamins (about a million) in capitalist Japan. Now some empirical results of studies seem to be available to re-examine the above formulations.

It is alleged by Dalit groups that some activist scholars do not accept the paradigm that the few upper castes constitute a group of exploiters. They also refuse to admit the formulation that all the Dalits, Adivasis and some OBCs are the real proletariat by citing isolated cases of Dalit civil servants (1 per cent) who have climbed the few steps of class ladder. It is difficult to understand why do they not collect data on a hundred families from each caste in a unit to identify how many of them are exploited and have remained poor and how many are exploiting others among each caste group to relate it to an analysis of classes. Further, the own account entrepreneurs among the Dalits may include hair-cutting saloons, laundry owners, fish stalls, vegetable vendors, etc. Now we have data from field studies to negate the thesis of presence of Dalit/OBC capitalists in the emerging capitalist economy.[20]

An attempt has been made by a corporate consultancy firm to study the representation of SC/ST/OBC employees in the private sector as part of CSR activities. The results are not available for public comment, but it is known through informal sources that 63 per cent of the topmost listed companies refused to give information and those who signed a memorandum of understanding (MOU) for diversity (like the USA) have performed very poorly in the implementation of what is called affirmative action.[21] This is further corroborated by a study of three young scholars from Canada, which shows that out of 9,052 board members, 4,167 or 46 per cent are *vaishyas* and 4,037 or 44.6 per cent are Brahmins. OBCs constitute 3.8 per cent and SCs/STs constitute 3.5 per cent.[22] The study concludes that 'caste is an important factor in networking. The small world of corporate India has interaction only within their caste kinship'. What else do we need to confirm that caste plays a dominant role in the capitalist development of 21st century India?

THE CASTE MODE OF PRODUCTION IN INDIA

The discussion on the role of caste in the economic transformation of India through globalisation made us assume that a caste-like MOP has been in operation in India. The MOP debate in social sciences is a serious academic exercise undertaken by scholars to understand the successive stages of development of particular societies. There are several competent Indian scholars of international repute who have participated in this debate and enhanced the capacity of the scientific world to understand the unexplored. In this context, the debate on the Indian version of development is explained below with the introduction of a new MOP as an illuminating exercise. The economic structure of the Indian society during the colonial period and the stagnant nature of this structure were explained in terms of a "colonial mode of production."[23] The construct was found to be essential as the existing analytical tools of feudalism or the state MOP were found to be inadequate to explain the Indian situation. In fact, the debate has opened new vistas in the area of political economy of agriculture in India. However, the debate was not carried further, particularly after the globalisation theories gained momentum. It is in the tradition of explaining the unexplored areas of social formation in Indian society that an attempt is made to formulate the caste MOP as an important analytical tool. It is sincerely thought that the essential feature of the Asiatic MOP, with reference to India (the dominant player in Asia), is the caste mode of production (CMOP).

WHAT IS A MODE OF PRODUCTION?

The concept of a MOP is a dialectical method through which the structure of institutions and their relationships within a society can be explained in a historical outline. Scholars have so far identified nine modes of production. Though the MOP is a Marxist tool developed by Marx himself, the concept has been adopted by both Marxist and non-Marxist scholars. It consists of four important analytical parts. In the process of production, people use different implements and tools such as ploughs, axes, lathes, labour, etc. These are known as the means of production. The second component is productive forces. No machine or single factor can produce anything by itself. This requires labour power, skills, experience and knowledge to put the means of production in motion. In the process of production, people necessarily enter into certain social relations known as production relations. This third component is dictated by the ownership of the means of production. The fourth component is analysed by Jairus Banaji by distinguishing relations of exploitation and relations of production. The surplus is appropriated from the labourers in colonial mode, not as rent but rent in kind through extra-economic coercion. This relationship is only a relationship of exploitation and it is a very important component to understand the MOP. All the four components are combined together in explaining a historically determined society. In each of the modes of production, a dominant class emerges and controls the means of production. For instance, in the state or the Asiatic mode, the state is the dominant category; in slavery it is the slave; land is fundamental for feudalism as capital is for capitalism. Though Marx has mentioned the communist, Asiatic, slave, feudal and capitalist modes of production as successive stages of development of a society, scholars have been unearthing different other modes by studying different societies within the Marxist mould. The studies of Frank, Amin, Weiskoff and other Third World economists have brought out clearly that the characterisation of some of the Latin American countries as capitalist or pre-capitalist is not a satisfactory explanation. They have significantly contributed to the Marxist intellectual tradition by introducing the dependency theory along with the centre-periphery imagery to explain the specific conditions of their societies. In India, attempts have been made by scholars to make India correspond with other European societies in its process of development by identifying similarities in these societies without recognising the specificities. In fact, Marx himself was struck by the peculiarities of the Indian society with the limited information available with him and called it the Asiatic MOP. Later, economists and historians realised the distinguishing features and introduced concepts such as the colonial mode, the Asiatic mode, etc. Even these scholars have not been able to succeed in capturing the whole process of production in India. They hardly touch upon rural India, particularly the caste system. Social anthropologists have studied these problems as issues in village studies without any explanation as to why do they survive even today. The CMOP seems to be gaining importance since the straitjacket stages of MOP are found to be in trouble after the fall of Soviet Union and the socialist mode, etc. On the other hand, India and some Latin American countries struggle for their independence from the Anglo-Saxons and their models of development.

FEATURES OF THE CASTE MODE OF PRODUCTION

It is necessary to identify the fundamental and differential features of the CMOP. Marx recognised the economic influences of caste and recorded its dominance in his main text, *Capital*, Vol I. It is at the stage of explaining the division of labour and manufacture, that Marx mentions the caste system. He says that, "the whole mechanism discloses a systematic division of labour, but a division like that in '*manufacture is impossible*' (emphasis added)." He further elaborates,

[T]he law that regulates the division of labour in the community acts with the irresistible authority of law of nature at the same time that each individual artificer, the smith, the carpenter and so on conducts in his workshop all the operations of his handicrafts in the traditional way but independently and without recognizing any authority.... This simplicity supplies the key to the secret of the *unchangeableness* (emphasis added) of Asiatic societies. The structure of the economic elements of society remains untouched the storm clouds of the political sky.[24]

It can be seen that the fundamental feature of a CMOP is its *unchangeable* feature. It was recorded by Marx himself while explaining the division of labour. Like several scholars who were looking at India, including the Indian authors, through a window of their own, however, did not touch the 'untouchable' in their framework. We can find in Indian history that the occupational mobility of certain artisan castes (some are now considered as OBCs) and the conditions and life styles of the untouchables have remained the same through ages. B. R. Ambedkar recognised this and identified the untouchables with slavery and related it to Hinduism. Had he used the economic explanation of its existence, such as the MOP or some other, he would have enhanced our understanding and a solution could have been found. He said,

> [M]ost parts of the world have had their type of what was called the lowly. The Romans had their slaves, the Spartans their helots, the British their Villains, the Americans their Negroes and the Germans their Jews. So the Hindus have their untouchables. Slavery, Serfdom, Villianage have all vanished. But, untouchability still exists and bids to last as long as Hinduism will last.[25]

This is one way of explaining the existence of untouchability and discrimination. The unchangeableness of the conditions of the Dalits (untouchables) needs to be sought in the MOP. However, his explanation that castes are stagnant classes (borrowing it from S. V. Ketkar from his study on caste) or the division of labour does not directly explain the concept. Division of labour, as elaborated by Adam Smith and explained by Marx, is a practice where the process of production is divided into different stages, such as 18 sequences for pin making, and each stage is perfected by one. This raises productivity. But in India, each occupation is held by a caste and the finished product is produced by the family or caste by following all the processes by members of a single caste occupation. This does not allow any change as noted by Marx. Interestingly, this problem has not been considered by Indian scholars for further study, perhaps limiting our understanding of the CMOP.

The social relations between the mainstream and the untouchables have been maintained through a MOP, otherwise they would have emerged as an independent social group as has been observed in the case of artisan communities in the mainstream. They are deliberately maintained as untouchables. But social interaction has continued to make use of their productive forces. That is why, untouchables are found to be surviving, yet without any improvements in their living conditions. As the productive forces play a dominant role in the MOP, the labour of Dalits is used in it. But the developments in the mainstream are restricted to the Dalits to contain their value through extra-economic coercion known as the caste restrictions. The productive forces of the Dalits have remained constant as they were forbidden to enter the mainstream, enter literate learning and own property. These three important restrictions made them stagnate with what they originally possessed as an 'indigenous community'. The situation did not alter very much as anticipated by Marx during the British Raj. It was said that the British, "fulfill a double mission in India: One destructive; the other regenerating—the annihilation of Asiatic society and the laying of the material foundation of western society" (Marx, British Rule in India, p. 40). The British, in fact, recreated and strengthened caste discrimination by rediscovering their Aryan roots in Hinduism and improved the productive forces of the Brahmins and other dvijas (William Jones). Therefore, we see in India the development of different modes of production existing side by side without any contradiction, but at the same time replacing one another without any difficulty. As production was characterised in the colonial MOP, the economy and the productive forces were drained without affecting the mainstream elite. The colonial mode as analysed by scholars did not identify the groups who were responsible in collaborating with the British as 'agents' or managing agents. It was the same 'dvija' communities which acted as the 'collaborating elite' by making use of their English education, technology, Western culture, etc. At the same time, the artisans and the Dalits were exploited and their capacities drained. However, no scholar of repute has elaborated these peculiarities as unique features of India.

The CMOP was sustained with the 'jajmani' system and the unequal exchange between different communities in the villages. Most social anthropologists have examined the self-sufficient nature of the village. But, the village was never self-sufficient. It was the self-sufficient agriculture that was sustained by the Dalit labour and the labour of artisan communities in providing infrastructure for the self-sufficiency of agriculture. There were interactions between villages (*gramam*) and occasionally resulted in *sangramam* (disputes) due to unsettled issues. The remarks of some scholars that there was no interaction among villages are not well founded. The rent on caste was devised in a meticulous way via the restriction of the numbers of 'dvijas'. In the Hindu social order, there was no possibility of entering the 'dvijahood' by others. One could aspire or even use the symbols to call themselves with the pseudonym called '*Viswa* Brahmin', etc. But, it was never accepted. The number of untouchables has kept on increasing as it is a residual category and anyone can be thrown into it. This process has created surplus people and the premium paid on the use of their labour has remained constant and a subsistence wage was paid. Marx has used the concepts of use value and exchange value distinctly to indicate that exchange value contains a component of socially useful labour. But in India Dalits or untouchables never constituted a part of this arrangement and the values of commodities produced by them have remained at the stage of use value with low premium. It is strange that both historians and economists never looked at this Marxist formulation and D. D. Kosambi has complicated the whole issue by emphsising that the 'Brahmin as a pioneer' had reduced administrative cost without being part of production.[26] While the Brahmin has been kept on enjoying a higher premium with all advantages including their numbers, they have extracted rents with the increase in population and demand for their services. One can see the constant and sometimes ever increasing demand for the services of Brahmins in the Hindu order, not only in India but even in the USA. Therefore, the occupation of the Brahman has remained untouched by others and their mobility is unrestricted due to the premium. The Bania and Kshatriya, the other two sub-groups of dvijas, have lost their original ritual status once they broke their traditional calling entering into secular jobs. However, all the three have had their grip over the system with their constant organisation for unity and upgradation. The Dalits and others were pushed into 354 occupations, mostly into lowly paid jobs in the post-independent period. Even today the untouchables are not allowed to share (a) crematoriums, (b) water and (c) shrines, indicating the continuation of the CMOP. Table 4.1 shows the offences and atrocities committed against the SCs over a period of 34 years, 1979–2013. It is more than doubled during the period, particularly after liberalisation. The caste-based index of discrimination (CID) calculated by K. S. Chalam in 2004 has clearly demonstrated and supplemented the increasing caste-related

Table 4.1

Main Offences and Atrocities Committed Against the Scheduled Castes (1979–2013)

Crime Category	1979	1983	1993	1997	1999	2013
Murder	388	525	510	513	506	676
Grievous Hurt	1,441	1,362	NA	3,860	3,241	4,901
Rape	430	641	798	1,037	1,000	2,073
Arson	10,313	982	369	389	337	189
Other Offences, & PCR ACT	10,703	11,324	23,296	22,145	20,009	31,569*
Total	13,975	14,834	24,973	27,944	25,093	39,408

Source: Ministry of Social Welfare, Government of India, 2014.
    The Source of record of crime against Dalits—National Crime Records Bureau, Ministry of Home Affairs, New Delhi.
*Includes SC, ST Prevention of Atrocities Act.

atrocities recorded for all India by the CRBI using data from the field.[27]

The argument by some sociologists that some positions in the public sector are occupied by the Dalits (SC and ST) through reservation is an indicator of occupational mobility which needs to be understood as an external force (State) and not as an autonomous act of the CMOP. The change of guard in Delhi in the 2014 elections did not change the structure or the direction of reforms. But the social consequences of the same were dormant in the previous regime that never came out in the open. Now there is open and serious social unrest, which may have been deliberately created to divert the attention of the people from the immediate economic problems. Or it is possible to construe as the outcome of the fascist content of reform based on self-interest, not necessarily designed in India, and by default ensembles the present regime that advocates certain ideology akin to it. No Dalit is reported to have been benefitted by the policy as not a single individual out of 5,814 foreign direct investment proposals (by 1997) was accorded to them in India. Table 4.2 shows the poor representation of

Table 4.2

Caste-wise Distribution of Indian Corporate Board Members (2010)

	Caste	Numbers	Percentage of Total
1.	Forward Caste	8,387	92.6
	Of which (a) Brahmin	4,037	44.6
	(b) Vaishyas	4,167	46.0
	(c) Kshatriya	43	0.5
	(d) Others	137	1.5
2.	Other Backward Classes	346	3.8
3.	SC/ST	319	3.5
4.	Total (1 to 3)	9,052	100.00

Source: Ajit, H. M. Dankar and Ravi Saxena, *Economic and Political Weekly,* 11 August 2012.

OBCs and SCs in corporate governance. Most of the benefits of globalisation including shares in multinational corporations (MNCs), disinvestments, scams and the like are appropriated by the Brahmins, *banias* and other dvijas, indicating the strength of the CMOP even in the 21st century. It is also reflected in the demographic profile of the country with the caste-related HDI.

There seems to be an extension of the CMOP wherever the Indians have migrated. This is a typical character that prevails even if the forces of production are not conducive for its survival in capitalist countries like the USA where the Indians have created caste cleavages and are able to persist even in the 21st century. It is problematic to imagine how the CMOP survives in a country like the USA with Indian migrants, where productive forces, the base, are different from that in India.

The analytics of the CMOP appears to be static while the MOP is related to a dynamic process of change in different phases of history. This is not new. Even Marx in his reference to caste has said, "[T]his simplicity supplies the key to the secret of the 'unchangeableness' (emphasis added) of Asiatic societies, an unchangeableness in such striking contrast in the constant dissolution and re-founding of Asiatic societies, and the never-ceasing changes of dynasty."[28] Interestingly, he has cited examples from Java in the footnotes to indicate how the internal economy remains unchanged. Java was colonised by the East India Company in the 6th century AD and must have introduced some social institutions. In other words, the status quo or ossified social structures continued for ages without any tampering either by the Muslim rulers or by the Christian missionaries of the East India Company. Thus, it comes out openly that whenever the ruling dispensation is totally regulated by the dvijas, particularly the Brahmin (not necessarily the priest class), the social structure was allowed to continue. This phenomenon has created animosity among the non-Brahmins in the South (Periyar EVR) and in Maharashtra (Jyoti Rao Phuley) to wage a war only against the Brahmin while all the three castes are in unison with this arrangement.

The present violence against Dalit Muslims and Dalits who are termed as beef eaters seems to be an old story repeated once more, indicating the deep prejudice and economic control over resources in one location. We can cite here the studies on the Hindu State in Travancore where caste was used as a mode of control.[29] It is reported that Marthanda Varma had killed 42 rebel leaders and their women and children were made outcasts. Pepper trade was organised and wealth accumulated through the collection of taxes. The accumulated wealth was hoarded in the Padmanabha Temple. Mahadev Desai, secretary to Gandhiji, noted it in 1937 that the Raja was made to carry the palanquin in which Nambudri Brahmins were carried as late as in the 1930s since the king was declared the servant of Lord Padmanabha and in turn a slave to Brahmin. The accumulation of wealth or primitive accumulation of capital through religion was never considered by the Marxist scholars as an important point to strike at the enormous power of religious fundamentalism in India. It is dubious logic, maybe advocated by wily experts, to say that religion is super structure while the whole process of development in Asia was located around the places of worship. For instance, the Travancore Royal Family was in the news in 2015 relating to the wealth staked in Anant Padmanabha Sway temple in Trivandrum.[30] In fact, the case was pending before the apex court for a long time and in July 2012 the Supreme Court of India appointed an expert committee to evaluate the riches stacked in vault A that was expected to be worth ₹10 trillion. The total wealth stacked was reported to be in trillions, much more than what was alleged to be stashed in Swiss banks. Interestingly the media stopped reporting on this issue and the proceedings of the Supreme Court have been made confidential. There are several such chambers in the temple and no one knows how much the total wealth in the temple is. This indicates that there seem to be a permanent institution of a particular caste or social assemblage that recreates of its own volition, by birth, generation after generation for thousands of years to maintain its hegemony, be it external rulers in the past or MNCs in the globalised world today. This trend seems to be not so deliberate in other societies where the priest class is open ended. This may be one of the reasons for the unchangeableness of the Indian social structure, apart from other contributing factors[31] as noted by Marx. Interestingly there seem to be few studies emphasising on this crucial link, though several research studies do point out the exploitation of SCs, the artisan castes and Adivasis as they do not fit into the class framework. Even international scholarship is over whelmed by the presence of a particular social group either in Marxist or renegade studies on India. If someone makes an independent attempt he is either killed or ignored with the traditional conspiracy of silence.[32] The fact that it never occurred to the scholars to look at India from CMOP rather than devised concepts such as feudalism from below and from above and so on is enigmatic in scholarship. It seems, there is some rethinking in the academic world in the post-colonial studies once the subaltern group collapsed by its own weight.

SOCIAL CONSEQUENCES OF FOREIGN INVESTMENT

We have examined how international trade has widened economic inequalities in the previous chapter. We may reflect here how the investments from abroad would affect the social life of India. India, as narrated by a section of the professional historians and even amateurs, has some kind of unconscious longing for the Western side of Indus. It has consciously entered the policy-making after 1991 to link India with the West through trade. Ever since the new economic policy was implemented, the country was thrown open to pre-colonial conditions of entry of foreign investors seeking profits here. The economic history of some of the poorest nations of the world, mostly from Africa, tells us interesting stories of how they became poor. India, being one of the growing and so-called future superpower, may not come under this category. Regrettably, India is not a homogenous country and there are many nations within the category of 'nation' and, therefore, one can comfortably make theories or models that may not be applicable to all and definitely be useful to the nations to which they are addressed with a hidden agenda. In this context, the recent debate on the advantages and disadvantages of FDI in retail trade has attracted the attention of every stakeholder, including Dalit icons. If one looks at the whole issue, it is not new. The National Democratic Alliance (NDA) government that had sincerely adhered to the reforms initiated by the Congress under the leadership of P. V. Narasimha Rao seems to have expressed its assent to the proposal. But, now, maybe the coalition has more inputs on the issue, so it is talking differently.

The MNC prize-fighters have descended on the economic columns of various newspapers with their excellent stories of how it is going to benefit the poorest of the poor and the ex-untouchables. They have now supporters and research inputs to tell us that there are already millionaires from these social categories, and some of them would one day become Tatas and Ambanis. Why bother about the reservations in private sector? The issue is not how many of the social categories are benefitted by this one issue of FDI but, the whole foreign investment as such. The Ministry of Commerce and Industry has revised its guidelines on foreign investments, based on the past experience in October 2011. It has permitted 100 per cent investment in several sectors, including agriculture, mining, coal, etc., with the usual riders. It has prohibited FDI in retail trading, lottery business, gambling, etc. The interesting part of it is that 100 per cent FDI equity is allowed in cash-and-carry wholesale trading. The guidelines are very clear that Indian retailers will be benefitted by this policy and all that is credited to Wal-Mart can be obtained by this facility as it has an automatic entry route.

But have the experts making optimistic remarks on Wal-Mart contribution to employment considered why it has failed to arrest unemployment and dissent in the USA where it was born? It is very curious to find that someone doing international business is concerned about one's own country now.

The WTO rules do not permit, and there is a lot of process of paper work involved even to get the most favoured nation (MFN) status. What makes them endure is their international outlook and cosmopolitanism in managing (grabbing) the conditions to succeed. Therefore, one need not look for ideas on how to protect the identity of the nation. Economists, particularly those working with international organisations, are part of this and are supposed to provide models that suit the conditions and interests of the investors.

Unlike in the textbook models that we teach in the classrooms, economists are supposed to develop a forward-looking and broad-based outlook to find out opportunities of profitable routes of investment. They need to identify the engines of growth in an economy and help link it with international trade (including the invisibles), irrespective of the social consequences in the host country. All nations are not endowed evenly. Similarly, all of them have their own institutions and legacies unique to each nation. For instance, India gets its 60 per cent of GDP from the non-corporate sector, out of which it gets 36 per cent from the service sector; agriculture contributes 19 per cent and the manufacturing sector gives only 4.5 per cent. Further, it is reported that in recent period the manufacturing sector has recorded negative growth. How has this happened? What are the social consequences?

Foreign investment, whether through FDI or FII or share market (temporary), goes to those sectors that are found to be profitable. It has nothing to do with the priorities, and factor endowments of the host country. Out of the 6 trillion of foreign investment that entered our country, 21 per cent was in financial services, 8 per cent in computer software, 8 per cent in telecom, 7 per cent was in housing and real estate, and another 7 per cent was in construction.[33]

The manufacturing sector, like automobiles, has only 5 per cent of this amount. If we consider that foreign investment brings technology and skills to accelerate growth, how could this small amount infuse confidence in the real estate sector? The service sector in India was riding on the financial bubble created in the USA and Europe. Experts in money markets have said that India and China have acted as buffer when the US and European countries were in financial crisis. Now the whole world is in economic turmoil and the results are echoed in India.

The most striking consequence of the foreign investment can be seen in terms of the regional imbalances it has created in the country. Out of the total foreign investment, 35 per cent has gone to Mumbai, 20 per cent to Delhi, 6 per cent each to Chennai and Bangalore, and Hyderabad comes in the sixth place with 5 per cent. Interestingly, 42 per cent of the investments came from Mauritius alone, followed by 10 per cent from Singapore, with the USA and the UK with 7 and 5 per cent, respectively. We have read enough about these dubious circuits and the crisis they have created in our public life. Table 4.3 shows the per cent of FDI equity originating from different countries. It is striking that 69.17 per cent of the FDIs come from tax havens, making the allegations of opposition parties that the Indian black money is routed through this group of countries seem to be a reality.

The social economy in India is built around caste and village communities. They have developed several institutions which some of the Western-trained economists refuse to recognise. There are 44.35 million non-agriculture enterprises with employment potential of about 80 million people. There are 15 million retail traders. Most of them are in the unorganised sector. The data on the own account enterprises (OAE) has revealed that there are about 1.7 million SC entrepreneurs (with low economic base) and around 5 million OBC and Muslim units under this category. They are not, of course, millionaires. It is common knowledge among those who frequent villages that an old woman near a dilapidated hut sells peanuts and little things for the passers-by and survives. The fisherwomen, most of whom come under the category of the SCs in North India, are the outlets for the fish gathered by men folk. It seems they do also come under the category of OAE. What will happen to them if retail trading is given to the

Table 4.3

India's FDI Equity Inflows: Top 10 Home Countries Share (in Percentage)

S. No.	Country	Aug. 1991 to Dec. 2000	2001 to 2004	2005 to 2009
	(1)	(2)	(3)	(4)
1.	Mauritius	31.51	38.81	49.62
2.	Singapore	2.76	2.22	11.33
3.	USA	20.10	14.36	7.28
4.	UK	5.44	7.80	5.64
5.	Cyprus	0.20	0.18	4.41
6.	Netherlands	5.19	9.48	3.83
7.	Japan	7.41	7.32	3.22
8.	Germany	5.61	4.13	2.61
9.	UAE	0.08	0.66	1.75
10.	France	2.59	3.22	1.24
	Sub-total	80.90	88.19	90.80
	Others	19.10	11.81	9.20
	Total FDI Inflows	100.00	100.00	100.00
	Memorandum Items: Nature of Source Country			
	(i) Premier Tax Havens	7.57	6.27	18.79
	(ii) Mid-Range Tax Havens	31.94	39.26	50.29
	(iii) Minor and Notional Tax Havens	0.01	0.02	0.09
	Sub-total Tax Havens (i+ii+iii)	39.51	45.55	69.17
	(iv) Others	60.49	54.45	30.83
	Grand Total	100.00	100.00	100.00

Source: K. S. Chalapati Rao and Biswajit Dhar, *India's FDI Inflows: Trends and Concepts*, ISID, Delhi, 2011.

MNCs? India had sufficient experience with the mechanisation of fishing and the displacements of traditional fisherfolk, growth of fish tanks leading to job losses for Dalit agricultural labourers, vanishing LIDCAP, etc. emerging as new sources of displacement.

Failure to understand the diversities in the national character of disadvantaged groups due to the excessive generalisation of the experiences of one or two so-called advanced caste(s), and their leaders in developed areas such as Mumbai, Delhi or in isolated pockets, creates more problems than solutions. If investors are blind to such marginalised groups and only concerned with the slowly emerging thin layer (created due to excess heat and not creamy layer) of the system, then it is cronyism of another kind and not development. If the government considers these consequences and is willing to spend billions (indirect subsidies to MNCs) later to safeguard the interests of the poor, then why should anyone have objection to FDIs? This may be considered as another side of rent-seeking behaviour of MNCs and MCCs under the invisible foot of state.

EDUCATION BECOMES A PRIVATE GOOD

The provision of education and health has been considered as the primary function of the State. One important argument advanced in favour of the formation of the State is for the provisioning of indivisible public services such as education and health to the citizens. They are called merit goods and can be provided by an institution that stands for sovereign political power. World Bank economists have used their intellect to distinguish between public goods and private goods even in education. They term school education as a public good, while higher education is called a private good as it provides benefits to the individual, and not to the public (even if one becomes a Nobel laureate, the concept does not allow to claim him or her as a citizen of a country). That even such a distinction did not save school education in India is a different matter. It is known to experts that higher education is not uniform and can be broadly divided on the basis of the shelf-life of courses, some long life and the ones promoted by the private sector for profit as short life courses or skills. Those who are familiar with the American higher education system would know that around 72 per cent of students are provided with free education through scholarships. Private universities survive through munificent endowments and research projects that their distinguished alumni get from the private sector. However, these are very few. The situation in higher education in advanced countries varies from country to country. Now the Indian government is seeking ideas and recommendations from concerned citizens, business groups, etc. on how to expand higher education for meeting the growing needs of the economy.

Indian higher education was initiated by the British to meet their requirements and to help create an elite class that would help them to survive and run the state once they left the country. This fact needs to be viewed in conjunction with a report given by a group of business persons-cum-educationists recently in Delhi on private participation in higher education. It is reported that the committee wanted land free of cost (on lease for 999 years like the Mulla Periyar dam) from the government and a 300 per cent deduction from taxable income. The wish list continues: a 10-year multiple entry visa for foreign students; a national loan fund of ₹1 trillion; no space index for institutions in urban areas to start campuses (like one-room universities); and that the Prime Minister should personally write to the business houses to take part in higher education.[34]

It appears that no educationist has opposed the recommendations that would impact the future generations and some experts who have made the recommendations are being considered by a section of the media as great Intellectuals and educationists who have brought a turnaround in the system. Critics and analysts do consider them as body shoppers with a naked craving for money and success. It is also alleged that some of the self-styled educationists have brought disaster to the system as they influenced the whole education system to concentrate on the production of men-machines or so-called software personnel to meet the lower-level skill requirements of the USA and other advanced countries in their transition from manufacturing economies to service providers. The froth of golden age of ICT and service sector jobs is gone now. There is some kind of homogeneity and a guarantee of minimum salary structures comparable to some Central government jobs now in the software sector for a select few. The repugnance for these courses is reflected in the closure of several colleges in the South. Can a developing country, with less than 15 per cent enrolment in higher education and a dropout rate of around 70 per cent at school stage, afford this?

Funding agencies such as the UGC, AICTE, state departments of education, etc. have been providing grants to maintain institutions that are generally declared as non-profit organisations. But, a majority of these institutions that came in the boom period with the support of political and business interests have made money out of the demand for a certain category of education. Some of these institutions have flouted norms and put all kinds of pressure on the regulatory authorities to get their licenses renewed. As a result, a few of the regulators are in jail and several professors are going round the CBI, Central Vigilance Commission (CVC), etc. for their extraordinary service rendered to higher education. A majority of these people are involved in the operations as educationists and are being unmasked as pseudo educationists. Amusingly, some of the professors who never taught in a school are producing textbooks for school children (rather than the school teachers) with factual errors that have created ripples in the Parliament.

PUBLIC VERSUS PRIVATE SCHOOLS

The controversy on the role of government schools (public school) in generating Naxalites versus private schools producing 'swayam sevaks' is an interesting issue on which there seems to be little discussion among academics. Most of the private schools in India are strangely called as public schools. It is a misnomer. However, the debate on public education is as old as the movement for self-respect and modernisation. Mahatma Phule, who is credited for the backward class movement, was the first person in modern India to apprise the British about the parochial nature of English education. In his memorandum (reproduced in one of my books) to the Hunter Commission in 1882, Phule questioned the rationale of restricting public education to the dvijas and denying the same to the shudra and *ati-shudra* farmers who had contributed to the education of others through special cesses. B. R. Ambedkar has further elaborated the argument in his Bombay Legislative speech on education.[35]

School education became public in modern India after the implementation of the recommendations of the Hunter Commission (1882). Thus, the debate on public and private schools is not new and has always been there to reflect a deep-rooted prejudice against the universalisation of education in India. The apathy and indifference in implementing the constitutional directive of providing free and compulsory education during the five decades after independence compelled the government to introduce the Right to Education (RTE) in 2009. The rules were prepared and individual states were asked to produce rules for the implementation of the act. The Central government has made a budgetary provision for the RTE through the Sarva Shiksha Abhiyan with a provision of not less than ₹200 billion in each budget.

In fact, policy-makers have delayed the RTE for decades, quoting that it would be difficult for the government to find funds for its execution. Now funds are available, yet the allocated funds for the SSA seem to have not been fully utilised; if spent, they are stories of embezzlement. What does it really indicate? Let us for a moment go back to the cultural history of our country to understand the low levels of literacy and underdevelopment. While most of the East Asian countries, including Japan through the Meiji restoration, achieved almost universal literacy by the end of 19th century, the goal is still eluding India. There are still pockets of high-levels of illiteracy (around 80 per cent), while the 2011 census has estimated an average literacy of 75 per cent for the country as a whole. But, illiteracy in rural areas is still a problem due to lack of schooling. It is not difficult to identify the groups and we need not spend millions on research to find out the reasons. This possibly could be attributed to our cultural ethos that invokes education as a prerogative of men and for a chosen few. This characteristic perhaps unconsciously guides our policy-makers. Therefore, we cannot find fault with some of our gurus and corporate babas for reflecting the popular sentiment.

In this context, we find Andhra Pradesh as a unique state with the dichotomy of a large number of higher educational institutions simultaneously flourishing with one of the lowest levels of literacy (lower than Odisha) in the country. The hullabaloo over the public or government schools and private schools in Andhra Pradesh in 2013 is due to the well-entrenched involvement of the private corporate sector in school education. Naturally, they would find ways to undermine government schools like the statements made by some babas in whom they have invested to create a brand value.

The sentiment that government or public schools produce Naxalites would make the parents even in rural areas withdraw their children from such schools. This would enable the private corporate sector (they have already produced a document on business possibilities in education) to enlarge its tentacles. Nowhere in the developed countries, including the UK, the USA and the OECD, is primary education left totally to the private sector. In the USA, schooling is compulsory. The state, through local governments and educational districts, manages institutions with necessary funding.

It is reported that the enrolment in purely private and non-profit schools in capitalist America comes to around 10 per cent. Even these schools are supposed to follow certain standards laid down by the government as they are identified as denominational with the church or other such groups. The situation in

India, particularly after debates on compulsory primary education and Article 45, and now the RTE, has become trivial. The enrolment in private schools now stands at 35 per cent of the total in elementary sector. This is not an urban phenomenon. The *Economic Survey 2012* mentions that enrolments in the private primary schools in rural areas range between 30 to 50 per cent of the total. This is preceded by the fall in standards where 48 to 54 per cent of students in Standard V cannot read a textbook of Standard II. Meanwhile, it is alleged that some high courts have interpreted that the 25 per cent reservation of seats as per RTE in corporate schools include economically weaker sections.

India is not the USA, not even Pakistan in terms of its diversity and plurality. It is exactly for this reason the British had introduced a secular grant-in-aid code for educational institutions to discourage denominational and communal orientations in education. The Indian republic stands for a secular state and the education system here needs to comply with the same through a uniform curriculum and goals. It was found in a study conducted by us about three decades ago that our education system is class-oriented. A municipal or panchayat school is for the wretched of the earth, the so-called public schools or convents for the rich and the aided schools for the middle classes. The students would perhaps never meet and share the sublime dreams of our founding fathers who wished that India should emerge one day as a single nation and not one with multitudes of classes and nations through schools that promote parochialism and discordant culture.

POLICY CRISIS IN EDUCATION

The confusion in higher education after the litigation of Unnikrishnan J. P. versus Andhra Pradesh in the apex court in 1992 and its impact on the policy framework is far-fetched.[36] In this context, the apex court directed the government in 2012 to follow a uniform fee structure in all professional colleges.

There are several implications of the above 1992 judgement. But, the damage alleged to have been done to higher education, particularly in the professional stream, during 1993–2002 and in 2012 is inconceivable. Policy-makers seem to have concentrated on lucrative professional colleges and neglected other streams of university education. The criticism was vindicated by the apex court again that declared the Unnikrishnan order as unconstitutional by a bench consisting of 11 judges chaired by B. N. Kirpal in 2002.[37] Without going into the legal implications of the case, one can comprehend that this case created new categories, including the NRI quota, free seats and payment seats in professional education. The irony is that the disarray is still haunting the state in the form of fee reimbursement. It has repercussions for a socially significant area that is supposed to be clear in its mandate, but landed in crisis due to judicial over indulgence and political opportunism?

Among the south Indian states, Andhra Pradesh is considered as one of the advanced ones in matters concerning the expansion of higher education during the period 1991–2011. (Ironically this is the only state in the south that has low literacy and high dropout rates in school education.) It is also recorded that half of the total private higher educational institutions including deemed universities in the country are located in the South as per the UGC survey in 2014. It was remarked by a commentator about the growing menace of private engineering colleges that suddenly the poultry farms, dairy farms, workshop sheds in the southern states disappeared and voluntary activity proliferated in a highly cultured sector. There was no immediate predicament with the trend. But, the backward classes started experiencing the heat as a majority of them were not able to get into private corporate colleges nor in the nationally recognised institutes such as IITs, IIMs, etc., as there was no provisioning for OBC reservations there. The protagonists of OBC reservations have raised the issue in the Parliament and the UPA-I government brought in 27 per cent reservations for OBCs in higher educational institutions. The post-Mandal litigations started once again in the courts. The agitations of the backward classes and the litigations forced the government to reappraise the system. An Oversees Committee under the chairmanship of Veerappa Moily was appointed, who in turn used the services of Anand Krishnan to gather data to formulate a policy for the implementation of reservations for OBCs under the guidance of the apex court. Higher education in the country started getting funds from the UGC, AICTE, etc. to create 54 per cent places in all universities to implement the 27 per cent reservations to safeguard the prospects of the non-reserved communities. This was a wonderful compromise that benefitted higher education which was for long suffering neglect. We come across examples like the UK where the government has introduced a teaching grant and subsidised loans schemes with a ceiling on fees in 2004.

Under the given circumstances, some states like Andhra Pradesh seem to have overplayed the drama through the student fees reimbursement (to help private players) under the guidance of imprudent advisors. They have introduced student-based subsidies in higher education through fee reimbursements rather than the institution-related grant-in-aid system. If a thorough inquiry is made into the system of reimbursement, it will become clear that it is neither the student nor the parent that was the beneficiary of the subsidies, but rather the managements of some worthless private colleges. The crisis is part of a larger game and the people know what it is. As the excitement of fee reimbursement unfolds through media reports, one can see the role played by interest groups in college management that are facing the heat of dwindling enrolments, while some poor backward classes undergo pain in silence (due to opportunities foregone or the opportunity cost).[38]

India being one of the most ancient civilisations and a substantial contributor of mind power in the area of abstract speculations and indigenous endowment in the form of *Siddha*, Ayurveda, etc., in medicine, mathematics, physics, chemistry and astronomy, is not far behind. We can definitely find a place for India in the world of science, technology, engineering, medicine and other areas of modern advancements in the 21st century. The country achieved self-sufficiency in food, developed indigenous missiles such as the Brahmos, formulated pharmaceuticals, etc. through its own research efforts. We today have world-class research laboratories developed by DRDO, CSIR, DST, Biotechnology, ICMR, Space Science and other departments of the government carrying out collaborative research with various universities.

The shift in accentuation from manufacturing to service in the West has modified university research from the fundamental to applied areas. This can be seen in terms of the kind of unfair combinations of narrow fields of study that have very limited application in practice, which are emerging at an enormous cost. The West (with its putrid wealth) could afford it. We must learn lessons from China that has built its economy on cheap products with the help of companies like Wal-Mart and is soon going to face the music once the level of development of society and its aspirations ascend, thereby demanding quality products. Higher education has an important social function of envisioning the future and maintaining stability through its innovative courses that suit our history, resources and culture. Let us hope our university system would soon meet the expectations!

UNIVERSITY RESEARCH TAKES A BACKSEAT

The idea of research and development was initiated in India along with the university system. It provided an excellent background for scientific innovations and produced brilliant minds and some Nobel Laureates too. Even now, research results of universities dominate publications as compared to earmarked research conducted by state-funded organisations. While schools are supposed to receive knowledge and transact and disseminate it to the students, teachers in higher education need to create and experiment with knowledge while teaching the students. Some of our aged experts of the government have overshot this difference and failed the universities. Universities in the country, particularly the state universities, have suffered from neglect, apathy, nonchalance and discrimination for almost three decades. The teachers or professors of the universities, including the affiliated colleges, have also contributed for these piteous conditions in the system. Most of them have become fatalistic in their attitude and seem to have not protested the decadence. The teacher's unions have become defunct. The militancy of some of the organisations in participating in the problems of the people and considering themselves as part of the community has been buried except at times for economic benefits like salary, perks, etc.

A few intelligent and smart professors have left the system after getting initial training in India. They have been encouraging the private sector to flourish. A World Bank document in 1986 has distinguished between higher education and school education by calling the former a private good and the latter a public good, and this seems to have been accepted in principle by policy-makers. Thus, the policies of the government both at the Centre and in the states have further strengthened the dichotomy between higher education and school education (as of private and public goods). Economic reforms in the country have cultivated the interest of the private sector in higher education through the Ambani and Bajaj report to the Vajpayee government. The mushrooming of private universities and so-called deemed universities has slenderised interest in university research. It is in this context that we can cite the concept of 'pseudo-university,' interrogated by higher education expert Professor Philip Altbach, as one that offers narrow and specially designed curriculum.[39] Most such universities have come up keeping in mind the demand for few specific courses, mostly in the USA and the West. These could be called short half-life courses as per the World Bank. They have very limited research component in their curriculum. There is now a growing fashion among many influential families to get university status for their institutes first, to enable assigning the position of chancellor to the head of the family and to make the younger sibling the vice-chancellor. This claim for university status is for a single discipline college and even for narrow sub-disciplines. Keeping the need to encourage and diversify courses through advanced research in emerging areas, the UGC has made a provision for deemed university status, particularly for those that are state funded and of national importance. This clause has been abused with the willing cooperation of the people in the system as revealed in the criminal cases filed against the Chairmen of AICTE, MCI in 2012–14. In order to support their argument, some of them have quoted out of context a recommendation for the commissioning for 1,500 universities in the country. In fact, we would have more than that number if some of the colleges are converted as deemed or autonomous. The commission itself was devoid of any university teacher or expert in higher education and failed to understand the US system where there are no affiliated colleges and India in which an affiliated college is as big as a university such as Columbia (11,000), St George (700) or MIT (4127) in the year 2014.

The Indian universities have failed to attract talented and hardworking bright boys and girls for several reasons. Now the legislators are debating whether scholars, students and teachers need to be given freedom of speech on the campus or to allow only free speech for a few and put some of those who debate on national and international issues passionately behind bars.

The promising and brilliant faculty in the universities has used the resources of the system for their initial learning and research, and thereafter left the system. Most of those Indian-born Nobel laureates in the USA or in the West have migrated from the same universities. The state or higher education agencies did not try to bring them back. An attempt was made to develop a strategy to provide incentives and other conducive conditions to attract our own scholars back home in 2006 sent to PMO was perhaps thrown into the dustbin without the courtesy of any acknowledgement due to bureaucratic indifference to new ideas. The academic situation in the country after the body shopping business revolution or the so-called business process outsourcing (BPO) or ICT upsurge have crippled the best brains. It is neither brain drain nor gain. It is simply 'crippled brain' as the finest brains in their formative years are diverted to simple tasks and for the so-called soft skilled jobs rather than trained for the scientific, technological and engineering needs of an emerging economy. The parents are contented and the ICT business groups are happy as the remittances are multiplied by 50 or 60 times in Indian rupees. But no one has ever calculated the opportunity costs of forego-ing the best brains of a few generations that are lost not being able to use them for the good of the country.

Teaching and research are interrelated in higher educa-tion and it may be for this reason that a teacher with adequate academic standing in any university is called a professor (one who professes profound ideas). In some countries, the posi-tion is restricted to universities and in many it is extended to senior faculty of a college and/or university. After the Fifth Pay Commission, teachers in universities were designated Assistant Professor, Associate Professor and Professor in place of Lecturer, Reader and Professor. The same was extended to colleges affiliated with postgraduate teaching and research activity. Now there is widespread criticism that research is given tepid treatment. University teachers are paid to teach and conduct research that supports or complements teaching. This is different for instance, from certain Western universities where teachers are paid only for 10 months and are supposed to earn their residual income through research or consultancy. Some private universities like Harvard have huge endow-ments, the value of which is equal to the combined GDP of Jordan and Sri Lanka. This is not possible in India where there are separate agencies such as the CSIR, DRDO and others to conduct or sponsor research. The universities depend upon grants from agencies such as the UGC, AICTE, ICMR, ICSSR, etc., which, in turn, rely on government.[40] The research fund-ing for science or social sciences is also not without prejudices, as reported by Wallerstein in his Gulbenkian Commission report on social sciences.[41] It is affirmed that funding decisions in countries like the USA are riddled with institutional biases, programmatic preferences and other considerations. We cannot say that it is not true in the Indian situation.

There are caste-like leagues in the system from top to bottom and they cling to power in Delhi as advisers or experts to sponsor candidates even after reaching the senile age of 80. They become stumbling blocks to progress in higher education. In a country where adulation is a social value, it has serious implications for governance. This can be seen in terms of the attitude of the elite to higher education in India. It has been a prerogative of the few who get educated with state support but mislay interest in it once the private sector has absorbed them. It is noticed that in many State universities about 50 per cent of the teaching posts have remained unfilled for decades. This has seriously dented teaching and research. The concept of contract lecturers has gained significance in most universities based on the private colleges' experiment of 'somehow complete the syllabus'. But, everyone in the system knows that contract teachers do not undertake research, nor are they sufficiently qualified and inclined to take up research. This then impacts the quality of products of the universities.

There have been complaints of discrimination and dissuasion of scholars from certain social categories. The number of suicides committed by students and scholars in the so-called quality institutions for several years got exposed with the Rohith suicide in Hyderabad Central University. It seems that those who talk about the low-level output of our research do not bother to look at these conditions in the universities. The research output in science and technology needs to be converted into patents. This requires a lot of expertise, entrepreneurial abilities and support from the industry. In fact, the research effort of our private sector is very low and sometimes the attitudes are counterproductive. Private sector sponsored research projects are few in our university system compared to the USA. Some of the scholars work as adjuncts of a foreign

funding agency or conduct research without much significance to the people. The major faltering chunk appears to be
in the area of selecting a topic, the methodology, the equip-
ment, research assistants and funding to sustain the project to
reach its logical conclusion. Lack of support for fundamental
research and low enrolments in basic sciences due to the mad
rush for application-oriented courses have created a dearth
of research skills among students of the younger generation.
Some of these conditions make the researcher either migrate
or become a successful entrepreneur. Some brave hearts only
implement the mandate of the system to inspire students to
become scholars through their dedication to teaching.

It is reported that China, with an investment of 1.33 per
cent of its GDP on research and development (R&D), generated 62,063 scientific articles abstracted to a standard data base
(SCI-E) compared to 26,810 for India with an investment of
0.69 of GDP on R&D, while the USA had 205,320 of the same
with an investment of 2.62 per cent of GDP on R&D. There
are 1,387,882 full-time researchers in the USA compared to
1,118,698 in China and only 115,936 in India. Of course, we can
find several biases in this trend as three-fourths of the journals
are published in the USA and 85.3 per cent of the journals use
English as the medium of writing.

There appears to be a rethinking in the government giving
hope to the possibility of getting a reasonable way out of the
present impasse in higher education policy on the basis of a
dispassionate exercise, rather than leaving it to the market
forces for a solution. It appears that the Government of India
is thinking of replicating the mission mode used for universalisation of school education for higher education. RUSA as
a mission mode seem to be on the cards to replace some of
the functions of regulatory bodies such as the UGC, AICTE,
etc. that have become notorious for corruption, red-tapism,
etc. However, this model appears to be developed by bureaucrats who lack the necessary academic grounding for research
and teaching at the university level as their thrust appears to
achieve the numbers to get the tag of 30 per cent enrolment by

2015. The NDA government has already initiated a process of formulating a national policy of education and it is believed that it might reflect the ideology of the ruling dispensation with little bureaucratic tinkering.

SOCIAL INFRASTRUCTURE

Infrastructure is the basic framework of a system or organisation and stands fundamental for the development of a nation. It consists of not only roads, buildings, power grids, communication systems, hospitals, etc., but also the necessary manpower to be generated through educational institutions. Public health care is generally understood as the science and art of prolonging the health of individuals and groups supported by the State. The definition given by academics may be different from what we normally think of the public health (government) care system in India. It is not limited to communicable diseases, as the common people expect the state to provide health care to prevent any kind of disability due to physical or mental suffering.

One of the important gifts of human civilisation is that prevention of disease is transferred from the individual to the group or society as a social practice. Therefore, the tradition of providing health-care facilities in all civilised societies until very recently has been provided by the organised state. This tradition is now replaced by private service providers or insurance companies, which charge a premium to come to the rescue of the client when he or she becomes a patient. This has grown as a big service sector that runs into trillions of dollars across the world. It is estimated that the medical market in India is worth ₹3 to 5 trillion per year. To convince individuals and governments about the painless and cheap method of providing health care to people, corporate interests have been relentlessly working through various lobbies, foundations, etc. and have succeeded to a large extent. Thus, India has emerged as the world's most debilitating country as far as health services are concerned. There are several reasons for this, and liberalisation is alleged to be one of the causes for reducing health care to that of a commercial service. Public outcry and civil society activism made the government present a White Paper recently in the Parliament to state the health of the economy in terms of the black money or parallel economy. The White Paper did not bring out anything new other than what has already been explained earlier by economists and, therefore, does not merit a detailed comment. What the process makes us to feel disheartening about is that no one has so far asked for a White Paper on the status of health of our people. Interestingly, the analytical reports presented by foundations and some civil society organisations appear to be dubious in terms of the credibility of intentions of some of them as they are alleged to be conduits for black money, as per the White Paper. Most of these foundations or trusts, etc. are alleged to be getting linked with international bodies, possibly to supply necessary data on the social sectors to expand their business interests in India. Fortunately, there are still divine and self-sacrificing persons who always remember the Hippocratic Oath. Unfortunately their number is dwindling. Modern medical professionals were in the beginning trained by the British during their rule through their allopathic system by offering courses through colleges affiliated to universities. The notion of a quack was made popular to make the indigenous systems inferior till the state introduced the Ayurveda, Yoga and Naturopathy, Unani, Siddha and Homeopathy (AYUSH) in 1995. Even those who have undergone training in these traditional courses prefer to settle in cities. A majority of students who get into the colleges by paying huge sums of capitation fees and years of prolonged education for obtaining PG diploma, certificate, etc. to be able to attract enough clientele, do burn out or reach middle age by the time they start practicing. Some of them may think that rural areas are not resourceful enough to recover the costs of their training. Some of them seem to be deficient in knowledge about the disease regimes of the rural areas and the poor. These could be some of the reasons for lack of response to the government proposal to incentivise rural service with 10 bonus marks per year to get admission in postgraduate (PG) as a new policy. There is a shortage of 14,000 doctors at the primary health care level. Some senior professors complain that the students care less for para-clinical subjects in their anxiety to prepare for the PG entrance exam.

The knowledge base of several students, mostly from private colleges, is so poor that degrees from Russia and Eastern Europe are now considered as better choices in terms of employment opportunities in the management of corporate hospitals. It seems the Central Ministry of Health and Family Welfare, along with the MCI, is seized of the problem. The proposals to conduct the NEET, a two-month foundation course, a three-year rural-oriented medical degree, etc. appear to be some of the strategies conceived to overcome the challenges of providing sufficient health professionals. But, the crisis in public health care is so grave that these measures appear to be inadequate. The ministry has recognised in some of its reports that the out-of-pocket expenses on health care are the highest in the world and the hospitalised Indians spend on an average 58 per cent of their total annual expenditure. Over 48 per cent of hospitalised Indians fall below the poverty line because of hospital expenses. The average expenditure for a below poverty line (BPL) family in a private set-up is estimated to be ₹5,638 and even in public hospital, it amounts to ₹2,700 (2004). The solution offered by policy-makers in term of privatising health care has been evaluated by scholars. It is found that it has raised the out-of-pocket expenses of the insurer, and that the experiments through Arogyasri have ultimately helped the corporate hospitals. The Central budget expenditure on health in India is the lowest, with less than 1 per cent of the GDP compared to 6.2 per cent for the USA, 2 per cent for China and 1.6 per cent for Bangladesh. How could tinkering with medical education (of course, in the right direction) without increasing the budget and regulating the private sector, cure the ailing public's health?

It is not only in relation to the privatisation of health and education, but also with reference to the kind of urban and modern ways of living through conspicuous infrastructures, that we need to learn from the experiences of the West. Detroit city, the birthplace of American car industry, is in the news, driving towards bankruptcy. The governor of Michigan, Rick Snyder, has appointed a black expert, Kevin Carr, as an emergency manager to find out ways and means of overcoming the current crisis. The city is not able to provide street lighting; there are no benches in the pathways and parks; 60-year-old trams have not been replaced; old buses ply on roads; pay pensions have been defaulted to, etc. Further, the city has lost around two-thirds of its population between 1960 and 2013, from 2 million to around 700,000 by now.[42]

The provision of public utilities in Europe and America was based on their climatic conditions and the bounty they received from the colonies. Unfortunately, Indians have tried to copy them without any external colony of their own. Perhaps the policy-makers instinctively realised the existence of internal colonies (social and marginalised groups) and planned the infrastructure accordingly after liberalisation.

People are happy with the quadratic national highways across different regions and cultures by marginalising local needs. These highways were aimed to link the four corners of the country for the free flow of goods without any hurdles to reach the ports passing through several special and export processing zones. They are considered as comparable to any other infrastructure in America or Europe in style and structure. They comprised a high foreign exchange component with very good margins for the contractors who became legislators in the course of time. This seems to be a good model of development in the capitalist mode where facilities are provided to people and, at the same time, give leadership to the nation. The models used here are the ones that were used during the time of Eisenhower and Roosevelt. Some American commentators tell us that Eisenhower spent money from the defence budget to create facilities to move troops across different states as a general during the Second World War. He was visionary as the future President to create the interstate roads and infrastructure to connect 50 states to become a strong United States of America. But the problem, according to President of the American Society of Civil Engineers (ASCE), B. D Leonard, is that "we are still driving on Eisenhower's roads and sending our kids to Roosevelt's schools." It means that the country has not invested on the maintenance or repairs or simply no provision has been made for depreciation on the capital. It is estimated that there is a backlog of $2.2 trillion infrastructure in the country.

It is not only in the US but in several European nations that huge infrastructures were magnificently built when they were riding on high growth, to showcase their vanity (beyond their need). They have now started crumbling, not only due to the downturn of the same economies but also the declining size of the population leading capacity to be underutilised. On 1 August 2007, the I-35W Mississippi River Bridge collapsed killing 13 people and around that time the San Francisco–Oakland Bay Bridge repairs became grave. It is reported that during the period of recession, the percentage of expenditure on public construction as a proportion of the GDP in America declined. The *Global Competitiveness Report 2012–13* estimates that the infrastructure score came down from 6.1 to 5.8, placing the USA at 25th rank.[43]

India, being the third largest economy in the world in terms of the size of GDP is ranked 87th with a score of 3.8 in infrastructure capacity (in the same report). Perhaps, keeping in mind this score and the need for world-class infrastructure to facilitate free movement of wares, our Prime Minister wanted more investments into this sector. It also has the capacity to absorb more investments and create new jobs. FDIs are, therefore, most welcome. But, we may reflect here on the kind of experiences the advanced countries have had in the era of free trade, the wealth so created and the consequences therein.

Detroit can be taken as a case in example to project the kind of complications awaiting us. Detroit is in distress, not due to any natural calamity but due to a man-made disaster and faith in a model. It is easy to develop a model of growth based on free trade to benefit from comparative advantage or factor abundance of a nation. It has also been noted in the theories put forth by various economists that factors move in search of efficiency and productivity to yield higher rates of return in a no holds barred situation.

The kind of huge infrastructure projects, including unwieldy irrigation, road, transport, flyovers, arty underpasses of contractor-based projects, need to be reviewed and only the relevant and cost-effective projects need to be selected to unburden the future generations. We need not replicate what others are doing if they do not suit our capacity and conditions. This is common sense and we do not need sophisticated models or advice of paid consultants for the same. We now have a situation where Hyderabad city would likely become a metropolitan centre sucking the resources from the underdeveloped hinterland, and the experience of the city of Detroit is a clear message to be considered by the present government for a careful urban planning.

WORLD BANK POLICIES AND THE DIVISION OF A STATE

It is a dramatic irony that both P. V. Narasimharao, the PM and pioneer of liberalisation, and Chandra Babu Naidu, the Chief Minister who has sincerely implemented the policies, originated from two different regions of Andhra Pradesh. They did not know the social consequences of the policies adopted in 1991 and the state got divided in 2014 citing inequalities and discrimination in development that took place during the period 1991–2014. Andhra Pradesh, as the third largest economy in the country in terms of gross state domestic product (GSDP), is vast enough to attract investors and investments.

Therefore, analysts are always interested in knowing about the expected rates of growth of its economy in general and various sectors vis-à-vis their interests. Andhra Pradesh has been considered as the 'rice bowl' of India with 75–80 per cent of the irrigated water being used for cultivation of paddy. In fact, the emergence of the state as a dominant player in the country is due to the skilful handling of the agricultural surpluses to get entry into business and from there to become lumpen capital is considered by some experts as an Andhra model. The basis for the development of an emerging capitalist class as crony capitalists is due to their proximity to the political power in the state. It is here that one can ponder over how the resources of the state, through budgetary and non-budgetary operations, have been used to get into the present trajectory of growth.

There is a perceptible change in the approach of the government towards various sectors of the Andhra Pradesh economy. This can be examined broadly from the contributions of different sectors of the economy as a proportion of the GSDP. During the early part of the state's formation (1960–61), the primary sector consisting of agriculture and related areas contributed 70.7 per cent of the income and the secondary sector or industry was about to gather momentum (its contribution was limited to 9.1 per cent) as per the Socio-Economic Surveys of the government for various years. The rest was added by tertiary sector or services sector, etc. The agriculture sector has continued to play a dominant role in state domestic product (SDP) being 57.2 per cent in 1970–71 and 46.6 per cent in 1980–81. The services sector seems to have played an equally important role contributing 29.4 per cent and 36.8 per cent respectively to the state's income during the same period, compared to industry that was confined to less than 20 per cent. The structure of the economy was balanced, seen from the proportion of income originating from the sectors traditionally classified as primary, secondary and tertiary.

Except in places like Visakhapatnam and some pockets of Hyderabad where public sector units are located, the overall emphasis of industrialisation of the state was absent. It has been either an agriculture-based or agro-processing-related economy for a long time as the state, according to some scholars, had no traditions of usury, mining, trade, etc. for a sustained period. Therefore, the successive governments diverted the state's resources for the development of agriculture to benefit few pockets of Coastal Andhra, and implemented people-oriented policies like ₹2 rice scheme (with surplus food grains) that reduced the poverty levels.

Assured irrigation is a precondition for achieving higher rates of productivity and output from agriculture as farmers are considered as the most efficient in India. The government has used the planning process as an important basis to put in resources in irrigation projects. The people are fortunate to have several perennial rivers passing through the state of Andhra Pradesh, creating opportunities to utilise the runoff for irrigation potential. The Nagarjunasagar Project was considered by Jawaharlal Nehru as a modern temple and it has given the necessary impetus to agrarian development in the four districts of East and West Godavari, Krishna and Guntur which once experienced severe drought and famines before Cotton's initiative. The importance given to irrigation and power could be discerned from the allocations made to this sector in the plan budget. The highest per cent of 60.9 of the total plan budget was used for irrigation and power in 1969–70 and it came down to 54.82 per cent in 1971–71. It started declining thereafter, indicating the shift in priorities of the government. It stabilised at around 40 per cent in the 1992–97 budget and stood at 34.24 per cent during the Eleventh Plan with a ridiculous amount of 0.45 per cent allocations for power (due to privatisation). Irrigation and power were almost combined together along with flood control in all budget allocations, indicating the highest priority given to agriculture up to the 1990s. Subsequently, the allocations for this sector started dwindling with the generation and distribution of power given a different orientation by the government.

It was during the period 1991–2004 that policies were vetted by international funding agencies and thereafter priorities started changing. However, the lives of the common man, the customer, the worker and the agricultural labourer have not been affected, particularly so in the rural areas. This can be seen in terms of the poverty figures generated by statisticians on the basis of modified methods given by Tendulkar. It is largely due to the state policy towards agriculture, power and land. The land put to non-agricultural use and food grains production have shown growth in inverse directions during the period. The land put to non-agricultural use was 1.351 million hectares (ha) in 1955–56 and it stood at 2.771 million ha by 2010–11 while food grains production doubled from 9.99 million tonnes in 1980–81 to 20.34 million tonnes in 2010–11. This was largely due to assured irrigation water. The subsidised water and power to agriculture seem to have made the state self-sufficient and helped some contractors to emerge as national players.

A Canadian research institute has estimated that the irrigation subsidy was to the extent of ₹428 million in 1980–81 and increased to ₹8,402 in 1999–2000, contributing ₹2,424, 21,778 and 1,928 per hectare under the NSP, SRSP and TBP. There seem to be pressure on the government now to offload the subsidy for power, etc. The consequences of such recommendations on the supply of power are well known. The regulatory mechanisms eulogised by policy-makers to achieve efficiency in the private sector have ultimately resulted in the regulation of the state in determining the tariff in favour of the supplier. This has impacted the economy. The economy seems to be stable due to decent infrastructure and ICT and not necessarily due to reforms.

The industrial development and expansion of the service sector were concentrated in Hyderabad city. It was a strategy alleged to be dictated by the World Bank through the PSRP and Vision 2020 document. In fact, the stratagem was not specific to Andhra Pradesh; it was universal in outlook depending on neoclassical theories that dictated that, "governments should limit activities to sound macroeconomic management and the supply of public goods, while other economic functions should be left to the private sector to pursue under free market competition."[44] This was sincerely followed in Andhra Pradesh during 1991–2014. The outcome of this policy is reflected in the widening of disparities among different sub-regions of the state. Development was concentrated in few pockets that were convenient for the investors. Apart from the historical and cultural divides, the people of rural Telangana, Rayalaseema and Uttarandhra were extremely deprived of opportunities. These led to violent agitations demanding the bifurcation of the state during 2008–14. The state was divided on 2 June 2014 into two states of Telangana and Andhra Pradesh.

The reasons for the demand for such a bifurcation can be judged from the Justice B. N. Sri Krishna Committee Report which noted that the per capita district domestic product by regions during 1993–94 and 2007–08 was not uniform. "Hyderabad city draws most of its income 82 per cent, from the services sector followed by industrial sector while the shares of Rayalaseema declined and Coastal Andhra has remained constant."[45] The per capita incomes of the three regions have also varied during the same period. But, the overall growth of the combined state was higher than the national average, out doing some of the neighbouring states. The aggregate growth did not look at the regional disparities or social disconnect that had been the ammunition to trigger the unrest, social tensions and human tragedies in one of the most well-governed and highly monitored state by the World Bank, indicating how the policies prescribed by aliens would create social disasters, if not related to the ethos of the land. Development in the 21st century through the manipulation of economic parameters is possible, but its social implications and consequences might become grave in a pluralistic country like India. This highlights the relevance of social economics.

NOTES AND REFERENCES

1. K. S. Chalam, *Governance in South Asia: The State of Civil Services* (New Delhi: SAGE Publications, 2014).
2. J. Moij, *Politics of Economic Reforms in India* (New Delhi: SAGE Publications, 2005).
3. J. A. Schumpeter, *Capitalism, Socialism and Democracy* (New York: Harper and Collins, 1942).
4. K. S. Chalam, *Education and Weaker Sections* (New Delhi: Inter India, 1988).
5. Frankfurt school was responsible in developing critical theory and has questioned the notion of objectivity in knowledge as it is embedded in historical and social process. It was not received in India with enthusiasm due to its methods of social criticism. However, some literary theorists seem to have adopted it and used it in cultural studies. Its use in social sciences seems to be lukewarm.
6. E. Said, *Orientalism* (New York: Vintage, 1978).
7. K. S. Chalam, *Economic Reforms and Social Exclusion* (New Delhi: SAGE Publications, 2011).
8. K. S. Chalam, *Education and Weaker Sections* (New Delhi: Inter-India, 1988).
9. Nicos Poulantzas, *Classes in Contemporary Capitalism* (London: Verso, 1978).
10. Harish Damodaran, *India's New Capitalists: Caste Business and Industry in Modern Nation* (Delhi: Palgrave Macmillan, 2008).
11. Vakulabharanam and others, "Patterns of Wealth Disparities in India during the Liberalisation Era," *Economic and Political Weekly*, Vol. 42, (September 2007): 3855–63.
12. Sankara Narayanan, "Sitting Ducks for Dwija As Well As Non-dwija Rulers," *Janata* (August 30, 2015).
13. J. K. Arrow, "Some Mathematical Models of Race in the Labour Market," in *Racial Discrimination in Economic life*, ed. A. Pascal (Lexington: Heath Books, 1972).
14. G. S. Becker, *The Economics of Discrimination* (Chicago: University of Chicago, 1957).
15. G. Akerlof, "The Economics of Castes, Discrimination and of the Rat Race and Other Woeful Tales," *The Quarterly Journal of Economics*, Vol. 90, No. 4 (November 1976): 599–617.
16. S. Bowles, 'The Production Process in a Competitive Economy', *American Economic Review* (15th March 1985): 16–36.
17. C. Shapiro and J. E. Stiglitz, "Equilibrium Unemployment as a Worker Discipline Device," *American Economic Review*, Vol. 74(June 1984): 433–44.
18. Samir Amin, *Unequal Development: An Essay on the Social Formations of Peripheral Capitalism* (New York: Monthly Review Press, 1976).
19. A. G. Frank, *Capitalism and Underdevelopment in Latin America: Historical Studies of Chile and Brazil* (New York: Monthly Review Press, 1967).

20. Ashwini Deshpande and Smriti Sharma, "Entrepreneurship or Survival? Caste and Gender of Small Business in India" (working paper 228, Delhi School of Economics, New Delhi, 2013).

21. Tata Consultancy Partners in Change, Delhi has conducted a study in 2012 to show that presence of Dalits in private sector BSE listed companies of India is almost zero.

22. Ravi Saxena, Han Donker and D. Ajit, "Corporate Boards in India," *Economic and Political Weekly*, Vol. 47 (August 2012).

23. Jairus Banaji, "For a Theory of Colonial Mode of Production," in Utsa Patnaik (ed.), *Agrarian Relations and Accumulation* (New Delhi: Oxford University Press, 1990), pp. 119–132.

24. Karl Marx, *The Capital Vol. 1* (Moscow: Progress Publishers, 1977): 338–39.

25. B. R. Ambedkar, *Dr Baba Saheb Ambedkar Writings and Speeches*, Vol. 5 (New Delhi: Dr Ambedkar Foundation, 2010).

26. D. D. Kosambi, *An Introduction to the Study of Indian History* (Bombay: Popular Prakashan, 1975), p. 313.

27. K. S. Chalam, "Offences and Atrocities against Scheduled Castes in Andhra Pradesh: An Empirical Investigation," *Social Action*, Vol. 54 (2004).

28. Karl Marx, *The Capital*.

29. *The Indian Express*, "Dadri: Outrage after Mob Lynches Man for Allegedly Consuming Beef" (1 October 2015).

30. Kosi Kawashima, *Missionaries and a Hindu State: Travancore 1858–1936* (New Delhi: Oxford University Press, 2000).

31. *One India*, 5 July 2015 Padmanabha Temple's vault–A has riches worth ₹10 lakh crores? www.oneindia.com/padmanabhatemple, accessed in August 2015.

32. We are expecting dozens of scholarly studies on this issue, both in India and abroad, condemning this formulation.

33. The current Professor Kallburgi murder by the so-called Hindu "fringe" organisations for ventilating critical or rational comments by the writer is being denounced by very few writers and limited number of scholars are reported to have joined the protest or the media blue walled.

34. Government of India, *Economic Survey 2013* (Delhi: Department of Economic Affairs, 2013).

35. Narayana Murthy NR of Infosys was appointed as the chairman to recommend measures to implement the Foreign Universities Bill, if it is passed in parliament it becomes an act to allow foreign universities in India, Planning Commission, Government of India 2012.

36. K. S. Chalam, *Modernisation and Dalit Education: Ambedkar's Vision* (Jaipur: Rawat, 2008).

37. Supreme Court case No. SCC (1) 645, 1993 Unni Krishnan VS state of Andhra Pradesh.

38. Supreme Court case No. 317 of 1993 TM Pai Foundation and Others VS state of Karnataka and others. 31 October 2002.

39. K. S. Chalam, *Finances, Costs and Productivity of Higher Education* (Delhi: Inter-India, 1986).

40. Philip G. Altback, 'The Startling Rise of Pseudo Universities', *Times of Higher Education* (28 November, 2003).

41. Immanuel Wallerstein, *Open the Social Sciences: Report of the Gulbenkian Commission on the Restructuring of the Social Sciences* (California: Stanford University, 1996).

42. K. S. Chalam, *Economic Reforms and Social Exclusion* (New Delhi: SAGE Publications, 2011).

43. Reports in Times of India, The Hindu during the month of June 2013.

44. Donald Kettle, 'The Looming Infrastructure Crisis', www.goveng.com, accessed 21 June 2013.

45. Government of India, *Committee for Consultation on the Situation in Andhra Pradesh Report*, Chapter 2 (Delhi: Ministry of Home Affairs, December 2010), Chairman B. N. Srikrishna.

5
Marginalisation of Agriculture Sector

Students of economics are familiar with the statement, "corn is not high because a rent is paid, but a rent is paid because corn is high." This famous sentence written by the classical economist David Ricardo and his quarrel with his friend T. R. Malthus on the possibility of a glut and on the Corn Laws reminds us of the debate over the economics of agriculture in the classical period. Though the present generation of students is not inclined to read about the debates, Former Finance Minister Pranab Mukherjee perhaps kept in mind the debates when he announced that without agriculture and its development inclusive growth was empty.[1] It seems the government is now paying special attention to agriculture.

The notion of economic rent referred to above as the compensation for the use of original and indestructible powers of the soil is transformed, by and large, as the payment made for use of any property today. The more significant aspect of it is the concept of quasi-rent developed by Marshall and extrapolated by modern scholars as the surplus earned by manmade factors in the short period, over and above opportunity costs. The concept of quasi-rent became a subject of great debate when liberalisation was advocated and arguments against unnecessary payment made to an artificially created scarce service or good through misusing or abusing of state power became a dominant discourse. The focus on agriculture seems to have lost.

DIVERSITY IN AGRICULTURE: A NECESSARY CONDITION FOR INCLUSIVE GROWTH

Agriculture being the direct beneficiary of natural resources is considered as a significant segment of the primary sector of an economy. Though mining, extraction, forests and fisheries do come under this sector, agriculture has become visible as the primary sector in India. In fact, India's contribution to world agriculture output is equal to (7.1 per cent) the size of the European Union and almost double the size of the USA. While the advanced countries subsidise their agriculture to remain competitive in the world markets, Indian farmers and the agricultural sector are deprived of this benefit as per some activists.

It is argued that the agriculture sector that has been protected under the State needs to be freed so that it can grow in the world of great opportunities. Further, India being a signatory of the WTO is obliged to open up its agriculture sector sooner or later to international competition. It looks like some intelligent people both in policy-making and in business thought that agriculture means the production of wheat, rice, fish, dairy products, etc. that have an international market. They were also of the opinion that India, being an ancient civilisation with a long history of agriculture, can compete in the international markets and reap the benefits of comparative advantage.

The social economy of India is prominently connected to agriculture and the rural setting in India. The vestiges of the jajmani system are still present in the form of caste relations and in a majority of instances are reflected in urban slums and habitations. It seems that sociologists and anthropologists who have revisited the village in India have looked at the process of transformations at micro and macroeconomic levels. But, it was striking to notice that Jan Breman et al. in their 1980 village study and the 1997 introduction to his work brought out a very significant historical point that is still consciously postured in the contemporary parochial outbursts of some groups. Citing Maine Henry James (1887) studies, they declared, "[O]ur contemporary ancestor could more easily be recognised in the Aryan peasants who populated the Asiatic land scape than in the primitive peoples of Africa and America who lived in tribal lands."[2] Following this example, publications in the Netherlands have compared the Javanese *desa* with the Teutonic *mark* and the Slavonic *mir*. Regrettably, very few of our social anthropologists have recorded that the caste system is being recreated in the process of development in the rural areas through agricultural development and in urban slums as a by-product of industrial development.

Neoclassical economists in general and those following in their footprints in India as development economists in particular, have been more concerned about the two sector models of growth without looking at its social upshot in rural India. The village, as previously noted, is an ossified caste order, with the social exclusion of some groups from others as an ideal of Hinduism and other satellite beliefs. Interestingly, it is recreated time and again through the process of maintaining the proportion of the toiling social groups in rural areas the same, despite the transformation of agriculture through high yielding varieties (HYVs), mechanisation, technology, etc. It is instructive to look at data for 60 years presented in Table 5.1 on the growth of the population in rural areas and in the agricultural sector in India. Though the population has grown over 2 per cent per annum up to 1991 and later stabilised at the replacement rate, the proportion of population in the rural areas has not declined as expected at the same rate.

The striking element of Table 5.1 is that the number and proportion of the labour force working in the agriculture sector has been increasing over the period 1951–2011. How is this possible? It can be expected, as per the neoclassical

Table 5.1
Population and Agricultural Workers

(Pop Million)

Year	Total Population	Average Annual Exponential Growth Rate (%)	Rural Population	Agricultural Cultivators	Workers— Agricultural Labourers	Total	% of Agricultural Workers to Rural Population
1	2	3	4	5	6	7	8
1951	361.1	1.25	298.6 (82.7)	69.9 (71.9)	27.3 (28.1)	97.2	32.5
1961	439.2	1.96	360.3 (82.0)	99.6 (76.0)	31.5 (24.0)	131.1	36.4
1971	548.2	2.2	439.0 (80.1)	78.2 (62.2)	47.5 (37.8)	125.7	28.6
1981	683.3	2.22	525.6 (79.9)	92.5 (62.5)	55.5 (37.5)	148	28.1
1991	846.4	2.16	630.6 (74.5)	110.7 (59.7)	74.6 (40.3)	185.3	29.3
2001	1,028.7	1,097	742.6 (72.2)	127.3 (54.4)	106.8 (45.6)	234.1	31.5
2011	1,210.8	1.5	833.7 (68.9)	118.7 (45.1)	144.3 (54.9)	263	31.5

Source: Registrar General of India and Agricultural Statistics at a Glance 2014, GOI.
Notes: 1. Figures within brackets in column 4 are percentage to the total population.
2. Figures within brackets in column 5 and 6 are percentages to column 7.
3. Min wages range between ₹85 for women in Tamil Nadu—skilled workers ₹249 WB, Mizoram ₹349.

models, that the unlimited supply of labour from rural areas was absorbed in the advanced sectors of the economy thereby reducing the dependency on agriculture. Pranab Bardan,[3] M. S. Swaminathan,[4] Hanumantha Rao,[5] Utsa Patnaik[6] and several others have written on issues relating to agricultural relations, but not necessarily on this typical phenomenon. One of the reasons for this appears to be the social structure created on caste-based artisan occupations that have been made redundant in the modern economy, and those who have been displaced finding employment in agriculture as labourers, which in turn may not be explicated by neoclassical theory. In other words, agriculture has been a great source of support for those belonging to the lower castes who are either displaced or thrown out of work under structural unemployment. Further, it provides reprieve to the poor whenever displacements in the urban industrial sector take place and then the lower classes/ castes return to their native villages. It has been reported in one of our studies on the NRF in Visakhapatnam that those who were given the golden handshake or voluntarily retired in public sector units, sooner or later joined their traditional occupations such as carpentry, handlooms, smithy, etc. or got back to the village to join the army of the agricultural force.[7] In other words, the lower castes, particularly the artisan and Dalit groups, rely on the agricultural sector, unlike in other societies. Column 6 in Table 5.1 indicates that the proportion of agricultural workers was around one third of the rural population in 2011 (Column 8). This proportion of the labour force remaining constant seems to be a unique social phenomenon that the neoliberals have overlooked or have not been able to account for in their development models. Thus, the incidence of social exclusion of a different kind associated with our agrarian structure needs to be addressed with special and innovative schemes for the upgradation and modernisation of traditional skills to meet the changing needs of growing economy. Schemes such as the National Rural Employment Guarantee Programme (NREGP/NREGA) and Prime Minister's Rozgar Yojana (PMRY), no doubt, provide incomes and sustenance to the poor, but do not supersede the low social status and inclusion of such groups in the mainstream.

AGRICULTURE IN ADVANCED COUNTRIES

The underlying assumptions of the advanced countries and their champions who have been advocating free trade that would help agriculture and facilitate free competition possible are shattered now. The Doha Round of talks of WTO in 2001 is a clear indication of the lobby of the advanced countries to protect their agriculture and insulate competition from others The two decades of liberalisation and the neglect of the agriculture sector have ultimately made the government to realise its folly when the growth rates of agriculture have come down. Now policy-makers in Delhi are thinking of introducing the second Green Revolution with the support of the market and little participation of the stakeholders. It is too early to predict anything now. But by the time an evaluation is taken, to quote J. M. Keynes, "[W]e are all dead in the long run." One can sympathise with successive governments that have sincerely implemented the policies prescribed by the advisers and policy-makers. So far, no government has ever penalised an adviser, policy-maker or even a statistician for miscalculations. It is the zealous politician or the executive who is supposed to take the final call. In this context, we can see that the policies pursued by the government since 1965 in terms of the minimum support price (MSP) of the CACP for about 25 agricultural products, particularly wheat and rice, have shown mixed results. In fact, we can see this strategy of MSP as part of the Green Revolution emanated almost at the same time. It was to protect the poor and illiterate farmers from dubious business interests that the CACP was created. There are half a dozen such commissions in one of the largest departments of the central government (agriculture) for providing assistance and technical advice for the use of modern methods of cultivation, calculating the cost of production, recommending the MSP, etc.

It seems the CACP is supported by the data generated by the Directorate of Economics and Statistics of the Ministry of Agriculture in arriving at a reasonable figure. After receiving the recommendations from the CACP, the government fixes the final price of the product based on which the whole machinery of procurement, subsidies, public distribution system (PDS), etc. moves. The postulate that the MSP would protect the farmer seems to be either naive or pedantic. It is the experience of every Indian farmer that the prices recommended by the government are alleged to be influenced by lobbies. The political economy of agriculture or grain trade analysed by some scholars has insinuated how class interests influence the whole issue of MSP. It is a serious, deep and complicated issue. However, paddy-growing farmers of the South, especially in Andhra Pradesh, have always been complaining of improper attention. Prices realised by farmers, particularly paddy-growers, are higher than the MSP. The MSP, it is alleged, has become a stumbling block for the ordinary farmer to bargain in the open market to get a reasonable price.

The fact that the MSP takes care of the margin of around 20 per cent between the cost of production and the recommended price has failed to convince the marginal farmer, whose experience is different, because he is close to reality, unlike the so-called average farmer of CACP who does not exist in reality. It was anticipated that the terms of trade would favour agriculture (with HYV) against industry. In fact, Ram Manohar Lohia was one of the earliest to argue for terms of trade in favour of agriculture both within the country and in foreign trade. Further, the contribution of the agriculture sector to GDP where majority of the rural population of about 65 per cent eke out their living has come down to only 14 per cent of the GDP. The growth of the labour force in the non-farm sector has also declined from 4.66 per cent to 3.35 per cent during the period 1993–94 to 2004–05. It means that the rural labour force, particularly the Dalits and Adivasis, is increasingly relying on a sector that is fast missing its sheen.

THE INDEBTEDNESS OF AGRICULTURAL HOUSEHOLDS

As noted above, agriculture and its related occupations provide employment to around 70 per cent of the rural population in India. There may be states like Tamil Nadu where 40 per cent per cent of the population resides in urban areas, and in other states of the East, for example, a large proportion of people live and depend totally on the rural setting. India still lives in villages known as 'sink of parochialism and cesspool of outdated traditions'. The social structure is recreated and sustained with State-supported development programmes, keeping the lowest and the highest groups in the social order unchanged for generations. Social economics is more concerned with the two extremes and in finding ways to reduce the disparity and discrimination in economic transactions and to bring equity in society. However, the liberalisation and modernisation projects looked down upon agriculture as a sunken segment of the economy (may be relying on the West) with step-motherly treatment meted out to this sector in terms of public policy.

There are several committees that have recommended the need to raise investment and capital formation in agriculture to enhance the capability and productivity of the sector to remain competitively at an advantageous position in the foreign markets. But the major hitch in taking the recommendations of such committees to the small and marginal farmers is the lobby of land holders who hive off the provisions for themselves. The poor marginal and small farmers remain neglected. In fact, the number and proportion of such farmers have been increasing and the dominant capitalist farmer is all pervasive now. Marginal farmers constituted 39.1 per cent and the small farmers 22.6 per cent (together 61.7 per cent) of total farming community in 1966 which increased cumulatively to

80.6 per cent by 2002–03. More than 55 per cent of the operated area is now in the hands of less than 20 per cent of the big landholders on record in 2004. Therefore, most of the programmes addressed to the farmer without qualifying him in relation to the size of farm are actually cornered by the big farmers. It appears that some of them are traditionally traders, and therefore, the middleman in connivance with the trader is ultimately benefitted when the agricultural prices rise due to several structural rigidities in the system.

The amount of investment made in infrastructure development and other complimentary factors that contribute to increases in productivity is called gross capital formation (GCF). Indian agriculture is said to be backward due to low capital formation and with the contribution of the public and private sectors to GCF not being very encouraging. It is noted that out of ₹760.96 billion GCFA in 2004–05, the contribution from the public sector was only ₹161.87 billion and private contribution was ₹594.09 million. The combined amount of public and private sectors reached 7.5 per cent of the total GCFA in the economy, although the public sector has contributed one third of the GDP. It has almost remained constant, reaching 7.4 per cent of the total in 2010 and 7.7 per cent in 2012–13. The amount in current prices looks significant at ₹2.34270 trillion in 2012–13, while its proportion in GDP has remained less than 3 per cent and has shown a decline from 1990–91. The small and marginal farmers account for 70 per cent of operational holdings, they, however, do not have surplus to GCFA.[8] In other words, the GCF in agriculture has not received the attention that it deserved during the liberalisation period, making agriculture vulnerable not only to natural calamities but even to market tyranny.

There have been series of tragic events in Telangana, Andhra Pradesh, Vidarbha, Madhya Pradesh, Rajasthan and other parts of the country where scores of farmers have committed suicides.[9] One of the factors inducing them to take the extreme step is said to be indebtedness. The highest proportion of indebtedness among agricultural households is reported to be 92.9

per cent in Andhra Pradesh, followed by around 89 per cent in Telangana, Karnataka and Rajasthan, respectively where the incidence of suicides is very frequent. Table 5.2 gives data on the indebtedness of farmers by different size class of land possessed. It can be seen from the table that more than 85 per cent of indebtors/loanees possess less than 4 hectares per household. The average outstanding loan amount ranges between ₹31,100 to 54,800 and ₹94,900 for the 2–4 hectare size, bringing home the point that any waiver of loans would benefit the rich farmers more. In the scheme of the neoclassicists, the small farmer is inefficient and lazy. If the amount of subsidy given to farmers in the USA and the OECD countries is compared to India, our farmers deserve a better treatment and package

IRRIGATION WORKS CONDITION THE SOCIAL STRUCTURE

The debate on irrigation works and their relationship to social formations has created several controversies in the social science literature. According to one theory, India being a part of the hydraulic societies such as Mesopotamia or Iraq (and other Central Asian countries) owes its unique civilisation to natural resources, particularly the availability of water. The formation of the State and its totalitarian structure has been attributed to irrigation works here. But, scholars are no more interested in studying the relevance of such theories, particularly due to lack of sponsorship and academic market, although the force of the argument makes some of us to ponder over it. It is in this context that a case study of Srikakulam district in Andhra Pradesh, one of the most backward and socially unique due to its Kalingan background and peoples struggles, is reflected here for the present work. Does the physical setting of the district, including its geological formation, have something to do with its backwardness? Have the bounties of nature (Eastern Ghats) made them complacent about mainstream developments or the Jain and Buddhist traditions internalised by the

Table 5.2

Indebtedness of Agricultural Households (All India) by Size Class of Land Possessed

Land Poss. (Hectares)	Estimated Number of Agricultural Households (Millions)	% to Total in Each Class	Estimated No. of Indebted Agricultural Households (Millions)	% to Total in Each Class	% of Indebted Agricultural Households to Total	Average Outstanding Loan Amount (₹)
1	2	3	4	5	6	7
0.01	2.389	2.65	1.002	2.1	41.9	31,100
0.01–0.40	28.766	31.89	13.597	29	47.3	23,900
0.01–2.00	15.458	17.14	8.611	18.4	55.7	54,800
2.01–4.00	8.435	9.35	5.61	12	66.5	94,900
4.01–10.00	3.302	3.66	2.52	5.4	76.3	182,700
10 and above	.371	0.41	.292	0.6	78.7	47,000
All India	90.21	100	46.848	100	51.9	47,000

Source: National Sample Survey (NSS) KI (70/33): Key Indicators of Situation of Agricultural Households in India 2010.

people made them develop a typical outlook towards life? Why have people here remained underdeveloped or rather undeveloped?

It requires a different kind of study to answer the above questions. For the time being we consider irrigation structures of the region and the agricultural techniques adopted by the people to suit their physical geography. About half a century ago (1960s), I had the opportunity to grow up in the region that was surrounded by three major tanks or *sagars* (lakes). Though the seacoast is about 20 km from the region, the area had Asarla sagar (it was Asurula sagar) in Temburu close to Sariapalli (an ancient Buddhist place close to Danta). It was called Asarla sagar by outsiders, may be because it was developed by the native Indians. About 20 km from the sagar there were two very big tanks developed by the Gajapthis of Parlakimidi as Sitha sagar and Rama sagar. People of the region knew how these sagars were very huge and systematically maintained by the Gajapathis. It was a British officer, Captain Randall, who later proposed the filling up of the tanks through the floodwaters of the Mahendra Tanaya River and the now famous Gotta barrage on the Vamsadhara (most of the sub-regions in the district contain similar locations).

This background is necessary to understand how the region had adequate water resources and how these were effectively harnessed for agricultural use. The region is also considered a half-tribal and half-plains zone after the Srikakulam uprising. It is located on a beautiful natural setting in the Eastern Ghats (known in the past as Kalinga Ghats) with perennial sources of water and aquifers on the Eastern Coast where some of the underground streams join the Bay of Bengal. In other words, it has been a self-sufficient region for generations. The lands have been commonly held under the jajmani system for a long time till the British Permanent Settlement introduced the zamindars as their agents. There was also a story that the local agents did not respond to the British demands of excess collection of revenue and, therefore, the region was categorised recalcitrant (in fact, the first rebellion against the British took place in the region when the local sepoys of Zamindars killed three British soldiers in 1780 at Visakhapatnam). It was possible for the local agents to remain like that, as they were self-contained, autonomous and inaccessible. Agricultural crops including different varieties of paddy, ragi, *korralu* and several local pulses were cultivated by farmers who knew the quality of the soil and the accessibility of water. There was not even a single incident of drought or starvation deaths in the region for a long time. But the resources were found to be insufficient when the population of the region increased.

It is very typical of the region that whenever there had been population pressure on land, people migrated to other areas. The history of colonisation of East Asia by the Kalingan seafarers did not get the attention of mainstream historians. One should notice that the united Andhra Pradesh did not provide any pull or push factors of succor to the people of the region, but it were the neighbouring Odisha, Bengal and Chhattisgarh that gave them possible relief in the form of providing opportunities of livelihood. This did not put pressure on the limited land and cultivation to create what is called an agrarian unrest. The so-called disturbance in the region narrated by some scholars was perhaps due to usury and the introduction of monetary transactions in the Adivasi areas.

Transition from a barter system to monetisation and usury shocked the Adivasis, resulting in various vicissitudes. The living conditions and the simple habits of the people were all related to the kind of agricultural practices developed there. Some of the water bodies were developed with innovative traditional structures with people's participation. It was not the so-called Adivasi way of living in tribal areas or conditions that made them to innovate in tribal areas, but it was the same type of organisation of life continued even in the plains. It appeared tribal or backward to outsiders and scholars who did not understand the history of the region and its ethos. Kalinga was considered as an advanced country even during the time of the *Rig Veda* and the Mahabharata and continued thereafter. It appears that the irrigation needs of the people were met from the small ponds, check dams, etc. developed to conserve water during the monsoon. Huge tanks like sagars were constructed where there were perennial sources. The average rainfall in the region was above the state average of about 1,100–1,500 cm per annum, 80 per cent of which is obtained just in few months for about a century.

The social structure of the habitations indicates that castes were the extensions of the Adivasi groups. Therefore, we do not find castes such as the Relli, Paidi, Dandasi, Kandra, Polinativelama and Kalinga, to name a few, in other regions of the state. We do not find even the unique Adivasi groups or the jungle kings in other regions. (In fact, the number of tribes and castes of the Odisha and Andhra border is the highest in India.) They have emerged in the region perhaps based on typical irrigation practices. The runoff from the steep hills till their confluence in the sea at a distance of around 200 km forced the people to get united instantaneously to store water for agriculture. The small size of structures such as ponds or tanks or *geddas* (channels) facilitated the organisation of small communities in and around them. This perhaps helped them to form coherent social groups not the competing castes found in other regions for sharing of scarce water. This shows how agricultural development in a region depends not only on irrigation but also on the political and social institutions that emerged from the material conditions complementing them.

THE SOCIAL ECONOMY OF IRRIGATION DAMS

The construction of dams on a running river was forbidden as per Hindu traditions, however, this was overpowered with the advent of modernisation projects during the British India and thereafter. The area under different sources of irrigation was 18.85 million hectares in 1950–51 and the same increased to 31.60 million hectares in 1970–71.[10] The period from 1970–71 was crucial and the sources of irrigation quickly reached 55.23 million hectares in 2000–01 and to 63.25 million hectares by 2009–10, an increase of 15 per cent over a period of a decade. Out of this, irrigation under canals increased from 15.81 million hectares to 16.51 million hectares during the same period. Irrigation by traditional source of tanks declined from 2.46 million hectares to 1.64 million hectares and irrigation through tube wells rose from 33.83 million hectares to 39.04 million hectares, compensating for more than the loss from other sources as per the data of the Ministry of Agriculture. Much of the irrigation potential created during the post-independence period was due to the construction of big dams and multi-purpose projects. The food grains production increased from 50.8million tonnes in 1951 to 264.77 million tonnes in 2013–14, raising the per capita net availability of food grains from 144 kg to 186 kg per year. The World Commission on Dams (2010) has estimated that agricultural productivity as a result of assured water in India is by 10 per cent, but government sources contested it and said that it is more. Tripathi and Prasad in their study on the determinants on agricultural development have produced results of increasing returns to scale and underlined that labour and capital have also significantly contributed to the output growth.

The current debate on the major irrigation projects like Polavaram not only in Andhra Pradesh but in other parts of the country as well, with the help of funding agencies, deserves attention. Dams were constructed in India from the very beginning and took a backseat when faith took precedence over others in governance. Some studies[11] show how projects were not allowed across holy rivers like the Ganga as damming of a live river was against the beliefs of many in India. There has been an overall change in the outlook of the devout with the advent of capitalist values. Therefore, while there were only 300 major irrigation projects in 1947, we have more than 4,000 by 2014. The projects were also necessitated by population pressure and agrarian reforms. It is claimed by experts that almost all the projects are undertaken to increase food grains production and to reduce poverty and deprivation. Flood control was secondary. Have these objectives been achieved?

Andhra Pradesh has the advantage of several perennial rivers that join the Bay of Bengal. But there were very few dams in the region before 1850. It was the vision of the colonial civil servant Sir Arthur Cotton to develop the Krishna and Godavari basins in the Madras Presidency that changed the history of the region. Though Cotton as an East India Company officer got the dams constructed for economic reasons (in his reply to the British Parliament after impeachment) without considering the riparian rights of either the Visakhapatnam or upstream farmers, it changed the landscape of coastal Andhra. The political economy of assured irrigation underwent a change once the impact of the projects got reflected in agricultural productivity. Once, Ganjam, Visakhapatnam and the ceded districts, or the Rayalaseema region used to play a prominent role in the power politics of Madras Presidency; but they had to slowly give way to the coastal districts by the time the state was reorganised. Telangana was not a part of it. The Krishna and Godavari delta started playing a leading role once the Nagarjunasagar, Srisailam and other projects started yielding fruits.

The subsidised irrigation water for agriculture has helped a new class to emerge in the region. Instead of the erstwhile zamindars, landed gentry, it is the contractor, kulak and other hard-working castes of the region who have started playing an important role in the social economy of the state. Interestingly, due to political manoeuvring, the benefits of assured irrigation were not extended to the regions (like Rayalaseema Telangana and North Andhra) that really deserved them. It is a political and economic strategy of deprivation of other regions executed by the beneficiary group through water politics that had far reaching implications for the social economy of the region. It is being analysed by scholars now how the contribution of the Bhakra Nangal Dam to the Green Revolution is marginal and its contribution to power politics in Punjab, Haryana and in the North substantial. Therefore, the deprivation of a major irrigation project, like a big dam, is not confined to the displacement of the Adivasis, Dalits and other marginalised groups in the project area alone. It goes beyond income, employment, health, education, housing, living environment, culture and other deprivations. It is forfeiture of political empowerment and uprooting of an identity.

INEQUITIES IN IRRIGATION

It is in this context that the underdevelopment of North Andhra or Kalingandhra (Kalingaseema) is reflected above to relate the irrigation needs of the region. Some politicians and activists are not aware of the fact that the title Godavari is owed to North Andhra. The river originated from Maharashtra as Goda. It gets its name once river Sabari of Visakhapatnam joins somewhere near Kunavaram. It is not only Sabari, but rivers such as the Indravati, Sileru and other tributaries of the Godavari that originate in the Eastern Ghats of North Andhra. The runoff at Rajahmundry or even at Polavaram would be nominal without the perennial contributions of the Eastern Ghats of North Andhra. In fact, most of the perennial rivers, such as the Mahanadi or Narmada at Amarakantak, originate from here (Eastern or Kalinga Ghat). The region has 16 river systems. However, no one talks about the irrigation needs of Uttarandhra. Telangana, it is said, got divided on the basis of the argument that they were discriminated in the provision of irrigation projects to the region. In fact, this inequity in the sharing of water in the Telugu country began during the East India Company with Sir Arthur Cotton's projects on Godavari and Krishna. As the Nizam state was not a part of the East India Company, Sir Arthur Cotton seems to have misconstrued the demand and provided water only to the right side of Godavari and Krishna districts and not even to North Andhra which had riparian rights on the flow in Godavari then and even now flows from Eastern Ghats. It is strange to notice that the left bank of Godavari where tribals inhabited, water which could be given through gravitational flow was not planned, as it was not commercially viable (in terms of the levy calculated by Cotton). The needs of the farmers and the revenue accruals after the completion of the projects were estimated to justify the construction and not the social and regional inequities that benefitted the delta. The inequitable distribution of water has remained the same even after independence with the dominance of one region over the others, indicating unfair administrative action that keeps on haunting Telugu people even today. (Those who are benefited by the irrigation might think differently, but its social implications are complicated.)

The project report of the big dam at Polavaram with ₹170 billion does not speak about the legitimate irrigation needs of North Andhra. It is found to be overwhelmed by the additional requirements of the Krishna, Godavari (with 71 per cent irrigation and water logging), Pennar and Kaveri basins. The Bachavat Committee (1973) had also referred to them and not to the needs of the most underdeveloped regions of the state. Irrigation and social issues have been flagged to the government through political and economic interests. Therefore, it is necessary to look at the social economy of a big dam in terms of not only the cost-benefit ratios but also the overall deprivations in the most neglected regions like North Andhra.

Srikakulam district, located in the North-eastern part of Andhra Pradesh, is in the news very frequently for all the wrong reasons. The district and the people of the region have witnessed the bloodiest turmoil in post-Independence India (Naxalbari movement) for reasons known to government agencies and scholars. But, the lynching of five Dalits in the district in the year 2012 indicates two emerging trends in the area. It is a clear departure from the history and culture of social harmony for which the region is known. The minor and medium irrigation projects in the district seem to have helped the district become a part of coastal Andhra for the exploitation of feudal relations. The typical caste politics of the district have been dictated by three dominant castes (Kapu, Kaalinga and K/P Velama claiming to be backward classes stretched in different directions). The land tenure system in the region is one of meander that began as freehold to that of zamindari, inamdari to Ryotwari, etc. due to the fact that the region had the largest number of medium to small size estates in the Madras Presidency.

Zamindars leased out land to the tillers on the principle of equity so that everyone could get some land and remain loyal. Thus, the conditions did not permit large farmers to emerge, as the holdings were modest. Though the issue is not about agrarian relations here, the zamindars of the region were not able to maintain the estates, particularly after the 1930 economic crisis, and voluntarily appealed for their abolition in the Madras Legislative Assembly (Adapa Satyanarayana). Some of them auctioned forests, *porambogs*, etc. at throwaway prices without proper titles just before the advent of land reforms in the state. This created lot of mystification in the tenure system as land became scarce and fragmentation of holdings went on unabated with increasing population over time.[12]

The geography of the North Andhra region is very typical in the country as a major part of the Eastern Ghats, including parts of Dandaka, with the largest part of the 950 km of the state's coastline being located here, has lured grabbers after 1990. Most of the area is covered with forests and fallow lands. For instance, Srikakulam district has an area of 583,700 hectares, of which only 278,713 hectares (47 per cent) is available for agriculture that includes fish and prawn culture. The situation in Visakhapatnam district is worse where forest cover is much larger and only 25 per cent of land is available for agriculture. The per capita land used for agriculture in Srikakulam in 2001 was 0.109 hectare and it further fell to 0.103 hectare as per the 2011 census. The situation in Visakhapatnam is grave as the per capita agricultural land fell from 0.074 hectare to 0.066 hectare between 2001 and 2011. These figures from government sources point out how land has become scarce in North Andhra. The figures do not include the land wrecked by the state in the name of development projects in this region, which has further accentuated social tensions here. We do not have sufficient data on the land markets in North Andhra, except the urban markets in Visakhapatnam where land is alleged to have been transferred from the poor and ignorant local land-holders to the powerful in the name of urban development and industrialisation. The information on the land transfers in the region is very complicated as there are ongoing litigations and poor maintenance of settlement records.

An informal conversation with some senior local leaders revealed that coastal settlers, some of them employees and ex-bureaucrats, have started buying and acquiring land, including D form *pattas* from the Dalits. The data on the operation hold-ings is one of the curious manifestations of having less than 0.5 hectare held by the maximum number of landholders (50 per cent in the total holdings) in the district of Srikakulam in 1981. The proportion increased to 55.63 per cent in 1995–96. The craving (hunger) for land can be seen in terms of an increase in the fragmentation of holdings and a contraction of viable holdings of 4 hectare and above during 1981–2006, the period in which some major changes also took place in the district. Almost 80 per cent of the holdings in the region, particularly in Srikakulam district, are in the range of less than 1 hectare. This cannot be compared with the holdings of the coastal dis-tricts where the productivity is much higher than the North Andhra (NA) region due to the availability of irrigation water and other input subsidies.[13]

The working class of the region is hard-working and is made up of seasonal migrants. Like the Bihar and Odisha labourers who made Punjab a grain bowl, the labourers of Srikakulam and Vizianagaram have been toiling in the fields of the rice bowl of Andhra Pradesh. A majority of the migrant labour-ers are Dalits along with some service and occupational castes as most of them are landless. The assignment of lands to the Dalits was limited to 3,221 families to an extent of less than 0.70 acres per family in 2006 in Srikakulam. The situation in the region seems to be undergoing a change after the construc-tion of Gotta barrage and medium irrigation projects in the region with the entry of the dominant castes in state politics. The proportion of canals as a source of total irrigation was only 28 per cent in 1971 and it increased to 66 per cent in 2005 placing increased pressure on land in Srikakulam.

The Lakshmipet incident in Srikakulam suggests the formation of a typical caste-based bourgeoisie to take on the Dalits in irrigated areas in order to displace them through terror and to grab their lands. The Dalit Mahasabha says that there are half a dozen villages prone to such incidents. Agriculture is no more considered as a viable activity and its contribution to the SDP/GDP has significantly diminished. The intelligent farmers either lease out or sell their lands in the villages and shift to other activities. The SCs in the plains and the STs in the forests are left with the land that is unproductive and encounter the economic and social brunt of reforms. Most of the atrocities on SCs and STs are taking place in the agriculture setting after liberalisation where big landlords lease out land and shift to lucrative business leaving the risk-prone agriculture in the hands of the middle classes/castes in rural area. The economic tensions of nonremunerative prices and social prestige of holding lands led to new tensions in the agrarian sector that seem to be different from the pre-1990 period in this region. Interestingly, the region gets irrigation projects after the ruling castes appropriated lands of the locals in different garbs, while the locals are thrown out and migrated.

THE GREEN REVOLUTION: FACT AND FICTION

The 2013–14 budgetary (Central) allocations for agriculture raised hopes of many, particularly of those who hail from rural areas. The Twelfth Five-year Plan (2012–17) outlay has increased by 18 per cent due to the decline in the rate of growth of agriculture last year. It was in this context perhaps, the finance minister was referring to the Green Revolution in East India to increase productivity of paddy with an outlay of

₹10 billion. The re-emphasis on the Green Revolution in the budget shows the intention of the government and indirectly accepts the fact that the earlier Green Revolution in a few districts of advanced states has faded. What were the conditions under which the so-called Green Revolution was initiated and what was its content? There have been several revolutions within this Green Revolution, such as the blue, white, red, etc. The finance minister spoke about five missions which were earlier part of the Green Revolution. The food security mission, sustainable agriculture mission, oilseeds mission, agriculture extension mission and the horticulture mission can be considered as the strategies to bring in the second Green Revolution. It is indicated that funding through an increased credit of ₹5.75 trillion with a subvention of 3 per cent interest to those who repay on time was announced. This appears to be different from the first Green Revolution of the 1960s.

Jawaharlal Nehru, as chairman of the Planning Commission, reviewed the progress towards the objectives of socialism and reduction of inequalities in the previous Five-year Plans in 1961 and found that the country needed immediate self-sufficiency in food grains and agricultural development. C. Subramaniam was the agriculture minister who took M. S. Swaminathan as adviser. There was already a debate on the need for self-sufficiency in food to reduce hunger due to population boom when C. Subramaniam took charge of agriculture and scientists were encouraged to find solutions. It was an opportune time for scientists like Norman Borlaug, who was conducting research on crossing Mexican wheat with the Gaines Dwarf developed by Washington University. He was invited by the government to extend the results of his research to Indian agriculture. Meanwhile, the USA offered a massive aid programme in the name of PL480.

The PUSA centre was used to extend the results of agricultural studies to farmers in select districts. In fact, PUSA is not a place name where these activities were concentrated; it is short form for PL480 of the USA. Former United States Agency for International Development (USAID) Director

William Gaud coined the concept of the Green Revolution. Rockefeller and Ford Foundations have originally located it in seven districts, including West Godavari in Andhra Pradesh, Punjab, etc. The contributions of B. P. Lal, the first director-general of ICAR, scientists of ICRISAT, IRRI and agricultural universities need to be remembered to assess the increase in production and productivity of wheat and rice, the basic two crops that are said to have revolutionised our food stocks. The initial support provided in the form of HYVs of wheat and IR8 rice in the select districts of Andhra Pradesh was extended, for instance, to other neighbouring districts such as Krishna, Guntur and Nellore where assured irrigation facilities were created. The impact of the American-supported Green Revolution in India has been assessed in hundreds of studies and the results are available now. However, there are very few who would acknowledge the context and the indigenous institutional support that was created to make the first Green Revolution a success.

Several factors contributed to the previously mentioned success such as community development projects, Krishi Vignan Kendras, model farms, land reforms, extension workers and, above all, the involvement of the community and the farmers in translating the vision into reality. It was undertaken under the direct supervision of the State or supported by its agencies and therein lay its significance. Some rational voices have contested the positive impact of the Green Revolution. According to some of the critiques, it was a capitalist strategy to introduce capital-intensive agriculture in a Third World country. China did not follow this strategy, yet it achieved self-sufficiency in food before India. The so-called benefits of HYV, as made out to be by the propaganda machinery, seem to not have considered its social costs.

For instance, the Green Revolution did not substantially improve the net availability of cereals and pulses that impact nutritional status. It is reported in Economic Survey 2012 that the net availability of cereals and pulses was 469 grams per day per person in 1961 when the population was 440 million and it did not improve when the population became 650 million in 1971 and came down to 438 grams in 2010. There is no doubt that it improved our food grains stocks. But this happened at a heavy price like the opportunity costs of public investment, damage to indigenous crops, etc. that the future generations are made to forgo. In fact, activists such as Vandana Shiva and others have argued that heavy doses of fertilisers, pesticides and herbicides, with equally heavy amounts of scarce water resources, have mopped up not only soil capacity but also the indigenous crops in India. Studies in agriculturally advanced states like Punjab, conducted at PGMIER, Chandigarh, have proved that the excessive use of chemicals in agriculture has increased the incidence of cancer in the state. Several social tensions are also associated with the iniquitous and feudalist tendencies in the State. In fact, wheat and paddy have emerged as hegemonic and destroyed the indigenous and locally used varieties that are considered by scientists as the biodiversity wealth of India.

An important dimension that seems to not have been mentioned in mainstream discussions is the redundancy of cattle (bovines) due to the introduction of machinery such as tractors, harvesters, etc. The bovine population (304.4 million) is more than double the size of human population and consumes equally important scarce resources and remains idle. We have religious sentiments for half of this population like the cow to be diverted to other uses and the farmer has a serious problem of maintaining them where grazing lands and common property resources have disappeared. In other words, the first Green Revolution seems to have solved the problem of food security but created problems for human welfare. It is against this background that the government is contemplating to usher in the Second Green Revolution in East India, consisting of Assam, Bihar, Bengal, Odisha, Jharkhand and eastern UP. Interestingly, the strategy seems to have already been put in place in the form of the so-called PPP mode with the support of GM crops and other capital-intensive techniques. This causes misgivings, as the area selected for the experiments is the most impoverished and politically sensitive region to realise the dream.

CORPORATE CULTIVATION A LA COOPERATIVE FARMING

India, being a Third World–compliant country for experiments of the advanced nations, is now being targeted for innovations in the farm sector as reflected in Doha round of talks of WTO. There seems to be a proposal, maybe a policy decision, to introduce corporate farming in the country, if it is not already in force in a different guise. Therefore, one need not be surprised to get a regime of corporate farming in the country when the government is in crisis and the policy-makers push through their agenda. It seems that important administrative resolutions are taken in the country whenever the governments were in trouble as seen from the record of reforms during the last two decades. If the past record of events is of any use for prediction, corporate farming seems to be certain.

There are enough farm and business lobbies with intellectual inputs from experts that would substantiate the need for corporate farming. It has been demonstrated by scholars and management experts that small farms and fragmented of holdings are the bane of Indian agriculture as they are unviable and economically disastrous. This is supported by data that marginal holdings of less than one hectare of land on an average have remained at 0.4 at the national level and at 0.44 hectare in Andhra Pradesh. The proportion of such holdings to the total holdings in Andhra Pradesh has increased slightly from 61.59 to 63.59 during 2005–11. Therefore, it may be sensible to go in for corporatisation of farming in states like Andhra Pradesh where the proportion of marginal holdings is very high. There is also the argument that marginal farmers have failed to bring in technology and innovations to improve the productivity of agricultural operations; as a result, farmers have remained poor and underdeveloped. What is the harm if small holdings are given to a corporate body which brings technology, investment and remunerative prices through access to international markets? The above argument is not sustained by productivity data. For instance, the productivity of rice was 3,011 kg per hectare in 2003–04 and it increased to 3,148 by 2011–12 in Andhra Pradesh. The productivity of *jowar*, an important crop in the state, was 1,102 kg in 2003–04 and it substantially rose to 1,749 in 2011–12. If the farmer was not getting remunerative prices, it was not due to the unviable nature of his holdings, but due to other economic and policy-related constraints like land and agrarian reforms. In fact, around a century ago, economists have pointed out that it is not the size of the holdings but the amount of investment made on the piece of land that is to be taken into consideration in measuring productivity.

Arthur Lewis and later Ranis-Fei, Hayami and other economists have reasoned that the supply of food and labour for the sustenance of industry are important as they not only create demand for industrial goods but also bring in foreign exchange through agricultural exports. India is not the USA or Japan to reduce the role of agriculture to less than 5 per cent of GDP as 60 persons out of every hundred depend on it. The role of the manufacturing sector in creating jobs is not encouraging (NSS survey) in absorbing the surplus agricultural labour in industry to throw away the babe along with the bathwater. Notwithstanding the arguments of some economists, the policy-makers and economic managers have introduced sufficient policy packages to encourage corporatisation of cultivation in a phased manner. In fact, a variant of the commercialisation of agriculture has been in place in the form of contract farming. This is a kind of vertical integration of farmers to supply a given quantity and quality of products at an agreed price to the buyer, mostly involving corporates. There are 10 top corporate houses such as the Tatas, Ambanis, Bharati, Agrigold (AP) and IEEPL, apart from MNCs who have been in this business quite for some time. They are now lobbying for corporatisation of farming and linking it with FDIs and international cartels.

Now consider the experience of contract farming, a prelude to corporate farming. Harish Damodaran, in one of his reports in *Business Line* in June 2012, has reported that the corporate ventures in agriculture are failing. He has given a case study of Tata Chemicals in the area of fresh fruits and vegetables in Malerkotla, Punjab, where it shut its operations for not achieving the planned scale of operations. We have the Kuppam experiment in Andhra Pradesh, where economies of scale were shown as a prerequisite for corporatisation during 2000–04. Yet, experience on this front has not been encouraging. Look at the ideology of cooperative farming whose ideological genesis rests with Robert Owen and the subsequent Cooperative Credit Society Act (1904) in India. The idea behind the movement was to develop the spirit of mutual help and social harmony, equity and empowerment. Though it was confined to credit and the expansion of sugar, milk and a few other subsectors in agriculture, it provided the necessary impetus for the development of innovations under the guidance of the state.

It is reported that there are 550,000 cooperatives (PACs, etc.) with a membership of 220 million in India. We may attribute the limited success of the so-called first Green Revolution to the spirit of public interest imbibed by the cooperative spirit among the people who participated enthusiastically in it. Interestingly, the Central government brought the 97th Constitutional Amendment and added Section 43B to promote the voluntary formation, autonomous functioning and democratic control of cooperatives in 2011. It also enacted the Multistate Cooperatives Act in 2002 to facilitate the interstate operations of agricultural cooperatives. The Eleventh Plan envisages tenancy reforms to enable leasing out of land to 'others'. We have yet to see the impact of the initiatives of the State on the economic efficiency and social upliftment of the farmers. Billions of rupees have been invested in the development of infrastructure, including public irrigation, technology, KVS, etc. and billions earmarked as subsidies. Then why the sudden shift in policy towards privatisation and corporatisation of the farm sector? If some experts feel that private sector is more efficient, let them consider the private sector and FIIs restrict their operations in areas uncovered by cooperatives and low technology zones (the government should make a law to that effect). Let the private sector bring capital and technology without encroaching on public resources and improve the welfare of farmers, thereby also not repeating what they have done in Brazil, Ethiopia, Sudan, Tanzania and other Third World countries (with adverse consequences).

THE SAGA OF NUTRITION AND POVERTY LINES

Agriculture is a primary and vital sector of the Indian economy, absorbing around 60 per cent of the labour force and providing food for everyone. Poverty and nutritious food are interrelated. The Right to Food (RTF) debate in India is concerned with both. Though the allegation that economists have dominated the field is partially correct, they have made the subject a source of great professional interest by incorporating dimensions of measurement to it. In fact, the issue of poverty was first taken up by nationalist leaders like Dadabhai Naoroji who had published *Poverty and Un-British Rule in India* (1901) where he calculated the cost of 'rice or flour, dhal, mutton, vegetables, ghee, oil and salt' in the range of ₹15 to 35 at 1867–68 prices in different regions of the country.

Ram Manohar Lohia, an economist by training, gave figures on poverty and discussed them in the Parliament. However, the concept of poverty has somehow drifted from its original notion and is now going round the statisticians and nutritional experts, attracting the wrath of the common person for failure to address the existential reality. The theory of poverty entered the public domain through the Planning Commission that has been using nutritional standards or calorie intakes as the basis to measure poverty since the 1970s. It is considered that a person in rural areas with hard labour needs 2,400 calories per day while the urban norm is fixed at 2,100 calories to deem anyone living below that level as poor. The calories are then indirectly obtained from different items of consumer expenditure data of NSS. Though the idea of nutrition is scientific and is being used by scholars to determine the health and well-being of people, its application in India to estimate the poverty levels has been a subject of great controversy. The noted economist V. K. R. V. Rao has opined that the poverty line thus calculated was only a 'nutrition line' and someone called it a 'starvation line'.

But, the enlightened administrator N. C. Saxena, in his report on poverty to the Ministry of Rural Development, used a broader concept that included 13 indicators. It seems the controversy about the basic data obtained to estimate the priority, general and excluded groups to provide subsidised food under RTF has not been resolved largely due to the disagreement among the researchers. Experts in the area of poverty studies, mostly the World Bank–sponsored studies, have concluded that economic reforms in India have substantially increased the rate of growth and consequently reduced poverty levels. This is the sum and substance of the 600-page anthology, *The Great Indian Poverty Debate*, published by Nobel laurate Angus Deaton and Valerie Kozel.[14] Interestingly, except for S. D. Tendulkar, no other article in the book touches the core of the poor in India: the Adivasis, Dalits, service castes, minorities and women. It seems that some of the nutritional experts (not from NIN) have opined that Indians are now adapted to a sedentary life and are of low physical stature and, therefore, the norm of 2,100–2,400 calories is very high and outdated. They have suggested reduced values of 1,776–1,999 calories and helped Tendulkar to arrive at his figures on poverty. This is a strange caloric norm and far from everyday experience. It is common knowledge that 60 per cent of the population in India still depends upon agriculture and, even if allowance is given to mechanisation in some pockets, majority of the farm workers engaged in hard labour need more calories. In the urban areas, workers who come under the BPL category engage in manual labour.

The average height and weight of some social or ethnic clusters are found growing with different statures in some genetic studies. The low average weight or height or stunted growth is precisely due to lack of sufficient food. Further, we have pockets of fluorosis, endemic tribal regions that need special attention for nutritional intakes. Therefore, some civil society groups have argued for a norm of 2,700 calories. Strangely, some experts from the urban elite, influenced by their environs and habits, come to such obtuse conclusions of reducing the calorie norm for the poor. Or, it may be due to a scheme to certify that the promise of economic reforms lessening poverty is realised. The draft bill on the RTF has said that, "[M]alnutrition is a condition which develops when the body over a period of time does not receive or absorb adequate and appropriate calories, proteins and other nutrients for good health, growth and maintenance of the human body and mind." The third 2005-06 NFHS data shows the impact of malnutrition on the growth of the human body, mortality rates, etc. The recommended dietary allowances (RDA) tables for different age groups are prepared by the NIN and are guided by the standards set by the WHO, United Nations Children's Emergency Fund (UNICEF), etc. However, what seems unclear is the kind of food items that people with different social, cultural and ecological backgrounds eat and their nutritional values.

The Government of India, under the Ministry of HRD as a nodal agency, is implementing the Mid-day Meal Scheme for children in the age group of 6–14 in government and government-assisted schools. An amount of ₹100 billion is being spent on the scheme on 120 million children in 1.25 million schools. It is alleged by civil society groups that the MNCs are now eyeing this segment to capture it in the name of supplying micronutrients. The apex court and the government seem to have recommended a nutritional diet that gives 650 calories to a primary school going child and 900 calories to an upper-primary school going child, plus

20 grams of protein per day. However, there is a nutrition or calorie gap in this argument here. Most children are from socially deprived groups. The NIN and other agencies have recommended dietary allowances for a child of 6+ years as 1,350 calories per day and in the age group of 7–14 years of about 1,690–2,100 calories per day, depending upon the sex of the child and his/her body weight.

How do they meet the calorie gap? Adivasis, mushahars (Bihar Dalits), etc. and other indigenous groups have their own methods of meeting satiety by eating rats, 50 kinds of leaves, 46 fruits, 15 flowers, 14 tubers, 11 seeds, 4 gums, fish, beef, pork and other items.[15] The question is: Do they consume them with human dignity that is fundamental in a paradigm of rights, or are they forced to eat them so as to stay alive like any other animal? Thus, the RTF in India is caught in a quagmire of the so-called myths of poverty lines and exuberance of statisticians. Therefore, experts should come out of their delusion of lines prescribing norms that are irrelevant to our conditions and a genuine and sustainable policy should be formulated at least now after five decades of research.

FOOD TABOOS AND NUTRITIONAL DEFICITS

There are studies to scrutinise the quality of supplementary nutrition of food such as *upma*, *khichdi* and halwa in place of modified therapeutic food (MTF) powder. The study of K.R. Venugopal is related to the health status of the child and mother, early childhood education, caste discrimination in the supply of food and several other issues in a select district of Andhra Pradesh.[16] It is found how the package of services in the programme is "inadequate, ill conceived, remised, vandalised and conspicuous by its failure to meet the stated objective: Providing nutritious food supplements to children." The important contribution of the study is that the author has related the findings with the NFHS-3 survey on infant mortality rate, morbidity rate, maternal mortality rate, etc. that have bearing on malnutrition and the so-called push outs in pre-school education in Andhra Pradesh.

The special focus on SC children and their nutritional status brings us to another very interesting issue relating to our food habits. Most children from disadvantaged families are found to be wanting in nutritious foods due to the non-availability or may be social taboos or food habits in our society. This takes us to another very interesting event of a food festival in Osmania University that became newsworthy with headlines and later a national issue. Food and drink patterns have evolved in each society over a period of time and there is a history behind every festival that involves special food preparations.

Food taboos are universal in all ancient societies due to either a custom or a religious sanction, often without any valid reason. Interestingly, the taboos are socially accepted. In a country like India where there are several ethnic, social, reli-gious and maybe racial and cultural groups, each group has evolved its own norms, taboos or styles of living. But, the most contentious issue in our society is that a small minority of the so-called settlers have been trying to impose their values on the majority of native Indians just to exhibit their hegemony and constrain a democratic right to choose food. This is seen in recent debates on the Telangana movement also.

It is difficult to examine why someone has chosen to be a vegetarian and how that person can be forced to accept non-vegetarian food simply because it is the norm for the major-ity. Though the Constitution has not guaranteed any type of food as universally accepted, it is possible and competent for our apex court reasonably to give that guarantee of right to food under Article 21 (protection of life). In the normal course, the so-called *pedakura pandaga* or beef festival in Osmania University campuses is not new in the state. But, the cow became a holy issue in the 1990s when it became a political subject for sections of a party and an identity problem for some social groups. The country was undergoing a great disturbance in mid-2016 on the issue relating to cow vigilantes with refer-ence to Acts made on the basis of Article 48 of the Constitution.

But, the Constitution has not referred to the so-called holy cow alone. In fact, the major contributor of milk and horse power in India (in South Asia) has been the black water buffalo, the local animal. But how is it that holy cow is becoming a centre of controversies? It is reported that the alien (from the steppes) cow is replacing the native animal and led to elimination of lives in the battle for caste and social hegemony, representing the symbols cow and buffalo two different cultures.

In the Directive Principles of state policy under Article 48, it has been that, "[T]he State shall endeavour to organise agriculture and animal husbandry on modern scientific lines and shall, in particular, take steps for preserving and improving the breeds and prohibiting the slaughter, of cows and calves and other milch and draught cattle." Unfortunately, some states have given importance only to the cow and passed Acts to prohibit its slaughter and endured lynching of humans to protect it. It is in this connection that one can refer to the noted historian D. N. Jha's book, *The Myth of Holy Cow* (proscribed in some states), to understand the historical facts behind beef eating and also D. D. Sankalia for archaeological evidence of cow.

It is distressing to note that the parochial and intolerant attention is paid to an issue without understanding its context in our country in the 21st century. Article 47 of the Constitution is relevant here wherein the state has been directed to raise the level of nutrition and bring in prohibition for intoxicating drinks. Those who are conscious about the welfare of some animals have paid scant attention to the needs of the poor and the disadvantaged.

Apart from religious sentiments and the hegemonic manoeuvring of the food habits of people for political reasons, the issue of providing nutritious food to the poor whose original sources have disappeared due to modern techniques of farming and vanishing of common property resources is relevant. The nutritional intakes of the poor and the disadvantaged have drastically gone down due to use of pesticides and extinction of mussels, crabs, fish, etc. and green leafy vegetables that were once freely accessible. Now the threat of lynching for the sake of cows has further dented their entrée to nutritious food available traditionally. It is noted that 100 grams of beef has 30 grams of protein, 56 grams of sodium and other nutrients and the milk of a water buffalo has more energy than cow milk. Advanced countries like the USA in whom some of our Hindu, Christian, etc. patriots look for succour and guidance lob the highest amount of beef of 80 pounds per capita; they do also produce the largest number of Nobel laureates. Should they tell us how to overcome the deficit in nutrition of the poor while protecting the cow?

THE FUTURE OF FOOD SECURITY

There has been a continuous debate on the provision of adequate food to all in the country ever since the Supreme Court directive, based on a Public Interest Litigation filed by the PUCL, Rajasthan, in 2001. The NHRC has commented that the RTF is an integral part of the fundamental right to life under Article 21. Further, the International Covenant on Economic, Social and Cultural Rights of 1966 reiterated the responsibility of every State in making everyone free from hunger. This has become an enforceable right by virtue of Article 32 of our Constitution. For that reason, the RTF campaign can be broadly translated as a movement for food security.

The Millennium Development Goals of the UN and civil society activity seem to have put pressure on the government and the NAC to draft the National Food Security Bill 2011 (NFSB). Interestingly, several issues came up for consideration in the process of litigation and public discourse both in the judiciary and in the legislative debates on the RTF. The executive, through the aid and advice of expert groups of different persuasions, has participated in the deliberations and the future of the bill is now hanging in balance between the libertarians and the egalitarians. Rights of any kind are not sanctioned or ordained just like that in any part of the world; they are fought and won by those who are passionate about the wellbeing of humankind. The story of food security in India appears to be following the same course. There are several ad hoc programmes and schemes drafted either by the Planning Commission or by the individual departments of the government to meet the scarcity of food for the vulnerable groups in different parts of the country. The major concern in all these schemes appears to be the addressal of immediate threats such as droughts, famines, tsunamis, etc.

The discourse on food security or the RTF seems to be more about providing food than the kind of food habits of people, the cultural backgrounds of the beneficiaries and the content of food. Unlike in some Anglo-Saxon countries, food habits, ecological conditions, culture, etc. are not uniform in India. It is, therefore, not possible to make a homogeneous prescription on the content of food for all Indians. The draft bill has defined under 2(k) that food can mean any article used for human consumption. It has further indicated that any article, flavour that enters the preparation of food or is declared by the government as food, comes under the category of food. But, rice, wheat, millets, sorghum, maize, etc. are considered food grains. It seems most activists and some experts are uncomfortable with the definition of food grains and are anxious about the supply, as well as the cost involved in procuring them. It is alleged by civil society groups that the bill has been kept pending because there is no consensus on the amount of subsidy and the proportion of people (poor) to be brought under the priority, general and excluded categories.

With expert, policy-makers are examining the RTF issue within the framework of a free market paradigm, rather than as a Constitutional and welfare consideration, it appears difficult to arrive at a meaningful solution for the same. The debate has clarified, "[E]very person shall have physical, economic and social access at all times, either directly or by means of financial purchases, to quantitatively and qualitatively adequate, sufficient and safe food which ensures an active and healthy life" (Article 4 NFSB). The unambiguous mention of access to adequate food is a cause for concern for some experts who are in the know about the performance of the agricultural sector for the last few years. The march of the Green Revolution seems to have slowed down after 1990. In fact, the negative growth rates of the agriculture sector for some years is a great source of anxiety and even experts started looking at clouds (monsoon) for solutions. The *Economic Survey* of 2011 reports that the compound rates of growth of the yield and production of rice, wheat and coarse cereals during 1981–2011 were not uniform and showed a declining trend (Chapter 8). Even investments in the agriculture sector have declined during the same period, while 60 per cent of the population relies on agriculture for succour (even in 2011).[17] One cannot be blind to these facts while examining the NFSB. In fact, such details could provide the vision for a different framework, probably specifying the right to land and security of common property and livelihood resources. There is no trade-off between food security and the loss of livelihood and common property resources of people who have been displaced. The displaced people have surrendered their natural rights under liberalisation and, therefore, food security is not charity, it is a right.

There is no doubt that the rate of growth of the economy and its global orientation, particularly to Western lifestyles, has changed the consumption pattern of the population during the same period (1987–2010). The *Economic Survey 2012*, quoting the data from the NSS 66th Round, highlights how consumption expenditures on cereals, in both rural and urban areas, has declined. There is also a marked change in the consumption habits of people as more money is being spent on milk and milk products while the expenditure on pulses has remained plummeted. Fascinatingly, there is marginal change in the expenditure on non-vegetarian food items such as eggs, meat, fish, etc. One can draw different inferences for the food security of people who have different habits in obtaining proteins rather than through a package of vegetarian items like pulses. In fact, people in rural areas obtain protein foods with their own effort and find it hard to retain them due to poverty and exchange them for other low-cost calories (such as fowls, stall-fed goats, etc. sold out). The whole debate on the RTF is based on a minimum basket of food grains and seems to have lost sight of the cultural and social diversity of food habits and their nutritional values. Therefore, civil society might insist on a revision of the NFSB to make it a National Food and Nutritional Security Act and not just a Food Security Act. This would definitely help sustain the agricultural sector as an important contributor of succour to the socially marginalised in rural areas.

NOTES AND REFERENCES

1. Pranab Mukherjee, *Budget 2012–13* (Delhi: Government of India, 16 March, 2012).
2. Jan Bremman, Peter Kloos and Ashwani Saith, *The Village in Asia Revisited* (New Delhi: Oxford University Press, 1997), 20.
3. Pranab Bardan, ed., *Conversations Between Economists and Anthropologists* (New Delhi: Oxford University Press, 1989).
4. M. S. Swaminathan, *From Green to Ever Green Revolution; Indian Agricultural* (Delhi: Academic Foundation, 2008).
5. C. H. Hanumantha Rao, *Agricultural Growth, Farm Size and Rural Poverty Alleviation in India* (New Delhi: Oxford University Press, 2005).
6. Utsa Patnaik, *Agrarian Relations and Accumulation: The Mode of Production Debate* (New Delhi: Oxford University Press, 1980).
7. K. S. Chalam, "National Renewal Fund and the Welfare of Working Class," *Economic and Political Weekly*, Vol. 31, No. 49, 1996.
8. H. R. Dave, "Capital Formation in Agricultural—A Policy Priority and Expectations from Bankers." Special address at college of Agricultural Banking, Pune, 20 November 2014.
9. Over 3,000 farmers' suicides in the last three years reported, *The Hindu*, 27 June 2015.
10. A. Tripathi and A. R. Prasad, "Agricultural Development in India since Independence: A Study of Progress, Performance and Determinants," *Journal of Emerging Knowledge on Emerging Markets*, Vol. 1, No. 1, 2009.

11. V. Misra, *Hinduism and Economic Growth* (New Delhi: Oxford University Press, 1962).
12. K. S. Chalam, *Political Economy of Under-Development in Kalingandhra* (Delhi: Zenith Publications, 2008).
13. TSDF, *Eradicating Under Development in North Andhra* (Hyderabad: TSDF, 2014).
14. Angus Deaton and Valerie Kozel, *The Great Indian Poverty Debate* (Delhi: Macmillan, 2005).
15. K. S. Chalam. Paper on RTF of NHRC 2014, Delhi.
16. K. R. Venugopal, *Integrated Child Development Services* (Hyderabad: Council for Social Development, 2012).
17. Government of India, *Economic Survey 2011* (Delhi: Government of India, 2011).

6
Social Implications of Political Process

There seems to be broad an agreement on the emergence of an American type of electoral process in India. Democracy is the foundation for electoral politics. Some of our intellectuals refer to India and the USA as two very popular democracies, yet there are a lot of differences between them. Indian democracy has a long history of rajas (kings) being elected by representatives even during the time of the Buddha, whereas the USA has had a very typical colonial past with different streams of European groups settling there by replacing the Native Americans. The settlers seem to have slowly adapted to the civilised forms of organisation over a period of time. It has a bloody history. We have oversimplified history here in order to compare the two systems and to find out the significant differences between them. Further, the American presidential form of democracy is devoid of any role for an organised political party with a declared ideology. The federal system and elections are quite different from India. The American system of democracy is not purely representative while the Indian federal system has well-laid-down Constitutional provisions.

There are around 230 registered political parties reflecting the diversity of India while not even 5 per cent of this exists in the USA. America has not yet reached perfection in the democratic spirit of representing the will of the majority, as the Electoral

College system for electing the president, even according to Americans, is defective. It is strange to find that only 50 per cent of the voters participate in the presidential elections (the highest participation was 61.2 per cent during Barack Obama).[1] In all other elections, it is reported that less than one-third of the electorate participates. How can the American democracy then be considered the same as that of India? Political pundits and pollsters have been analysing data from the 1952 elections to indicate voters' perceptions about political parties, people, government, context of political choice, voting behaviour, etc. in India. Often they fail to predict the outcomes, indicating the complexity of the so-called mindset of our voters. But, in the USA it is possible to predict the possible outcome, depending upon the amount of money invested and the involvement of the powerful corporate lobbyists in elections. It is on the basis of this experience in the American electoral politics that some political economists have theorised that much of the political activity is rent-seeking resulting in considerable waste of resources in the less developed countries.

A recent survey in the USA has shown that only 23 per cent of the people had given their consent for the federal government.[2] Perhaps we may get similar results if a survey is organised here. In other words, slowly electoral politics is becoming a big economic affair and someone might say that it is better to outsource it! The political process in India in the past has been definitive as a majority of those who participated in the freedom struggle or those who had an urge to serve the people used to contest elections. The elected members used to be sincerely present in the houses of Parliament to participate in debates on behalf of the people. There were also occasions when big business houses used to go around politicians or sponsor candidates in elections. There used to be very few millionaires in the Parliament. MPs or legislators used to discuss issues seriously, both in committees and in sessions of the Parliament before arriving at a consensus. There used to be pressure groups, such as the FICCI, CII, etc. to approach the government before the budget session with their wish lists.

Sometimes the prime minister or the finance minister would entertain the delegation, but there were very few occasions when their wish list was taken as the basis for budget preparation or policy-making.

The situation underwent a change around the 1980s. Scholars like Francine Frankel,[3] Pranab Bardhan,[4] Atul Kohli[5] and others have explained how policies were formulated and implemented by different regimes, parties and governments. They have analysed and explained how radical departures in the political processes have taken place in India. Some scholars have pointed out the nexus between contractors, bureaucrats and politicians in seizing public resources. In other words, formulation of policies is not a part of the parliamentary procedure now but goes beyond that. There is a substantial change in the composition of the Parliament today. It is reported that around 250 billionaires or millionaires are in the Parliament today (maybe around 70 per cent) and, interestingly, the remaining have claimed that they are either social workers or civil society activists in their election affidavits. Under these circumstances, parliamentary procedures have also undergone a change where business interests are directly reflected in the committees with representative members, it is alleged, representing their private interests. For instance, if a Parliamentary committee on civil aviation consisting of MPs from the private aviation industry sits in judgement, what kind of decisions will be taken to protect Air India? (An example is the story of Kingfisher Vijay Mallya.) After all, the spirit of democracy should ultimately be reflected in the participatory process of decision-making on public issues. This is not happening today in India as the political class has slowly transformed to represent the economic interests of a few. This is reflected clearly in the recent scams or frauds involving the politicians both at the Centre and in the states. We may also consider here the social implications of these developments in a fragmented society like India.

The thin layer between politics and business seems to have disappeared and the institutional mechanisms of a capitalist democracy like the USA are well entrenched now in India. Given this background, it is time that the common man in the USA and the aam aadmi in India comes together to sustain true democratic values and culture!

THE SIGNIFICANCE OF 'BRAND' IN POLITICAL MARKETS

The political process in India in recent times appears to be mimicking Western democratic techniques. It has adopted some of the methods that the market capitalist democracies have adopted to suit the economic interests of a few big players. It is also noticed that studies in social sciences, particularly in the sphere of political economy (Chicago), have been backing such political adventures. The theory of public choice/social choice had a remarkable influence over the theories of democracy developed with reference to the voting behaviour of citizens. About half-a-dozen Nobel laureates in economics, including Amartya Sen, have been associated with the emergence of a subject called 'social choice' contributing to new thinking in public affairs, replacing or enhancing the old ideas or studies on democracy, markets, the state, etc.

Public choice theory has impacted crucial policy-makers and government functionaries who, in turn, have evangelised political parties that play political games. The theory has examined how public servants, including bureaucrats, are not benevolent to work for the common good of society. Deducing from the famous articulation of Adam Smith that the self-interest of an individual functions as an invisible hand in the exchange of goods in the market, James Buchanan (Nobel laureate) has affirmed in his studies that people, societies and communities do not exist in reality.[6] Acknowledging another Nobel laureate, K. J. Arrow, that there is no mechanism for collective choice and the impossibility theorem, Buchanan has advocated a greater role for the market. Buchanan and his followers were able to formulate theories in public policy that have been generally accepted by institutions like the World Bank.

Representative democracy, according to the above group, is nothing but the tyranny of the minority. In most elections, the voters are poorly informed and interest groups play an important role in the outcome of the first-past-the-post system. It is said that interest groups or industrial lobbies trade their votes in exchange for support for benefits such as agricultural subsidies with other group that appear to be in conflict of interests, but make adjustments in such a way that they secure a majority to get both their bills passed. Therefore, it is better to rely on an efficient institution like the market for arriving at conclusions rather than the inefficient state in the supply of public goods. In fact, the group of political economists or the Chicago boys have provided convincing arguments for reducing the number of public goods to very few and sufficiently orienting policy-makers to make policies in such a way that supply is left to the private sector.

Buchanan has said that voters always weigh the costs of taxes to the citizen and the benefits that they get through the transfer of income or public goods in the proposed budget before going to the polling booth to vote. Many scholars and policy-makers in India subscribe to the ideas of the Chicago school and have made attempts to formulate amendments to our democratic political process. Some of them have been functioning in a way to replicate the American system in India.

Amartya Sen has contested the arguments of the group, specifically the impossibility theorem that indicates the difficulty in arriving at group decisions and provided a simple solution to it saying that it depends on individual preference.[7] We are sentient to the fact that the theories developed by some scholars are based on a society (built after eliminating native groups) which is individualistic in content and selfish in approach. But, ancient civilisations like India that had developed several institutional structures that give importance to groups rather than to Individuals, cannot accept such radical departures.

Sen, in his Nobel lecture on 'the possibility of social choice' (and in other works), has provided an answer to the riddle, saying that "[W]hen people cluster in parties with complex agendas and dialogues involving give-and-take as well as some general attitudes to values like equity and justice, the ubiquitous inconsistencies can yield ground to more congruous decisions."[8]

Sen has further argued that in a matter of national outrage like famines, the electorate may be reasonably univocal and thoroughly consistent. Despite the riposte, the behaviour of some of our politicians, maybe due to corporate influences, has not changed and they continue to imitate the market economies. They seem to be employing management consultants from Harvard and other business schools to design campaigns to win elections rather than depending upon the congruent people-oriented manifestos or programmes. This has changed the content of our electoral politics.

It appears that some of the dominant players in the national and regional elections consider the theories advocated by market fundamentalists relevant in India once they get elected. Therefore, they are using the market model to fight elections. The protagonists of market economy seem convinced that democracy in India is approaching what the Chicago boys have assumed in their formulations, a political market. Politics is considered, as per their formulation, another sector for profitable investments. Naturally, all the techniques of planning and executing the ideas of concept, pricing, promotion and distribution facilitating political communication should be made possible. But, the Indian electorate, unlike the American voters, is drawn from the socially and economically poor cohorts and, thus, it is felt that it is better to attract them through market strategies. Marketing is not the cup of tea of economists.

Management experts, particularly the marketing gurus, are in great demand in politics. One of the strategies that they generally suggest is the creation of brands to easily connect with the customer, albeit the voter. A brand is not just a symbol; it is more than just fulfilling promises and meeting customer satisfaction. It involves advertisement campaigns, event sponsorships, media manipulations including paid news, social networks, etc. to create a brand as in business. Therefore, personal brands, such as Anna,[9] Ramdev,[10] and several corporate babas and film stars, have been in great demand in the political market. It was found by scholars that in the 2004 elections the feel-good factor and India Shining campaigns did come under this category. It seems all political parties active in parliamentary democracy are now involved in creating human brands of their own for future use.

Each political party is trying to generate a few good brands at the national level and only some at the regional level. A few brands are created and kept pending for the future while some brands are used sparingly, depending upon the market density or voter turnout in a region. Political parties are now putting more confidence in the media and marketing research houses rather than the psephologists. If the present trend continues, voters in a poor country like India would have no recourse to ameliorative manifestos from political parties that are obliged to make some promises but smug with the brands as they do with consumer goods!

INDIAN DEMOCRACY AND THE OLIGARCHY OF CASTES

Democracy is generally understood as a form of government. There are different meanings attributed to it. Democracy, according to Abraham Lincoln, is a system of government off (of) the people, buy (by) the people and far (for) the people. Though the prepositions in the parentheses may be the original statement of Lincoln, but, of late, it has been reduced to what is actually indicated in the sentence. Therefore, the working definition of democracy is usually taken from Schumpeter from his outstanding work, *Capitalism, Socialism and Democracy*.

Democracy, according to him, is an "institutional arrangement for arriving at political decisions which realizes the common good by making the people itself decide issues through the election of individuals who are to assemble in order to carry out its will."[11]

This is considered as a real and practical definition to understand the working of democracy in different forms and institutions now. We do also consider the presence of liberties, rule of law, elections, etc. to qualify a country as a liberal democracy.

Indian democracy, according to scholars like B. R. Ambedkar, is as old as the Buddhist sanghas. However, in the modern period, it was the British who introduced the contemporary form of democracy in India. Interestingly, the adult franchise was restricted to the propertied classes and no one argued for universal franchise with the British until B. R. Ambedkar approached the Southborough Committee in 1919. Political democracy has been limping with several contradictions thereafter. One important dichotomy, as noted by him, is that there is one-man-one-vote in politics and in the social and economic life too many values. This contradiction has not reached a boiling point to blow up the parliamentary form of democracy in India as anticipated. Instead, the caste system has changed itself to the changing contours of a liberal democracy. The people in whom statesmen like Ambedkar had reposed confidence in throwing off the system have slowly compromised and adjusted to the whimsies of parliamentary democracy. We now have a so-called liberal capitalist democracy in operation. The most important feature of a capitalist democracy is its compromise with the concept of private property. Further, such a Western capitalist democracy has been applauded as the one system that replaced slavery in the West. However, it has allowed socio-economic inequalities to persist. The development of cronyism is its inherent weakness. Crony capitalism is thriving in India due to the internal contradictions in society, particularly the endurance of the caste system.

The Western model of liberal capitalist democracy has degenerated to such an extent that it wouldn't survive without support from the market. It seems that both the institutions are intertwined to a degree that it is very difficult to tell which institution stands for which. It is easy to find freedoms guaranteed in the written Constitution in some of the democratic countries without adequate provisions for equality of opportunity. Therefore, resolving the contradictions between private property and political, social and cultural freedoms is the greatest challenge before the judiciary of the modern State. Consequently, the political apparatus has created several alternatives like interest groups, corporations, lobbyists, power brokers, etc. as a compromise between the various rights. The situation in India has been studied by several social scientists to characterise the Indian State, its economic policies, constituents and the processes during the post-independence period. There are different generalisations. But, one important observation on the mobilisation of lower castes, particularly the Dalits, as a 'secular upsurge' by a scholar has an implicit assumption that the State, market and civil society are autonomous and have allowed the upsurge. This appears to be incorrect. The Indian State is a caste state. To be precise, it is an upper-caste state that has a record of meddling with all. Therefore, one can see the bias in the formulation of policies from the very beginning down to the present day through 1991 reforms.

In each of the Five-year Plans, a particular social group is liberated to join the modern economy. For instance, the abolition of privy purses so as to convert them into capitalists or industrialists with the cash in compensation rather than keeping the group as feudal lords; providing opportunities to the educated upper castes through globalisation and ICT to enter the service sector in the post-Mandal period, etc. This has its impact on the composition of the ruling class. The mere representation of a person in a constituency through reservation or under the tutelage of a dominant caste party does not qualify one to be a part of the ruling class. How much command or demand one has on the party in getting economic resources for the caste he/she represents alone should decide his/her status.

In this context, the OBC–Dalit combine that came to power and fell apart in UP in the past gave us several lessons. Now both scholars and laymen belonging to the Dalits appear to distrust the OBCs and, unfortunately, they see in every OBC a Mulayam Singh Yadav (even if someone pretends as a convert). The fallout of the above experiment in the North is due to the emergence of dominant castes in each state to capture power.[12] This has given enough opportunities to the resource-rich dominant castes to emerge as the big players in each state. Instead of the caste-neutral and secular political parties in a well-defined liberal democracy, it is caste that has emerged as a big player. If we look at the political leaders in power in each state, we understand that it is through the manipulation of one or two castes or an oligarchy of castes that many are on the saddle.

Let us start from Jammu and Kashmir; it is related to few families, Punjab and Haryana Jat Sikhs, Delhi Brahmin-Bania group, UP Scheduled Caste-Brahmin combine, Bihar BC-Modi combine, Bengal Bhadralok, Maharashtra Marathas, Gujarat Patel-Bania mix, Odisha Patnaiks and Mahants, Andhra Kamma-Reddy combine, Tamil Nadu Thevar Brahmin League, Karnataka Lingayat/Vakkaliga, etc. This is only an illustration and we might have missed some details. It is for experts to ponder over and clarify or dismiss the formulation! This is not a new phenomenon. It happened in the past in Great Britain during the Whig Oligarchy in the 18th century. It was during the leadership of Robert Walpole (1720–40) that the British Whigs wanted to increase the base of the party by bringing in the underprivileged feudal and middle classes, with the aristocracy backing it. Later, the Tories appropriated the oligarchy. There is a lesson for intellectuals and leaders of various castes to learn from this episode. The groups should not envy too much by looking at each other and miss the common agenda altogether, leaving scope for the very fundamentalist forces to capture power and take the country backward like the Tories.

LIMITS TO BAHUJAN POLITICS

The results of the Assembly elections in 2012 in five states, particularly in UP, induced political pundits to make different conjectures. One important message, according to some, was that UP was becoming another Tamil Nadu, making national parties redundant in state politics. This may be a farfetched hypothesis that needs serious empirical study following an Indian approach for a better understanding of a native phenomenon. Others say that the BSP did not make any impact on the results and the euphoria created around Mayawati was blown over after 6 March 2012. This does not seem to be based on facts. The vote share of the BSP has remained almost constant ever since Kanshiram experimented *bahujan* politics with Mulayam Singh Yadav in UP. The difference between the winning Samajwadi Party (SP) and the defeated BSP was around 3 per cent votes polled and the BSP came second with 209 seats. Significantly, the BSP pockets of the Agra and Bundelkhand regions seemed to have remained intact. Then why the defeat? Caste and religion have become so sensitive in recent times that a dispassionate attempt to analyse the issues at hand with academic interest is not appreciated. Yet, public discourse on issues of contemporary importance needs to persevere. It seems that the status quo of our society is maintained due to the failure of some groups to cut a few traditional mores. But, in a dynamic situation they feel frustrated and make the onlookers rueful.

In this context, we can see that some groups develop obsessions with entities that make them comfortable as long as they are not challenged, such as the obsession of the orthodox Hindus' with the Vedas, the fetish of literate Dalits with Ambedkar statues, etc. The issue of the erection of statues is referred here in connection with the onslaught of the Mayawati government in UP during 2010–11. It was the beginning of a protracted battle against her government by all parties that eventually made her vacate the seat. No one is willing to recognise the greatest service she has done to Lucknow by beautifying the whole

Gomathi area and making it perhaps the only magnificent secular-public place developed in post-independence India. S. A.
Iyer, in his column in *Economics Times*, called it the 'Lutyens of
Lucknow' (it is more imposing than Rajpath).[13] In fact, it has
emerged as a pilgrim centre for Dalits. But, we are told that
many groups among the Dalits have not accepted Mayavati
leadership and there are several green-eyed activists who
started an undercurrent of hate campaign against her. Maybe
the style of functioning of Mayawati was responsible for that,
but, is the Dalit leadership not mature enough to endure it like
they have been bearing others for ages? Or is it the limitation
of the exclusionist politics that she was forced in and could not
traverse? The present NDA government seems to have taken
a leaf from Mayawati in appropriating Ambedkar by putting
billions of rupees to deify him rather than investing the money
in projects for the emancipation of Dalits.

Democracy, according to one commentator, is about
numbers. In a country like India with caste, religion, region,
language, etc., garnering the magic figure of winning somehow is now considered as successful politics. Ambedkar
knew this more than anyone else; therefore, he wanted separate electorates for the SCs. He had to compromise with
Gandhiji in 1932 as per Dalits to save his life and the SCs
have been compelled to contest in reserved seats and solicit
the votes of non-Dalits who constitute nearly 70 per cent.[14] It
means that the SC and ST candidates contesting in reserved
seats need to perpetually depend upon others to get elected
and need to be loyal to the party that gives them the ticket.
This is similar to the erstwhile jajmani system of the feudal
period where one needed to depend upon those who commanded resources and people. Realising the constraints
of the existing political framework, Kanshiram shifted his
place of work to UP (from Pune) in the 1980s. Those familiar with social statistics recognise that the concentration of
Dalit pockets in the mainland Aryavarta of UP, Punjab, etc.
does cross around 30 per cent of the population in some
districts and in Punjab 30 per cent at the aggregate. This

is also true in Bengal. But, Kanshiram concentrated on UP and worked hard in the regions where Muslims, Dalits and lower BCs comprise around 50–70 per cent. But, his experiments did not give results and he finally designed the *sarvajan* formula realising that Brahmins constituted around 10 per cent of the population and were clever, unlike in other areas. In other words, Kanshiram went ahead with the so-called identity politics to capture power. But, he could not witness the triumph of his politics in 2007 (one year after his death in 2006).

This was a very inopportune time for Mayawati as she was dubbed by Dalits as the one who mortgaged the self-respect of Dalits to the Brahmins. The Dalits have failed to see the distinction between social movements and political strategy for winning elections. It is alleged that Mayawati was forced to slowly estrange the symbol of upper castes, Satish Chandra Mishra, by 2012. Now the BSP is restricted to UP and may be to a sub-region in the future, if the present trend continues. The competing politics in UP made the SP, one-time a Lohiate party, to become worldly wise in making the affable young man Akhilesh Yadav the new chief minister. The SP was originally like the BSP, but slowly it graduated to becoming a bahujan party by bringing other castes into its fold. The upper castes in UP first encouraged the BSP against the SP; and now by supporting the SP against the BSP, they seem to have permanently lost the ground in UP politics for ever to be dictated by these forces. This attitude of some ruling castes using one caste against the other sustains the caste system in India through electoral politics. But, the future depends on how the BSP prepares its strategies. The reading that the SP won 58 out of 85 reserved seats in 2012 to show that Mayawati has lost ground with Dalits is not entirely correct. Dalits, or any single caste, on their own in any constituency (including reserved) do not win elections without support from others. Therefore, the number indicates a general trend of some kind of a swing in favour of the SP, maybe due to the Muslim shift. However, the BSP has pockets of Dalit concentrations where it can get a minimum of

70 seats and a peak of 90 with its own vote bank. But, that does not bring victory. It has to play inclusive politics. In fact, no political party, including the BSP, SP, DMK, RPI, etc., which speaks about social engineering, has ever experimented with sharing power with the minorities within the social groups and tried out constructive programmes to unite the bahujans, sarvajans and even the numerous Dalit sub-castes.

The Dalit vote bank of the BSP is alleged to be a divided house with disruptive behaviour, leg pulling and finding solace with non-Dalit leadership considered as some of its shortcomings. This is the greatest limitation of bahujan politics as of now. Further, the SP has shown that there is an alternative leadership in the party. But Mayawati has a problem of stewardship as the Dalits are disorderly and are too many to claim leadership. Fortunately, Mayawati has no family to fall back upon and future politics in India appears to be heading towards consanguinity rather than consensus politics!

Constitutional protection has helped some groups to politically mobilise their numbers, first in the South and later in some parts of the North, to replace the traditional dvija rule. By the time the non-dvija rule started yielding returns, mostly to those who were in power, two incidents shook the country. The Kilvanmani incident in 1969, when the DMK was in power, in which 42 SCs (Dalits) were burnt alive in. A few years later, nine STs were murdered by the Bhumihars in Belchi in Bihar during the Karpoori Thakur government. In both the incidents, the Dalits were the victims while the so-called backward castes were in power. One may say that these were fortuitous incidents as neither M. Karunanidhi or Karpoori Thakur was responsible for the ghastly incidents, the feudal forces were the culprits. But, this gives out a clear message that the empty rhetoric of social solidarity disappears in testing times if the cadre and the social proletariat are not ideologically and practically prepared. It is alleged by Dalit activists that the unenlightened leadership from these parties ensured that the Dalits did not get protection under their rule. This appears to have been repeated in the case of Andhra Pradesh where the emergence of shudra rule caused two incidents in Karamchedu and Chundur, helping to propel leadership roles among the Dalits in the 1980s and some of them later alleged to be co-opted.[15] It seems they were all fragmented by the time the Lakshmipeta incident in Srikakulam (see previous chapter) took place.

A dispassionate analysis of the events, particularly after the recent episode in Parliament on reservations without any discussion on Dharmapuri in 2014, or such violent incidents elsewhere is critical. The so-called alleged quid pro quo of the possible passing of a Constitutional amendment and granting of disputed Indu Mills land costing about ₹40 billion to an Ambedkar memorial in Mumbai and a better package in Andhra Pradesh through SC/ST sub-plan are to be scrutinised to find out what is in store for the poor Dalits? Dalits are not bahujans and the sarvajan experiment has remained rhetoric rather than internalised by the cadre of BSP. It appears that one group wanted only social reforms so as to achieve political power and authority, while the other group really wished for the abolition of the inequitable system through the annihilation of castes. This dichotomy in the social movement at least in the North could not be clarified properly and resolved by the leaders and its persistence presence might create problems of adjustment in the future. In other words, the social and economic agenda of emancipation project for the Dalits and OBCs as bahujans has surfaced as a split philosophy each reading differently from the same needs to be revisited by scholars who are in social science research.

The 2014 incidents involving the so-called backward castes like the Vanniyars in Tamil Nadu and the Yadavs in UP for caste mobilisation may not necessarily be representative of the aspirations of a majority of the groups that they represent. But, it is as dangerous as the anti-reservation movement launched by Youth for Equality against the whole caste-based reservations during Mandal, as the all non-Dalits-unite call given by the PMK in Tamil Nadu, and an anti-SC reservation in promotion game plan of the SP. In both the cases, they seem to have been remotely influenced by a dogma of divide and rule. There seems to be some kind of an emerging situation where the Dalits can bargain with the ruling classes as in the past with the dead bodies on their laps and the backwards can establish their mighty by arm-twisting the Dalits as muscle power of the mainstream social norm even in the 21st century. This seems to be structurally designed in our social hierarchy where some castes are given economic concessions but not social status and the natives are denied both, to prolong the hegemony of caste order.

The conflict between Dalits and OBCs would not alter the traditional situation as long as these two groups are made to fight while the wealth of the nation is amassed by a few. Unless both the groups who had common ancestors in history and in their culture sit together, keeping all kinds of false pretensions aside, to arrive at a common minimum social and economic programme, it is difficult to engage a formation that has already emerged as a raucous system with international support. There seems to be some anticipation that the middle class or petty-bourgeois in the urban areas under the influence of the ICT is slowly reckoning the existence of the Dalits and their leaders. The prognosis became real in the 2014 elections through the use of ICT and political marketing by Modi and the so-called aam aadmi taught lessons to those who were arrogant and vile in power.

PSEUDO-SECULARISTS VERSUS FAKE HINDUS AND MUSLIMS

Secularism is a charming concept usually flaunted during elections in India. The expressions 'pseudo' and 'fake' are being used increasingly in public discourse in the context of social and secular affairs in India. We have seen during recent elections how political party functionaries keep talking about their version of secularism and denounce the opposition party as communal or pseudo-secular. If a particular party is close to one religious group with a genuine desire to improve the socio-economic conditions of the people, the other political party calls the adversary pseudo-secularists or accuse them adopting appeasement tactics to please a group. The political party under attack calls the opponent communal or fundamentalist. In fact, both or all those who are using the political space for reconciliation or conflict seem to be insincere in translating the Constitutional values or vision. It is a great fraud on our Constitution as the issues of secularism, equality, freedom, etc. are inflected by political class keeping in mind the vote bank and not the legitimate aspirations of the people. One can be considerate to those who genuinely take up the issues of minorities (belonging to different religious groups) at the risk of being targeted by the majority. In a country where identities are artificially manufactured for obvious reasons, the terms minority and majority are found to be false.

India is considered a Hindu nation by some, while many claim that it had a *Sanatana Dharma* and the notion of Hinduism was constructed only during the 19th century based on structures like Christianity (Romila Thapar).[16] Missionaries, scholars pointed out, had also their share of sins in adapting to Indian social mores. However, if a Hindu believes in *Vasudhaika Kutumbakam* and acts against its tenets, is he/she not a fake Hindu or a pseudo-Hindu? Similarly, a follower of Islam, who believes in equality and brotherhood, but, in practice, defrauds his conscience is also a fake. The common man has nothing to do with the fakes and their frauds. What he/she needs is the opportunity to use his/her abilities to pursue a comfortable life irrespective of his/her descent and belief.

We have adopted a Constitution and parliamentary form of democracy. They are not based on our so-called dharma but on alien values. You cannot say that we need one value for governance and another for social intercourse. It is a mockery to claim that we are modern in our economy, governance and polity, and traditional in our social life. If someone wants to practise such values, it is not possible in public life. The freedom to practise one's beliefs is protected at the personal level with reasonable restrictions. This is possible only in a secular, democratic and socialist country. Those who oppose these values are pseudo-religionists and are a threat to the majority who are always non-partisan native Indians. A nation is created over a period of time through the process of assimilation of factors such as language, culture, ethnic origin, historical, geographical and other considerations. The contemporary world bears witness to several movements fighting for national identities both in the Middle East and in Latin America due to the Anglo-American hegemony in the name of globalisation.

Interestingly, there is an undercurrent of a deal based on primordial and questionable identities shaping in India. Yet, the egocentric clout with the aid and support of corporate entities is promoting certain beliefs and fads to uphold the alleged supremacy of a particular thesis of the cultural unity of India. Globalisation and its contents are being used very systematically to spread the virus across the globe. Though mankind had seen such imprudent plans met with disastrous ends in history, the cruel minds continue with their acts. Unfortunately, India of late has become a centre of this malice through media and money. The basic principles of the Indian Constitution seem to rest on non-interference and not the so-called protection of *mathadipathis* like Kesavanada Bharati.[17] We had a legacy of pluralism because of our long history of colonisation by different alien powers and imposition of different belief systems on native Indians. It appears that no civilised world promotes institutions based on the ideology of graded inequality, as a predestined consequence, as we witness every day in India. The recent political drama of the ascendancy of a particular social group in power and its collusion with international capitalist expansion remind how the historical process of colonisation of India by alien powers occurred in the past. As literate knowledge is forbidden to the lower castes and opportunities are denied once again with privatisation, it appears that very few studies would be forthcoming to record this trend as the traditional exclusion from literate learning is going to be thrusted upon by deceit after liberalisation. One should appreciate the fact that the local beliefs of common people, who are in a majority, follow their traditional practices; if necessary, they translate Allah, Jesus and Vishnu into their own forms of worship. The common folk are so secular in their outlook and just do not mind adopting some alien elements as seen in the practices of the Peerla festival, incorporating Muslim and Hindu practices in the South. The common people are not fundamentalist in their approach as it is one of the many events in their cultural life and not a fulltime activity as in the case of the religious fundamentalists. It is noticed that fundamentalists keep on inventing different kinds of festivals, rituals and stories with the support of obtuse urban Intellectuals like the Nandis, Bhatras, Tiwaris, Khans, Pauls, etc. to perpetuate their hegemony. The secularists and so-called Leftists who claim to be non-partisan have failed to develop an alternative culture and allowed religious fundamentalists with soft pedaling to flourish with the aid of modern technology. We have seen debates by some Marxists in Kerala defending religion on dubious grounds as they have failed to practise what they preach. This is contrary to the idea that religion will disappear with the advent of capitalism and modernisation. India is different from other nations where one or two faiths survived. We have dedicated social groups innovating and perpetuating faith as a business activity with billions and trillions of rupees spent and invested. Is there any country in the world where a god's birth, marriage, nuptial, love affairs in different guises and in different regions with diversity, interpreted as a universal value to carry out rituals/ceremonies throughout the year? They are all now being broadcast and televised with innovative and creative works in dedicated TV channels and via special programmes in regular networks. This has a cascading effect on the gullible and ordinary people as seen from the fact that the amount of money spent on religious festivals has increased enormously after the advent of the ICT revolution as reported by the NSS study.[18]

It appears that no social psychologist has studied the impact of technological innovation on the religious intolerance of people. On the contrary, we have several scholars and prize-fighters justifying the acts of religious fundamentalists.

Secularism has become a way of life in India, unlike the European version where religious crusades forced them to end up in secularism there. Our secular culture is purely based on the Indian value system founded on its geography and history. However, the country is undergoing a transition from traditional to modern era without much transformation in social life due to religious control over the lives of people. There is hope in the will of the common man who does not care for the professional fundamentalists. Secularism along with socialism and democracy would help reinforce the vision of our founding fathers. The ideals are to be translated into action through constant efforts by intellectuals, government, political parties and civil society.

DALIT–MUSLIM RELATIONS IN PRE-PARTITION BENGAL

It is noted by scholars that between the economic base and religious super structure, culture plays an important role in the area of human relations. Economic elevation may not directly alter the relation as one to one order. Hindu–Muslim relations in India and the presence of diverse sociocultural groups and identities might have influenced the founding fathers to suggest a secular form of republic. It appears that it has its influence on the drafting of constitutional objective in India while Pakistan had adopted a different piece of constitution. However, history tells us that most of the nations in South Asia have a common ancestry and legacy. It would be interesting to learn about their unique history. Indian historiography today is facing several challenges, including the selection of social categories to narrate changes in the recent past. It is only by studying contemporary history and relating it with the past that we can save/sustain the discipline of history in India. The existing studies on Partition, mostly on Northern India, have presented the problem of nationalism in terms of Muslim–Hindu relations. But some scholars like Sekhar Bandopadhyay[19] believe that it was possible because the Dalits of UP and Punjab did not identify with Hindu nationalism and were not targets of violence. But, the situation in pre-Partition Bengal was different. It is for the first time Sekhar Bandopadhyay, a popular historian and social scientist, is bringing out the real categories into focus through an analysis of the conditions of caste in the subcontinent and not in terms of the imagined European class. He pointed out that "[W]e need to introduce the category of caste into this discussion as Dalits participated in Partition politics and 'were equally victims and perpetrators of violence." Dalit participation, Dalit–Muslim and Dalit–Hindu relationships in pre-Partition Bengal will have to be understood within this heterogeneous context of political response to fast-changing historical contingencies.

Dalit identity politics in the colonial period started around the 1870s and was intimately connected with two Dalit groups, Namasudra and Rajbanshi in Bengal. They are numerically strong, despite their assimilation by dominant religious conversions, and as a result West Bengal today has the second largest concentration of the SC population in India. The previously mentioned two numerically large castes were spread into two geographical regions in pre-Partition Bengal: the former in Bakarganj, Faridpur, Jessore and Khulna and the latter in Rangpur, Dinapur, Jalpaiguri, and Coochbehar. The two castes provided leadership to the Dalit struggle for land in 1872. They fought for reclamation of the marshy lands of the Sunderbans, questioned the dominance of Brahminism with the support of the Sahajiya-vaisnav sect and started joining the mainstream nationalist movement. But when riots broke out in 1911 and 1930 between the Hindus and Muslims, they were not a part of Hindu nationalism and joined the Muslims later to fight caste Hindu landlords. They remained silent, noted Sekhar Bandopadhyay, resulting in the Congress getting only 7 seats out of 32 reserved for SCs in Bengal.

The communalisation of Bengal started with the Hindu Mahasabha that campaigned for Dalit votes. The 1941 Dhaka riots took place perhaps with the active participation of the

Namasudras. There seemed to be internal disquiet between the Namasudras and the Rajvamshis that persisted after the emergence of Jogendranath Mandal[20] and Radhanath Das, each supporting different viewpoints.[21] Jogendranath Mandal of Bengal was a towering personality, comparable to B. R. Ambedkar in Bengal, and got elected to the Constituent Assembly from Bengal. He became the chairman of the Constituent Assembly of Pakistan after partition as Law Minister and resigned from the Parliament with disillusionment almost about the same time as Ambedkar.[22] But, neither historians nor mainstream Dalit scholars have given him proper space. Sekhar has narrated how Mandal took an aggressive stand against the partition and a pro-Muslim stance with the argument that the Dalits and the Muslims were of the same economic position and a separate autonomous united Bengal would be helpful for their advancement. But, Mandal became despised for his pro-Muslim stand and his rivals Radhanath Das and P. R. Thakur joined the Congress to get 26 out of the 30 reserved seats in 1937. By that time, the Hindu Mahasabha had a strategy to create a Hindu majority province in West Bengal which was endorsed by the Congress at the Tarakeswar Convention on 1 April 1947. The country got divided. The Rajbansis aligned with the communists in the Tebhaga share cropper movement. But, it was a movement against the Rajbansi Jotedars by Rajbansi Adhiars (share croppers) and led to rupture in the caste coalition. The noted historian says different layers of social relations converged and cut across caste, class and communal boundaries in rural Bengal.

The study of Sekhar Bandopadhyay brought some interesting lessons for the contemporary struggles in India. It has brought out very clearly that Jogendranath Mandal's support for the partition did not solve the Dalit problems in Pakistan. One of the greatest damages done to Dalit solidarity in Bengal was the fragmentation of the Dalits as a group. Some were kept in East Pakistan at the time of the partition without much relief and, therefore, migration took place later in waves after 1947. By 1950–51, aggressive discourses of Islamic nationalism forced the Dalits out of Pakistan, while the dominant Hindu discourse in India tended to absorb them into a 'Hindu refugee' identity. But, Hindu nationalism was/is not willing to offer full citizenship to them and the unrest in the region still continues.

The migration of Dalits from East Bengal had one of the most pathetic stories of splitting of a community in recent human history which no historian has so far recorded. Dalit refugees were denied land in Bengal and were dissipated into different parts of the country, including the Andamans and Dandakaranya. Interestingly, the non-Dalit refugees were accommodated in the 24 *paraganas* and other important places in Bengal with land and support. Thus, "organized Dalit voice consequently disappeared from Bengal public sphere leading to all-powerful political myth that caste does not matter in Bengal." Interestingly, the discourse on reservations for OBCs and the Dalits in India by the so-called Hindutva parivar uses the same language as of their opponents, left and liberals in private conversations for some time (got alienated from the lower castes).

COULD A MUSLIM BE SECULARIST?

The Muslims of India are as natural citizens of India as anyone else and they keep projecting as the true inheritors of a composite cultural legacy. This is contrary to the stereotyping of Muslims. In fact, religion never united Muslims. Otherwise, we would not have seen the partition of Bangladesh from Pakistan or the Arab problem. Why is it that the so-called secularists have not recognised the importance of the statement of Ali Khan, the Khadim of the Ajmer Dargah, who protested against Pakistan PM visit in March 2013, even if there were some theatrics in the statement on the occasion of Pakistan PM's visit to the shrine? Are Muslims not qualified to be patriotic and at the same time remain secular in their approach to international relations? Had not Modi become secular for Americans after the NDA win?

In fact, most of our current debates on secularism are superb examples of political drama and intellectual disgust without any practical programme of action to sustain secularism in a pluralistic country. Then what is the harm in appreciating the Khadim? The situation was different during the freedom movement. Scholar-statesmen such as M. N. Roy, B. R. Ambedkar and a forgotten Telugu scholar K. B. Krishna, had provided sincere and honest analyses of the Muslim problem and the need for secularism in India. K. B. Krishna, who taught Marxism to A. K. Gopalan in jail, was a Harvard University scholar who produced a dissertation on 'Communal Representation in India' for his PhD degree in 1935. He added some essays and published *The Problem of Minorities or Communal Representation in India* in London in 1939.[23] After a survey of the situation in different countries in the British colonies, including Kenya, Krishna concluded, "[T]he only solution is to demand independence for India from British imperialism." He analysed that, "Hinduism and Islam represent different stages of human development. The Islam of immigrant Moslems was divorced from its natural surroundings and transplanted to Indian surroundings. The association of Moslems with non-Moslem communities in different localities created different situations and outlooks. This also accounts, in addition to educational and economic factors, for the cleavages of opinions and interests in the political classes of the same faith."

The differences between general Islam and Hinduism and between particular local Islam and Hinduism are expressed in the relationships of classes belonging to these faiths. Moral ideas are the outcome of material needs. Religion is the organisation of such moral ideas. "At some stages of human development moral ideas and needs coincide. The contradictions between morality and practice are becoming deeper with the growth of class antagonisms." Around the same period, M. N. Roy also expressed a similar opinion and lamented that we do not try to understand the conditions and the situation of our own Muslim neighbours and alienate them. B. R. Ambedkar has, in a way, drawn some of his insightful thoughts from the experiences of Muslims and his dialogues with Mohammad Ali Jinnah and others. He has narrated how "every change, executive, administrative or legal inflicted a series of blows on the Muslim community." The exclusion of Muslims from political power was 'the essence of the distinction' between the ruling group and the subject group. Thus, he had an inexplicable longing for the Muslim community.

It also shows that Islam, compared to other religions, is far-off from open proselytisation. In fact, religion is not a full-time activity of people, except of the priestly class and most of the conflicts are confined to the vested interests amongst them. K. B. Krishna said, "[T]he Arab-Jew problem, like the Hindu-Muslim problem, is neither racial nor religious. It is a struggle between two classes belonging to different faiths accentuated by the political policy of imperialism."

The imperialists have left us officially in 1947 and we do not know who has stepped into their boots now? Abundant wisdom had gone into the Constituent Assembly debates in formulating certain Articles relating to the secular nature of the state. Though secularism was added as part of the Preamble during the Emergency, there was already a basic structure existent to entail secularism and socialism. The Constitution-makers were not guided by the medieval feudal practices of some Muslim or Hindu princes and even English officers having wives from different religious groups to declare their religious tolerance. It was a depraved kind of approach to a serious issue that was later alleged to be theorised as 'Sarvadharma samabhava' by some disingenuous scholars. In a country which was converted as a colony of several alien settlers and their belief systems, it was inevitable for the native Indians to absorb unfamiliar practices, sometimes with persuasion and many a time with force.

There are very few studies to show how the lower castes were converted to Islam. But there are few studies on Christian conversions. Those lower castes who got converted to other faiths seem to have remained poor and excluded practising the adopted dharma sincerely. One is worshipping an animal while the other is abhorring it. How could both be treated with the same reverence? The principle of equality of treatment of all religions does not work like this. The two groups should be allowed to practise as per their conscience according to Article 25 of the Constitution without interference of the State. Samadharma samabhava might operate among those classes or groups who were from the same stock, but spread into different faiths over a period and have come to an understanding to rule together.

The internal social division within the Muslim community is not openly discussed either by those who rely on their strength or those who oppose them on religious considerations. Yet, the fact remains that the Hindu social division is reflected not only among Muslims but also among all those who got converted from lower castes in India. There seems to be no social interface between the minority disadvantaged groups and the Hindus, particularly the Dalit converts known as Arjals and Ajlafs. The common agenda of bringing out a social cohesion among these groups to end the vilification of the minority community would need to go a long way.

This would enable them to obtain the necessary power to expose the antagonism of some groups who are actually resisting help from the government to these groups due to their low social background and not their religion. This process should make them united for reservation in public jobs and subsidies offered to the socially disadvantaged. But leaders of the minority community oppose any sub-division within the group as that would reduce their political manoeuvring. However, the leaders have done precious little for this community. In this context, the victims should notice that the common ground of all the upper echelons as a class is the same irrespective of their religion.

Therefore, the socially marginalised should learn from their antagonists to get united to ask for a separate sub-plan within the national plan for their amelioration. It is time that we need to practise rigorously what secularism stands for to bring in development programmes that are earmarked for the poor. This is possible if one detaches from personal beliefs and practices from all public/State functions and confine to secular transactions. It is neither disbelief nor irreligious to be distinguished from that of vulgar display of personal beliefs as we see frequently now. There is no other way as of now and no public servant, including the judiciary, should be spared for violating this value. It is the principle of proportional representation in a democratic polity based on the equality of economic opportunities, together with a scientific temper that would ultimately make religious problems trivial. Until then, we need to cultivate constantly the feeling of brotherhood in an unemotional environment to build a nation called India.

THE GUJARAT MODEL OF DEVELOPMENT

The Gujarat model of development became popular after the 2002 riots against Muslims. It became the key campaign mantra later when Modi took reins of power to usher in the much eulogised trajectory of development. It is on the same plank that he was projected as the prime ministerial candidate in 2014 elections against the UPA-II.

Gujarat, known for its outward-looking trade, built the first dry-dock in human history at Lothal in the first millennium BC indicating its long experience with trade and business. The business caravans of Gujarat entered important trade routes of Africa even during the mediaeval period. Gujarati businessmen, including Muslim traders, are spread in different parts of North America, Africa and other countries. The Gujaratis do carry their traditional identity and practices wherever they go and would like to visit their ancestral homeland at least once. Thus, the rich culture and customs of the Gujaratis are distinctly different from those of other regions of the country.

Narendra Modi came to limelight for a dubious reason and would have remained only as a great organiser of business and economic activities in the state, had he not sported his ambition for a national leadership role. The Gujarat economy had been on the growth trajectory ever since liberalisation was introduced in India. The huge expansion that has taken place in Gujarat is due to the liberalisation agenda of P. V. Narasimha Rao and Manmohan Singh. Though Modi has coined 'Gujarat Khamir' (resilience) to create a brand image for the state, the development was not entirely due to his or the successive governments of the state. There is no evidence on record to show that the state has introduced innovative programmes of its own except the ones given by the Centre.

Modi has sincerely implemented schemes like SEZs in 60 areas during his tenure as CM and seems to have introduced only a scheme known as Special Investment Regions (SIRs). It is an extension of the concept of SEZ with huge enclosures covering 100 km radius in 13 places given to each industrial zamindar. The state is blessed with the largest coast of 1,600 km, with around 35 river systems to provide sufficient water, and has abundant resources of soda ash, bauxite, lignite and other minerals. It is a low-density state with 234 persons per sq. km compared to 325 for all India around 2010 and a large number of NRIs are ever willing to invest in the state.

Several scholars have found that the highest rate of growth was observed during the tenure of Madhavsinh Solanki; it was around 25.32 per cent in 1981–82, 12.6 in 1990–91 and is around 9–10 per cent during Modi as CM. Thus, the rapid growth in Gujarat is not due to any single politician but is due to favourable economic conditions. Nevertheless, there are states such as Tamil Nadu, Haryana and Kerala whose development is considered to be much faster and inclusive than that of Gujarat (Planning Commission, Delhi).

An important fact about the social structure of Gujarat is not publicly discussed. It is the only state in the Fifth Schedule where the largest population of Adivasis inhabit in three-fourths of the districts. There are seven districts where the Adivasi population is more than 30 per cent and in the Dangs district the population is 93.76 per cent. The grave issue is that in districts like Baruch, Valsad and Dahej, the SEZs and SIRs are located in Adivasi areas without much protection to the locals. Though the Modi government claims that it has devoted around ₹40 billion for tribal sub-plan during 2013, it is not reflected in the descent of poverty levels or atrocities on Adivasis. On the contrary, NGOs claim that 96 per cent of the accused in the SC and ST atrocity cases are acquitted (see CRBI reports).

Further, irrigation water through mega projects like the Sardar Sarovar seems to have not been used for agriculture in terms of its contribution to the SDP being only 10 per cent. The huge investments in infrastructure such as roads, sub-sidised water and power (one of the surplus states) are only benefitting industrial houses as anticipated by scholars long ago. Although the impact of the rapid growth in sectors like petrochemicals (26.26 per cent), pharmaceuticals and chemi-cals (21.33 per cent), and ship-breaking contribute more than half of the income of the state, it has resulted in increasing incidence of silicosis, respiratory diseases, etc. in the state. Hiraway Indira reports that the share of wages as a per cent of net value added declined by 3.5 per cent per year from 11.8 in 1998–2000 to 8.5 per cent in 2008. Another important devel-opment under the reform in Gujarat has been the increase in the value of "subsidies, incentives and favours to the corporate sector, with the result that not much revenue is left to redistrib-ute for the purpose of including the excluded."[24]

The change of guard in Delhi with Modi occupying the seat of power would bring change in the social relations as he claimed to be an OBC. Contrary to the expectations, the tensions between Muslims and Hindus, mostly OBCs, have been ampli-fied. Even beef eaters are not only marginalised but lynched to signify the hegemony of a section of the vegetarian dvijas during 2015–16. It is unimaginable to note that such barbarous acts are possible in the so-called capitalist economy. However, the Modi government has very good relations with the beef eating US and European investors. This dichotomous nature would never be explained by the libertarians as they did not bother about the social outcomes of their policy prescriptions.

Gujarat is being vaunted by scholars as a model state to be emulated by others as it has attracted the largest chunk of FDI and houses the top business houses and the high-status IIM-A. In this context, the issue of FDI initiated a debate on several related concerns and movements, some to strengthen it and quite a few to divert attention from its adverse impact. It is said that the liberalisation agenda is a package consisting of intellectual, civil society and political interest group activities to have control over properties of independent nations. It is believed that FDI would enhance the productive capacity and wealth of those nations whose resources were either unutilised or underutilised. Several scholars and activists are now referring to the advantages of FDI, particularly with reference to Wal-Mart in China. Yes, one can learn from the experiences of China, but one should know the history and the conditions under which the FDI operates there. Until 1982 there was no right to private property as the communists believed in Proudhon saying that 'all property is theft.' But Deng Xiaoping, in his reformation program, brought the 1982 Constitution with a provision for private property facilitating communes to own land.

China brought in an Act on private property in 2007. Yet, all land in urban areas is owned by the State and the foreign investor is not allowed to buy land. FDIs go to regions/ places that are identified by the State for their economic activities and not beyond. If it were in India, our experts would have created precedents (like SEZs) to make the courts/revenue officials pass orders to transfer titles (in the name of mutation) even in Adivasi areas to non-tribals. This is happening despite the abolition of Article 31 (private property) with the alleged help of Article 300-A, and invoking eminent domain. The implementation of the Right to Fair Compensation and Transparency in Land Acquisition, Rehabilitation and Resettlement Act, 2013 is still undergoing hurdles. In fact, the whole issue of private property is a very interesting subject that needs attention in the context not only of FDI but even issues of territorial and regional identities. No private firm or MNC in China is given property rights over land beyond 30 years and the CPC is the dominant player both in government and politics.

THE JUDICIARY AND THE CONSTITUTION

The Indian judiciary seems to have acquired the character of Brahma, the Almighty, who is *Swayambhu* (creates himself) and has developed a notoriety that abrogates accountability to anyone under the sun. The judiciary is given the mandate that the law laid down by the apex court is binding on all. Therefore, it has utmost responsibility to do justice to the people of India. However, legal experts and social scientists do generally attribute the current crisis in higher education, reservation of jobs, concentration of wealth in a few hands, particularly, to judicial orders that are 'unfair' not only to the profession but even to the Constitutional morality. Regrettably, some of the judgements in social litigation have not bothered to look at these provisions. On the contrary, some of the orders have created opportunities to expand the privatisation of higher education in the name of equity and without asking the state how much of the GDP is spent on education.[25] During the last two decades, millions of poor among the upper castes and SC, ST and BCs have been deprived of higher education, as a result opportunities in emerging sectors of the new economy.

India is considered as one of the leading democracies with a written Constitution and a stable government. It is reported that some chief ministers, at the January 2015 meeting in Delhi on the proposed National Counter Terrorism Centre (NCTC), wanted the Constitution to be reviewed to accommodate perhaps their grievances in a federal set-up. Similarly, the Supreme Court, in its fresh order on reservations in promotion, has made the political class appeal to the prime minister to amend Article 16(4), maybe for the third time in a decade. These developments make us sad due to the exiguous respect paid to the Constitution by those who are supposed to revere and uphold its values.

The constitutional history of India indicates how we evolved and adopted it in November 1949 in the Constituent Assembly. The federal structure of the country was already in place in the 1935 Act. The chairman of the drafting committee,

B. R. Ambedkar, was the only person who was eminently qualified at that time to take a view on the federal structure as he had already done his PhD on 'federal finance' under an eminent economist in the USA in 1918. Even B. N. Rao, adviser, was not an economist in the sense of B. R. Ambedkar in dealing with not only economic issues in a federal set-up but even the structural and ideological concerns. Ambedkar used to refer to India in all his writings as the United States of India, indicating the federal nature of the country. In this connection, one may find a few disconnects here and there in the federal composition that may not call for a review. The chief ministers' conference, NDC meeting, etc. are forums where such issues can be sorted out if a hard-headed home minister is considered as an issue, but not a review of the Constitution.

The Constitution is generally defined as a 'framework of political society organised through and by law, in which law has established permanent institutions with recognised functions and definite rights'. The apex court has, in the past, delineated the basic structure of the Constitution. Though legal luminaries and political executives like Shivashankar have expressed very serious reservations on such judgements due to the tilt given to the Mathadipathis and the elite, the fact remains, however, that we are now following the arrangement. In fact, the partial view given to the structure without considering the social vision of the Constitution and the Preamble has been a subject of academic discussion for quite some time. It is in this context that the history of the social clauses put in the Constitution need to be viewed.

The country would not have emerged as the so-called nation on 1 January 1950 without certain agreements and reservations in the framing of the Constitution. It is relevant to refer to the agreement reached between B. R. Ambedkar and Gandhiji in 1932 and the first amendment to the Constitution under Article 15(4) in 1951 due to the agitations in the South for caste-based reservations. The guarantees given to the minorities under Articles 29 and 30 can also be considered as serious concerns for the nation. They were very fundamental for a nascent nation that was emerging with several dichotomies in its social and political life. We should consider these provisions as a 'social contract' between the minorities (the vulnerable) and the majority or the ruling classes. If these agreements were not respected, the ideal of a unified nation would collapse at any time.

The visionary judges of the apex court, in the formative years of independence, showed great insight into the Constitution with their wide experience, learning and maturity in delivering judgements dispassionately keeping in view the country's future. It is difficult to find such a class of people now due to the quality of legal education, training and recruitment. Judges are appointed to the High Courts from anyone who has "for at least 10 years been an advocate of a High Court or of two or more such courts in succession", or "a judicial officer for ten years" [Article 217(20)]. According to one estimate, 67 per cent of judges come from the category of advocates. It appears some of them occupy chairs in the apex court with limited exposure. Otherwise, how do we explain the disarray in social jurisprudence in the country, particularly in relation to caste-based reservations and privatisation?

Apart from judicial orders that are a fraud on the constitutional morality, the liberalisation and privatisation of the economy have deprived the reserved communities from entering the organised sectors as they are not taken in the private sector. The private sector is mostly managed by the dvija castes who have a sufficient number of people to manage and can afford to deny jobs to others in the pretext of merit and efficiency. The higher courts are not free from caste biases even among the brother judges who come from lower castes, as the February 2016 incidence of Justice Karnan case signifies. The Constitution under Article 312(1) speaks about the All India Judicial Service and it is alleged by lawyers for social justice that it was never implemented as it would create opportunities for the reserved sections to enter higher judiciary. The elite judiciary is so powerful that while other constitutional functionaries are prohibited from taking up post-retirement jobs, they are always on post-retirement assignment through the process of creating positions while processing bills, superseding of other constitutional bodies, does not augur well for the judiciary. This would entice the political class to resort to amendments to the Constitution to show their authority as in China where the judiciary is made subordinate to the ruling party.

CORRUPTION AND THE CIVIL SERVICE

The civil service system in India is linked with the state power and political process as the Indian bureaucracy from the time of Chanakya is considered as a permanent structure. The class of civil servants, irrespective of their caste background, is found to be elitist.[26] There is a close nexus between the politician and the executive in formulating and executing policies that are mutually beneficial. The notoriety of the politician, contractor and bureaucrat combine leading to several scams in recent years is well known.[27] In this context, the tainted Indian Administrative Service (IAS) couple, the Joshis, in Bhopal were asked to pay ₹1.35 billion as tax. The IT department appraised the value of unaccounted property of the couple at around ₹4 billion. However, Anna's team against corruption did not quote the incident (first reported in 2010) in their campaign against corruption, but concentrated on the whole bureaucracy, particularly the lower rung, articulated public anger. The Parliament debate on the Lokpal Bill ab initio unresolved to conclude the shape of the act.[28] The shrewd politicians had the last laugh.

Public discourse on corruption began against the public servant. We must congratulate the Anna team for capturing public attention on this malicious evil in our contemporary social life. The concept of the public servant includes the political executive and now they are misplaced altogether. Only the civil servant who runs the system is left as the scapegoat of the discourse on corruption. It is not always true to say that the whole system is corrupt. Let us assume that there are Joshis in every state cadre and in all categories, including the central services. The IAS cadre has a strength of around 5,000 and the Indian Police Service (IPS) force is about the same number. Group-A services in the Central government do constitute a fewer in count in each department. The all-India service officers are well organised, like our Varna system, compared to other services. If we assume that the Joshis are everywhere, what is their proportion? For instance, in the united Andhra Pradesh cadre of around 700, hardly 20 officers could fall under this category which does not comprise even three per cent of the total. We do not consider a hundred all-India service officers are found corrupt through the ACB or CBI net in the state to make it above 10 per cent of the total strength. A technical report of the CVC on the IAS cadre (India) for 1998–2000 has found that there were 133 cases of discipline reported, of which only 10.53 per cent were related to disproportionate assets or corruption. The number may be a little higher for IPS and other services. This is not as alarming as it is made out to be. Vilification of the civil servant through public debates would demoralise the cadre to carry forward important development and welfare schemes of the government. It is the initiative of the civil servant through his/her informed and experienced nuances that a policy is formulated. When the formulated policy is discussed with the political bosses, it finally gets the nod as per the business rules of the government. Then it becomes an official policy. If the civil servant develops cold feet or is imprudent in his/her advice, the system will collapse.

We may now look at the magnitude of the damage done to the system and the country by some of those who were not corrupt but were deviant and arrogant compared to those who have acquired assets disproportionate to their known income. It is strange that the debate on public servants never highlights the sacrifices and the contributions made by dedicated men and women, both in the political executive and in the civil service. It was the committed public servant and his vision for an equitable and just society as per the constitutional mandate that helped the country develop during the first few decades after Independence. The country became attractive even with the Hindu rate of growth for foreign investors due to the infrastructure, human and natural resources developed by these great public servants. At the same time, there were reports of committees and commissions to indicate how public resources were used and concentrated in the hands of a few business houses with the connivance of some motivated public servants. In the 1990s, the economy was made to respond to the needs of the industry, private investments and the greed to accumulate so as to create more wealth and the public servant was asked to facilitate this process.

The crisis today is largely due to the mismatch between the nature of the job and the moral code of conduct of the civil servant. Those who entered the service around the 1980s were sent to Western universities, mostly business schools and or international funding agencies, to acquire skills to manage the economy rather than to govern the people. The role of the administrator, thus, became that of a facilitator rather than a policy-maker or decision-maker. It created ethical dilemmas and dichotomies in the system. The developed West was very clear about their so-called materialistic outlook and the conventions of public behaviour. In fact, the OECD has formulated 12 principles for managing ethics in public service. One of the important principles is that there should be clear rules defining ethical standards to guide the behaviour of public servants dealing with the private sector. It also emphasises transparency and open scrutiny for decision-making processes in the government. We are aware that some of our public servants who are feudal in their outlook and demeanour would never allow such democratic practices to be implemented or followed in our public life.

Another dichotomy in our superior idealist culture is that not everything is accessible to everyone. There are certain things that are accessible to some and some are kept secret (once Vedic knowledge). This has created dual standards and values. The honest young civil servant is baffled and those who are perfidious tend to survive and outshine others to occupy important positions. As of now, there appears to be no transparent system in the state(s) to assign positions based on integrity and performance. Ethical values, as distinguished from religious morals and practices, have evolved over a period of time as culture in a pluralistic country like ours. But, several contradictions and dichotomies in the public behaviour of our leaders tend to influence the work ethics of civil servants. Some of them have evolved their own standards in the absence of code of ethics (not conduct rules) in the changed circumstances. For instance, the constitutional morality of working for a secular, socialist and democratic republic could prick the conscience of some civil servants when they asked to make a policy to facilitate private sector expansion. To resolve some of the dichotomies, the second Administrative Reforms Commission under the chairmanship of Veerappa Moily in 2010 has given a report on ethics in the public service.

The Prevention of Corruption Act 1988 contains 31 clauses and four chapters to deal with corruption cases. It has defined a public servant under Clause 2C (1) very widely to cover, "[A]ny person in the service or pay of government or remuneration by the government by fees or compensation for the purpose of any public duty." It also includes NGOs that receive aid from the government. In order to operationalise the act, the CVC was created through an act in 2003. The definition of corruption under the CVC is different from the World Bank concept of using public office for private gains. If one looks at the CVC website and the manuals laboriously prepared for its effective functioning, the huge bureaucratic structure and the number of cases registered, it would clearly indicate the assurance of the government on corruption. It is not even one decade old in its operation to boast of results. In addition to the provisions of the act, there are stringent service rules specially prepared for civil servants and all-India service officers. Hundreds of officers, including ambassadors, have lost their jobs due to misconduct or misdemeanour.

The highest constitutional authority to advise the president on the discipline of government servants is the Union Public Service Commission and its decisions are respected by the apex court. Cases against hundreds of delinquent officers are pending in courts. Corruption has been rampant in recent years because of the fact that the so-called 'license permit raj' has been replaced by the 'contract and tender raj'. It is naive to say that corruption is prevalent only among the bureaucracy while the corporates use both the political class and the executive to loot and amass wealth at the cost of the poor and the future as revealed in cases like Coalgate, Davis, etc.

THE SUCCESSFUL ENTRY OF POLITICAL MARKETING IN INDIA

Political marketing as a sub-discipline of political management in some Western universities became an academic success after globalisation and the expansion of market democracy. It looks that the subject has not yet attracted mainstream academic disciplines such as political science, political economy and public policy in India. The recent amazing landslide of the BJP, particularly through its Prime Minister (PM) designee, is a marker to be noted by every social scientist. Though there is a small study on the political marketing of BJP in the Delhi elections, it has not attracted the attention of many. The role of the media, internet, technology, consultants, etc., is very important in understanding the concept of political marketing. Applying the subject of commercial marketing here, scholars such as Kotler and Levy, Mac Ginnis and others in the 1960s and 1970s have published extensively on political marketing. It is now a thriving business for consulting firm in the USA. It is noted that the services of famous political marketing consultants, such as James Carville who was the strategist for Bill Clinton in 1992, Karl Rover for George W. Bush in 2000, Philip Goulder for Tony Blair in the UK, and Mark Penn for Hillary Clinton in 2007, were accessed to win elections mostly in the market democracies. *Business Today* in its October 2013 issue informed us that our PM designee Narendra Bhai Modi had employed advertising firms such as McCann World, Ogilvy & Mather, etc. to seize power in Delhi while the Congress Party had relied on some bureaucrats who had degrees in management and the AAP had psephologists, etc.[29] The left is averse to the idea of market, as devastated in 2014. In other words, it is now a full-scale service activity that can be hired by political parties.

The market is understood as a place where buyers and sellers meet, not necessarily in physical setup to transact, but also through e-marketing. "Political marketing is about political organisations (such as political parties), adapting techniques (such as market research and product design) and concepts (such as the desire to satisfy voter demands), originally used in the business world to help them achieve their goals (such as win in elections)." Ever since Anthony Downs published his famous book, *Economic Theory of Democracy*,[30] that stimulated James Buchanan, Gordon Tullok, George Stigler, Jagadish Bhagwati and others who in turn attacked the institution of the state and made it vulnerable, the market entered all human activities. India is credited as one of the developing countries which have followed the model of growth prescribed by funding agencies. Though some of our commentators acclaim our leaders and policy-makers for this, it is not their ingenuity that facilitated the turnaround of the economy, but meekly following the model set by them. Now, it is anticipated that with the involvement of the market in the political games, we may also attain the cultural status of the West soon. At the same time, it is possible to make them imitate some of our institutions so that we can proudly say later that we are parallel in our structures and tastes. This is a win-win situation that pleases most of our leaders in Delhi, Hyderabad, etc. and their corporate clients.

Political marketing requires some basic things such as the product, brand image, political consumers, communication, delivery, etc. Among these fundamentals, product design is very important. In order to get to the brass tacks, analysts are supposed to get the feel for market demands by talking to party members, holding focus group discussions, opinion polls, segmentation of voters/consumers, views of the public, etc. to design the product. Product design and development based on market intelligence is crucial here. It is said that Reagan made his product design using the slogan 'peace and economy', Bush on 'no tax rises', Clinton on 'change and economy' Obama on 'yes, we can', etc. We have seen Narendra Modi using the language in several campaigns including the one in the L. B. Stadium, Hyderabad in 2014. After the product is designed with slogans such as 'development and change', 'Congress hatao', etc., branding becomes vital. Branding is about how the political organisation or individual is perceived overall. If the organisation is found to be redundant, it is better to rely on an individual and focus all resources for making him/her the brand equity. Brands are essential in the electronic age to create a feeling of identity, help consumers/voters know about the party and its policies and distinguish the brand from the brand of a competing party. Above all, it is possible to examine the life cycle of the product and make changes when better products dominate the market. In the recent elections of 2014, NaMo was found to be a robust brand that captured the market compared to others. We have seen the media honchos using these terms in their election coverage.

It is noted in the studies that there are two categories of parties, the sales-oriented party (SOP) and the market-oriented party (MOP). The former relies on the method of persuasion to change the mindset of voters while the latter responds to the views and demands of the voters. However, both depend on market strategies of communicating with the voter through brand images. The 4Ps of product (campaign platform), push marketing (grass roots efforts), pull marketing (mass media) and polling (research) are used to communicate with the voter by using all means of communication. We have seen the use of not only the internet, electronic screens, etc., but also massive live in programmes using TV channels, print media, etc. The glamour of film stars as in the case of consumer products has been extensively used to improve the brand image of parties who may be co-opted into the party later. The technique is, of course, very expensive involving expert teams from abroad. In a way, it is good that elections and political parties are slowly moving into a regime that makes all this process standardised so that it can be monitored or regulated from any part of the world.

Branding of political leaders and the product image of a party need investments to attract the young, smart phone wielding, web surfed and TV addicts. But, what is missing in the whole exercise is the message that the leader may want to convey, with the manifesto and the response of the voter seems to be lost forever and may not be appropriate for a country like India.

It appears that the election results of Bihar are turning out to be the end of an experiment in India. But, the outpouring of explanations by political analysts for the victory of the *mahagathbandhan* by attributing it to a marketing expert who has earlier worked with the Modi team appears to be farfetched. The Bihar results have amply demonstrated that people value their caste and communal loyalties more than temporary emotions if an occasion of their devastation is affectively explained, as was ensured by Lalu Prasad, a Lohiate.

Thus, the political process in India though appears to be identical with that of other market economies like the USA, it has developed its own attributes like the oligarchy of castes and religious fundamentalism using technology to capture the imagination of the middle classes who have of late come of age in big numbers. It is possible to combine market strategies to capture her/him both as a customer and as a voter. This important change in the political process in the new era needs to be studied seriously to capture the implications for a pluralistic society.

NOTES AND REFERENCES

1. www.electionatlas.org/results (accessed on 1 July 2013).
2. www. idea.int/ve/countryview (accessed in July 2013).
3. Francine Frankel, *India's Political Economy 1947–2004* (New Delhi: Oxford University Press, 2005).
4. Pranab Bardhan, *Political Economy of Development in India* (New Delhi: Oxford University Press, 1999).
5. Atul Kohli, *Democracy and Development in India* (New Delhi: Oxford University Press 2009).
6. James Buchanan and others, *The Limits of Liberty* (Chicago: University of Chicago, 1975); *The Calculus of Consent* (Ann Arbor: University of Michigan, 1962).
7. A. Sen, www.nobelprize.org/nobel-prizes economic-sciences (accessed on 1 November 2013).
8. Ibid.
9. Anna Hazare a civil society activist who initiated a movement against corruption with the support of some NGOs and others. The corporate media created euphoria on the movement and individuals for about a year and later kept silent once their hidden agenda pushed through.
10. Baba Ramdev is a yoga guru. He developed some interesting business models that made him a billionaire overnight.
11. J. Schumpeter, *Capitalism Socialism and Democracy* (New York: Allen and Unwin, 1976).
12. Kanshiram was the founder of BSP and Mulayam Singh Yadav was of SP. The former comes from a Dalit background and the latter an OBC. Both of them have joined in UP to topple the upper caste government and later fell apart in a short period.
13. S. A. Iyer is editor and columnist of the *Economic Times*.
14. See, *Dr Babasaheb Ambedkar Writings and Speeches* (New Delhi: Dr Ambedkar Foundation, 2010), Vol. 17, pp. 464–69.
15. Chundur is close to Amaravati, new capital of Andhra see *The Times of India*, 19 September 2015 mentioned about Bhumi pooja at Amaravati.
16. Romila Thapar, *Early India* (Delhi: Penguin, 2002), p. xxix.
17. Kesavanada Bharathi vs state of Kerala wp 135/1970 Supreme Court of India.
18. *The Hindu*, "Muslims Poorest among Religious Groups," 20 August 2013.
19. Sekhar Bandopadhyaya, *Caste, Culture and Hegemony* (New Delhi: SAGE Publications, 2004).
20. Jogendranath Mandal, like B. R. Ambedkar of India, was the chairman of the drafting committee of the Constitution of Pakistan. Being a Dalit, Mandal secured reservations for Pakistan Dalits.
21. Radhanath Das was as Dalit leader of the United Bengal.

22. Jogendranath Mandal, Chosen by Jinnah Banished by Bureaucracy, *Dawn*, daily, 4 November 2015.

23. K. B. Krishna, *KB Krishna Selected Writings*. Birth centenary celebrations committee (Guntur: Nagarjuna University, 2007).

24. Hirway Indira, Amita Shah and Ghanshyam Shah, ed., *Growth or Development: Which Way Is Gujarat going?* (New Delhi: Oxford University Press, 2014).

25. T. M. Pai Foundation and others VS State of Karnataka, in S C 377, 11 August, 1995 Supreme Court of India.

26. K. S. Chalam, ed., *Governance in South Asia: State of the Civil Services* (New Delhi: SAGE publications, 2014).

27. Ibid.

28. The Lok Pal Bill is a federal government initiative to establish an Ombudsman to supervise and discipline the corrupt public servants. There is already CVC a statutory body and UPSC a constitutional authority with a mandate to impose penalties on the basis of due process of law. Anna Hazare with superficial knowledge about the system under the influence of some NGOs and motivated individuals alleged to have misled the people. The movement lost its popularity once the media deflected him and some others floating a political party.

29. *Business Today*, "A Namo Smartphone, Namo Apps and Games Are Boosting BJP Prime Ministerial Candidate's Campaign," 27 October 2013 and a report in *Livemint*, 14 October 2014.

30. Anthony Downs, *Economic Theory of Democracy* (New York: Harper and Row, 1957).

7

Caste Prejudices and Human Dignity

Human dignity as a notion appears to have been prevalent in all speculative philosophies of the human civilisation. Yet, there could be deviations from the basic idea of "all men are born free and equal in dignity," from country to country, depending on physical conditions and metaphysical expositions. Thomas Paine's remarkable book, *Rights of Man*,[1] denounced by his contemporary Edmond Burke's eloquent justification for inequity among humans, was a great leap forward in human social evolution. The French Revolution, the American War of Independence and subsequent developments further strengthened the longing for equity and justice grounded in the principle of common elements of existential conditions of man. Marxism and humanism, as distinct from capitalism and hedonism based on self-interest and development, respectively, have provided us with theories as to how we can attain harmony with nature and society. Different schools of thought in India have elucidated the need as well as methods for attaining liberation from the self and social bondages. Though there have been materialistic and humanistic philosophies prevailing in India, giving primacy to the existence of the human being rather than a supernatural force from the time of the Lokayatas in the ancient period and elaborated by D. P. Chattopadhyay, M. N. Ray, Rahul Sankrutyayan,

Amartya Sen and several others, their views, however, were marginalised and suppressed in mainstream discourse. The conflict between the materialistic and idealist views of life and between alien and indigenous schools of thought is continued unabated, spilling over to contemporary disputes and occasional violence.

The idea of human dignity was articulated by social groups who have been marginalised and excluded from the mainstream development process in India. The intensity of the struggle for dignity has been more pronounced in the recent past due to global support for both the ideologies noted above. Globalisation and the expansion of capitalist development relying on efficiency, merit and 'karma' have strengthened the argument that men are intrinsically and metaphysically unequal and they are destined to be so. On the other hand, the popularisation of democracy and human rights as a part of the paradigm of dignity has secured the struggles of the oppressed and the marginalised. The two extremes of the contemporary situation in the world, particularly in the political economy of India, are creating social tensions. It is irony that those who have been advocating for a special identity for the country have joined hands with the global powers that uphold the principle of inequity (social and economic) as a natural process to espouse efficiency. This serious contradiction in our social life is being stifled by diverting the energies of the oppressed to mystical and devotional pursuits by those who oppose the victim's intrinsic parity with others. This is possible in India where there is a structured and permanent institution of the caste system that sustains this contradiction due to the fact that there is a perpetual collective that works for their own self, interestingly with the resources of the deprived.

The situation can be interrogated within the framework of human dignity and rights. Robert Adorno in one of his papers on bioethics has brought out the contradictory nature of the reductionism of a person as an ensemble of chemical elements under the biotechnological power, over human being as a natural person.[2] Human beings, by birth, possess a unique and unconditional value that is intrinsic and inviolable. It means that dignity is the same for all humans. "Because it depends on the being of the person, and not on his behaviour, it cannot be gained or lost; it does not allow for any degrees."[3] Bringing the theoretical difficulties in establishing human dignity under the genetic diversity within the UNESCO 1997 Universal Declaration of the Human Genome and Human Rights, Adorno underlined the fundamental unity of all members of the human family. The notion of dignity is inclusive and does not privilege humans over other species. "Each person deserves to be admired and wondered at with a new freshness" by employing the 'eyes of heart' and not the 'eyes of flesh.'[4]

The notion of dignity based on the intrinsic worth of a person as member of humanity is antithetical to some schools of thought that evaluate individuals on the basis of their behaviour or *gunakarma*. The idea of dividing humans on some pretext or the other is itself a negation of the universal value of human dignity. Though the Constitution of India, being a supreme document prepared by the founding fathers after the Universal Declaration of Human Rights in 1945, did recognise dignity and rights, however, we need to walk a long distance to reach the goal due to the bogey of the past. Articles 14 and 15 of the Indian Constitution are cited time and again by the judiciary and others to deny dignity to members of society who are socially, educationally and economically deprived and excluded, rather creatively and innovatively using the provisions to expand dignity. It is possible to attain an enlightened status if our judiciary, policy-makers and social leaders use 'eyes of heart.' We are trying to look at the efforts of our nation in providing what kind of dignity or discrimination to our own people who are termed as Adivasis, Dalits and OBCs in the following pages.

Human development as the composite index of education, health and income is an important advance in economic reasoning. The HDI has replaced the GDP as an indicator of the development of a nation or even a group. Keeping the social division of the Indian population, the Planning Commission commissioned a human development report for India in 2007 and provided data by the socio-economic background of the population. Several state governments have also published reports on the lines of the India-HDR. However, the first attempt to estimate the human development by caste category and the positive contribution of caste-based reservations to human development was attempted by K. S. Chalam.[5] In other words, scholars and government agencies have recognised the caste element in the process of human development. But, there seem to be very few attempts by the state as an agency to reduce the inequalities and discriminatory practices in the provisioning of public education and health particularly after 1990. The *Human Development Report 2013* of the UNDP was released with HDI ranks of different countries. The theme of the 2013 HD report is "human progress in a diverse world," which appears to have a covetous tone towards the rise of the South or developing countries. We are aware that the HDI is popularly used now in all debates to indicate the development of a country and not the GDP, because the HDI gives a better understanding of human progress achieved in a country than mere income expressed as the GDP. The HDI is an aggregate estimate of three indicators, namely life expectancy, educational attainment and income of a country during a year. The UNDP has been publishing the annual HD reports from 1990, incorporating new and innovative ideas in each report.

The Indian subcontinent takes pride in the intellectual inputs contributed by Pakistani and Indian scholars Mahbub Ul Haq and Amartya Sen for the popularisation of the concept Human Development, which is universally accepted now as an annual record made available by the UNDP. The subject matter based on human capital theory in the West later seemed to have been twisted in the hands of one group of scholars and Nobel laureates (like Schultz, Buchanan, Becker and others) who considered education as private investment in man. The premise on which the theory of human capital developed has enabled World Bank scholars to reduce education, particularly higher education, to that of private investment and made countries like India play a nominal role in public provisioning. One of the reasons for the present crisis in higher education seems to be the studies that led to this plunge. Yet, it has also enabled scholars like Haq, Sen and others to take it to a different level and produced a civilised concept called 'human development.' The 2013 HDI report makes an important statement that, "[N]o country for which data was available had lower HDI value in 2012 than in 2000."[6] It adds that there is convergence of HDI values across the countries in the world. The issue here is whether it has enhanced the dignity of human beings.

HUMAN DEVELOPMENT AND DIGNITY

A key message of the 2012 HDI report is that economic growth alone does not automatically translate into progress in human development. Therefore, it is necessary to concentrate on four important issues, namely enhancing equality, including the gender dimension; enabling greater voice and publicity of citizens, including the youth; and managing demographic change. The report demonstrates using data and regression analysis to show how inequalities hold back human development in many countries. While discussing individual countries, it is pointed out that, "India's performance in accelerating HD, however, is less impressive than its growth performance."[7] Indeed, Bangladesh is doing well at 1.83 per cent during 1990–2000 compared to India's rate of growth of 1.23 in HDI during the same period. The report presents HDI ranks for different countries over a period of three decades 1980–2010. India is ranked 136 in 2012, and the rank has been lingering around 131–136 during 1990–2012, during the above period. Among the BRICS nations, India is the only country that is not even close to any one of them: Brazil, 85; Russia, 55; China, 101; and South Africa, 121. The HDI value of India was 0.345 in 1980, which increased to 0.410 in 1990 to 0.507 in 2000 and stands at 0.554 in 2012. If the ranks are adjusted for inequalities, the value of the HDI comes to 0.392, a loss of 29 per cent during the above period.

What it is like to be a human being is given in Box 1.3 of the HD report referring to dimensions of freedom, well-being and deprivations along with the classic paper by philosopher Nagel Thomas on 'the experience of being a bat.' But, the authors have failed to grapple with philosophical nuances of the essence of man in the context of freedom from fear as an important human value. It is here that the authors of the report mentioned about human emancipation from human conditions, like Auschwitz (Poland), the place where millions of Jews were butchered during the Second World War. Are there similar or broadly related issues, maybe less malicious practices, perpetuated even in the contemporary world or in India?

Human dignity seems to have something to do with the essence of man. It is farfetched to discuss the metaphysical elucidations of Emanuel Kant or Indian sages Adi Sankara or Ramanuja here to convey that spirit is outside mind and body to care for mundane human dignity. Is it consciousness or higher feelings beyond the self that comprise the essence of man? Alternatively, is it a sense of deduction of the feeling that we are all basically same humans? The West has tried to address this question and come up with the idea of human dignity. In fact, the Frankfurt school scholars such as W. T. Adorno, Horkheimer and others have published volumes on this question. But the mundane sciences such as biomedical and human genome project have brought out future issues like how the human species is endangered, which is a threat to human dignity. However, the human genome project has clarified that the human DNA is 99 per cent common with chimpanzees and only less than 1 per cent of its genetic information is typical. Therefore, it is the intrinsic worth of human beings, which is inalienable, irrespective of age, sex, religion, colour, social group, caste, nation, etc. that seems to be identical everywhere. Then, why is it that there are more poor people in India than in China, Brazil, Cuba or Albania? Are social institutions and practices responsible for this?

As part of the human dignity paradigm, the HDRs have introduced a concept called the Gender Empowerment Measure (GEM) in 1995 to identify how women are discriminated against. Interestingly, it has never occurred to our scholars to use a similar methodology to produce a caste-related development index (CDI). It is noticed that a research paper (first of its kind, presented in ISEC, Bangalore, and published in ICSSR journal in 1999 and also in a book in 2000), highlighting the unique contribution of the reform movements in the South for gender equality, education and social mobility, etc., was totally ignored in a government-sponsored study report of a South Indian State in 2007 indicating either deep prejudices or fear of plagiarism. Therefore, human dignity could become an important measure of human advancements in the future, if the HDIs are expected to converge in a diverse world. India, being a country with several contradictions, should learn from others and excel in ensuring dignity and fairness.

The Indian Constitution has recognised the existence of the SCs, STs and socially and educationally backward classes. The above categories constitute more than 50 per cent of the population. The progress record in providing dignity and human development to these excluded sections over six decades of planned development is analysed below.

Adivasis as Sub-humans

The Adivasi or tribal problem is unique to India as we have the world's largest concentration of tribal population at 8.2 per cent of the Indian population in 2011. The concept of a tribe, like that of a caste, is a colonial construct. Interestingly, anthropology as an academic discipline was developed by the colonial rulers to study the populations in India which they considered were different from theirs.[8] It was British civil servants such as H. H. Risley (1891), J. H. Hutton (1963), Edgar Thurston (1901) and others who developed concepts to study the peculiar characteristics of the Indian population. In fact, they were studying the populations that were different in colour, languages, belief systems, etc. to explain to their country men in their own notions that were alien to them. They developed the concept like a tribe to describe populations that were not intelligible to them, but never used the category for describing any of the English or European populations that were more backward and scattered than any of our so-called tribal populations (17th century). That is why some of the Indian sociologists like Deepankar Gupta call the caste and tribe as census categories and have developed their own theories to denounce that caste is not race. This dichotomy of Western and Indian notions in our intellectual tradition has created problems in the international forums to deny the fact that India had indigenous populations. The government has not accepted the concept of indigenous to be given even to tribals, the Dalits or the so-called native Indians particularly at the World Conference Against Racism held in Durban in 2002. This attitude has led to several ideological overtones and political manifestations in our public discourse on caste.

The notion of a tribe can be traced to the Roman civilisation and seems to have been derived from the Latin word *tribus* to mean those who were members of a big family with common occupation, interests and habits. But, the description has neither a derogatory meaning nor any inferior ascription as was ascribed for the natives by the Anglo-Saxon colonialists. The classification of populations as tribal, non-tribal or civilised, un-civilised and other typologies seems to have been part of an expansionist imperial or colonial mindset found throughout history. It is strange to find that the idiom has remained the same even during the so-called enlightenment period. It was further strengthened and codified with the advent of missionary activities in the ruled nations. In this context, we may refer to the studies of Lewis Morgan[9] who has written extensively on 'Iroquois,' the Native American people and published, *Ancient Society*. It is in this work that Morgan has divided the process of development of human society in to different stages such as savage, barbarian, etc., which were also taken as the basis by Marx and Engels[10] to formulate their mode of production theories. Though Morgan has used the Iroquois and Athenian societies for the formulation of the linear development model of society, Marx took the initiative to extend it to the whole world and Engels completed it to become a universal dictum. Even Indian scholars like D. D. Kosambi[11] followed this model to examine the unique Indian society. This may be one of the reasons for the limited light thrown on the native Indians who, unlike the Iroquois, had kingdoms of their own, state apparatus and extensive cultures as native rulers or tribal janapadas and other institutions in the past and also in the present. However, it was never considered by scholars as unique due to the colonial mindset who had adopted the European models to understand a non-European society like India. The social science discourse of some of the Indian scholars seemed to be an extension of the European project and there were very few attempts to understand our people with models based on our conditions. Therefore, the colonial concepts, ideas and theories were repeated even after independence in areas that needed unique approaches to enhance our understanding of our economy and society. It has been pointed by Andre Beteille, the well-known social anthropologist that,

> [T]ribal society faces problem in the context of Indian society. There is first of all the problem of discriminating among related and overlapping modes of tribal organization. There is also problem of drawing clear lines of demarcation between tribal and non-tribal society. In India the encounters between tribe and civilization have taken place under historical conditions of a radically different sort. The co-existence of tribe and civilization and their mutual interaction, go back to the beginnings of recorded history and earlier. Tribes have existed at the margins of Hindu civilization from time immemorial and these margins have always been vague, uncertain and fluctuating. Hindu civilization acknowledged the distinction between tribe and caste as the distinction between two kinds of communities, *jana* and *jati*, one confined to the isolation of hills and forests and the other settled in villages and towns with a more elaborate division of labour. The transformation of tribes into castes has been documented by a large number of anthropologists and historians.[12]

Thus, the perplexity among anthropologists and social scientists in their definition and description of tribes in India was anticipated. Unfortunately, the hegemony of imperial academic approach to social issues has continued and the colonial hang-up lingers on some of the social scientists in the neo-colonial globalisation agenda.

The situation in the USA is not different. But, the colonial rulers there accepted that they were migrants and settlers in a region inhabited by the Native Americans. The term Native American is defined as those who were born in America as distinguished from those who migrated there. They have also been using the term indigenous to denote those who inhabit a geographical region with earliest known historical connections to the region. In India, some discussion was carried by creative writers like Mahasweta Devi (late popular Bengali writer) about the indigenous people of India. She calls all the so-called tribal populations of India as indigenous and, therefore, can be called as Adivasis. Some of the writers who have very intimate knowledge about the tribal and local people, unlike several of our present generation of scholars and policy-makers, have found many appropriations made by the mainstream society. The elephant totem Ganesha, Shiva, deities, tantric practices, herbal medicines, art forms, etc. were adopted and used in mainstream religious practices and, over a period of time, claimed as our own.[13] Later, incursions into their belief systems began with mainstream Hinduism and cunningly the local practices were termed as primitive, animist, little culture, etc. It is noted by few scholars that the original Indian and alien Mediterranean denominations were forced to unify indigenous practices to deny their original native claim that they were a distinguished category of India.[14] This is different from the USA and other regions where there were attempts to assimilate the natives, but they revolted and repudiated the settlers/aliens. The assimilation process in India seems to be cunning and subtle to deny the claim that there is anything unique (once the core is appropriated) in the native culture. The devastation has gone to such an extent that the native Indians today do not have anything that is of their own. It appears that the process can be compared with that of a colonial plunder. It is not only internal colonisation but also destruction of the identity of the unique categories who are the original people of this country. In the USA there are still 560 federally recognised tribal autonomous regions, but in India we have not been able to decide the indigenous character of our tribal populations though Article 244 of the Constitution speaks about their autonomy. It may be because 56 per cent of the total mineral wealth of the country is in the forest area where 71 per cent of the inhabitants are Adivasis. The strategy of TSP and the creation of ITDA seem to have failed to alleviate the tribal from exploitation and neglect.

The problems of land settlement started in India when land was by and large commonly held by the communities till the British brought in the Permanent Settlement in 1793. It was further strengthened with the Land Acquisition Act 1894 with the draconian 'eminent domain' clause to appropriate community properties. It is estimated that around 20 million people, mostly tribals, were displaced using the above laws by 2000.[15] Now the government has brought the Forest Rights Act 2006 and is in the process of implementing it to confer titles on the Adivasis and to permit them to use minor forest produce, etc. This is very interesting as the process is typical in its content, as the titles are given to those who have been the owners of the land and the protectors of the forests for ages and so they are the legitimate claimants of major and minor produce. However, it is imperative that the belief systems and knowledge practices of the Adivasis are to be recognised as unique and significant and their legitimate access to the resources should be conceded first, as it gives them the moral strength that they are the real inheritors of the wealth of the country. It is a known fact that the concept of private property originated as a colonial construct, particularly in relation to land holdings with the advent of the Permanent Settlement as noted above. Land was commonly held by the communities and there were different types of holdings in different regions of the country before the British introduced different laws to transfer lands from the original inhabitants to their cronies. It is weird to notice that the tribals, Dalits and other marginalised and powerless social groups in the country have been deposed out of their lands and habitations under the Land Acquisition Act 1884 in the name of development for the last 120 years and a new act was enacted only in 2013. Despite all these protections and Constitutional guarantees under Articles 16(4A), 244 and 342, and the 5th and 6th Schedules, etc., as noted above, more number of Adivasis and Dalits are displaced in India in the name of development than in any other civilised nation during the 20th century.

There are 84 million Adivasis or tribals in India as per the 2011 census. They are spread among 635 tribal groups, speaking hundreds of languages and dialects. As the most ancient inhabitants of the land, they are the legitimate inheritors of the Harappa, Mahenjo-daro and other unidentified and undeciphered primeval civilisations. Some Western scholars and their followers in India have formalised that these civilisations are not historical and might be barbarian due to the fact that they did not have a written word to record their facts of history. They do not entertain questions regarding why only written words are considered as facts of history and not the recording of events in terms of alternative means of communication such as cave paintings, tablets, cuneiforms and other nonverbal communication techniques as developed by the ancient people before the development of language. It might have been a colonial ideology not to allow any credit of ancient civilisations to the native subjects as the colonialists' own history is hardly of a thousand years' old compared to the natives that they colonised and would appear to be ridiculous to teach history and culture to the natives.

It is established beyond doubt that the land and civilisation of India should have been acceded to the so-called tribals rather than eulogising the alien marauders. We have adopted a tribal policy from the time of Jawaharlal Nehru in the 1950s and the Tribal Sub Plan Strategy, 1973 as a part of planned development. We know the progress achieved by the Adivasis during the last six decades of planned development. The union minister for tribal affairs took a proactive stance during 2013–14 asking the governors of states to implement the Constitutional provisions relating to tribal areas. This unexpected position of the minister was considered by commentators as a very significant move since no one prior to him sitting in the chair had the guts and knowledge to use the provisions enshrined by the founding fathers of Republic of India.

The Adivasis are the most deprived and malnourished group with 43.8 per cent living below the official poverty line as per 2014 data. The literacy rate is as low as 2 per cent at the mandal/tehsil level in districts like Visakhapatnam. There are some tribal groups like the Savara (Sabari) who are present in several states. For instance, they are found in the Eastern Ghats spreading across Andhra Pradesh and Koraput and other districts of Odisha are ancient people who are going to be affected by mining in Visakhapatnam district. The group is also present in Sabarkantak in Gujarat which seems to be noteworthy as the rivers Sabarmati and Godavari as Goda plus Sabari are derivatives due to their presence there. It is in this context that the issues of licenses for mining to outsiders in the Eastern Ghats spread in tribal areas of Andhra Pradesh which is alleged to be one of the serious violations of Constitutional position. Apart from the environmental, social and cultural degradations that it might cause in one of the most beautiful and bio-diverse regions of the country, which the Telugu people are proud of, the economic dimensions have not been discussed so far.

We have forest coverage of 78.2 million hectares in the country, where 70 per cent of the tribals are living. Most of the mineral resources of the country are located in the tribal areas, including the Araku valley and Galikonda of Visakhapatnam in Andhra Pradesh where the proposed mining was planned and is being cancelled now after protracted struggles of tribals with the support of the Left. Given the socio-economic status of the Adivasis remaining the same, and the fragile environment that would affect not only the Adivasi inhabitants but the people of the most backward districts of Vizianagaram and Visakhaptnam, the decision of the ministry to cancel the sanction of license is justified during the year 2015.

In fact, a proposal was mooted about two decades ago, when Giridhar Gamango was union minister, to treat the mineral resources of the country as the Provident Fund (PF) of the Adivasis. The concept was to facilitate the government in making use of mineral resources like the PF of its employees being used through planning processes for the development of the country. The government pays interest (at 9 per cent) for the use of PF accumulations. It is possible to estimate the value of the mineral resources used to arrive at the amount of royalty or compensation to be paid to the Adivasi inhabitants (keeping in mind environmental concerns). It is estimated that there are about ₹400 trillion worth of mineral reserves (excluding coal and oil) in our country with self-sufficiency in several minerals such as iron ore, magnetite, copper, zinc, etc. The annual value of exports is about ₹2.26552 trillion and is considered as an important resource for our rapid rate of economic growth.[16] The Mines and Minerals Bill 2011 has made a similar proposal of sharing the returns with Adivasis, but is not yet cleared. Thus, the Ministry of Tribal Affairs has not only prepared a rationale for its order but also provided reasonable grounds for future policy-making, to treat the minerals located in their areas as PF to help provide succour to the hapless Adivasis. If the economic conditions of the Adivasis are improved, automatically, the demand for other features of development such as education, health, income, etc. will follow.

It is also necessary to learn lessons from the tribal development policies adapted in the USA, Australia, etc., where the European colonisers are still in power and their policies seem to have not benefited the natives. The struggles waged by the natives or the indigenous people at international forums from these advanced countries clearly indicate that the claims of the governments are short of any sincerity and honesty. It is known that some of the so-called Red Indians (Native Americans) in the USA are given gambling contracts/casinos to manage, but not a share in the wealth of the nation. It is reported that 50 per cent of the Native Americans live below the poverty line). There are 4.5 million NA in the USA and about 60 per cent of them live in urban areas.[17] But, the gaming business seem to have not helped a majority of the natives, although there may be few millionaires to show case the policies of the federal government.

Thus, it is left to the policy-makers in India to pursue innovative and fresh policy frameworks suited to our conditions, where majority of the Adivasis are still living in inaccessible and mineral rich forests and jungles. The international experience with tribal development suggests that we should never thoughtlessly follow the prescriptions of others to solve our problems.

CASTE PREJUDICES AND THE DALITS

The SCs as ex-untouchables were listed and attached to the 1935 Act and have been called as Dalits by the leaders of the community (Ambedkar) who opposed the Gandhian term 'Harijan.' During the post-independence period the Dalit community, it is alleged, was used as a 'vote bank' in politics with appeasements such as extension of constitutional provisions for political reservations, scholarships, job reservations, etc. Yet, the socio-economic status, particularly the discrimination against the community, has not weakened as projected by some scholars. K. S. Chalam, in his study on education and weaker sections, has proved that there is no change in the ranks of the varna castes, though the values of ranks as obtained by sociologists like Chibber changed but not their relative positions. Dalits have continued to remain at the lowest rank even after several decades of ameliorative measures.[18]

The caste prejudice in India is internalised through childhood formations shaped at home and superimposed by social conduct. Therefore, one can see the atrocities on the so-called untouchables growing every year even in the ICT age. The recent dreadful incident in the Paris of Andhra and pride of upward mobile shu-dras of Andhra Pradesh, Tenali, made all of us who love the town hang our heads in shame. A 45-year-old woman was killed in the presence of her daughter for preventing some young upper caste-brutes from sexually abusing her daughter, a good-looking BTech student. In the eyes of the beasts, the pretty mother and daughter were found without a male companion as hapless Dalits. They were returning from shopping when the incident took place just opposite the statue of the Father of the Nation. Though the media has not revealed the background of the incident, circumstantial evidence leads us to the specifics that they were easy prey due to their social background.[19]

The incident in Tenali, Guntur, after a gap of around two decades in the neighbourhood of Chunduru, amply shows that economic growth has not brought any social change, but has led to further nasty feudal depths of despair. Now we have entered a different dimension of caste atrocities. This reminds us why Ambedkar wanted annihilation of the castes. In his most famous speech, prepared but not delivered at the Jat-Pat-Todak Mandal, Lahore, in 1936, he cited a press report of 4 January 1928 about the conditions imposed by upper caste Hindus on Balais, a Dalit caste in 15 villages of Indore district.[20] Out of eight conditions imposed by caste Hindus, two were related to women; that they should not wear gold and silver and fancy gowns, etc., perhaps to keep them as their slaves. Is there any change in the mindset of people as far as women, particularly those from the lower castes, is con-cerned? The Khairlanji incident where the women were brutally butchered in the home state of Ambedkar is a saga of Dalit depri-vation of human dignity.[21]

Several studies indicate how the lower castes have fought against the so-called upper-caste/Brahminical values. It is recorded by Hardgrave Robert that the lower caste Nadars and Ezhavas of Tamil Nadu and the Travancore presidencies resisted inhuman conditions like the womenfolk of the community being made to wear no upper garments, to entertain the lust of the upper castes.[22] The leaders of the Nadars and Ezhavas appealed to the British and defied the upper caste dictates by wearing upper jackets. This hurt the ego of the dominant castes leading to a caste battle during 1818–19. The army was called in by the British to control the situation. Of course, this revolt of the Ezhvas and Nadars made them unite under Narayana Guru and they shifted their traditional occupation to other callings to emerge as one of the most upward mobile communities in post-independence India. We just do not have instances of such revolt from lower castes or Dalits in Andhra. Does Sunila of the above Tenali episode symbolise this? In this context, we may reflect on the notion of beauty and aesthetics in relation to the social composition of our society. It is strange that the younger generation with the so-called development-oriented mindset think about the beauty and glow of women in terms of the standards offered by the Anglo-American or white skin cultures. They opine under the influence of the beauty market that all others like the dark-skinned African-Americans are slaves meant to serve the rest. Hindi channels (some Telugu too) have almost banned dark-complexioned people. There seems to be no change in the attitudes and values of people even in an era of globalisation. However, the local people with dark, brown, etc. skins have proved the indoctrinated upper castes wrong through their intelligence and charm, when opportunities are opened up to them as demonstrated in Olympic medals won by Karnam Malleswari and others.

In fact, Ram Manohar Lohia, in his article 'Beauty and Skin Colour' published in March 1960, has narrated how the greatest woman of Indian mythology, Draupadi, was dark and charming. He narrated the beauty of fish-eyed Meenakshi of Madurai telling the rest of the world how her beauty 'bit more to the heart than the eye.' The grace of Tambaram Lalita, a Tamil beauty, seems to have attracted the attention of Lohia who lamented how the aesthetic judgement of the white-skinned Europeans dominated the world and distorted our aesthetic sensibilities. There are historical records to evaluate native Indian beauty and wisdom of the womenfolk.[23] I remember that I had an occasion to officially interact with the most beautiful woman I have ever seen who was a dark person and I could relate her to the Yakshini kept in the Patna museum.[24] The Yakhshini figure, a first century AD sculpture, was a chance discovery of a British officer who found it in a *dhobhi ghat* about a century ago and took it to Patna. The woman I am referring to was also a Bihari and there are absolute resemblances of the living beauty to the Yakshinini of ancient India. It is appropriate to bring to focus that the native Indians or the so-called lower communities were more attractive than the settlers who came here and enslaved the locals resulting in the destitution and physical devastation of people. It is with the advent of a democratic government and adequate food, that some of the downtrodden were able to slowly recover from the damage and restore their original charm.

It is not only in physical elegance but even in the illumination of their knowledge and wisdom that the women belonging to the lower community is exemplary. There are competent cabinet ministers from this community both in the Centre and in states, apart from Mayawati. This shows that women of the lower communities are as competent as anyone else, if given the chance. This trend appears to be the crux of the problem.

The upper caste offenders of Tenali in Andhra Pradesh referred above seem to have a crush on the women and were waiting for an opportunity to pounce on them. Interestingly, there is very little analysis by our intellectuals who were very critical about the increasing menace of Dalit lumpen elements when the Chunduru incident occurred. Is there any parallel in recent time where a mother lost her life defending the honour and chastity of her daughter? Is it not our responsibility to make Sunila's sacrifice a symbol of self-respect and esteem of the new generation of women which we should be welcoming!

SEXUAL ASSAULTS IN DELHI—PAST AND PRESENT

In the ritual status of Hindus, it is not only Dalits but even women of all castes are treated as inferior shudras. Therefore, women are considered as sex objects to give pleasure to upper-caste men. The lyrics sung by classical poets and pundits are cited often by a section of the literati to show how they were treated in the past, which is only to gloss over the cruel treatment meted out to women in contemporary India. We read in the newspapers and electronic media time and again how even babies as old as 5 years are raped in different parts of the country and reported widely from the metros. Interestingly, the media took a proactive role in the cases of rape to express their social and professional concerns and at the same time get sufficient TRPs. These were wonderful opportunities to satisfy both the obligations of pay and profit where some of the reporters get recognition and are remunerated. We can infer from this how ethical norms have been governing a section of the so-called 'wild media' in the national capital city for the last one decade. It is noticed in the cases of Arushi, Nirbhay, etc. that the events as identified by corporate media projected as national and can be flashed as international as against the Khairlanji and Tenali brutal episodes in terms of the prompts given by background scores to glee or clap. The media think that the people have lost their instincts and common sense to react to concerns of public order and social obligation and therefore have taken it on to themselves as the representatives of the people. Alas! Some of them pose as if they do not represent the corporate interests (investments). Delhi-based media and their regional cohorts know why every single event in Delhi is becoming a national concern just before or during a Parliament session and once the match fixing is over, everything becomes normal.

Delhi is also known as Indraprastha and has several sobriquets. The noted archaeologist B. B. Lal tried to identify Hastinapura near Meerut, 100 km from Delhi. It was the capital of the Kauravas as Indraprastha was for the Pandavas. There are five *prasthas* in the Mahabharata including Sonepat, Panipat, Pilpat and Bhagpat in and around present Haryana. Delhi was considered as the gateway to the Gangetic–Yamuna doab and remained the capital city for several dynasties such as Anang Pal till the national capital was shifted from Calcutta to Delhi in 1911. The city used to have a cosmopolitan stance till recently with all the dimensions of Indian culture. It is common knowledge for every Indian that the first assault on a noble woman took place in Hastinapura and she is none other than the great crowned queen of Indraprastha, Draupadi. C. Rajagopalachari in his English Mahabharata, under the section on Draupadi's grief, narrates how Duryodhana turned to his brother Dushasana to go and fetch Draupadi to the assembly even if he had to drag her. Then, "Panchali rose trembling, heart-stricken with sorrow and started to fly for refuge to the inner apartments of Dhritarashtra's queen. Dushasana darted her, caught her by the hair and dragged to the assembly." Later Karna, speaking on behalf of Duryodhana, said "[E]ven the clothes they have on are now Sakuni's property. O Duhsasana, seize the garments of the Pandavas and the robes of Draupadi and hand them over to Sakuni."[25] We all know what happened thereafter. There is an interesting reference to the robes of all the Pandavas in the text. But the Pandavas were not disrobed, only the hapless lady was their target. Scholars, poets and pundits may interpret so many things from this. But we are interested here to know why Draupadi was the target. I got an explanation from The Discovery of India by Jawaharlal Nehru.[26] In the chapter on the 'Mahabharat,' Nehru interprets the process of the assimilation of the aliens (Aryans) with the local native Indians. Draupadi, according to him, through the institution of polyandry, represented the local Indians. It appears as if the local people particularly their womenfolk then and now are meant to satisfy the lust and pleasure of the. The events in Delhi, UP, Khairlanji, Tenali, Punadipadu and several other places relating to women demonstrate the verity behind the ancient myth.

The data on crimes in India maintained by the Crimes Records Bureau reveal that Delhi has emerged as the crime capital of India during 2010–11. But, the city obtained this dubious distinction only after the 1980s. There were 10,419 crimes reported in the year in 1957 and 27,196 in 1970 and 35,648 in 1980. The number shot up to 68,075 in 2000 and settled around

55,959 during 2010–11, the highest among the metros. The distressing part of the measure of crimes in Delhi is that there were 56 cases of rapes in 1980, 223 in 1995 and shot up to 572 in 2011. It was Bombay that stood first in 1957 and it is replaced by Delhi now. As per the CRBI 2011 report,[27] the victims of rape in the country were a total of 24,206, mostly reported from the North (see Table 4.1 in Chapter 4).

The age distribution of the victims under IPC 376 shows that the age group of 18–30 is the most vulnerable victims of abuse and then comes the age group of 14–18. Children below the age of 10 and women above the age of 50 are also found to be victims of the male chauvinist pigs (MCPs). Delhi again comes in the first rank with 572 cases, of which 57 are in the age group of below 10. The records may not contain cases of rogues who lure the victim with their machinations and later use their creative intelligence to dump them and might later pose as crusaders or reformers. There seem to be no provisions for such crimes of the cheats in social relations in the IPC, except 420 (relating to property). There seem to be some misperception about the idea of rape among the Adivasis. The culture and ethos of tribals or Adivasis are different from mainstream society and the prevalent laws have limitations in capturing the tribal concept of rape. Therefore, we can find from the crime records that the highest incidences of rapes are in the tribal regions of Madhya Pradesh, Chhattisgarh and Andhra. But UP, Delhi, Punjab and Haryana are exception to this, living in Gangetic plains with less proportion of Adivasis and more of Western outlook but epitomising and carrying the legacy of the patriarchal society from the time of Draupadi up to the Khaps, etc., signify low female ratio in the region. The low female ratio suggests the dignity of women.

There is a dark side about the episodes of rapes in India. The incidences of rapes and molestations against Dalits have been increasing over a period of time and stood at 1,557 in 2011. They are reported only under the PCR Act and, therefore, miss everyone's attention. Interestingly, we rarely come across civil society activity anywhere in the country against this inhuman recurrence except the Dalits themselves fighting a losing battle.

The suicide of a Dalit scholar, Rohit Vemula, who dreamt of becoming the Karl Sagan of India, on the campus of the University of Hyderabad, shook the conscience of the world as he raised the issue of caste humiliation.[28] Yet, some groups subscribing and conspiring to bring their feudal ideology into focus in public discourse with the support of a section of the media to make the incident trivial speaks about the cruel nature of the legacy that is against all norms of human dignity.

NOTES AND REFERENCES

1. Thomas Paine, *Rights of Man* Reprint (New York: Grove Press, 2008).
2. Roberto Adorno, *The Paradoxical Notion of Human Dignity*, www.revista-persona.com.ar/9 (accessed on 20 December 2005).
3. Ibid.
4. Ibid.
5. K. S. Chalam, "Human Resources Development in South India," *Journal of Social and Economic Development*, July–December, pp. 291–313 (2000).
6. UNDP, *Human Development Report* (New Delhi: Oxford University Press, 2013).
7. Ibid.
8. Crispin Bates, "Race, Caste and Tribe in Central India: The Early Origins of Indian Anthropometry," Edinburgh Papers in South Asian Studies Number 3 (1995).
9. Lewis Morgan, *Ancient Society* (London: MacMillan, 1877).
10. K. Marx and F. Engels, *The Holy Family* (Beijing: Foreign Languages Press, 1936 reprint).
11. D. D. Kosambi, *An Introduction to the Study of Indian History* (Mumbai: Popular Prakashan, 2009).
12. Andre Beteille, "Tribes and Castes," *The Telegraph*, 24 June 2008.
13. D. P. Chattopadhyay, *Lokayata* (New Delhi: Peoples Publishing House, 1959).
14. Naval Viyogi, *The Founders of Indus Valley Civilizations and Their Later History* (New Delhi: Blumoon Books, 2006).
15. Walter Fernandez, *Development-Induced Displacement* (Guwahati: North East Social Science Institute, 2007).
16. Annual Report of 2011–12, Ministry of Mines, Delhi, 2012.
17. www.ssrdqst.rfmh.org (accessed in October 2012).
18. K. S. Chalam, *Education and Weaker Sections* (New Delhi: Inter India Publications, 1988).

19. *The Hindu*, "Woman Dies in Tenali Protecting Daughter from Drunken Youth," 13 April 2012, and also see *The Times of India* on the same date.

20. B. R. Ambedkar, *Dr Banasaheb Writings and Speeches* (Delhi: Dr Ambedkar Foundation, 2010).

21. Kharlanji is a place in Maharashtra where the wife and daughter of one Dalit Bhootmange were butchered and their private parts mutilated on 1 October 2006.

22. Robert Hardgrave, *The Nadars of Tamilnadu* (Berkeley: University of California Press, 1969).

23. Mastaram Kapoor, ed., *Collected Works of Ram Manohar Lohia* (Delhi: Anamika, 2010).

24. A. L. Basham, *The Wonder That Was India* (Delhi: Rupa, 2004).

25. C. Rajagopalachari, *Mahabharata* (Mumbai, Bharatiya Vidya Bhavans, 2012).

26. Jawaharlal Nehru, *The Discovery of India* (New Delhi: Oxford University Press, 1985).

27. Government of India, *Crime Records Bureau of India* (Delhi: Ministry of Home, 2011).

28. Rohit Suicide Case, *The Indian Express*, 2 February 2016.

8

Language, Culture and Social Inequalities

Social economics, a branch of mainstream economics, is concerned with the 'social dimension' of human well-being. A comprehensive understanding of human nature as a constituent of social being with ethical and moral dimensions of behaviour to attain common good is a *sine qua non* of the subject matter. While economists quite often disregard this essentiality of human transactions, social economists, however, consider the culture and social institutions, including language and literature, which reflect the inner dimensions of a society, as important. We can notice the influence of progressive ideas on the worldview of people inspiring them to take up struggles as they evolve. Marxist or post-Marxist writers of the traditional type to a large extent have sidelined culture, including literary depictions, as part of the superstructure and ignored them in the mainstream analysis. However, with the advent of critical theory and the Gramscian influence[1] over social science discourses, a remarkable change in the mode of thinking and writing in the recent past has been witnessed. India, being a country of several contradictions and conflicts, needs to be approached through humanistic dimensions represented by its literature and culture that have economic and social implications. We have considered in this chapter some well-known Telugu writers as representatives of the trends that they have signified.

The 21st century knowledge society has facilitated access to information to those who have the capacity to own or use ICT. At the same time, it is obliged to repose confidence in the customer or user to have free entry that is either seemingly available without cost or at a price. This requires radical changes in the institutional structures that have evolved over time and are responsible for the identity of nations. One may consider this as an element of transformation in post-modern societies or the hegemony of neo-imperialism. Already, the WTO regime is in place with its GATS making even 'expressions' capable of getting a patent. It is against this background some cultural theorists as noted below conjectured, culture, knowledge and several other forms of intangible goods are packaged and marketed. Therefore, culture needs a marketplace to trade. In a situation like this, international literary festivals in countries where there are potential customers and subjects are received with great enthusiasm. Publishing industry both in India and elsewhere has a multibillion market, but economists have limited their analysis to Economics of Information and knowledge without looking at their social spillovers.[2] UNESCO has been publishing data to indicate how several languages and cultures are disappearing much faster under globalisation today than before.[3] There is a perceptible change in the attitudes of people in traditional societies, particularly the middle classes who are becoming targets of the media as a great source of market, brand creation, infotainment, etc., which is seriously disturbing the living conditions, leisure time activities and erosion of traditional values.

Post-modern and post-colonial studies on culture have gained prominence in the era of globalisation. Writers, philosophers and commentators of the Third World countries mostly, with the pre-colonial awareness or knowledge have started reflecting on the status and conditions of people who by definition are free citizens. The commodification of culture and the so-called knowledge and ICT products with Western and seemingly colonial hangover started invading the cultural space more rapidly and deeply today than ever before. There are different groups of scholars who have been reflecting on the history, culture, language, life styles, habits, etc. after assigning India to the USA and other Western countries since 1990.[4] The impact that the trends in post-colonial global culture have created in India is remarkable, but the resilient Hindustani identity got resurrected and an artificial synthesis using Western concepts with Indian content conscripted by some scholars as noted above has emerged. It was anticipated by some scholars like Gail Omvedt and others that globalisation would ultimately liberate the mindset of people who are deeply engrossed in traditions and customs that are becoming hurdles in the way of economic liberation from the Hindu rate of growth.[5] Interestingly, the economy as per the official economists has acquired sufficient growth but, according to their critics, not justice. The neoclassical economists who are concerned about the quantitative aspects of growth have ignored the sociocultural consequences and kept on moving ahead with their policy prescriptions. The compromise between Western economic thought with Indian ethos started creating contradictions resulting in violent eruptions in the social life quite often.

The world was dismayed when a popular litterateur and former vice-chancellor of Karnataka University, Kalburgi, was killed by some unidentified terrorists, for his views on religion and literature, in Dharwad on 30 August 2015.[6] The west coast of India has been a hotbed of religious intolerance for the last few years as reported in the media relating to two other activist scholars murdered by the same brigade. This is quite different from the frequent lynching and killing of Dalits and Muslims in Uttar Pradesh, Haryana and other parts of the so-called cow belt or north India during 2014–15. The Kalburgi killing is relevant here in view of the fact that writers and scholars have been enjoying the so-called freedom of expression under Article 19 guaranteed in the Constitution and this event reminded us of the dark emergency years without formal declaration. It also reminds us why literate learning was forbidden and harsh punishment was prescribed against those who disobeyed the prescriptions of Hindu Dharma sastras in the classical period (Manu and other law-givers). Though dissent seems to have prevailed in the past, it was not taken on record for any kind of reflection and only one version of the views of the literati prevailed for generations in the mainstream India. Therefore, the freedom of writers to express views and creatively produce literary works against the status quo, orthodoxy and inequities is applauded and the enemy was provoked to see the physical end of such argumentative Indians like Kalburgi.

Ever since the concept of hegemony of Gramsci[7] was accepted in cultural studies that critically looked at institutions such as religion, education, family and the media, scholars in India have been reflecting on them to understand the typical Indian ethos. The notion of hegemony as ideological domination under the Foucaldian[8] concept of power relations in the use of discourse by the ruling class enabled scholar activists to interrogate the 'system of social networks' in operation as in the case of Kalburgi and other incidents. Cultural hegemony as manifested in the killing of writers and rebuking intellectuals in India today needs to be understood by an analysis of the context as depicted in the language, cultural forms and institutions including new forms of worship and control by the power elite. This would enable us to appreciate the complexity of Indian capitalist democracy, particularly after 1990. If we miss this background, we may fail to understand the events unfolding in the JNU, HCU and IIT campuses where the elite rule the roost.

THE CHAR DHAM DISASTER: DELUGE OF FAITH OR MARKET MANTRA

Culture in the form of religious discourses and command over the lives of people in India has been playing a defining role in both public and private relationships from time immemorial. Its influence was more than significant in the few months before the *Char Dham* incident. Hardly four months after the tragic death of about 40 people in a stampede at Allahabad when the devotees of Kumbh were on their way home in the month of February 2013, the great tragedy of Char Dham took place during the last week of June. The horrible experiences narrated by the survivors to the media points out the sudden and unexpected suffering of the pilgrims who were brought there by tour operators.[9] Though it is a sensitive issue, with undue media reach, a dispassionate academic discussion on the commercialisation of faiths is essential to envision the future in order to avoid such incidents. Leaving the evolution of *Chota Char Dham* from the original Char Dham as part of the transformation process of conversion of Shiva *sampradaya* in to militant Vaishnavism, the role of Adi Shankaracharya needs to be reconciled here. Even today, the Rawals (traditional Hindu holy men) of Kedarnath are drawn from Karnataka and Nambodris of Kerala for Badrinath (built on a Buddhist temple). Interestingly, not many pilgrims from these two states from the South are found in the present episode and only Telugu folk are in large crowd. It is reported that about 10,000 people have already registered in Hyderabad for Amarnath *yatra* in 2013. Is it voluntary?

There are several paradoxes in the Char Dham episode. The Himalayas are known for lord Shiva, and all the river systems including the Ganga are devoted to him. It is out of place here to know how phallus worship of the Indus valley civilisation transformed in to Rudra, Muruga, Shiva or Eswar. But, a perceptible observer can find out the defilement of traditional norms of calling Hardwar the gateway of Lord Shiva as 'Haridwar' seems to be a bit niggling about the conspiracy of silence on the subject. In fact, the whole Nath tradition of North India is related to Shaivism and *tantra* where majority of the followers were drawn from the so-called lower castes (see D. P. Chattopadhyay, N. N. Bhattacharya on *Tantra*) in the past. South Indians claim Siddha sampradaya in contrast to North Indian Nath traditions. Some of the tantric traditions are incorporated as part of Badrinath and Kedarnath rituals. We do not know who the multitude of Nagsadhus descended every year on the Kumbha are.[10]

The popular belief systems of the people of the South were influenced by saints, Nayanars (Shivaite) and Alvars (Vaishnavite). Some of them seem to have migrated from Kashi during the 7th–8th centuries after Sri Shankaracharya cleared the way for their arrival. This was a turning point in our history and the Dakshinapath lost its identity and was linked with the pan Indian ethos. The North Indian saints and pundits have influenced local languages in Telugu and Kannda lands and brought uniformity with their use of Sanskrit. The hegemony of the elite language as a unifying force facilitated conversation with local people (who had different belief systems) and Hindu sects before the Abrahamic beliefs descended in the medieval and modern periods. Thus, South Indians, particularly the Telugu-speaking populace, are found to be fond of pilgrimages to the North due to their proselytisation in the form of literary contributions in the mixed language. It appears every Hindu in the South believes that one should at least once in their lifetime dip in the Ganga and visit the dhams so as to attain *jeevanmukti* or physical deliverance (*bondito kailasam*). There are instances or episodes of old people thrown into the Ganga or corpses burnt on the banks to attain salvation. But, people never realised that pious Godavari, Krishna, Kaveri and other river systems of the South do equally deserve attention of the North. (After the advent of electronic media and the exuberance of faith market with political patronage, the Krishna and Godavari Pushkarams evoked huge presence of piligrims in 2015–16.) We hardly find any one from the North revering them, indicating the disregard or bias in our credence of faith. In other words, some kind of grading like national gods, state gods, regional gods and local goblins have already emerged depending on the status of the patron.

While anxiously watching the TV for clues about some of our kith and kin in the Char Dham episode in 2013, on one occasion it was seen that advertisements were being telecast alongside on a Hindi channel about trips to Char Dham. It is a very interesting show where a baba was sitting on an altar sermonising on the mundane and spiritual benefits one gets in a pilgrimage to Badrinath, Kedarnath, etc. The hostess in her beautiful attire gives a commentary as to how to get a reservation, the facilities and other arrangements provided by an agency along with the phone numbers. Of course, our media created a wonderful space of scrolling beneath and above the main content as Breaking News to attract the attention of the viewer. Today, traditional temples are also using ICT facilities like e-*darshan*, e-*prasad* and other e-related services to reach out the customers rather than the devotees. As far as Telugu devotees are concerned, they have more advanced information through regular and special devotional channels all the time. In fact, there are special babas, gurus, brothers, matas and priests who have emerged and sustained themselves through media coverage. After all Telugus are in the forefront to declare that they have come of IT age. Commercialisation and packaging of faith is prevalent among all the religions in India. Thus, faith and devotion related services are packaged and sold in the market better than many other items or goods.

The impact of television, ICT and other complimentary developments in the so-called service sector that includes religious tourism after liberalisation has enhanced the contribution of this sector to GDP manifold. As noted an earlier chapter, the number of places of worship in India has increased four times over a period of two decades that stood at around 3 million involving billions of rupees worth of properties and business. Almost all faiths in general and Hinduism in particular (due to its size) have accumulated huge properties in all the important holy places and cities (people know of only of the Anantpadmanabhaswamy temple in Trivandrum). Most of the properties are *benami* and are emerging as a source of concealing black money. Though, we have sincere and honest philanthropists and devotees, some of the criminal minds are behind several dubious operations of the religious trusts and endowments. However, the growth of faith in terms of quantity is found widespread while the depth of spiritual commitment is shrinking.

It is in the context of the Char Dham disaster, certain distressing events have been reported in the media in 2013. How do we understand the incidents where wades of missing cash in the hands of some babas and the raping and killing of the hapless mother and daughter (lost pilgrims) who were searching for help? The influence of the growing market culture on religious practices seems to have distressed contemporary life and living. The tragedy in Char Dham, viewed in this context, poses several issues for reflection such as avoiding media publicity to attract pilgrims, regulating the visits as guided tours, controlling the commercial elements for profit at places of worship, etc. by concerted citizens and leaders including sane religionists.

Uttarakhand, where the Char Dhams are located, is a very small state of about 10 million people planned about a decade ago. It might boast of several natural resources, but most of them are subject to the vagaries of the weather and climatic changes. The state has 13 districts and 15,761 inhabited villages with 70 Vidhan Sabhas and six Parliamentary constituencies in 2013. Though the state is part of the Himalayas, it does not come under either the 5th Schedule or 6th Schedule since it has only 2.6 per cent Adivasi and 16 per cent SC population. Yet, the Hindu population of the state is about 72 per cent. The literacy rate is above 80 per cent with several premier educational institutions located here. The per capita SDP of ₹48,114 is above the national average. Interestingly, 47 per cent of the population lives below poverty, indicating the precarious position of the population relying mainly on tourism.

The Char Dham disaster about which everyone is concerned needs to be analysed scientifically. It is necessary to know that the Himalayas in which the Char Dhams are situated are the youngest and the highest mountain range in the world with an age of 70 million years on earth (which is 4.54 billion years old). The earth scientists have noted that the Himalayas were formed when the Indo-Australia plate collided in to the underbelly of the Eurasia plate. Thus, it is geologically unstable and seismologically active. It has 15,000 glaciers providing a perennial source of water to the Indus, Ganga, Brahmaputra, Yangtze and several other rivers. The sedimentary and metamorphic rocks of the region seem to be responsible for fragile slopes and landslides and are also exposed to occasional cloudbursts. Uttarakhand is the abode of not only Hindu shrines, but the state had ancient Buddhist and indigenous sects inhabiting here Sikh and Muslim places of worship developed over a period of time. It has a limited carrying capacity with fragile environmental implications. The region is considered as a '*devabhumi*' and some of the people are called as *paharias* or hill people, referring them as innocent in the ordinary transactions of others. They love the land and the forest and, therefore, when deforestation was initiated in the name of development, a counter movement such as the Chipko Movement was started to stall it in 1978. However, a large number of hydro-electrical projects in the region including the highest and controversial Tehri dam, Srinagar dam, etc. have been completed, making the region prone to geophysical disasters.

It has been reported in the media during the period of disater that a Right to Information (RTI) question has revealed plans for constructing 557 hydropower projects on the pious rivers of the region. Interestingly, most of the contractors are South Indian operators such as GVKR, Lanco, GMR and others, but the NTPC project in 2010 was scrapped due to people's resistance. The state government seems to have developed tourist destinations with the support of some operators as the demand for trips to these dhams beyond Rishikesh has increased several folds as per the government website. It is reported that there are about 10,000 beds available for use by the tourists in different categories of hotels, *dharmashalas*, etc. The number of tourists who visited Uttarakhand during 2010 amounted to 31.1 million, three times the size of its population which was hardly in thousands a few decades ago. One can imagine the amount of pressure put on the fragile natural resources of the region by around 2 million visitors particularly in the Alakananda, Bhagirathi and Mandakini river banks where the dhams are positioned. Given the hydrogeological formation of the region and the river systems, the state had an average of 1,606 mm rainfall. It is noted that the rainfall in the region on the fateful day was 380 mm. An activist scientist has alleged that the forest cover of 53,483 sq. km of the state was 84.9 per cent in 1970 and has reduced to around 50 per cent by 2013. Thus, scholars and activists who had been studying the region had anticipated the tragedy.[11] The International Panel on Climatic Change has already warned of extreme weather conditions and, of course, the CAG of India warning to the state government for not following the guidelines of licenses for hydro projects is now in the public domain.

Thus, the 17 June 2013 disaster was a consequence of a vicious circle of leisure time activity promoted by market strategies, capitalist industrial expansion for cheap power and unworldly religious jingoism together with surplus cash invested in mindless construction in an ecologically sensitive area. This is substantiated by the statement of a priest of Kedarnath, Sri Vagesh Lingachar, after the incident (in June 2013) that tourist operators and the business interests have made the area a virtual market place that masked the temple that could be seen from a distance a few years ago. This is an emerging situation where faith is conditioned by the market and if it becomes a practice, one can surmise the end of the significance of religion as a spiritual force in our society.

WRITERS, SCHOLARS AND THE FREEDOM OF EXPRESSION

Economic reforms and its contents seem to have influenced the content and method of presentation of literary works in India due to the influence of the West. However, critiques like Leela Gandhi[12] and others call it a post-colonial or post-modern trend in our culture and language, seeming to have no impact on the attitudes of writers towards the socially marginalised groups, except those who sympathise with them for ideological reasons. The controversy over the statement by a non-teaching professor (Hon. Fellow in Centre for the Study of Developing Societies) is to be looked into in the broad context of the changing times and the intolerance against certain excluded groups.[13] It is not for the first time that the country has witnessed such outbursts by people on social or cultural issues. We have a long history of fights and duels in our country over petty issues such as endorsing the status of a particular caste and inter-faith, and intra-sect issues trickling out in public discourses and ending in legal battles. But, the present issue relating to a cartoon on Ambedkar in NCERT book appears to be due to a misunderstanding or confusion in making a distinction between the statement/utterance of a writer and the proposition and observation of a scholar. The open spurt or clash of ideas can also be interpreted as a phenomenon of social change (good or bad).

Increasing markets for leisure time activities, owing to the rise in incomes and alternative sources of entertainment has encouraged publishing companies to publish what is popularly called 'non-fiction' categories. Otherwise, how do we account for the attendees such as Ashis Nandy, Binayak Sen, Barkha Dutta, Dalai Lama, Gurucharan Das, Nandan Nilekani, Kiran Bedi, etc. at the recent Jaipur festival?[14] There are some creative writers, poets and sundry authors who might have participated or visited the venue to showcase their writings. But, how do we evaluate or understand this phenomenon? Writers are generally considered as those who write books, stories and other types of creative writing to appeal to the 'senses or emotions' of the readers or people. They are not bound by any restrictions except to correspond to the aesthetic values. Literary critiques have developed several theories about the evaluation of literary pieces based on the aesthetics developed in each country, grounded in its culture and society. Indians are fond of *rasa* theory while the Western, African and other nations might have their own parameters to judge creative writing, including poetry. Scholars are those who have specialised in a discipline and have the aptitude for deep study and reflection.

The writers can be broadly divided into scholars of social sciences, humanities, and physical and natural sciences. There seems to be a design in the policy of the government and funding agencies in recent times to marginalise and outwit the social scientists who raise issues of social concerns, particularly in the emerging unipolar world. Therefore, we have a deep crisis in social science research. On the other hand, there are writers who get involved in discourses without sufficient theory, data, methodology and deep study of the problem. Scientists are responsible people and bound by traditions of the profession to defend their argument or make it clear that they are only making a protocol statement subject to verification and falsification. Therefore, they are not generally seen discussing issues in public except in the classrooms or informed groups or gatherings. Unfortunately, the decadence is seen happening much faster in social science research today with competing claims by everyone, including civil society action research based on limited and sponsored agendas. The post-liberal society has invented several notions and categories in social science discourse based on their experience in the market economies of the OECD and pushed them into developing countries like India. It is now debated that the concept of civil society, as originated in the writings of Hegel, Marx and even Gramsci, is being inverted to provide primacy of market over the state with the support of libertarian public intellectuals (PIs). But, PIs are neither serious scholars nor organic intellectuals, but are those who can translate complex ideas into simple language. In that sense, every thinking person, including media persons starting from a stringer to a camera operator who can project the degradation of basic human values, should be considered as a PI.

However, we know the standards of some of our PIs who privately manipulate and twist issues, depending upon the reciprocal value of the transaction. Do we have PIs like an Edward Said who questioned the hegemony of the West? Freedom of expression is the lifeblood of democracy. The corporate media and a section of the national press cite Article 19 aptly to sensationalise certain select issues is guilty of ignoring many social issues of importance. Why has it not been used or distorted the Imrana case, or the Khairlanji or the case of a Dalit professor being attacked in Dhule, Maharashtra, for taking a class on the reformation movement in college?

Freedom of 'opinion and expression' is different from what is incorporated as Article 19 in the Universal Declaration of Human Rights of UNO and not in the Indian Constitution. There are studies by Yoginder Sikand and Avinash Mishra[15] show how corporate media houses, particularly the dominant ones, restrict the freedom of expression of citizens by manipulating and distorting facts as episodes, or what Chomsky calls the 'manufacturing of consent.' Some of them either confuse or deliberately use statements of persons like Ashish Nandy as conduits of their depraved feelings and abuse the freedom of expression of citizens. It may also be due to the willing cooperation of PIs who degenerate or get pampered by sectional interests and create ruckus out of nothing for perishable news value, but not as durable commodity of expert opinion. The recent debate about events in JNU and on the issue of Kanhaiya Kumar and others, both in the Parliament and in the streets, is a case study how the freedom is interpreted in India.

THE RECOGNITION SYNDROME OR IDENTITY CRISIS

Amartya Sen, in his famous book *Identity and Violence: The Illusion of Destiny*,[16] observes that the false notion of a solitary identity is resulting in violence in the contemporary world.

The debate on political reservations for various caste groups in the State legislatures once again brings the issue of identity into public discourse, some scholars terming it as identity politics. The notions of freedom, identity, violence, choice, etc. are generally used in debates of caste-based politics in India.

Therefore, it is necessary to examine the relevance of some of these ideas in the context of caste-based reservations. Does the present debate come under the broad framework of freedom to choose a leader or select someone within narrow confines like caste? Reviewing Sen's book *Identity and Violence* for *The Guardian*, John Gray raises philosophical limitations to understand contemporary society. Gray cites the experience of Isaiah Berlin who narrates how he witnessed a terrified man being killed by a crowd in Petrograd during the Russian Revolution that remained a lifelong horror of violence and compares it with Sen's experience of how in his childhood he saw a Muslim daily wager killed before his eyes. Gray has argued that Berlin considered freedom only as a universal value, but not an overriding human need. Gray was critical about Sen's conceptual therapy, perhaps ingrained in Sen's concept of freedom, to remove the deep-seated traits of man.[17] Perhaps, Gray missed what Sen meant that, "violence is fermented by the imposition of singular and belligerent identities on gullible people" through propaganda. The solitarist fallacy of identity in the Indian situation, if extended further, leads us to spot out the inhuman and irrational social institution called 'caste' as a marker. The philosophical discourse of Sen on identity can be applied to our social situation. There is no doubt that humans would have multiple identities as parents, children, workers, classes such as rich, poor, Hindu, Muslim, Buddhist, Christian, etc. But, they are all subsumed under the dominant and inherited identity called caste.

Sen has attributed the fallacy of identity to intellectual error. It is necessary to qualify what Sen intends to refer to as intellectual error: judgement or beliefs on issues of social significance. Considering that caste, as a belief, may be a false belief, is it possible to reduce the intensity of this identity through reasoned public debate as Sen wanted us to do? We have historical narratives of not only public debates but even caste wars to bring people around public reason, with little effect. Thus, Sen, according to his critiques like Gray and others, has failed to provide a reasonable solution to the problems of multiple identities. As remarked by Sen, violence creates identity as much as identity creates violence. Caste as an identity is not a simple social or cultural institution, transformed from generation to generation as a legacy, but it is a political tool to keep a select few in power and several others outside it. It has never remained the same. It has had its own ups and downs passing through some historical processes. The Western or occidental concept of class as equivalent to caste got imbibed in us in social science discourse to look at it as a static phenomenon. Some scholars have cited narratives to show that caste has undergone mutations. Yet, the dominant ideology or what Sen describes as propaganda in his above cited work seems to have remained the same, in terms of 'they' and 'we,' the ruling castes and the ruled with an experimental group of residuals or untouchables. Therefore, in order to come to power or enjoy patronage within the system or to demand a rightful share in power, people have tended to use the social category of caste, as an identity. In this context, the debate on why the backward classes should not be given their share in politics in proportion to their representation in the population appears to be legitimate. The debate has also other spillovers like the related issue of recognition and self-image of individual leaders who have been championing the cause of the victims, but never got public attention. The social reform or renaissance movements in modern India from the time of Jyothiba Phule, Ayothi Das and others have produced several leading lights such as B. R. Ambedkar, Periyar E. V. R., R. M. Lohia, Karpoori Thakur and several others who have struggled to get recognition to a majority of the socially disadvantaged. Nevertheless, solitary belief of some because of the propaganda that the leaders of the marginalised are inferior due to their birth has been blitzed through brainwash of religious or social bigotry in India. This could, in the framework of Sen, come under unethical or wrong identity of humans who are supposed to have several identities. But the single most significant identity in social relations in South Asia still remains the caste.

The individual who defies established social norms and makes sacrifices for the larger interests of the community/caste and brings tangible gains for them should be considered as a leader. There are always self-centred and egotistic persons who get into social movements for recognition. There is no problem with them as they do tend to contribute to the development or enhancement of the social cause. But, the problem is with those who claim that every success of a social movement is due to his/her indulgence. There are episodes of some leaders who conduct themselves as a symptom of abnormal condition of superciliousness and prone to inability to treat others as humans and co-workers, landing ultimately in a syndrome. It is alleged by commentators that the syndrome is widely prevalent today among social activist groups (SC/OBC) or civil society organisations that fail to absorb or assimilate other similarly placed individuals and their contributions. The kind of decadence in leadership styles is increasingly creating divisions and subdivisions and might damage righteous intentions. Social activists must be very careful in analysing such tendencies in persons and leaders as they might shape up as stumbling blocks of emancipation movement in future. There are instances from the political and social history of Andhra Pradesh during 1990–2015, about how the elite of one caste forged unity and assimilated other castes that were close to them to wield social power and ultimately political supremacy. However, one need not be carried away by the public gossip of internal bickering of the ruling castes, as they are manipulative (arranged) to confuse others as everyone knows that ultimately they get united when their power is about to dissipate. We have witnessed several of such bickering among different caste groups by means of organising caste summits in coastal Andhra just before elections or for political power in 2014.

The identity problem is not confined to the precincts of a nation state. It is a cross-border phenomenon and includes the Indian diaspora. The term diaspora originated from the dispersion of Jews from Israel since the time of the Old Testament and particularly after the decimation attempt by Hitler (seems to be their long lost kin) during the Second World War.[18] There are scholarly studies on the fascinating aspects of the South Asian diaspora including the economic networks that have helped in hastening globalisation in recent times. But, the issues relating to the South Indian are hardly discussed though Telugus were the first to widen diaspora outside the peninsula in the historical past. It is really painful to observe that some of us keep on talking about the migrants of the North West or Jammu and Kashmir (like the Pandits or the Sindhis) while keeping speechless when our own South Indians are being killed or persecuted at the time of Srilankan genocide in 2009. It is necessary to bring to the fore the facts relating to Tamilian dispora. Tamil diaspora is not limited to a single language speakers group as most of the South Indians outside of Madras Presidency were known as Madrasis or Tamilians before the 1960s, though Madras Presidency had Telugus, Kannadas, Malayalees and Tamils. It is irony that the same is carried in the diasporic studies though several of the tea garden workers in Srilanka still consist of Telugu speakers but lumped together with Tamilians. We are referring to this sensitive issue here to open up the issue to raise the predicaments of not only the North-western Indians but also about our own people when incidents of victims of genocide are discussed (in the South). The history, culture, language, politics and even cross-border issues are deliberated as North or North-western India as if nothing exists beyond the Vindhyas or even in the east. In fact, the border with other nations is much longer on the coast and in the Himalayas than on the western rim. No one appeared to be perturbed when the IPKF forces from Visakhapatnam suffered causalities during 1987–90, and tensions prevail in the East or down South at Kacchativu or when the fishermen of the South and East are being persecuted on a daily basis on our continental shelf. Are they not Indians?

The Tamil problem, as it called in Sri Lanka, is neither of a recent hitch nor did the so-called Tamils migrated from mainland India. We had a long history as old as the concept of the diaspora of Jews. Those who have an alien mindset or imaginary cultural roots with the cow belt of Sumeria while sustaining with the local resources for generations in the South, is responsible for this fallacy. Sri Lanka was once a colony of India and, according to some sources, both the Sinhalese and the Tamilians were migrants from India. Professor Sudarshan Seneviratne[19] has shown that there are some native indigenous populations in the island. The Andhra/Telugu people had a long link with Sri Lanka from the time of the Satavahana period when Hala, the 17th monarch, met the Sri Lankan princess Lilavati and married her. It was Pallavas who built the Kovils there and Rajaraja Chola I annexed Sri Lanka as part of his empire. It is said that Mahinda and Sanghamitra left for Sri Lanka through Kalingapatnam and the left canine tooth of the Buddha was taken to Anuradhapura from Dantapura (Srikakulam, Andhra Pradesh). However, the plantation workers and indentured labourers were exported from the coastal south from ports like Visakhapatnam, Baruva, Korangi, etc. during the 19th and early 20th centuries by the British. Thus, we have had long and cherished relations with the island that should have rattled our Telugu conscience when the issue of the Tamil diaspora surfaced for public debate during 2014.

There are two categories of Tamils in the island of Sri Lanka. The original Sri Lankan Tamils, known as the Elam Tamils, who have been there from the 2nd century BC, mostly in the north (Jaffna) and then the Tamil, deluge and Malayalee workers, popularly called as the Indian Tamils, who are alleged to be of recent origin and spread in different parts of the island. It is estimated that out of the 20.2 million population, nearly one fifth (18 per cent) of them speak Tamil. It is possible to conjecture that the social hierarchy prevailed in India had crossed the border along with migrants and have today around 20 *urai-kuts* (castes) in Sri Lanka. Though Sri Lanka does not officially recognise caste, the cruel design of the caste system prevails. It is reported in some studies that agricultural castes like Vellala, lower castes like Pariah, Pallar, Nalavar and the numerically strong Karaiyar (fishermen) along with the Brahmin sects like Salagama (Nambudri), Piraman, etc. do exist among the Indian Tamils. It is claimed that the De Silva or Rajapaksa titles signify Brahminical allusion.[20]

It is not only in Sri Lanka, but everywhere the Indian migrants went, either in the past or in recent period that the problems of divisiveness based on caste/descent have emerged. The problem appears to be serious in South Asia and America where their number is considerable. The divisive forces are further provoked by those who imagine that they are the descendants of Purus, Baratas, Huns, Parthians, Sakas, Pahlavas, Yavanas, Jats, etc. and came from outside and settled in India with the simple idea of 'divide and rule.' If we fail to find a way out and try to fish in the troubled waters, as is being experimented by the Sinhalese with the alleged support from crooks from India, the next war or Kurukshetra would be fought on caste lines. Is the world prepared for another discourse on *niti* and *nyaya* to be sermonised by Avatar Sri Kishan of Gita?

It is reported that the Telugu migrants to the USA and other European countries are maintaining close cultural roots with India. Yet, the identity crisis according to one commentator pushes them to stereotyping obsolete village Hindu social ritual practices of feudal era.[21] The number of temples and places of worship and cultural entities succinctly under each caste group in the USA smut the identity of the Telugu people. In this context, one should remember great reformers like Gurajada Apparao, Gidugu, Tripuraneni, Thapi and a few others who worked for the renaissance movement in Andhra Pradesh, fighting against caste and religious bigotry that made it possible for the present generation of migrants to cross the seven seas.

WRITER AS AN AGENT OF CHANGE: GURAJADA APPARAO THE UTILITARIAN

The role of writers to depict contemporary society through their works was not peculiar to classical writers in India in general and in Telugu country in particular during the 19th century. But, the introduction of English education through the utilitarian spirit inspired writers like Gurajada Apparao in the Madras Presidency to depict social decadence due to Brahminical overreach. His experiments with literary works (Bride Price) have attracted the attention of both English and Bengali writers like Rabindranath Tagore.

There was increased interest in the writings of Gurajada Apparao (1862–1915), the doyen of Telugu language and literature, on the occasion of his 150th birth anniversary in 2011 and it continued thereafter. However, there seems to have been little effort on the part of non-Telugu scholars to look at his writings and place him in proper perspective. There are no doubt several translations of his magnum opus, *Kanyasulkam*, or *The Bride Price*, translated into English. But, that is not the only contribution of Gurajada to literature and his other writings such as *Mutyalasaralu* (garland of pearls), *Putthadibomma Poornamma* (the golden doll Poornamma), short stories, dairies, comments, etc. need to be studied and commented upon to get a comprehensive view of his times, his response to his contemporary society and his vision for the future. This needs to be carried out by scholars who are well versed with current trends of literary criticism and need not necessarily be limited to litterateurs.

It is necessary to contextualise Gurajada and his writings to the time when feudalism was at its pinnacle with the support of the British East India Company which had introduced several landmark reforms in land tenure. One should remember here that the East India Company was formed when Great Britain was in the last phase of its feudalism. The concept of private property in terms of land and permanent tenure were introduced with the idea of exporting primary goods for external and internal markets. Industrialisation was in its nascent stage and, therefore, it would be too unusual to expect a Marxist in India as some critiques opined (see below) and much less in Visakhapatnam during the latter part of the 19th century. The introduction of English education and legal instruments based on local practices of the *dharmashastras* and the Shariat along with British laws for their citizens, started influencing social life. It is reported that the zamindars of Vizianagaram were motivated to conduct the Aswamedha *yagna* and a probable sati at the height of feudal decadence, a time that might be considered by some as the golden age of dharma. But, the social life where 90 per cent of the people remained poor, destitute and ignorant was detested by some enlightened individuals as immoral and undemocratic. There were members of the royal family with their wide experience and exposure to new ideas have started introducing reforms and encouraged pundits and literati to reflect.[22] Given the Adivasi and socially deprived background of a section of society and its long historical crusade against all kinds of incursions, the region was anticipating a rational and progressive crusader first to record the evils and provide possible solutions. The conditions eminently suited the emergence of a phenomenon called Gurajada.

Gurajada Apparao needs to be evaluated from the socio-historical and locational background of the Madras Presidency. Visakhapatnam and Ganjam were the two important districts that the British got under their sojourn after 1794 battle at Padmanabham (the region was known as Kalinga and beyond Mahanadi was Utkal or Kosal). One should remember that the region was at that time known as Kalinga or Trikalinga and was part of the Madras Presidency, while the neighbouring state was Bengal. There was neither West Bengal nor Orissa at that time. The physical proximity to Calcutta seems to have facilitated Gurajada and other modern scholars and reformers to get exposed to or interact with their counterparts in Bengal, a region that was a neighbouring state much nearer than Madras. He had also links with Madras, the Presidency

capital after the erection of railways between the two prominent presidencies of the British India in the 19th century.

The so-called enlightenment movement in India is said to
have been the prerogative of English education. The British
India government started implementing the Wood's Despatch
in 1854 by establishing three universities, namely in Madras,
Calcutta and Bombay. This facilitated the introduction of
modern English education in India on the model of London
University with affiliated colleges. Gurajada was born in 1861,
just seven years after the establishment of the Madras and
Calcutta universities, and sandwiched between two presidencies drawing abundantly from the flow of English and modern
ideas from the West through English education. Persian was
the court language during medieval period and it was an Indo-
Aryan language like English that was considered as Indo-
European (by William Jones) had a different cultural milieu,
perhaps helped to promote or sponsor the languages through
their local agents who were known as rajas or feudal lords. In
the middle ages, the promotion of classical language must have
helped to strengthen the native rulers to patronise *prabhandas*
on the lines of Persian or Iranian or Aryan roots (may be imagined) as legacy of Vedic knowledge. Therefore, by the time the
East India Company came to Surat (in 1619), there seems to be
some kind of unity in the vast country through the Muslim rule
(when Copernicus had not yet challenged the Hellenistic world
view to usher in renaissance). In fact, British colonialism in a
way brought ideas that were fresh from the Renaissance and
Reformation movements that followed Copernicus and Galileo
impact on modern ideas. The kind of innovations that were
native and indigenous, such as that of Aryabhatta (476–550
AD), Varahamihira (499 AD), Bhaskara II (1145–1180 AD), etc.,[23]
however, did not challenge the Aryanised or Hindu beliefs like
puranic cosmology till Meghnad Saha did so in the 19th century. Perhaps, the emergence of new ideas must have played an
important role in the worldview of the educated dvijas, mostly
Brahmins, who had already encountered another challenge
in the form of Islam. There could have been an independent

stream of transformation and reawakening in the country if the Lokayata, or Charvaka traditions had been allowed to continue. In fact, a majority of the dissenters in those traditions were Brahmin scholars who were brutally suppressed by selfish and self-seeking pundits in the earlier eras (see Lokayata). Some anthropologists, such as Partha Chatterjee and the Subaltern group whom our Telugu scholar Velcheru Narayana Rao[24] seems to have followed in evaluating Gurajada, appear to have overlooked indigenous native traditions and the persecutions without giving any scope for renaissance in India. This can be seen from the time of Adi Shankaracharya and the Vaishnavite traditions that brutally eliminated all kinds of heretic beliefs or theologies and brought unity in Hindu Theology. The greatest blow from the onslaught of Advaita hit Kalinga that was under Buddhist and Jain traditions and the assault helped conversion of the local shrines and *aramas* as temples in the Kalinga region, much deeper and extensive than other regions. Historians like H. Kulke and D. Rothermund[25] have recorded the Dark Age in Kalinga from the 7th to 11th century AD till the Eastern Gangas ushered in to restore Brahminical order in the region. Sri Krishna Devaraya in the South and the Peshwas later in Deccan (Maharashtra) further strengthened the hegemony of the Hindu or Brahminical order during the 15th to 17th centuries. They had created different epochs by the time the British entered and slowly controlled regions and established their presidencies. There seem to be similarities in the epochs between eastern India (mostly the Tri Kalinga experiences) and western India (that was challenged by Joti Rao Phuley). It is strange that no one has seriously tried to record the developments in the Madras Presidency, particularly in the region between Godavari and Mahanadi, where the Telugu renaissance originated and where Gurajada was the harbinger of that advancement. Unless scholars look at the root causes of the political economy of the developments in power structure, the culture or the literary sources would not be in a position to bring out the real from the superficial sketch depicted in narratives.

Gurajada was the recipient of first generation English education imparted through native colleges established by the zamindars. It was incumbent upon him to share his learning with his fellow citizens as well as own caste persons who had been deeply submerged in outdated traditions. As a teacher, it was his duty to tell his students including his patrons like Anand Gajapathi about the truth that he was discovering with his exposure to an English education. Unlike several dishonest and diabolic characters who were his contemporaries, Gurajada sincerely tried to use his knowledge for the emancipation of his Niyogi caste brethren first, and the masses at large.

Mahatma Phooley (1827–90), the first Mahatma of India who was 30 years older to Gurajada and resided on the west coast, had clearly brought out the fact that the education policy of the East India Company was not really bothered about the common man, as the British government had deliberately ruled that education was to be a preserve of the higher classes. Interestingly, Periyar E. V. R. in the Madras Presidency was 19 years and B. R. Ambedkar of Maharashtra 30 years younger than Phuley to carry the mission of one aspect of modernisation project through public education.

It is instructive to analyse the moorings of the leaders of the South, most of them have come from the teaching profession to herald renaissance or reformation movements in 19th century India. In the Telugu-speaking region of the Madras Presidency, it was Kandukuri (1848–1919), Gurajada, Gidugu (1863–1940) and others who were all drawn from the teaching profession and who were in the forefront for social change. It is not out of place to put it on record that utilitarians such as Bentham, J. S. Mill and later G. B. Shaw and their writings profoundly influenced these leaders and their ideas to a large extent were echoed in their writings.[26] According to Eric Stroke and others, due to the training which the British civil servants got under these schoolmen in England called the utilitarians that some of the officers carried the feeling of "greatest benefit to the largest number" as a value. The influence of the Fabians and the British Labour Party could be seen later in the ideas and ideology of liberals like Jawaharlal Nehru, B. R. Ambedkar and others.[27] As far as Gurajada was concerned, he was not only a contemporary of these influential people[28] and their writings but was a driving force in the Telugu region reflecting upon and indigenising modern outlook into a traditional society through his writings. Though Macaulay was maligned by a section of the nationalists for their own reasons and to some extent due to his uninformed utterings on Hindu knowledge systems, the intentions of Macaulay were very progressive at that time. This can be seen from his note, wherein he has stated,[29]

> I think it is clear that we are not fettered by the Act of Parliament of 1813; that we are not fettered by any pledge expressed or implied; that we are free to employ our funds as we choose; that we ought to employ them in teaching what is better worth knowing than Sanskrit or Arabic; that the natives are desirous to be taught English and are not desirous to be taught Sanskrit or Arabic; that neither Sanskrit nor Arabic has any peculiar claim to our engagement; that it is possible to make natives of this country thoroughly good English scholars; and that to this end our effort ought to be directed.

Gurajada definitely lived up to the expectations of Macaulay in the positive sense of his mission both as a teacher and writer.

The methods of English education are common in Great Britain and India. It, no doubt, created several tensions in our society that could be seen in terms of the Anglican and orientalist debates that led to the formation of the Brahmo Samaj in Bengal, the Arya Samaj in the North and the Theosophical Society in the South, depending on the conditions and social awakening. In fact, Gurajada has commented on the Theosophical Society for its duality in emancipating the lower castes and women in his writings.[30] Interestingly, the opinions expressed by Gurajada and the comments of Ambedkar later resemble the same sentiments, the voice from below. Being a Niyogi and an intelligent person working with Andand Galapathi helped Gurajada to articulate the voices of the subaltern as there were very few educated representatives from these communities to express views on their behalf. The initiative taken by literary persons like Gurajada who provoked critical thinking on the decadent society became a social movement later as seen in the writings and activities of Tapi Dharma Rao from the same region. Tapi and Tripuraneni (see below) championing the non-dvijas in the Justice Party in Madras Presidency have actively participated in the activities of the so-called non-Brahmin movement of the South facilitating Bobbili Raja to emerge as prime minister. All of them who worked for the Justice Party brought the first caste-based quota in the public service in India during 1925–30. The caste-based (all castes) reservations policy of the Madras government of 1925 helped to mobilise the lower classes to get the Constitution amended in 1951 to regularise reservations with immunity.

Gurajada seems to have been very sensitive to issues that were contemporary to his times and this can be seen in his comments on social issues either in his correspondence or in creative writings. For instance, he commented on the bickering between Kesav Chandra Sen and Devendranath Tagore of the Brahmo Samaj. One may wonder why Andhra literati had commented on issues related to Bengal. It needs to be remembered here that Visakhapatnam was part of Madras and its neighbouring state Bengal was close to Vizianagaram where Gurajada worked. Assessing a writer or reformer is very difficult if we place him out of historical context; Gurajada case is one where we could notice to what extent he was farsighted and his writings relevant to understand his contemporary society and his role in changing decadent feudal traditions. It is for this reason that the people of the region kept him in high esteem.

Gurajada Apparao's *Kanyasulkam*, the *magnum opus* of modern Telugu literature, was translated into English by Velcheru Narayana Rao and published in 2011 with a 45-page afterword. In contextualising the play, Velcheru tried to project how Gurajada did not represent a part of colonial modernity but a continuation of the past that had been alive until recently. Velcheru and his collaborators David Shulman and Sanjay Subrahmanyam[31] have argued in their writings that elements of modernity did exist from the 15th to 16th century Telugu literary texts and, therefore, *Kanyasulkam* should be seen only as a continuation of the past Indian or as the Telugu version of modernity.

There is no problem in accepting this position provided one recognises that the 15th–16th century writers and philosophers encountered a challenge from an alien belief system called Islam. Islam had advocated that it was the personal responsibility of the believer to reduce inequalities among its supporters. We have noted above how the transformation of South Indian society in the image of writers led to a radical departure from the then existing value system of graded inequalities based on birth, which had given rise to protest movements in the form of Bhakti in the beginning and other dissents like Justice Party political mobilisation on a large scale that possibly led to Indian modernity in the South.

Velcheru projected Gurajada as the one who wanted to carry the culture and spirit of India. It is here that he recalls Partha Chatterjee's assumption of an ahistorical and apolitical essence of India to substantiate his position against Gurajada. As social scientists, we feel this is another way of mystifying the substantial contributions of Gurajada. There is no need to present him as a nationalist of pure Indian origin as there seem to be no such characters even in Bengal. If it had existed for the Bengali bhadralok, it was soon absorbed by several competing movements including Shyam Prasad Mukherjee, Bengal division on communal lines, etc.[32] Gurajada Apparao was a product of his times and region. He was the harbinger of a new era, particularly in Telugu literature.

Yet, Gurajada is still living in Dalit poetry, women's liberation and other radical movements as he believed, "[L]iterature in the vernacular will knock at the door of the peasant and it will knock at the door of the Englishman in India. Its possibilities are immense." Gurajada, in his first version of the play, found the Brahmin *sulka* marriages and child marriages "scandalous, a disgrace to society ... literature cannot have a higher function than to show up such practices and give currency to a high standard of moral ideas."[33]

But in his revised version of the play, issued after 12 years, in 1909, the purpose was clearly stated,

> [M]y own vernacular, for me, the living Telugu, the Italian of the East in which none of us is ashamed to express our joys and sorrows, but which some of us are ashamed to write well.... A great writer must write and make it. Let us prepare the ground for him.[34]

Victims of tradition are overwhelmingly occupying this ground or platform of revolt now. As for the social reform among Brahmins of the region, Gurajada was aware of the Vaidika and Niyogi litigations and the problem of child marriages by quoting the numbers. He had appreciated the support received from the Madras High Court nullifying the *kanyasulkam*. Some Brahmins of our region are still going round the courts penniless.

But, most scholars are not aware that the reform movement of the non-Brahmins in the Madras Presidency originated in this region which later led to the so-called communal reservation policy of the Justice Party. Maharaja Ananda Gajapathi was the first to get the *Sudrakamalakaram*[35] translated into Telugu around 1890. This translation opened the debate on how the non-Brahmins were treated in the Hindu scriptures. The zamindars or landholders of the region were not drawn from upper castes as in other regions. Most of them had Adivasi backgrounds or belonged to other lower castes and were humiliated by the Brahmin hegemony in Madras. The lower castes and Adivasis revolted against the social and ritual inequalities observed in private and public life and actively participated in the formation of the Justice Party. C. R. Reddy was a prominent figure in the movement and through his writings it is apparent he had very good relations with Gurajada.

Therefore, Gurajada made the play a social drama by not confining it to a few Brahmin families, but rather a universal classic. Some literary critiques like K. V. Ramana Reddy did not understand this background and commented that Gurajada had unnecessarily brought in characters like Asiri, Siddhanthi and others (low caste) in the second edition of the play. Gurajada was a great visionary and harbinger of change, not only in making the spoken dialect the medium of a modern epic but deliberately introducing 'diversity' in literature! The progressive nature of his thoughts and their relevance can be evaluated not only from *Bride Price* but also from his numerous writings that reflected a distinct flavour, different from either Kandukuri or Ram Mohan Roy.

The post-colonialist writings on India are trying to reflect on projects that support the neocolonial agenda of modernisation that support or supplement market capitalism and commodification of culture including language and literature. Edward Said, the leader of anti-imperialist writings, in his book *Culture and Imperialism* has said, "The World has changed since Conrad and Dickens in ways that have surprised and often alarmed metropolitan European and Americans who now confront large non-whites, the migrants population among their midst. Impressive roster of newly empowered voices asking their narratives to be heard."[36] It is farfetched to note that Gurajada, almost a century before Edward Said and the post-colonialists, could imagine and provide the space for the subaltern voices of Madhuravani, Asiri, Bairagi and a host of others of lower castes in his writings to be the first to introduce diversity in modern literature.

THE DRAVIDIAN REVOLT IN TELUGU COUNTRY

The social economy of Telugu society cannot be appreciated without reading about the nuances as noted above in the previous section of a society that underwent tremendous advancements in all fields of life. There are creative writers in Telugu, Tamil and Kannada in the South who have depicted this in their works, but very few have written about socio-economic issues with ideological commitment and with a social science approach to describe the nuances. This reminds us about the inimitable service done to social science by a Telugu litterateur, Thapi Dharma Rao, whose 125th birth anniversary was on 19 September 2012.[37] He was the initiator of social science writings in Telugu through his famous column in *Prajamitra* of Gudavalli Rama Brahmam. His popular book, *Devalayala Meeda Boothu Bomma Lenduku* (why lewd figurines on temples?), was first published in the above-mentioned journal. The seeds of progressive literature in Telugu and the rebellious nature of social and cultural leaders, and thereby politicians of Kalingandhra, had a different geographical and historical background. Unfortunately, no historian from mainstream academics has ever done serious study on the region consisting of the Mahanadi-Godavari terrain, as do the present German scholars such as Burkhard Schnepel, H. Kulke and others.[38] It was broadly due to prejudice, as noted by Vincent Smith, "[H]itherto most historians of ancient India have written as if South India did not exist."[39] In this context, we should note that Thapi Dharma Rao perhaps had inherited the recalcitrant cultural traits of the region which was once, according to Godavarti Ramdas, a horror for Rigvedic Aryans.

There were three great centres of learning and the renaissance movement in the northern part of Telugu country during the early part of the 20th century: Parlakimidi, Vizianagaram and Rajahmundry, and most of the leaders were drawn from the teaching community who had worked there. It was in Parlakimidi that Thapi Dharma Rao studied his FA during 1905–06. The political and cultural developments in the region must have played an important role in shaping his personality. It seems he had worked in different odd jobs in the old Vizag district during his early days (the present three districts of North Andhra). Thapi can be considered a link between traditional literature (*Vijaya Vilasam*)[40] and modern progressive trends in Telugu. He chaired the first Progressive Writers Association in Bombay, was responsible for the organisation of ARASAM (progressive writers of Andhra) and in a way for VIRASAM (revolutionary writers),[41] and was also the president of the Sri Sri Shasti Poorti celebrations in Visakhapatnam. Thapi started the 'Andhra Sahitya Samajam' in Madras, edited the Justice Party journal, *Samadarsini*, in Telugu and was closely associated with the social justice movement in the Madras Presidency. He started the Veguchukka Grandhamala[42] and encouraged progressive literature. He provided, perhaps, routes for all modern trends, both in content and form in Telugu literature and culture. He revolutionised Telugu journalism and the use of the spoken word (as a student of Gidugu) and closely associated with Visalandhra and the left and rationalist trends till his last breath in 1973.

Thapi was closely associated with Telugu film-making by contributing scripts or stories for landmark progressive movies for social change such as *Malapalli*, *Raitu bidda*, *Drohi*, *Kilugurralu*, etc. It is difficult to find a comparable celebrity either during his lifespan or today, given the wide spectrum of his work under a school of thought of his own, namely the Thapi *bata* (path). There are very few reviews of Thapi in mainstream literature and a much smaller number among the youth (on the net) remember him. We have in poetry Adikavi Nannayya (foremost poet) and do not have a grandfather or *thatha* for literature (all forms) of the modern period. It is appropriate now to identify Thapi (who was popularly called as Thataji) as the 'Thataji' (grand pa) of progressive literature?

Tripuraneni Ramaswamy,[43] a leader of the Telugu renaissance movement in coastal Andhra, is considered here as a Dravidian icon and his statue was unveiled in Tenali by the secretary of the Dravida Kazhagam, Arivukkarasu, on 11 April 2011. It is not only a symbolic gesture but a significant recognition that Tripuraneni had close interactions with the movement. The first quarter of the 20th century discerned remarkable developments in our social and cultural life.

Though the emergence of modern society appeared to be a universal phenomenon, as a natural trail of the reformation movement in Europe, it had its spillover effect on other societies. It was during this period orthodoxy in religion had dwindled, and utilitarian and pragmatist ideas were freely exchanged in Europe. It had its impact on British India. Indians started going abroad, defying the religious ban on crossing the seas. Interestingly, children of orthodox families were among the few (like the present swadeshis going Westward) who got educated in London, Dublin, Cambridge and other liberal universities in Britain. Some of them went to England to appear for the ICS and to get licenses to practise at the bar. But, a majority of them became freedom fighters and freethinkers because of the prevailing intellectual climate in England.

A reasonable ambiance was created in India after the introduction of reforms in education with the Wood's Dispatch in 1835. Interestingly, the situation in the Deccan (South, including Bombay) and in East India was qualitatively different from rest of the country where the feudal princely states had control over social life (with exceptions like Baroda and a few others). Tripuraneni Ramaswamy left for Dublin under the refined circumstances. Tripuraneni cannot be evaluated in isolation of the legacy that he endured from a region (coastal Andhra) that was known for one of the earliest social revolts in India. He parodied the Gita to replicate the story of Palanati Brahma Naidu (12th century reformer who embraced Dalit Kannamdas as his lieutenant) and followed the traditional language in all his works, including *Sambhuka Vadha, Khooni, Kurukshetram* and others. Even his first edition of the Vivaha Vidhi was in the mixed classical Telugu language. There is a story in circulation like that of Periyar E. V. R. He would not be taught Sanskrit by a Brahmin as he was a Shudra. He learnt the language through other means and that was, it is alleged, one of the reasons for his vehement opposition to Brahminical scriptures.

Tripuraneni had very good contact with the Dravidian movement led by Periyar and participated in their meetings at several places. The binary Aryan and Dravidian are narratives as a phase of cultural divide, one representing an alien and the other home-grown. Tripuraneni appears to have championed the native and local variety representing the Dravidian movement in the Telugu-speaking areas. It is surmised that the establishment of A. C. College at Guntur and the introduction of English education in the region seemed to have brought rationalist and utilitarian ideas as compared to the neighbouring Krishna district where English education entered late. Unlike other members of the Justice Party in the Andhra region, Tripuraneni was not a landlord or a zamindar. It is noted that leaders of the Justice Party who were drawn from zamindari families have slowly disappeared after 1935 and the seeds of dissent grown in the region through leaders like Annadurai in the Tamil region gave birth to a Dravidian party to emerge later. But Tripuraneni did not live to see the fruits of independence nor a social awakening that resulted in identity politics in the region a few decades later.

In contrast to other non-Brahmin leaders, Tripuraneni and Periyar belonged to a different category of social activists. In fact, the first half of the 19th century produced two interesting reformers in the South (Deccan) unlike that of Bengal. They were Mahatma Phule in the Bombay Presidency and Pandithamani Ayothidasar (1845–1914) in the Madras Presidency. It was Ayothidas who popularised the concepts of the Dravida and the Sakya Buddhist society that helped to lay the foundation for a self-respect movement to be led by Periyar and one that even inspired B. R. Ambedkar. In fact, Periyar Ramasamy was influenced by Ayothidas and worked with him when he was young.[44] Similarly, Phule laid the philosophical foundation for B. R. Ambedkar (he acknowledged it in his writings on Sudras) to work in Maharashtra. But there was no such precursor for Tripuraneni after his death in 1943. M. N. Roy and Tripuraneni were born in the same year 1887. A meeting was arranged by Avula Gopala Krishnamurthy, the leader of the rationalist movement in the South, between M. N. Roy and Tripuraneni in Tenali around 1940. Both of them did agree on several issues of contemporary relevance during the British raj along with the strategies to educate people on humanism and rationalism. One of his ardent followers, Ravipudi Venkatadri, worked in the movements initiated by Tripuraneni, while another of his followers, Ravela Somayya, ended up with Lohia socialism, etc. We just do not have sufficient tools to appraise personalities like Tripuraneni; otherwise, it is easy to refer to the emergence of some communists, a regional party like TDP, cultural renaissance, including films, etc., as probable outcomes of his labour. Alternatively, we can at least conclude that Tripuraneni halted the decadence and religious bigotry in which the community was steeped in for few decades and turned their attention to reform and emerged as a political force in coastal Andhra to reckon with. The tragedy is that those who eulogised him once as the greatest reformer avoid uttering his name now lest the Dravidian ethos elude them forever.

The World Telugu Conference (2012) in Tirupathi was conducted after a gap of four decades. It was quite different from the previous one as it evoked criticism for its emphasis on feudal values in literature particularly of one section or region projected as a universal epithet of Telugus while Telugus of Telangana were on a warpath for identity. This is exactly the point on which some critiques are going to the extreme to discard Telugu as a medium of instruction and embrace English. It is important to understand why there is decadence or underuse of Telugu in the public sphere. Is it deliberate or a part of the dissolution or as a consequence of something else? Andhra Pradesh, where Telugu was once used extensively, was an agro-based economy, particularly in the deltas of Krishna and Godavari. Linguists say that language is a medium of communication of the times to posterity. It reflects the life, culture and socio-economic activities of the period. We cannot artificially protect it once the base is gone. The coastal districts in particular and others in general have shifted to other traditions and occupations, helped to patronise private schools and colleges (engineering) and promoted them to move boys and later girls to the USA where English is spoken. Interestingly, this is evidenced in some of the gatherings of Telugus like the one at Tirupati where contradictions are manifested between those who earn in the USA and wish to live in feudal Andhra in the name of the Telugu culture.

The Japanese scholar Yamada Keiko published an article, "Origin and Historical Evolution of the Identity of Modern Telugus," in the *Economic and Political Weekly*.[45] He was critical of how, under the colonial hangover, some Telugu intellectuals had developed an imaginary common historiography of the Telugus as Andhras, as an arbitrary exercise. He was referring to the issue of the emergence of the Telangana movement as a case in point about how language identity, if not inclusive (as noticed in the above episodes), did not protect the unity of people.

While the elite of the classical Telugu-speaking class celebrated at the World Telugu Conference at Tirupati to exhibit their meiosis, students from lower socio-economic backgrounds who took Telugu as medium of instruction experience extreme deprivation in university education. In this context, the death of Ramesh, a Telugu medium student of Nalgonda district at the Seethafalmandi station in Hyderabad in 2012, is one of the most tragic incidents in the midst of episodes of self-immolation for a separate state of Telangana. The suicide note left by Sankini Ramesh was reported to have mentioned that the cause of the extreme step was his failure to pursue an MSc in English medium. The details published in the daily papers indicate that he hailed from a village and might be from a poor socio-economic background. This incident brings out a serious malady in our education system that has been tolerated for decades to reach the present epidemic proportions.

There seem to be very few studies and media reports about the kind of troubles that the first generation of learners in Telugu medium encountered. (It may be true even in Hindi and other mediums also.) Yet, a majority of them have reached the highest echelons in their chosen fields and have contributed to knowledge creation and national development. The system of education in Andhra Pradesh has undergone a metamorphosis during the last three decades. School education has become a profitable enterprise with more than 60 per cent of children in general and almost all in urban areas in particular studying in English medium schools.[46] The mother tongue is now considered as a false notion, if not abusive, due to the fact that neither the mother nor the father is in a position to take care of children (there is only a school tongue). The entrepreneurs who were responsible for such trend and made millions have joined politics and are formulating policies now both at the Centre and in states.

The Constitution-makers (some of them Hindi zealots) did not dare to call any Indian language, including Hindi, the national language and tactically called Hindi and English official languages.

The issue of the medium of instruction is critical since there is no consensus among the stakeholders with diverse agendas to formulate a national policy of medium of instruction. But, one can think of identifying a common cause of providing sufficient ground for a language to be offered to the student in which he is comfortable to think, study and communicate. After all, language, according to Gordon Childe,[47] the legendary historian, is nothing but socially accepted noises or sounds. However, once a language settles as the official language, the cultural supremacy of the ruling classes through the medium of language starts impinging on the people. Interestingly, English, as the official language of the British, sufficiently entrenched itself in its colonies, thus, having adequate freedom to develop as a native language. Therefore, we have today Indian English, American English, etc. The limited job opportunities in American Business Process Outsourcings (BPOs) have been reduced to a business proposition by a few to make the gullible crave for general English, deriding Telugu as inferior in the state. Now electronic media is adding glamour to this.

We know how students are divided on the basis of the medium of instruction, Telugu medium being generally pursued by the lower classes (a double disadvantage) and, thereby, developing inferiority complexes at the college level in Andhra Pradesh. The victim, Ramesh, mentioned previously, belonged to this class. There are several studies[48] indicating how students would be comfortable to study in their mother tongues in the formative years and can move on to learning other languages after the mastery of their own mother tongue. Of course, sociolinguists have proved that each social group, in our situation each caste, has its own style, code and norm of language. Unfortunately, we have in Telugu more diversity than others for historical and sociocultural reasons explained elsewhere in the chapter. In fact, English has also attained the status of a symbol of exclusion as different styles are being promoted by different social and interest groups. Some of the publishing houses, journals and even newspapers, it is alleged, are encouraging a typical style of expression for those who come under their social or elite category at the exclusion of others. Therefore, the illusion that English is a social leveller needs to be taken with a pinch of salt. Giving an identity to a language is possible when you start respecting your mother tongue and openly demonstrate it so that people like Ramesh get courage and pursue education irrespective of what medium of study one chooses.

DELHI IGNORES SOUTH INDIA

In the imagination of Delhi intellectuals and the media, perhaps, the South, like in mythology, is inhabited by *rakshasas* (demons), although Phule Jyotirao called them *rakshaks*,[49] protectors of the homeland. The media in Delhi has grown in strength and capability in making the political class and even the civil service system listen to it on all matters. We are very happy that the media has grown in strength in a democratic society and is playing an important role in alerting the state not to make people suffer out of hunger. It has succeeded in using Article 19 of the Constitution guaranteeing freedom of speech. Though the article is very elaborate and clear, it is accessible only to citizens and not media, with provisions of reasonable restrictions.

Nevertheless, the media, particularly the big business houses (some of the small players became big after entering the media business) bring up issues that are least concerned with the common citizen. Of course, the responsible media is taking up issues on behalf of uninformed and poor citizens and working for a democratic process. The fact of the matter is that the media should represent the genuine concerns of the people and should not restrict itself to a few and project whatever they say as an important national concern. Is this freedom of speech (there is no provision for the freedom of press)? Article 19 is interpreted in the larger interests of the citizens whom the media has, of late, been misusing, according to some critiques.[50] There is a subtle discrimination in the Delhi media as far as incidents relating to the South are concerned.

It has become a media norm that, whenever the Parliament is in session, there is a possibility that before it starts taking up the agenda, trivial issues (or issues that are trivialised by the media) are fixated and sidelined the main agenda during 2005–15. Sometimes it is alleged that business houses themselves create an agenda to divert attention from their deeds so as to not be noticed by the legislature or to obscure the real issues of the people. For the last few years (2005–15), none of the important bills concerning the people were taken up for discussion and the sessions were made infructuous by the hullabaloo created by a section of the Delhi media for their own benefit. If one makes a content analysis, it will be revealed that the interests of certain sections of society, including individuals, are protected rather than there being any dispassionate attempts to project the real issues. Some friends in the Delhi Union of Journalists Ethical Council studied the infamous Imrana case and pointed out how waffling the Delhi media had been about the minorities.[51] The same treatment appears to have been accorded to the South in Delhi. Globalisation has benefited many, but it has harmed the interests of certain groups within the country. (For instance, observers say that the presence of efficient civil servants, scholars, media persons and public figures from the South and East were in Delhi a few years ago was different from what it is today.)

Interestingly, majority of the boys and girls from the South have gone to the USA and are living there abstemiously to send remittances back home. The South Indians are happy with the money and even argue for the recognition of those who were responsible for this. In fact, the damage done to the South through this brain drain appears to be incalculable as we are going to lose heavily in terms of policy decisions without the presence of capable persons from the South in the decision-making processes in Delhi. Most of the best brains from the South (I have called it brain crippled) have either left the country or are not interested in entering the public sector or government, leaving the space for others.

In fact, the South was once represented by Madras and it was shattered by the emergence of NTR and later YSR; in recent times, there are KCR, K. K. and Kavuri to reckon with.[52] This is not sufficient to withstand the onslaught of the North and the Hindi chauvinism which was once countered by Periyar E. V. R. It is all gone now. You do not find anyone talking about India beyond the Narmada and there are very few from the South to say that South Indians have a separate culture and languages to be projected as part of the Indian ethos. No one in Delhi thinks that the Tamil problem is as big as that of Jammu and Kashmir as the South has a more porous border with Sri Lanka just as Jammu and Kashmir has with Pakistan. The issues of the Tamil country, for that matter the fishermen of North Andhra in the continental shelf, are survival problems as those of the people of Jammu and Kashmir. But, the national media has never projected the issues as frequently as those of Jammu and Kashmir or the North India in Delhi.

The poor North Easterners are found humiliated and their girls are reported to be molested in Delhi.[53] This is really making many of the integrationists worried because of the negligence and subtle discrimination of the South and North East in Delhi and in the corridors of power. The Delhi media is ready to project anything that is happening in Delhi as national and the South is generally scandalous (episodes of A. Raja, Jayalalitha, Marans, Satyam, etc. and not much about Radiatapes, coalgate, etc.) enough to be overlooked. The notion of cultural hegemony depicting the power elite in Delhi in corporate media in projecting characters and band values of people against others does demonstrate the importance of writers, language and their social background in contemporary Indian discourse.

Thus, the language and culture of marginalised groups due to either the location of the people in a region or their caste have been considered as unimportant in the post-reform period. The economic viability, particularly the size of the market and its money worth, determines the importance. Nevertheless, they may turn out to be the real issues that might consolidate the affected groups under hurt feeling to trigger movements such as the Telangana, Bodo, Dravidistan, etc. It is the creative writer, the intellectual and the committed media that bring immediate reaction against injustice in analysing the power relations as intelligibly as possible to the victims who are dissuaded by multiple cultural products today. We have seen it in the South in the past and as recently as in 2014 in the creation of Telangana. Social scientists need to listen to them carefully to draw conclusions of their own rather than dismissing them as super structural issues.

NOTES AND REFERENCES

1. Antonio Gramsci, *Selections from Prison Note Books* (Hyderabad: Orient Longman, 1996) and Max Horkheimer, *Traditional and Critical Theory*, tr. Jeremy J. Shapiro (New York: Herder & Herder, 1972).
2. D. M. Lamberton, ed., *Economics of Information and Knowledge* (Harmondsworth: Penguin Books, 1971).
3. www.UNESCO.org/languages-Atlas (accessed in January 2015).
4. Leela Gandhi, *Postcolonial Theory: A Critical Introduction* (New York: Columbia University Press, 1998).
5. Gail Omvedt, "Capitalism and Globalisation, Dalits and Adivasis," *Economic and Political Weekly*, Vol. 40, No. 47, 2005.
6. "Kannada writer M. M. Kalburgi shot dead," *The Hindu*, 31 August 2015.

7. Gramsci, see note 1.

8. M. Foucalt, *Archeology of Knowledge* (London: Routledge, 1998).

9. "The Untold Story of Uttarakhand," *The Hindu*, 26 June 2013.

10. See www.en.wikipaedia.org/shaiva-siddhantha for details.

11. www.downtoearth.org.in/news/man-madereasons-uttarakhanddisaster (accessed in June 2014).

12. Gandhi, see note 4.

13. "Ambedkar Would Have Recognized the Humour," *The Times of India*, 22 May 2012.

14. *The Times of India*, 24 January 2013.

15. Yogindra Sikand and Avinash Mishra, ed., *Indian Mass Media Prejudices Against Dalits and Muslims* (Delhi: Hope India, 2010).

16. Amartya Sen, *Identity and Violence: The Illusion of Destiny* (New York: W.W. Norton and Co., 2007).

17. See www.theguardian.com/books/206/august5 for details.

18. See www.theindiandiaspora.com for details.

19. Srilankan High Commissioner in India, see his home page.

20. www.idsn.org/srilanka (accessed on 1 August 2014).

21. It is now popularly known in the USA about the Telugu diaspora split on caste lines and the obsolete ceremonies like half sari for girl child, etc. as a part of identity of some social groups.

22. See Gurajada Apparao's Preface to *Kanyasulkam*.

23. Aryabhatta was a mathematician, Varahamihira was an astronomer and Bhaskara II was a mathematician.

24. Velcheru Narayana Rao, *Girls for Sale* (New Delhi: Penguin, 2010).

25. H. Kulke and D. Rothermund, *A History of India* (Calcutta: Rupa and Co, 1990).

26. Eric Stroke, *The English Utilitarians and India* (New Delhi: Oxford University Press, 1989).

27. Nehru and Ambedkar were educated in England when there were rich deliberations about socialism, equity and other egalitarian ideas including the influence of Harold Laski on young minds.

28. These influential people include Charles Dickens, Havelock Ellis, P. Lakshmi Narasu and G. B. Shaw.

29. H. Sharp, ed., *Selections from Educational Records* (Calcutta: Government Printing Press, 1965).

30. A. P. Rajam, *A Century's Quest for the Footprints*, compiled by Ramu Naidu (Velugu Publications, 2015).

31. Narayana Rao, see note 24.

32. Sekhar Bandopadhyaya, *Caste, Culture and Hegemony* (New Delhi: SAGE Publications, 2004).

33. See Gurajada Apparao's *Kanyasulkam*. *Kanyasulkam* is a Telugu play written by Gurajada Apparao in 1892. It is one of the earliest modern works in an Indian language, and it is the first Telugu play to deal with social issues.

34. See Gurajada Apparao's Preface to *Kanyasulkam*.

35. Kamalakar Bhatt, *Sudrakamalakaram,* a Sanskrit treatise.

36. Edward Said, *Culture and Imperialism* (New York: Vintage Books, 1994).

37. Thapi Dharma Rao was a writer, journalist and scholar who took the spoken language movement in Telugu to its logical end and initiated social science writing with a socio-anthropological approach first time in Telugu language.

38. Burkhard Schnepel, *The Jungle Kings: Ethno Historical Aspects of Politics and Rituals in Orissa* (Delhi: Manohar Books, 2002).

39. See note 35.

40. *Vijaya Vilasam* is a Telugu Literary critical writing published by Visalandhra Publishing House, Vijayawada, 1980.

41. Sri Sri was a revolutionary poet of Telugus and known in the literary world through his Mahaprasthanam. He passed away in 1983.

42. Veguchukka Grandhamala was a publishing company to promote progressive literature.

43. Tripuraneni Ramaswamy educated in Great Britain embraced the rationalist thought in assessing the social practices in Coastal Andhra and at one time wanted to join M. N. Roy.

44. K. Veeramani, ed., *Collected Works of Periyar EVR* (Chennai: The Periyar Self-respect Propaganda Institution, 2005).

45. Yamada Keiko, "Sovereign and Historical Evolution of the Identity of Modern Telugus," *Economic and Political Weekly,* 21 August 2010.

46. K. S. Chalam, *Economic Reforms and Social Exclusion* (New Delhi: SAGE Publications, 2011).

47. Gordon Childe, *What Happened in History* (Harmondworth, Penguin, 1952).

48. "Children Learn Better in Their Mother Tongue." Advancing research on mother tongue-based multilingual education, www.lobalpartnership.org/blog (accessed in December 2015).

49. Phuley Jyotirao, *Gulamgiri* (Bombay: Government of Maharashtra, 1989).

50. Sikand and Mishra, see note 15.

51. Ibid.

52. N. T. Ramarao (NTR) was a non-Congress Chief Minister of Andhra Pradesh and unseated the ruling party with his Telugu Pride slogan. KCR, K. Chandrasekhar Rao, started the Telangana Rastra Samiti (TRS) to achieve the Telangana state. Kavuri Sambasiva Rao, a coastal Andhra contractor, is a Union Cabinet Minister. K. Kesava Rao is the former President of the Andhra Pradesh Congress Committee.

53. "Girl from Northeast Molested, Accused Film Actor Karn Pratap Singh," *Hindustan Times,* New Delhi, 25 March 2015.

9
Alternative Paradigms

Social economics as a branch of Economics was initiated during the 19th century in Europe. There seem to be different approaches to study economic issues dominant during the period of industrialisation and then during the colonial expansion of Europe. The English approach to development was supported by Adam Smith, as the 'wealth of nations' is different from the French from the time of François Quesnay (1759) who had developed a method to understand the circulation of wealth. It is also noted by scholars that the Germans did not evince interest in trade to accumulate wealth, but did use Frederic List's ideas to protect industry to provide opportunities for employment and growth. Thus, we have in the traditions of economics discipline different approaches to development, while the English hegemony continues to prevail in India due to its colonial past.

There has always been resistance to colonial rule in India from the very beginning. Patriotism and love for the land along with a subtle liking for traditions and the perception that the British were destroying some of the institutions were behind many of the revolts. At the same time, there were different schools of thought that advanced the ideas of revolt following certain ideological considerations during freedom movement in India including Dadabhai Naoroji and others relating to economic exploitation.[1] It is very heartening to note that Indians have contributed to the international understanding of colonialism, exploitation, liberation, development etc. We cite here some important contributions that appear to be fresh in their approaches to the understanding of the Indian economy and society and bring them under the broad rubric of the social economy. We are citing the works of well-known scholars and freedom fighters whose ideas appear to have been ignored or overlooked by mainstream social scientists in formulating alternative policy prescriptions with the hope that it may generate some debate now.

M. N. ROY: THE EPITOME OF THE FREEDOM STRUGGLE

The original name of M. N. Roy was Narendranath Bhattacharya. He was born in Khetput in Midnapur district of West Bengal.[2] M. N. Roy was perhaps the only Indian revolutionary who travelled both in the East and West to enlist support from allies to free India from British rule through an armed struggle. In the process, he became the founder of the Communist Party of India in exile on 15 December 1920 (Tashkent, USSR) and helped to establish the Communist Party of Mexico in 1919.[3] He was born in a region that has given some of the greatest leaders of the freedom movement, including Subhash Chandra Bose, Aurobindo Ghosh and Shyama Prasad Mukherjee. Roy was a student of Aurobindo Ghosh for a brief period in the National College and seems to have been influenced by him. Jatin Mukherjee, the great Bengal revolutionary who became a martyr fighting the British, was his guru. Roy left India in search of arms and financial help vaguely promised by the Germans, but landed in the USA in 1915. He became a Marxist in America and got his first wife there.

It is fascinating to study the adventurous life of Roy who spent almost two decades outside the country to become a political revolutionary and social radical. It is alleged by thinkers that it is easy to become a political revolutionary in India but very hard to find someone who can speak up and practise against the existent rigid social institutional structures. It seems Roy defied this presumption and become a scholar and a seer at the end of his life to prove the primacy of ideological revolution in India. He was one of the very few who were self-taught about Marxism, science and humanism. Lenin wanted comments on his theory of imperialism and in the process was convinced by Roy's analysis of colonialism,[4] particularly with reference to India. Roy argued that the colonial powers did not allow the national bourgeois to grow and liberate the proletariat; yet decolonisation was inevitable. His thesis to defeat the ecclesiastical inclinations of Gandhi seems to have remained uncontested till his death. It is, however, very intriguing to find that Roy joined the nationalist movement led by Gandhiji and Nehru after he was released from jail (he was convicted in the Kanpur conspiracy case in 1924). Leaving aside the criticism about his integrity and alleged secretive connections with America spread by Comintern and others, Roy remained a staunch supporter of the social and intellectual revolution in India. After a brief stint with the Congress party and association with leaders like Bose and others, he was reported to have been disheartened and started his own outfit, the Radical Democratic Party, in 1942. He however realised that the parliamentary form of government, formed on the basis of political parties, was a prisoner of its own ideologies with little scope for democratic practice. He thought that a party-less democracy was a better solution to reach out to the people even at the panchayat level and wound up his party in 1948.

Roy started an intellectual movement; he produced the 22 theses on radical humanism in 1948 and joined the International Ethical Union with headquarters in the USA in 1950. The journey of a radical from the Bengali bhadralok, it is alleged, has remained eccentric and superfluous to the Indian society as he was imbued with Western values of liberalism, seems to have ultimately ended him without tangible accomplishments. This is a limited assessment of Roy; his intellectual impact on India and elsewhere is yet to be assessed. If we were to evaluate his contributions to intellectual advances beyond communist theory and practice, and also assess the limitations and the historical context of any progressive movement in India, it is difficult to find a comparable personality. His contemporaries are great leaders such as Periyar E. V. R., B. R. Ambedkar, Ram Manohar Lohia, Jay Prakash Narayan and others with whom he had dialogue, but none of it led to any collective action. This is one of the historical slips of the Indian renaissance movement initiated by him and is still too enervated to emerge as a national movement. Yet, M. N. Roy will remain an enigmatic personality because of his social background and the historical circumstances under which he dabbled with so many issues in quick succession.

If we look back, unravel and notice that had the contributions of Marx, Darwin, Sigmund Freud and others who explained the contradictions in human society not available to mankind, the world would have been worse to live in by now. In this context, the role played by M. N. Roy is very significant and needs fresh reflection in the changed situation in the world today. But the Royist's or his followers who kept on nagging on a system called Soviet Communism that is almost lifeless and dead now requires a revisit. The writings of Roy in different languages amount to thousands of pages and a project initiated by Sibnarayan Ray seems to have been abandoned after Ray's death in 2008. Roy, in the last days of his life, realised the futility of radical programmes of transformation in a society that was deeply ingrained in tradition, superstition and orthodoxy. Unless there was a Renaissance movement like that in Europe, the future would be bleak and India would continue to live under various shades of subjugation. There is enough evidence in his writings on Indian materialism from the time of Lokayata and a clear analysis on 'Reason, Romanticism and Revolution' to develop a philosophy to carry on radical humanism as an alternative project. Unlike most of his comrades, Roy took it upon himself with a utopian mindset to get India, a nation that was not yet ready, to liberate from orthodoxy got in return a rude shock. He believed that a revolutionary is one who should carry the confidence of conviction that he would rebuild the world, better than today. This needs a sound philosophical and theoretical foundation for which he has elaborated several concepts and notions such as physical realism, reason is biological property, materialism can be sustained without dialectics and so on. However, his over-emphasis on libertarian freedom, perhaps carried with him from the days of his New York experiences, seems to have dented his unreasoned judgement on socialism, communism and democracy in India.

Like Roy, several scholars differed with Stalin Joseph, which included K. A. Wittfogel and the whole Frankfurt school of scholars who enriched Western Marxism. Many intellectuals reflected on the limitations of dialectical historical materialism, including the so-called Asiatic mode of production to Third World countries but none of them is as vehement as Roy who was against limitations of Marxism. On a hindsight it appears that Roy lost his moorings being an Indian while his contemporary in Italy, Gramsci, seems to have reinforced Marxism. The country lost an opportunity in Roy once again. Perhaps Indian intellectuals, particularly the secular and Left genre, paid little attention to his writings and warnings that he prophesied about the future of communism and alternatives he was suggesting. It is time that some of his ideas and rumblings on Indian science and superstition, thesis on freedom, state, democratic socialism, primacy of rationality and building grassroots radical democratic movement to achieve a stateless state deserve scrutiny.

DEVELOPMENT PHILOSOPHY OF B. R. AMBEDKAR

B. R. Ambedkar was one of the greatest thinkers of modern India who blended Western thought with Buddhist ideals.[5] It would be hasty to come to a conclusion about his contributions merely on the basis of his biography written by some individuals or merely going through his debates in the Parliament and in the Bombay Legislative Assembly. In fact, the maturity in his thinking and the philosophical thrust given to his political strategies reached its zenith by the time he completed *Buddha and His Dhamma*.[6] Therefore, one needs to relate his subliminal thoughts with his analytical approaches to understand India and learn how he provided solutions to the existing evils in the country. At the same time, one may notice the continuity in his thinking from that of his writings on social issues like *Annihilation of Caste* in 1937, through his economic writings and *Buddha and His Dhamma* in 1956. In Part IV of the book *Buddha and His Dhamma* relating to 'Enlightenment and the Vision of the New Way,' Ambedkar has shown that he clearly understood Gautama's dilemma. Ambedkar has said that when Gautama sat in meditation for getting new light he was in the grip of the Sankhya philosophy. As we all know, Sankhya is one of the enlightened schools of Indian thought that influenced the Bhagavad Gita. But, the problem with the Sankhya, according to Ambedkar, was that Gautama was riddled with how to do away with suffering. The Sankhya has limited tools to deal with this problem. In fact the Sankhya was one of the greatest schools of thought in the ancient period and even preceded Western thought as far as the methods of approaching truth were concerned. But it was least concerned about social issues. Therefore, Ambedkar came to the conclusion that the Buddha finally developed his own teachings without much reliance on the Sankhya. Thus, Buddha became an independent philosopher and teacher. Ambedkar has explained that there were four important distinguishing features in the teachings of the Buddha: (a) the mind precedes things, mind is leader of all its faculties, etc.; (b) the mind is the fount of all good and evil; (c) avoidance of sinful acts; and (d) real religion lies not in the books of religion, but in the observation of the tenets of religion. He goes on to explain the greatness of the Buddha and has said that the Buddha's doctrine of Anicca (transtoriness) is confirmed as modern science concept of universe is that of grouping dissolution and regrouping and (anatta) as egoless-ness.[7] Ambedkar seems emotional at the end of the book and says, "[W]ho would not say let such a one be our Master"? The essence of Ambedkar's work is that knowledge is essential to salvation and ignorance is one of the two main causes of failures to attain it and craving or attachment being the other limitation. Modern scholars might evaluate Ambedkar as an idealist in interpreting the importance given by him to mind over matter. But, definitely, he cannot be compared with that of Shankaracharya as Ambedkar himself has critiqued the latter in his writings. He may be considered to some extent as an epistemological idealist in interpreting the Buddha. But he had profound understanding about the materialist conditions of the people in general and Dalits in particular. Therefore, he gave a practical guide for achieving equality in an egalitarian or unjust society as he found in Buddhism "Sense of Equality and Equality of Treatment."[8]

There is some kind of a craving for Buddhism among sec-tions of Dalits and to that extent is idealising and sometimes indecorously reducing Ambedkar's position as a messiah. One must understand here why Ambedkar wanted Buddhism to be a tool for the emancipation of the Dalits. He was not inter-ested in giving the Dalits salvation or liberation from bond-age as there were several religions under which Dalits were already drawn into without either physical or metaphysical emancipation. He knew that the Buddhist approach to philos-ophy was largely borrowed from the native Ajvikas. Buddha had propounded the theory of *paticca samuppada*, dependent origination. This theory speaks about anitya and the process of continuous change, and elucidates that nothing such as ego, personality, soul, etc. remain. Therefore, no transmigration takes place. Then where is the need for varnas based on past karma. In other words, in one go, the whole edifice of caste, based on past karma and transmigration of souls, was devas-tated by the Buddha. This was a great revolution in the ancient period to denounce the existence of caste. It is still valid and is not available in other religions including Mediterranean Islam and Christianity. The reasons why Ambedkar embraced Buddhism can be explained by the fact that Buddhism demolishes metaphysical Hinduism that supports caste. And, at the same time, it provides sufficient grounds for the emancipation of the Dalits in modern society. But the same needs to be creatively used and not limited to the worship of an idol alone that makes Buddha as an avatar and is now being extended to Ambedkar himself.

It is noted that philosophical understanding is always necessary to sustain a programme. Unfortunately, some of the activists in the Dalit movement do not understand or are sometimes led away by competing religious discourses to come to divergent conclusions. We are of the opinion that, among the different communities in the country, it is only the so-called SCs or the Dalits who are in disorientation or divided on the basis of religion, sub-caste, region, language and other considerations. It is in the light of the above background and philosophical context that we have tried to bring out the programmes of Ambedkar which we consider are important. He has written books and made presentations in the Bombay Legislative Assembly as well as the Constituent Assembly and formulated policies as labour member in the governor general's council that gave him an opportunity to project a vision about the future of the Dalits during 1935–50. However, it is very difficult to find a specific theory of the Dalit development exclusively written by him at one place. Except in his detailed memorandum on the safeguards for the SCs for submission to the Constituent Assembly on behalf of the SC Federation in March 1947, nowhere did Ambedkar formulate any detailed programme for Dalit development. It is also true that most scholars and activists have focused more on the social and political contributions of Ambedkar than on his economic and educational ideas. In fact, Ambedkar had two PhDs in economics from two premier universities of the world in the early part of the 20th century (Columbia 1917 and London 1923). He was aware of the fact that economic development was essential for the survival of the Dalits. But, his existential condition and the social circumstances that prevailed during British India forced him to concentrate more on the problems of social exclusion and untouchability and made him fight for the human dignity of the Dalits. It does not mean that he has not written anything about the economic upliftment of the Dalits in India as there were occasions when he clearly formulated a vision for this. Some of the ideas are scattered in different parts of his writings. Therefore, it is the responsibility of scholars to bring all these together to bring out a vision of the great son of India for the upliftment of the Dalits in particular and the poor in general. The following are some of the sources from which a comprehensive vision of Ambedkar's Dalit development can be understood, namely his philosophical background based on his books *Buddha and His Dhamma, The Annihilation of Caste* and *Buddha or Karl Marx*; 'States and Minorities', 'Small Holdings in India and Their Remedies' and his economic writings; and his speeches delivered in the Bombay Legislative Assembly and in the Parliament.

The theories of development and growth appeared mostly during the decolonisation period, particularly with reference to less developed countries. Theories of economic development emerged as an important subject of study only after the Second World War and Ambedkar was deeply involved by that time in governance. Development during the colonial rule was understood as emancipation from want and destitution. During the 18th and 19th centuries, the Dalits were considered as destitute and depressed classes. Therefore, if there was any single theory propounded by Ambedkar about the economic emancipation of the Dalits in India, it was about state socialism. It was a philosophical and theoretical understanding of the fact that development was possible for the Dalits only through parliamentary democracy. In his papers on the Buddha or Karl Marx he has clearly mentioned that the root cause of *dukkha* in the Buddhist tradition was poverty. One could remove dukkha, Ambedkar said, only through the abolition of poverty with state ownership of agriculture, industry

and insurance. But, this was to be achieved not through violence but through a peaceful means of democratic socialism in
India. He evaluated the means through which socialism could
be achieved as per Marxist and Buddhist principles. He found
that it was through non-violence, following the *panchashila* and
the eightfold path of Buddhism, that it was possible to achieve
equality and socialism for Indians in general and the Dalits in
particular. It is said by S. G. Kulakarni that,

> [The] philosophical achievement of Dr Ambedkar consists in work-
> ing of a conception of individual without being an individualist of
> modern western brand conception of individual, which is not conflict
> with Nairatmya Vada. Dr Ambedkar has interpreted Buddhism as a
> vibrant world view and way of life to people who were systematically
> denied any opportunity for engaging in philosophy and religion. He
> made the traditional religion morally reprehensible in a society which
> has expected to emulate secularist values.[9]

In other words, he used Buddhist principles of equality to
blend with Marxist principles of the annihilation of classes
so that the Dalits would remain comfortable in a new society.
This framework should have remained as the back bone of his
vision of Dalits development.

Scholars like Amartya Sen are now elaborating on the
need for a democratic polity to sustain development.[10] In fact,
Ambedkar was one of the earliest to formulate the thesis that
development could be sustained only in a democratic set up.[11]
He has elaborated on the point that political democracy rests
on four principles, namely:[12]

1. That the individual is an end himself.
2. The individual has certain inalienable rights which must
   be guaranteed to him by the Constitution.
3. That the individual shall not be required to relinquish
   any of his constitutional rights as a condition precedent
   to the receipt of a privilege.
4. That the State shall not delegate powers to private persons to govern others.

In the stated principles, Ambedkar has observed that the rights of individuals are not negotiable, much the same for the Dalits. He knew that in a country like India, where groups of individuals were placed in a hierarchical order and were traditionally treated as unequal, it was essential that the primacy of the value that, 'all are born equal' be restored. It is difficult to envision development for all in India without first reinstating this universal value. That is the reason why Ambedkar insisted on state socialism which was to be adopted for the Dalits and others in an equal footing. This was to be achieved through provisions in the Constitution and not through legislative processes. That is the reason why he wanted to become the minister for planning so that he could implement this development programme. But Nehru did not give him this opportunity and made him the chairman of Drafting Committee for the Constitution. Ambedkar played his historical role very well in the job by incorporating Directive Principles of State Policy where socialism and secularism were enshrined.

Ambedkar worked on provincial finances in British India, for his doctoral thesis in Columbia and on the problem of the rupee in London and written treatises such as small holdings in India and their remedies, showcasing an economist par excellence. Ambedkar commented that justice in taxation was conspicuous by its absence during the British rule. He observed that, "[I]t was a cruel satire that the many, European Civil Servants who fattened themselves on pay and pickings were supremely exempted from any contribution towards maintenance of the government."[13] He also indicated in his dissertations that the most oppressive tax at that time was the salt tax which remained at 11–14 per cent of the revenue during the 1850–90. He explained how the income was not spent on the development of the people. He found in the study that around 60 per cent of the income was spent on the military during the period 1809–50. This, excess expenditure on military according to Ambedkar, was an imperial system which had drained the Indian economy. Therefore, he wanted India to have a federal structure, where the taxes were based on rational principles. If one were to be inclined to formulate a theory of development as developed by Ambedkar in his writings, his economic writings in the form of PhD dissertations published as books can be considered as the background on which a theory of development could be constructed. In fact, one article published in the *Journal of the Indian Economic Society* in 1918 on agriculture preceded the theories of Arthur Lewis, the Nobel laureate in economics whose paper "Economic development with unlimited supplies of labour" appears to be similar in approach.

The profound wisdom of Ambedkar relating to the economic upliftment of the Dalits can be seen in his memorandum on 'States and Minorities' submitted in 1947. In Article II, Section 2 on remedies against the invasion of the fundamental rights, Ambedkar has provided provisions of protection against economic exploitation. It means that he wanted state socialism by means of constitutional remedies against the economic exploitation of the Dalits. The text from his memorandum, 'States and Minorities,' clearly indicates what he wanted to provide for their economic development. He wanted both agriculture and industry to develop simultaneously. He wanted agriculture, insurance and industries to be nationalized within 10 years of the Constitution coming into operation.

State socialism, he said, is essential for the rapid industrialisation of India. Private enterprise cannot do it and, if it did, it would produce inequalities of wealth like what private capitalism has produced in Europe and which should be a warning to Indians. Consolidation of holdings and tenancy legislation, Ambedkar said, are worse than useless. They cannot bring about prosperity in agriculture. Neither consolidation nor tenancy legislation can be of any help to the 60 million untouchables who are landless labourers or solve their problem of unemployment and poverty. Only collective farms on the lines set out in the proposal of developing collective farms can help them.

The plan for development of the country, Ambedkar hinted in his 1947 memorandum, has two special features. One is that it proposes state socialism in important fields of economic life. The second special feature of the plan is that it does not leave the establishment of state socialism to the will of the legislature. It establishes state socialism by the law of the Constitution and thus makes it unalterable by any act of the legislature and the executive. The allegation that Ambedkar was responsible for Articles 15 and 16 to protect reservations in jobs is only half-truth as caste-based reservations had already been implemented in Southern states which got incorporated in the Constitution as a continuation of policy. But it was struck down by the Supreme Court in 1951 that led to street fights in the South to make Jawaharlal Nehru government to make the first amendment to the Constitution in 1951. But Ambedkar has provided substantial support for the weaker sections and the poor in Part IV of the Directive Principles of State Policy. Ambedkar defended this part of the Constitution in the Constituent Assembly, saying that it was instrument of instruction to the political party which may come to power through the democratic process and which it is obliged to implement. Articles 38, 39, 41, 42, 43, 45, 46 and 47 of the Constitution speak about socialism, right to education, right to food, etc. translated as part of Article 21A later, which are his contributions that shall remain as rights of not only Dalits but of all weaker sections to enjoy. Unfortunately, successive governments after Independence have paid only lip service and never tried to implement them fully, maybe due to the interference of the elite of the apex court. It is strange to notice that a section of the Dalit activists and the Left never referred to these provisions as his constitutional blessings.

Ambedkar never wanted that the Dalits remain in the scattered settlements of villages. He was against the proposal to make the village a unit of governance, while Gandhiji romanticised the village. In his Constituent Assembly debate, Ambedkar gave a strong reply to his critics who were very critical about him in not making the village as a unit of governance in the Constitution. In his reply he said, "[W]hat is a village but a sink of localism, a den of ignorance and narrow mindedness."[14] Though Ambedkar wanted the expansion of the public sector and the creation of opportunities for Dalits in the services sector, we have noted in the previous chapter that the opportunities for the Dalits after the 1991 Economic Policy have come down.

It is instructive to look at the proposal of industrialisation which Ambedkar had mentioned in his 'States and Minorities' here. It is good to find that the language and the tenor of his argument of an industrial policy which was based on the development of the public sector in key and basic industries became a part of the Industrial Policy of the Congress Government in 1948. The Industrial Policy Resolution of 1948 of the Nehru government is almost the same as that of Ambedkar's proposal made in his above-mentioned memorandum. It is this policy that had made the country strong economically and helped to achieve the rate of growth of around 5 per cent on average before 1990. After the introduction of the industrial policy in 1948, the Congress Government eulogised it as a *sine quo non* of socialism in their resolution at the Avadi Congress in 1956. This was a policy to translate some of the provisions in the Directive Principles of State Policy which Ambedkar had so laboriously developed and incorporated in the Constitution. In fact, Ambedkar was the first to start an independent Labour Party in India, maybe on the lines of the British Labour Party. In fact, both Ambedkar and Nehru and several Congress party socialist thinkers during pre-Independence period were influenced either directly or indirectly by the writings and speeches of Fabians of England.

Nehru–Ambedkar Socialism

There seems to be some misunderstanding between B. R. Ambedkar[15] and Jawaharlal Nehru as far as political issues were concerned and there was absolute convergence of ideas in their economic programmes. Was there a separate stream of socialism in Ambedkar or Nehru? It is difficult to discern from their writings, but one can find that both of them were trained in the liberal traditions of England, witnessed the emergence of the Labour Party while they were students in the UK and must have been influenced by the social democratic rhetoric of the preeminent position of the public sector. Nehru emphasised on the 'commanding heights' of the public sector for planned development,[16] while Ambedkar strategised that it was only through the expansion of the public sector that the weaker sections could enter in to the modern sectors of development. In fact, the industrial policies of the Nehru government, during the life time of Ambedkar, relied on state enterprises to create the necessary ground for development in the years to come. Ambedkar emphasised in the election manifesto of the S. C. Federation in 1951 that,

> While rapid industrialization of the country is very essential in the opinion of the Federation agriculture is bound to remain the foundation of India's economy. Any scheme of increased production which does not take into account the re-construction of Indian agriculture is doomed to disappointment.

He provided data to show that 93 million acres of cultivable wasteland were available in the country that needed to be made accessible to the scheduled castes to increase their income.[17] He has also noted that cottage industries along with electricity supply needed to be promoted to supplement agricultural incomes. In fact, some of the ideas were put in to action in the subsequent planning processes in India to raise the levels of income in general and through welfare measures for the Dalits in particular.

The policies of Nehru that are called as Nehruvian socialism with which Ambedkar had no quarrel were put in the back-burner by the P. V. Narasimha Rao government that opened the flood gates to FDIs, in the name of which the black money of the dvijas is stacked outside the country. The liberalisation policies from 1991 have continued without any change either by the UPA or the NDA governments, strengthening the economic and social base of the dvijas, and some shudra groups as in the south are co-opted in to the system by the present regime to make it a viable and enduring formation to rule India.

Dalits have a difficult time to decide to which way that they should go? If they want the whole community to be emancipated, the project on which B. R. Ambedkar devoted his life, they need to decide the strategy now, and if they want that Babasaheb memory is to be kept alive with the chosen few and forget about the rest, it is very simple, forget about his emancipatory project and join the band wagon. In any formation to succeed in public maneuvering, the unity and constructive action among all Dalit groups (as seen from the actions of Dalit adversaries) are to be built and demonstrated in great strength. Nonetheless, this is the most testing period for the Dalits even quite different from the time of B. R. Ambedkar (1880–1950) when the British were present to intercede and confer some concessions.

RAM MANOHAR LOHIA AND LEFT UNITY TODAY

Ram Manohar Lohia, one of the cherished leaders of the freedom movement and a great socialist intellectual, evokes interest among the common people in the country who are looking for an alternative today.[18] History is always dispassionate about personalities and detached from emotional connects. It has been proved time and again that individuals and personalities are mercilessly thrown in to oblivion when their work and ideas are a menace to contemporary society and bring characters of those whose sacrifices for the well-being of humankind are eternal to limelight (though they might have desolated during their lifetime). The relevance of the ideas and opinions of some intellectuals may be far-reaching and visionary during their lifetime and might be taken as incredible by their contemporaries, but that does not mean the knowledge and experiences remain futile. There is one group of evangelists in India whose profession is to make irrelevant ideas significant and earn a living whether they are useful or useless to the common people. Religion and faith based on hypocrisy and hegemony might make a few ideas always appear in the public domain, but have little relevance to aid the victims of the unkindness of time. We have in India indigenous thinkers such as Mahatma Phuley, M. N. Roy, B. R. Ambedkar, Ram Manohar Lohia, etc. in the modern times whose ideas as noted above were found relevant whenever society was dragged into chaos and bigotry.

The collapse of the Soviet Union experiment, the crisis in Europe, the emergence of neoliberal policies along with the resurrection of fundamentalism, the control of caste and cor-porate media and the inconsequence of the poverty of Indians in public debates call for a reflection on the ideas of Lohia once again. Though some scholars published fascinating papers and books on Lohia during his centenary year in 2010, it is an occasion which need not be burdened with any obligations to remember him as a custom, but to really understand his rel-evance today.

The critics of Lohia, particularly from the Left, used to call him as perhaps a petty bourgeois intellectual who was critical about Marx. Some of them might also think that his programme of action against caste supremacy and his short-tempered utterances against some communists were only passing remarks. But, four decades of experience both in India and in socialist countries have shown that he was to a large extent right in perceiving the problems of building socialism in India. It was unfortunate that Ambedkar, who took the support of the socialists and contested elections in 1952(54), had corresponded with Lohia, but passed away without get-ting their agenda fructified. In a way, the bourgeois and ruling classes succeeded in keeping the Left forces divided with their tricks, including co-opting and cajoling some of the diabolic individuals in the parties to indirectly support them to remain in power. But this did not yield any growth in the party cadres and, in fact, weakened the whole Left movement in India. Some analysts[19] indicate how the three types of Left with Marxist ideologies and people-oriented struggles are all made irrelevant with the ideology of globalisation and PPP model with temporary solutions to the victims with small goodies. Further the Left did not realise the power of the media, particularly the electronic channels under the control of corporate and caste power, as dangerous despite the fact that NDA came to power with Ramanand Sagar's Ramayana the first time.[20] And with 400 regional channels eulogising Hindutva hard and soft along with social media added in 2014 facilitated NDA-II to get total power now. Lohia, a shrewd observer and an intelligent communicator, seems to have anticipated about the role of media in Indian politics long back in one of his speeches in Guntur Hindu College in 1955.

Unlike several other leaders, Lohia did not go to England for his higher studies as he abhorred the Anglo-Saxons (although Germans do come under Saxons, they never claim so). He was trained by one of the foremost economic historians of his time, namely Sombart Werner[21] and his contemporaries including the famous Schumacher whose *Small Is Beautiful* derived most of his ideas from Mahatma Gandhi and the Buddha. His approach to the study of Indian problems was indigenous and critically drawn from Indian philosophical thought. It is very illuminating to read Lohia's book *Marx, Gandhi and Socialism*, as one of his very important contributions to Indian thought. Lohia used several examples from Indian thinkers such as Adi Shankara to illustrate his point on abstract ideas like the difference between worldly truth and absolute truth.[22] He was very critical about Marx, at the same time being a Marxist, and used his theory of surplus value for his analysis. His major criticism against Marx was that the latter had used his European background for the study of Asian or Indian problems that were different. Lohia was of the opinion that Marx's lack of knowledge about Asian society made him draw extreme generalisations that did not allow him to draw meaningful conclusions and in a way made him irrelevant in the Indian context. One of the examples that he used to attribute to Marx was the economic crisis and the appropriation of appropriators. This did not happen in the capitalist advanced countries of Europe, but only occurred in Asia and Russia. But he was an ardent supporter of Marx in saying "Marxism is quite accurate in its findings on capital accumulation, correct from one angel on questions of industrial crises, of monopoly, and socialization of labour, but factually wrong in the spheres of accumulating poverty, causal class struggle, and the world revolution."[23] In fact, the criticism in the last sentence is taken by some of the followers of Lohia to an unconstrained extent to denounce Marxism. Lohia's criticism about the Soviet Union of Stalin era did not last long. It is here that we need to revise some of our reflections on Lohia to make him relevant and up-to-date for the 21st-century India.

The critics and admirers of Lohia should not hesitate to recognise that the limitations of Marx and Soviet model and even China as noted by Lohia do not exist anymore today to prolong the criticism. Similarly, the Marxists who were critical about Lohia's approach to communism may consider the changed circumstances in the world and the relevance of the socialist programme advocated by Lohia, and the need for a reassessment of his ideas to bring all the progressive forces on one platform to fight capitalism and its Siamese twin fundamentalism. The frequently cited metaphor of Marxism by most Indian activists and intellectuals is about the base and the super-structure approach of studying capitalism or modes of production is not so important today to understand the emergence of imperialism with roots in capital and culture. It has gone to such an extent that some of the materialist interpretations of history by Indian activists have rejected the blatant reality of caste and hoodwinked intellectuals such as Ambedkar and Lohia as those who squandered time and resources on super-structure issues that would blow off once economic emancipation of the poor was achieved. We know now what really happened to that interpretation today. We have seen four decades of active participation of the Left in the parliamentary form of democracy and the content of their demands, activities, implementation of policies wherever they were in power are in no way different from what Lohia advocated. Then where is the point of departure? It appears that there are strong notions and thoughts about Marxism on both sides to differ on interpretations. Now the objective and subjective conditions and the assumptions about developments in India have changed. It seems that both the Left and socialist groups have lost precious time and energy in coming to terms to form a joint action to mitigate the miserable conditions of the poor and the socially deprived under globalisation. No socialist with Lohia ideology today would oppose or contradict programmes against neo-imperialism or economic globalisation which Lohia opposed during his lifetime. There is no scope for belligerent disputes between the communist Left and socialist Left to give space for neoliberal and fundamentalist forces who are now on the same side to enter all spheres of socio-economic life of the people.

Lohia spelt out his socialist agenda in terms of six programmes, namely maximum attainable equality, social ownership, small and indigenous technology, four pillars of state, decentralisation of industry, and world parliament and government. These goals, perhaps Lohia thought, could be achieved through his seven point revolution or *sapta kranti*. These included equality between men and women, shunning of colour discrimination, annihilation of caste and status based on birth, revolution against colonialism, revolution against private capital, revolution against armaments and the creation of a world parliament. Unfortunately, very few Left thinkers seem to have taken these ideas very seriously and never found interrogating them either in academic debates or on political platforms. However, his ardent followers are also to an extent responsible for this apathy, failing to raise these issues for public debate at the all-India level. The followers of Lohia were confined to the Hindi belt (UP and Bihar) and a few pockets of some social groups need to be widened to accommodate the socialist agenda of the Left not only during elections but in every aspect of public and social activity.

Some of the intellectual contributions of Lohia are found to be still valid after the emergence of the North Atlantic hegemony, which Lohia detested during his lifetime. Let us look at three of his important ideas: capitalism and imperialism, limited personality of Rama and capitalist production relations. Lohia, unlike some Indian Marxists, was one with the Latin American scholars who developed ideas regarding how the imperialist centre of the USA was responsible for underdevelopment of the periphery.[24] Lohia questioned Marx's formulation that imperialism comes in at the final stage of capitalist expansion. He did not agree with it and said that British imperialism was responsible for the development of British capitalism and that both were interrelated. He was perhaps anticipating Latin American scholars such as Wallerstein, Gunter Frank, Cardos, Arrighi, etc. when he said that exploitation was like the village being exploited by the town. Though Lenin elaborated on imperialism as a continuation of the Marxist analysis in 1916, interestingly, both M. N. Roy and Lohia gave a different analysis to this as far as India was concerned. This needs to be further studied to make Lohia relevant today.

The greatest price the Marxists and the so-called materialists of India paid for disregarding the potential of Hinduism and to derail the agenda of socialists should have been known to the activists when their camps are not only becoming empty but even threatened with annihilation. It was Lohia who took the Hindu ethos to task by questioning the limited personality of Rama and making him as the ideal of Hindus and have in the process prickled Gandhi's *Ramrajya*. Lohia was perhaps the only Indian Intellectual who raised his voice by coining a term called the Vashista tradition (Brahminical) being responsible for several of our ills. He was one of the foremost thinkers and statesmen who reserved party positions on the basis of caste and had foreseen the emergence of a situation like the one that we see today in Bihar, UP and elsewhere. The Indian Intellectual class, due to their control over the media and public discourse, never allowed any indigenous thinker like Lohia to come to the limelight who questioned their social dominance and observed a conspiracy of silence against him. They have been doing so from time immemorial and the same can be seen in the case of Phuley, Ambedkar, Periyar, Lohia and several others during the last century and are now witnessing the same in the contemporary period with ICT.

One of the important contributions of Lohia in the mode of production debate is his criticism of Marxist overemphasis on the destruction of production relations rather than the productive forces. Lohia's ideas can be interpreted to understand the collapse of the Soviet Union where there was continuation of productive forces along with their production relations that became a necropolis of socialist regime. The mode of production without much change in relations seems to have helped the development of bourgeois class who diverted social surplus from the USSR to the USA and Western Europe, and ultimately pulled down the system. It needs to be examined to what extent Lohia was right in this prophecy.

The recent debate in the Parliament about colour and gender discrimination targeting a Lohite seems to have been distorted in the media. But the fact of the matter is that Lohia spoke about the beauty of black people and explained the splendour of the personality of Draupadi. He was right in saying had the African blacks rather than the British whites were our colonial masters, black colour could have taken the place of white in our public discourse. One can notice that the color blindness is happening today in our electronic media and the ad industry with which our self-styled protectors of Indian culture are comfortable eulogising white and European colour and blondness.

Lohia was one of the ardent supporters of democratic decentralisation and power to the victims of the caste system. Perhaps it was in this context that he encouraged the lower castes in positions of party and power politics to provide adequate representation to the real proletariat. Unlike the Marxists, who proclaimed the nonexistence of caste and the presence of class in India, Lohia, being an indigenous thinker, correctly strategised his political moves to bring equity and equanimity (*samata* and *samtvam*) in a caste-ridden Hindu society. In this process, Lohia was far ahead of his mentor Gandhi and also the Marxists. The critics say that the Left in India has not learnt lessons from the dwindling numbers due to alleged caste composition of the party structures that reflect an upper-caste hegemony. The age old criticism persists that the lower castes are alienated from the Left, since they hardly see their comrades occupying positions in the party bureaucracy, but increasingly see the relatives of the caste oppressors occupying important party positions. This seems to be changing now as there are some reviews and rethinking in certain groups that may help bring course correction in the history of future India. There is wide spectrum of scope thrown open for building a united struggle with fresh and young people joining the pro-test movements in different forms to make India a democratic socialist and secular country with all the Left and democratic forces coming together. The life and mission of Lohia would definitely enrich all those who are interested in finding alter-natives to the present neocolonial conditions in the economy with Hindu fundamentalist character. The post-Modi era seems to have rattled several issues with victims cornered into a narrow social base. The situation has helped to trigger spon-taneous reactions from groups that were not known before in public discourse. It is reported that the Bihar Brothers (Lallu Prasad and Nitish Kumar) who were trained and patronised by Lohia could stop the onslaught of the so-called Hindutva while the Left is still licking the wounds of overconfidence and irrelevance.

PERFIDIOUS CHARACTERS IN COMMUNIST COUNTRIES

Like M. N. Roy, Lohia and others have subjected communism to scrutiny for its failure to give importance to human nature and the intricacies involved. In fact, some of them were justi-fied once the system started crumbling due to the despicable character of some leaders. One may say that it were the leaders who failed and not the system. But the failure to identify the weaknesses and limitations has been a theoretical omission. It is possible to substantiate this with case studies of episodes of corruption in the so-called communist countries while the American voters are preparing to elect the next president quietly. The media reports on Presidential elections in the USA for 2016 surprise us as to how the capitalist countries are unruffled by any of the scams or frauds (as no serious allegations reported) while all the immoral activities are happening in the traditional societies in their yearning to catch the secular West. In order to project the exemplary value system of the West, studies commissioned by their corporate bodies are being pushed into the public domain through media for public consumption in India. Those who are familiar with the 'World Values Survey' and studies on corruption kept for public debate for the last few decades after the fall of the Berlin Wall would realise the purpose of such reports. Economists, particularly the Indian breed, are the first to develop theories about the public enterprises or states' role in economic activities that promote rent-seeking tendencies among bureaucrats leading to rampant corruption in most of the Third World countries. The recommendations from the experts follow: it is better to privatise the economy to increase efficiency and opulence. But, our recent experience with corruption is quite contrary to what the experts have been campaigning for decades. A section of the intellectual community has established that bribery, cronyism, red tapism, inefficiency and several other shortcomings of a politico-economic system are rampant in communist and even in mixed economies like India. It is very hard to find democratic values or human rights in such countries as they are totalitarian systems that do not allow productive forces to enjoy the freedom to grow. This has resulted in their stunted growth and increased misery. It is reported that about 540,000 people have so far been sent to jail and around 40,000 corrupt officials involving 54 billion yuans are under trial in China in 2012. The recent events involving the Chinese Prime Minister Wen, Politburo Member Bo Xialai and military personnel in bribes and scandals of millions and billions of yuans speak about the magnitude of corruption in present-day China.

Since China is still carrying the red flag, CPC and the People's Republic, etc. to describe a communist regime in power, the crimes naturally go into their account. In fact, it is not only the present-day market socialist China, but even the so-called socialist bloc unleashed by Gorbachev through his perestroika and friendship with Reagan administration has provided a different story of communist experiment.

However, the amount of wealth accumulated and siphoned off to the West and other countries through mafias after the fall of the communist regimes does not substantiate the criticism that the communist regimes were inefficient and impoverished. In fact, the amount of wealth created in these nations was alleged to be the main motive for its enforced disintegration and capture. It appears, there is a different side of the story that the communists have failed to explain and turned remorseful. The media occasionally provides very little information on Cuba, Venezuela, Vietnam, etc. Poland was in great turmoil in 1980–89 during the communist regime and our experience with life and liberty of people in Warsaw was very interesting was documented by experts like Peter Schweizer.[25]

It is strange to find that the ideological debates became unipolar after the fall of the Soviet Union and the Third World countries lost steam to argue for an autonomous and socially relevant path of development. They were forced to accept neo-colonial methods of development. A great opportunity for the development of social economics was lost as neither the critiques of Marx nor the protagonists of socialism evinced interest in substantiating the alternative paradigm and practice available in the Nordic and other countries for record. Scholars like Vivekanandan and the Lohites have been arguing that the socialist concept of welfare state vision to promote key principles of social democracy like equality, freedom, democracy, justice and human solidarity in every society can be fruitfully promoted.[26] The findings of Michael Heinrich that the crisis theory as reportedly developed by Marx and defended by the Marxists, despite its shortcomings, can be attributed to Engels editorship (*Monthly Review*, April 2013) are to be read with caution[27] as the views were contradicted by G. Carchedo and Roberts in the December issue of the *Monthly Review* 2013. They have explained that, "between 1963 and 1975, the UK rate of profit fell 28%, while the organic composition of capital rose 20% and the rate of surplus value fell 19%. Between 1975 when the UK rate of profit troughed, and 1996, it rose 50%, while the organic composition of capital rose 17% but the rate of surplus value rose 66%. Finally, from 1996 to 2008, the rate of profit fell 11%, as the organic composition of capital rose 16% and the rate of surplus value was flat. All these three phases are compatible with Marx's law."[28] It is unusual to find that the development debate and civil society activities are concentrated around corruption of public servants, including their political bosses who take decisions for a consideration and not the system that promotes it. It is also noticed that studies sponsored by international organisations have brought out results that support the argument that poor people in the Third World, in order to survive, indulge in corrupt practices. The instinct of survival, it is reported, is so strong that it remains faith neutral irrespective of religious dogmas such as Catholic, Protestant, Muslim, Hindu, etc. It appears that some scholars wanted to promote the idea that, except market, nothing could save the nations (where a scandalous bunch of dishonest people is in office).

Interestingly, some of the experts just do not care to recognise corporate frauds or speculative manoeuvres, including incidents of insider trading, as immoral. They are perhaps part of the game and collect and accumulate whatever growth is obtained through reforms. Therefore, we keep on getting the billionaires' list each year by Forbes without the tag 'ethical earnings.' In other words, the ethical or philosophical accentuation that corporate capitalism promotes development is perilous for human survival as it is narrow and one-sided as revealed in hundreds of critical studies and reports produced by scholars, UNCTAD noted in the previous chapter. We face a dilemma now, whether we should desire growth with honesty or growth with perfidious public servants operating market mechanism and get involved in corruption and manipulations of contracts and other corporate frauds.

Let us examine some of the alternative experiments made on the basis of theoretical expositions as demonstrated by nations with their social consequences.

DEMOCRATIC CAPITALISM AND REPRESENTATION

Social democracy is different from democratic capitalism. Scholars and philosophers have tried to resolve some of the contradictions between them by discovering new concepts. For instance, John Rawls has defined primary goods in a capitalist country as those that constitute "all social values, liberty and opportunity, income and wealth and the bases of 'self-respect'".[29] These primary goods are distinguished from health and vigour, intelligence and imagination, which are natural goods. He has opined that these goods need to be distributed in such a way that the least disadvantaged tend to get the largest benefit. It is on the basis of this monumental philosophical work of Rawls that Amartya Sen has re-examined the question of inequality. These two works need to be articulated through the studies of Ambedkar, Lohia and others to find solutions for the question of the reservation problem in India. It is clear that India is now in the deep embrace of democratic capitalism. The question of justice is to be examined from the point of view of the disadvantaged and the circumstances in which they live. Rawls John opines, "[J]ustice is the first virtue of social institutions, as truth is of systems of thought."[30] He also maintains that inequalities in the distribution of wealth and authority are 'just' only if they result in compensating benefits for everyone, and in particular for the least advantaged members of society. In this context, the performance of the Constitution needs to be judged in relation to the poor in India (democratic capitalism) today. The Planning Commission has reported (2010) that in rural areas the STs had the highest level of poverty (47.4 per cent), followed by the SCs (42.3 per cent) and OBCs (31.9 per cent). It is estimated by the Planning Commission of India that out of 441 districts in the country (except Jammu and Kashmir), more than two-thirds of the districts with SC population had a literacy rate lower than the national average (52 in 2001) and It can be seen that across India, out of 152 districts with more than 25 per cent ST population, 28 districts have ST literacy below 50 per cent and 9 districts have female ST literacy rate below 30 per cent.[31] The data is cited to show that the same is the trend in allocation of land and other assets to Adivasis. Therefore, it is clear from the data that the reservation in jobs and positions of power, including the posts of judges in the Supreme Court, defence, etc. debated for publicity, seems to be not amenable to the compensatory principle of democratic capitalism, according to recent debate on the issue both in Parliament and outside. Then, is it possible to extend the analytical concept of entitlements, used by Amartya Sen, in the context of 'famines and poverty' here? As India has chosen the path of the market economy, such entitlements should work. An entitlement refers to the set of alternative commodity bundles that the person can command in a society, using totality of rights and opportunities in a market economy. These entitlements provide claims over primary goods to individuals and assume that these would ultimately create and enhance capabilities in people. However, these entitlements alone may not generate the declared capabilities to ensure justice. Here Sen has elaborated, "[It is the] actual freedom that is represented by the person's capability to achieve various alternative combinations of functioning's that will decide justice."[32]

It is important to distinguish capability—representing freedom actually enjoyed—both (a) from primary goods (and other resources) and (b) from achievements (including combinations of functioning's actually enjoyed and other realised results). To illustrate the first distinction, a person who has a disability can have more primary goods (in the form of income, wealth, liberties, etc.), but, lesser capabilities (due to handicaps). To take another example, this time from poverty studies, a person may have more income and higher nutritional intakes, but less freedom to live a well-nourished existence because of a higher basal metabolic rate, greater vulnerability to parasitic diseases, larger body size or simply because of pregnancy. Arrangements, such as reservations and quotas for women, the handicapped, etc. used in India as entitlements, need to be appraised under such a formulation. Entitlements of people must be sensitive to the respective impacts of the different systems on aggregative and distributive aspects of peoples' effective freedom and capabilities, within the contours of liberal capitalism. Elaborating on the principle of 'justice as fairness' by Rawls or its critical extension by Sen and others is within the framework of liberal capitalism and seems to be under certain assumptions like free competition, veil of ignorance, etc.

Liberal capitalism is inseparable from democratic institutions where the freedom to choose is guaranteed. In a market economy, goods are produced for the market. The market in theory, however, does not recognise the social background of the person who produces it. It is also necessary to see that these groups or communities are represented in both production and distribution to expand the base of the market and to enhance the capabilities of individuals. This is possible by drawing people into the system and by providing representation to each of the groups in various institutions.

The individual in India represents a caste or community and, therefore, it is necessary to ensure that each caste or community is adequately represented in the institutions through which the system operates. To make democratic capitalism function efficiently, all groups (both advantaged and disadvantaged) need to be represented (proportionally) in the organisations, whether they are public or private. It is exactly here that one must examine the representation of various groups in the emerging opportunities in India to find out whether it is really a democratic capitalist economy or a traditional caste-based system. It is estimated that the amount of investments that were brought into the economy during the post-liberalisation period amounted to few billion rupees.[33] It appears that none of the socially disadvantaged groups is represented in the corporate sector by opening opportunities to them. In fact, new institutions like multi-caste corporations (MCCs) are emerging with the association of influential castes. These caste cleavages would never allow liberal democratic institutions to function and, in turn, distort the traditions of liberal capitalism. To strengthen these democratic institutions and to broaden the market, affirmative action in the form of proportional representation needs to be extended to those sections that are inadequately represented in the economy.

The Constitution of India speaks about, "[The] provision for the reservation of appointments or posts in favour of any backward class of citizens, which, in the opinion of the State, is not adequately 'represented' (emphasis added) in the services under the State." The democratic principle of 'representative form' rather than the 'pure participatory' variety, seems to have guided the 'will' of the Constitution-makers. Given the recent scams like 3G, Coalgate, ONGC, etc. and the economic anarchy attached into the methods of selecting contractors and agents, it is difficult to judge the success of the entitlements in a country that pursues democratic capitalism. Alternatively, the representative form of democracy can be put into practice in the form of opportunities and entitlements for those whose presence is minimal in the government but their proportion is significant in the population. It is possible to provide representation to such sections or social groups in the public sector in the form of quotas or by devising some deliberate policies by the elected government. This, in principle, should be acceptable to the social economy.

DEMOCRATIC SOCIALISM

There seem to be a lot of experiments in managing governments and economies in the advanced nations after the 2008 economic crisis. Some of the European nations involved in the

Second International (1889–1916) have started renewing their ideas related to socialism. Interestingly, the Nordic countries still consider themselves as social democracies. The French have turned their attention once again to socialism in electing Hollande in 2012. In this context, the notions of democratic socialism and social democracy appear to be relevant to deliberate, though there are some fundamental differences between the two. For instance, social democrats believe in implementing welfare programmes through a democratically elected government, while adherents of democratic socialism believe in the nationalisation of the means of production in running the economy through a democratically elected government. Social democrats advocate peaceful transition from capitalism to socialism. While Jawaharlal Nehru was considered as a social democrat, his colleague in the Constituent Assembly, B. R. Ambedkar, was emphatic about state socialism. It appears that the compromise between these two ideas has been reflected in the Directive Principles of State Policy.

The principles of social democracy and/or democratic socialism can be interrogated in the context of the present situation in India. While inequalities in social and economic life of the people continue to be daunting, the country has adopted the Western model of development based purely on the invisible hand. India is now deeply involved in an era of liberalisation and an economic structure based on the market. The incorporation of socialism as a part of the Preamble of the Constitution is of no value in a system based on markets. Nevertheless, successive governments have argued that they have not abandoned welfare programmes and safety net schemes to bring relief to the socially disadvantaged. In other words, the governments seem to be buying an argument analogous to some of the European leaders, saying that they are still social democrats and would like to bring gradual change within the existing system.

This is different from democratic socialism where the means of production are under the control of the State and the principles of democracy are used to take decisions in running the affairs of the economy. In a social democracy, the production and distribution of goods and services rely on the efficiency and competitiveness of the market forces. In a way, the present version of market socialism as practised in China where the CPC controls everything comes under this category.

The Indian Constitution has given not only certain directions to the State to observe the rule of law but also certain obligations to the weaker sections as well as the socially and economically backward classes. How can the issue of caste-based reservations be operated as a mechanism to distribute income, privileges and power in a system that is based on the market?

In the present situation of a liberal market economy, according to some, making special quotas for certain people in jobs leads to inefficiencies and waste. Therefore, the rule of reservation in public employment that has been in vogue for the last century and half (from 1856) became redundant in theory and was struck down by courts at different stages of litigation. The protagonists of justice (as being fair) argue that special provisions in the form of quotas for the underprivileged and the unrepresented needs to be accommodated in a democratic society. In fact, reservations and quotas exist even in capitalist countries such as Malaysia and the USA to provide 'representation' to certain categories of people who are not adequately represented in public services in order to facilitate the true spirit of democratic functioning of the polity. The relationship between democracy and capitalism needs to be understood here to highlight the significance of the principle of 'representation.' It is believed that both have a set of harmonious and mutually supportive institutions, each promoting a kind of freedom in the distinct relations of social life.

The liberal democratic capitalist societies according to Samuel Bowels[34] are, "[T]hose two dozen or so nations whose social life is structured by a limited State that extends civil liberties and suffrage to most adults and an economy characterised by production for the market using wage labour and privately owned means of production." Generally, democracy is identified with liberty while capitalism is related to private property. There is a contradiction between these two. The conflict between these two values has been resolved in post-liberal democracies like that of the USA through the creation of corporations. The emergence of giant corporations, a majority of which later turned into MNCs, have done away with the concept of private property (at least in theory). The concept of the 'shareholder' was invented with limited liability. The democratic principle of representative form was introduced in the organisation of the corporations through the so-called elected representatives who took part in the decision-making processes as representatives of the shareholders. This invention is believed to have solved the contradiction between liberty and private property, but it never resolved the antagonistic nature of liberty and inequality.

The collective action undertaken by representatives, for instance, sometimes leads to inefficient decisions of resource allocation based on a majority rule. The costs involved in resolving such issues could be minimised if a unanimous decision is taken. This is possible when all the interests of the people or communities are properly represented. It is perhaps exactly to represent these diverse interests that our Constitution-makers introduced a set of collective choice rules in the form of the Directive Principles of State Policy. B. R. Ambedkar in his address in the Constituent Assembly in 1949 called them instruments of instruction to the government about 70 years ago. Is it possible to achieve equity through the creation of equality of opportunities? How it results in achieving social democracy if not democratic socialism with a change in the ideology of the ruling establishment(s) is a marvel to be seen in the years to come.

DISINVESTMENT AS A STRATEGY OF THE NEOLIBERALS

Democratic socialism promotes the public sector. The economic activity of governments through the public sector is considered as an investment in the security of people. In all modern economies, including the pure capitalist systems, the public sector exists at least to maintain public utilities and, in many a country, to provide economic and technological guidance to the private sector by the State. However, the neoclassical theories in the 1980s described public sector units as a drain on the economy, as most of them were considered in pure economic terms as loss-making units. Some economists also considered them as the foundation that promotes rent seekers. An important argument advanced by the critiques of the public sector for the withdrawal of the state or what was called at that time, as the "non-communist withering away of the state" was to avoid any economic drain owing to PSEs. The experts have also developed indicators, including efficiency, productivity, profitability, etc., to prove that PSEs are useless and it would be better to abandon them. Now the situation seems to have changed. It is possible to prove the need for the public sector on the basis of parameters developed by the same experts to show that the public enterprises are the lifeblood of developing countries like India in the current global situation. India pursued industrialisation and modernisation through the policy of public sector enterprises during Jawaharlal Nehru's government. Some of those who were associated with the policies of the government became turncoats-and the policies were dismissed as useless under liberalisation with some economic indicators to measure the performance of PSEs in the 1990s. Now, the same indicators that were used to make the PSEs as scapegoats can be used against them to prove that almost all PSE units are not only making profits, but also substantially contributing to the revenue of the government through taxes and surpluses. The economic survey reports that out of the 240 in the 1990s only 234 units are left employing a capital investment of ₹9.92971 trillion in 2013–14. They have realised a profit of ₹1.49164 trillion and contributed ₹1.63207 trillion to the exchequer through dividends, taxes, etc. The loss-making units have come down to around 70 in sectors crucial for society and the economy. The evaluation of public enterprises using financial ratios created by business managers does not take in account how the prices of the PSEs are determined. The prices of most of the units, including the oil companies, till recently, are guided by administered prices. The administered prices are calculated taking into consideration several issues, including the welfare of the people. For instance, the price of a life-saving drug manufactured in a PSE, as compared to that of a private company is not based solely on unit costs. It is necessary to look at the economics of PSEs where high depreciation cost that include not only plant and machinery but also social overhead capital as per norms are invested, making the margins lower than for private units. R. Nagraj[35] reports in one of his studies that over the last 40 years, public sector enterprise product prices never exceeded the overall price level and in 2003–04 the relative price stood just at 83 per cent of what it was in 1960–61. This means that public sector prices are growing slower than the overall price levels of the economy as a whole. Further, some of the PSEs are the ones that were making losses in the private sector, got into the government segment to provide social protection to workers as a model employer, etc. For instance, nationalisation of National Textiles comes under this category which is still in the red as per the parameters of performance indicators rather than using a separate set of measures to suit its character.

The government introduced a policy called disinvestment of public sector units in 1992 and institutionalised it with a separate department of disinvestment. If we look at the controversies that encircled some of the important privatisation bids like BALCO, VSNL, Centaur Hotel and 17 other hotels of the Tourism Corporation, the inherent intentions would be clear. Despite disagreement on the method, successive governments have gone ahead with disinvestment in all the PSEs, particularly in the *maharatnas* like ONGC. It is found that out of the total disinvestment of ₹821.99 billion as in 2011–12, the total amount during the first 15 years was ₹478.32 billion, making the remaining amount in just six years notwithstanding the protest from Left parties and others. Visakhapatnam Steel Plant (VSP) workers may be looking at it as nightmare.

Ever since liberalisation policies were pursued in India, there has been a demand for disinvestment from the public sector units that were built with the people's money. In the name of improving efficiency and to reduce the fiscal deficit, governments have been transferring public assets and properties to private individuals, often through questionable transactions. The VSP management took a decision to disinvest 10 per cent of its capital through an initial public offer (IPO) to the extent of ₹25 billion. The disquiet of the workers needs to be understood in the backdrop of the sacrifices that they made in protecting the public sector company which was once notified to the BIFR. Visakha Steel is the pride of Andhra Pradesh and an example of how workers of an enterprise can stand by its management to bring a turnaround, once declared as a loss-making unit. In fact, the Disinvestment Commission had recommended writing off the entire accumulated losses and a disinvestment of 51 per cent of its remaining equity in 2000. It seems that the decision to defer the BIFR proposal has made the company to turn around and earn ₹22 billion profit per annum (2006) within a short period and is now its net worth is ₹132.29 billion in 2012. It has a market share of 10 per cent of total sales in its segment. The VSP was implementing its expansion plan to produce 6.3 million tonnes and a future plan of 11.5 million tonnes with ₹220 billion. The expansion was planned with internal resources without any support from government. The magnificent achievement of the plant, according to the workers, could be made possible due to the industrial peace achieved and the struggles they waged against the government to retain it as a public sector unit. The present decision of the company to disinvest as part of its policy is opposed by the workers due to several apprehensions. It is in this context that we need to look at the performance of PSEs since they have been considered as white elephants in the past by vested interests.

Interestingly, privatisation was facilitated by the apex court in a landmark judgement in the BALCO case in December 2001. It is said: "[T]hus, apart from the fact that the policy of disinvestment cannot be questioned as such, the facts herein show that fair, just and equitable procedure has been followed in carrying out their disinvestment". Public memory is very short and some critiques know how this judgement and the subsequent developments in privatisation made the owner of BALCO emerge as a giant in a short period of time with control over government-augmented resources to articulate policies of the government.

THE FUTURE OF SOCIALISM

The notion of socialism entered India through the English-educated. The Fabian socialists and utilitarians in the liberal universities of Britain trained some of our freedom fighters. As students of economic systems, we have studied socialism and communism along with capitalism as three distinct forms of economic organisation. We learnt that C. E. M. Joad, a prominent socialist, said, "[S]ocialism is like a hat that has lost its shape because everybody wears it." In fact, pioneers of communism, Karl Marx and Engels, addressed the riddle of essence of socialism, as there were Fabien socialists, feudal socialists, petty-bourgeoisie socialists, etc. Therefore, a distinction between the socialism advocated by Fourier, Owen and Sismondi and Marxian view of scientific socialism was crafted. They explained the concepts both in the *Communist Manifesto* and by Engels in *Socialism: Utopian and Scientific* in 1880. Most of the analysts appear to speak about the pre-communist phase of socialism that was prevalent in 20th century Europe and in some developing countries. In fact, socialism became a universal value during the last century as no one had openly opposed it except a few who wanted the autonomy and liberty of the individual to prevail as a value of an open society. Even a fascist like Hitler advocated his own brand of national socialism in 1933 in the European context. Some people in the USA are critical about Barack Obama's policies as being socialist. However, those who defend the equality of outcome as well as the equality of opportunities can be clubbed together with socialists advocating that the means of production should be socially owned, as one class.

The communists are those who want the abolition of private property through a political process. Interestingly, the collapse of the Soviet Union and China's experiments with market socialism are considered as deviations and very few are willing to discuss about the epoch in academic circles now. Thus, socialism as an economic system is considered by many as a panacea for meeting the challenges of inequality, poverty and social development. Depending upon the stage of development of the economy and the society or simply the productive forces, each country has designed its own breed of socialism. Consequently, we have the Nordic countries calling themselves socialist, some European nations such as France, Italy, etc. claiming to be social democracies and Third World countries like India having the tag as democratic socialists (in the Preamble to the Constitution). All these countries have not abandoned the market as an instrument of economic transactions or declared war against capitalism. In some of the Latin America countries, particularly Chavez's Venezuela, it is reported that workers (including those retired) seem to have participated voluntarily in work with patriotic fervour during a sabotage attempt by adversaries to cause damage to the economy. The workers felt that they were the owners of the state-owned company PDSVA as Article 62 of Venezuela Constitution says, "[T]he participation of the people in forming, carrying out and controlling the management of public affairs.... It is the obligation of the State and the duty of society to facilitate the creation of the conditions most favourable to putting this in to practice." We have similar provisions in the Constitution under Articles 42, 43 and 43a. The advocates of socialism had anxiety about its future even during the early part of the 20th century. There was lively debate in the UK Labour Party after Anthony Crosland published his document, 'Future of Socialism,' in 1956 and its reissue in 2006. We have seen in India debates about the future of socialism and scientific socialism (communism) with different groups of activists, scholars and public men voicing their concerns about the disappearance of the culture of socialism, particularly after 2010.

It is increasingly being noticed that the economic programmes of the social democrats in Europe are accepted as socialist in nature without realising the fact that they have not solved the problems of capitalism. It is yet to be seen to what extent China has addressed the issues of poverty, inequality, environmental degradation, corruption, etc. through political control of the State. In its party Congress a few years ago, China reaffirmed its faith in democracy and added a new concept 'scientific development.' The use of the term development rather than socialism is a radical departure from the original ideological position. The concept of scientific development was elaborated as an approach that takes care of inequality, environmental sustainability, etc. and not necessarily equality of opportunity, with a firm commitment to resolve contradictions of private capital. This is a clear message that the Chinese are going to join the club of social democrats if they are already not attached to one. It needs to be evaluated as to what extent the principles of socialism are applied in social democracies, or democratic socialist countries or in the so-called communist countries. Would the change in the composition of the working class, the hegemony of the MNCs, the oversight of WTO for the arrangements, the strength and enormous influence of the mass media in carrying the propaganda of the MNCs, etc. dampen their emphasis on market?

Most of the parties whose agenda is socialism are participating in elections. According to Marta Harnecker,[36] Latin American activist scholar, the Left parties have electoral deviations in four areas, namely the tendency of getting elected as an end in itself rather than a means to work on a project of social transformation; linking up with popular movements only during elections and for electoral reasons'; individualism during the campaign, seeking funds and support for themselves and for the party; and internal conflicts over the elections as if other members of the party were their main enemies. As a student of Althusser, Marta Harnecker[37] has reflected on the new political movements and pointed out their limitations. She has said that, "[M]any of these theoretical debates resulted in splits because they divided the various forces even more". In this context, the position of the socialist (Left) parties, including the so-called centrist party like the Congress whose declared agenda is identical (socialism) in India, presents an impression that they are in the same league.

Socialist and market economies seem to have exhausted their capabilities to solve problems of the common people as the current situation unfolds. There is no doubt that reducing inequalities without affecting the sustainability of the environment is possible through socialism and the culture of give-and-take. Social democracy as practised in Europe, and seen to be experiencing a crisis, now seems to be a temporary phenomenon if understood as a phase of transition to real socialism wherein each individual is allowed to draw as per his/her need and contribute to the common good as per his/her capacity. But, convincing 'others' about the need to share appears to be a philosophical approach to life or world view. The present generation of youngsters needs to encounter this civilisation problem. The divided socialist and Left groups seem to not have realised this. As such, the future of socialism hangs in balance between the fortitude of the human attitude of sharing and the brutal disposition of acquisition. The sooner our leaders realised this dichotomy, the better for humankind.

SOCIAL WELFARE VERSUS SOCIAL SECURITY IN INDIA

Social economics is receptive to the paradigm of human rights as entitlements. In this context, we may notice some interesting judicial assertions in India. The Supreme Court directed the governments of Delhi, Andhra Pradesh and other states to provide night shelters to homeless on 23 January 2010 in a writ filed by the PUCL. The apex court cited the previous orders passed in 1981 and 1996 in interpreting Article 21 of the Constitution in this case. The Right to Life enshrined in the Constitution says that, "[N]o person shall be deprived of his life or personal liberty except according to procedure established by law." It was construed by the court that life is not merely restricted to the animal existence of a person, it means something more than this, and the homeless, particularly during winter, should be provided with night shelters. Behind this order, the court seems to have assumed that India is a welfare state to ensure the basic needs of life to people. But, there is no mention about a welfare state in the Constitution. Even the concept of human dignity has not found a place in constitutions like that of the USA. Therefore, it is likely that someone can get an order to that extent from a jealous judge in future as we have several such cases in our country.

The Indian Constitution is unique compared to many others in the sense that it contains the results of fine intellectual exercise and wisdom. While addressing the criticism and sarcastic remarks of some members of the constituent assembly in the making of Constitution (1949), B. R. Ambedkar said that in an era where we have about hundred written constitutions, we need to draw from them that which suits our conditions. He has also defended the Directive Principles of State Policy incorporated as Part IV of the Constitution where the concept of welfare is mentioned. He has further said, "[W]hoever captures power will not be free to do what he likes. In the exercise of it, he will have to respect these instruments which can be called directive principles. He cannot ignore them." This was a brilliant strategy where the judiciary and the executive were given the opportunity to interpret and direct the state to, "[P]romote the welfare of the people by securing and protecting as effectively as it may a social order in which justice, social, economic and political, shall inform all the institutions of the national life" (Article 38).

The concept of welfare derived from the Fabians, Benthamites and the British Labour Party seems to have inspired both B. R. Ambedkar and Jawaharlal Nehru in formulating the socio-economic policies after independence. It is recorded that Nehru used the Directive Principles as the motive to establish the Planning Commission in 1951 through an executive order. Ambedkar used the British Labour Party manifesto for articulating the aphorisms and his memorandum on states and minorities submitted to the Constituent Assembly in 1947. The concept of welfare was the bulwark on which the first few plans were drafted using ideas like growth with justice, poverty alleviation and several other such programmes of successive governments. Now, that has been slowly replaced with a new concept called social security which is very popular in the West and in America. It is very hard to find the concept of welfare in the policy documents drafted by the new generation of policy-makers who are trained in new public management. Even the Ministry of Social Welfare has been renamed as the Ministry of Social Justice and Empowerment under whose jurisdiction the provision of night shelters and other hundreds of schemes operates, are supposed to provide welfare or well-being to the people. There is an issue of legitimacy and propriety in using the new concept of social justice in our situation where the Constitution is supposed to guard socialism and secularism.

Social security, like the concept of social exclusion, is now widely used in development literature and is related to the present culture of the European society. The social problems in Europe are quite different from ours. For instance, asocial people, delinquents, single parents, etc. have not yet become serious issues though some of our experts are using the terms in our academic debates. In order to tackle such social problems, packages called health insurance, unemployment allowance or social security measures are needed as partial actions to tackle problems of alienation due to the capitalist policies pursued there. We have structurally and, in certain cases, historically given social conditions and problems that cannot be tackled with piecemeal packages like the ones in Europe where poverty and inequality are not as serious as in our society. Therefore, we need a welfare state to tackle the aggregate problems of our society. But, in the West, as economists have explained, the welfare function is an aggregate of the individual utility functions as the individual and his liberty to choose are more important than the society. Philosophers like John Rawls have tried to pose the issue of justice as a social problem and attempted to solve it through his difference principle called 'the greatest advantage to the least advantaged'. This is a little advanced compared to the Benthamite principle of greatest benefit to the largest number based on which the concept of the welfare state was designed in most of the Third World countries. Now this is slowly being replaced by the concept of social security. Both the concepts are used interchangeably by most scholars without realising the differences in the philosophical or ideological connotation. Social welfare is a much wider notion, an end in itself, and social security can barely be a means to achieve it.

ENSURING PUBLIC ACCOUNTABILITY OF POLICY-MAKERS

The libertarian principles of public policy are not confined to academic debates alone; they have entered governance in most countries like India through the expert advice of the motivated and jealous advisors and consultants. Most of the advisors whose ideas are sincerely implemented by governments do not carry any liability nor they have shown remorse if their advice fail to deliver.

Academic experts have made the idea of accountability popular ever since the use of the corporate mode of governance. This is used as a method of accounting the obligations of functionaries of a business organisation and is ensured through different methods. There is a blend of business accounting and democratic participation in the system to ensure that the organisation is accountable to the shareholders or partners. It is basically a bookkeeping function. The objective of transparency in decision-making is guaranteed through the annual statement of accounts, particularly in the profit and loss account to the general body (along with other financial statements). This is taken as one of the criteria to assess accountability in public affairs including public enterprises.

The development of public enterprises both as a part of the system of a mixed economy and also as a mechanism of democratic socialism played an important role in the 20th century to address some of our constitutional objectives. India, along with several other countries, particularly the so-called non-aligned socialist block, has used public enterprises to build their economies. What is deficient in the whole process is the absence of the application of democratic instruments of governance. The core of elections, voting, referendums, counter proposals, minority veto, plebiscite, etc. are totally missing in the instruments of public accountability.

It is obligatory for the registered companies or enterprises to present an annual report to the Parliament/Assembly and a proviso to raise questions, debates, etc. in the legislature. It is possible that details about the functioning of the enterprise could be elicited and such a procedure is construed as public accountability. There are several flaws in this method. In fact, scholars have provided alternative concepts such as external productivity, cost effectiveness, social cost benefit ratio, etc. which could be used to substantiate the usefulness of a project to society. Further, social responsibility or constitutional obligation seem to be more relevant and are within the concept of bounded rationality of democratic decision-making. Are the concepts really used to account for the activities of all the functionaries in the government?

Most of the decisions in the government are either taken or vetted by officers. The accountability of a government servant is ensured through two sets of service rules known as conduct rules and civil services classification, control and appeal rules. There are separate rules for the all-India service officers such as IAS, IPS, etc. and the code of ethics is not yet prescribed. The rules ensure that the term of office of the incumbent is protected under Article 311 and, at the same time, extract the work as per the norms and conditions of service. This is a requisite service condition for a clerk as well as a cabinet secretary. The method of assessing the work or making people accountable is done through the vertical (outside the state apparatus) and horizontal (within the state) structures of administration. The vertical forms of accountability are of very recent origin after the advent of the RTI, media, citizen's committees, civil society activism, etc. that are slowly picking up in India. Internal accountability is ensured through entries in the ACRs (1–10 grading), vigilance/CBI reports, performance management systems, disciplinary proceedings, comments of the judiciary and CAG, etc.

We should recognise here that the most significant job of a civil servant is formulating and or assisting in the design of public policy. Therefore, in democratic countries like the UK, civil service values are given importance. The civil servants are accountable to ministers, who in turn are accountable to the Parliament. Therefore, the civil service core values of integrity, honesty, objectivity and impartiality, together with political neutrality and anonymity, are said to be the hallmark of an efficient civil service. But, the Sixth Pay Commission in India has remarked that,

[T]he institutional structures of top down management and isolated managerial efforts have proved inadequate for satisfying performance i.e., delivery of results and outcomes. There is over-reliance

on Command models of administrative efforts for service delivery....
The importance of a systems' shift from top down monitoring to
stakeholder-citizen participation and co-production with transparency and checks is critical for better public service delivery.[38]

The Second Administrative Reforms Commission 2010 has
recommended a civil services code and ethics in governance
for ensuing accountability. It is, however, alleged that most of
the above principles are observed in its breach than in execution, which seems to be supported by the increasing number
of cases of disciplinary proceedings against officers by the
UPSC, CVC, etc. Legislators are accountable to the people, in
theory, at the time of elections. Interestingly, the judiciary is
not accountable to anyone except their conscience and still the
Judicial Appointments Act is not cleared by the apex court. Is
it not ludicrous in a democratic country?

The Sixth Pay Commission and the Moily SARC have recommended for the lateral entry of officers at the level of joint-
secretary and above to be recruited through UPSC. It seems
the rules are framed by the government to implement the recommendations soon. This is the time to reflect on an important
set of functionaries in the government, who are above public
accountability. They are the policy-makers and advisors in
the form of adjuncts to the ministers, the PMO, the Planning
Commission (not officers) and other non-descript organisations. They prescribe many things such as the crude price, coal
price, privatisation, etc. They are not amenable to any of the
instruments of accountability or the disciplinary proceedings
noted previously. In fact, the tyranny of some of the policy-
makers is so depraved that several controversial policies could
be ascribed to their policy advice and execution. Some of them
are not direct recruits and very few are from the mainstream
civil service (post-retirement). They enjoy absolute freedom
necessary in a democratic society but are not accountable
directly to the legislature or any democratic agency. The academics that earn and live in the West and give advice on Indian
affairs are also beyond the quagmire as they are the neo-dvijas

(two lives). This is typical of the Indian system of governance that evolved during the post-1991 period. It is also true in the case of the higher judiciary in India. Like the media, they are not bound by any rules, except their invisible conscience.

The policy packages of the government are to be deliberated and are supposed to be processed as per the business rules approved in accordance with Articles 77 and 78 of the Constitution. It is strange to note that most policy-makers are not aware of the constitutional provisions and, even if they know, they have contempt for it. We do not find the kind of confession expressed by scholars like Paul Samuelson (Nobel economist) who said, "[M]asters of financial engineering had been created a lot of them at MIT, some of them by people like me-there is no CEO who understands at all, a derivative". On the other hand, we come across persuasive arguments and academic publications to prescribe further liberalisation of markets in India when the country is in deep crisis. What does it mean? Is it irresponsibility or unethical course of action? Social economics with its commitment to common good alone can look at the shallow of the policies scrutinising them from the humanistic perspective of human dignity and virtue.

SOCIAL ECONOMICS AS AN APPROACH TO ALTERNATIVE PARADIGM

The thesis that there is no alternative to globalisation has been aggressively propagated like a brand in business models and has created anxiety amongst the commoners who are the victims of the system. The end of Soviet Union and China's relations with capitalist countries have further eroded the morale of the alternative paradigms explored by scholars, leaders and activists in different parts of the world. However, the seeds of the degeneration of the Washington Consensus (globalisation) is inherently present in the model got exposed after 2008 financial crisis. The economic fantasies popularised by the chosen few have adversely affected academic exercises in the spirit of scientific enquiry, and economics as a traditional discipline has been reduced to a subject in business management in several institutions of higher learning. Nevertheless, serious economic disasters in most of the OECD countries and in some Third World countries revitalise the free thinkers and socialists alike to look deep into the weaknesses of the model and shed light on the native or local models of emancipation. We have had in India both traditional and modern approaches that have been parallel to the Western models of development.

We have presented some important contributions made by our chosen leaders from the time of Gandhiji during the freedom struggle, and that spilled over to the post-independence period. Though some of their ideas were discussed in political clusters, they did not receive as much reflection as they deserved. Now, these ideas and the discontentment with models that were European and disconnected to the Indian situation are being studied and reflected. In fact, most of the thoughts and ideas of our indigenous thinkers are in the tradition of social economics and are found to be more relevant today than before. They are concerned with human well-being without any recourse to unusual agencies. Buddha, Gandhi, Roy, Ambedkar and Lohia can be called the leaders of such a tradition and it has the potential to enrich the social economy approach to development in India. The ideas of our leaders reflected with Western emancipatory ideologies give us an insinuation that the Hindu ethos is not confined to social relations, but it is all-pervasive to seize economic and political transactions under its dominance to dictate events and incidents. It is time to study, reflect and converge the relevant approaches that help to dissipate the present assault on our society and economy and evolve strategies to bring glory and freedom to the nation.

NOTES AND REFERENCES

1. Ajit K. Dasgupta, *A History of Indian Economic Thought* (London: Routledge & Kegan Paul, 1993).

2. M. N. Roy was a freedom fighter and a communist with close relation-ships with Lenin and other communist leaders of the world. He became a humanist at the end of his life.
3. https://www.britannica.com/biography/Manabendra-Nath-Roy (accessed on 12 September 2016).
4. Shibnaryan Ray, *Selected Works of M. N. Roy* (New Delhi: Oxford University Press, 1987).
5. B. R. Ambedkar, *Dr Babasahab Ambedkar Writings and Speeches*, Vols. 1–17 (Delhi: Dr Ambedkar Foundation, 2014), Vol. 13.
6. Ibid., Vol. 11.
7. Ibid., Epilogue, p. 597.
8. Ibid., p. 583.
9. K. S. Chalam, ed., *Relevance of Ambedkarism in India* (Jaipur: Rawat Publications, 1994), p. 11.
10. Amartya Sen, *Development as Freedom* (New Delhi: Oxford University Press, 1999).
11. B. R. Ambedkar, *Dr Babasahab Ambedkar Writings and Speeches*, Vol. 13.
12. www.Ambedkar.org/ Ambedkar writings/states and minorities
13. B. R. Ambedkar, *Babasahab Ambedkar Writings and Speeches*, Vol. 6.
14. 1949 Constituent Assembly debate and Ambedkar's response.
15. B. R. Ambedkar, *What Gandhi and Congress Have Done to Untouchables*, Vol IX (New Delhi: Govt. of India, 2014).
16. Rabindra Chandra Dutta, *Socialism of Jawaharlal Nehru* (Delhi: Abhinav Publications, 1981).
17. B. R. Ambedkar, Vols. 3 and 6.
18. Mastram Kapoor, ed., *Collected Works of Ram Manohar Lohia*, Vols. 1–9 (New Delhi: Anamika, 2010).
19. Rahul Varma, "Why the Left Has Not Been Able to Make a Pan-India Mark," *The Hindu*, 11 April 2016.
20. Aravind Rajgopal, *Politics after Television: Hindu Nationalism and the Reshaping of the Indian Public* (New York: Cambridge University Press, 2001).
21. W. Sombart, The Jews and Modern Capitalism (London: T. F. Unwin, 1913).
22. Mastram Kapoor, ed., Vol. 1, p. 386.
23. Mastram Kapoor, Vol. 1, p. 175.
24. K. S. Chalam, *Readings in Political Economy* (Hyderabad: Orient Longman, 1999).
25. Michael Heinrich, "Crisis Theory, the Law of the Tendency of the Profit to Fall and Marx's Studies in 1870," *Monthly Review*, No. 64 (2013, April).
26. B. Vivekanandan, "The Welfare State Vision: Pointing the Way for the Future Welfare of Humanity," *Janata*, 10 April 2016.
27. David Harvey, *Seventeen Contradictions and the End of Capitalism* (London: Profile Press, 2014).

28. Guglielmo Carchedi and Michael Roberts, "A Critique of Heinrich's, 'Crisis Theory, the Law of the Tendency of the Profit Rate to Fall, and Marx's Studies in the 1870s'," *Monthly Review*, 01 December 2013.
29. John Rawls, *A Theory of Justice* (New Delhi: Oxford University Press, 1993).
30. Ibid.
31. Refer to Census of India 2011.
32. Amartya Sen, *Inequality Re-examined* (New Delhi: Oxford University Press, 1992).
33. K. S. Chalam, *Economic Reforms and Social Exclusion* (New Delhi: SAGE Publications, 2011).
34. Samuel Bowles, *Democracy and Capitalism* (New York: Basic Books, 1987).
35. R. Nagraj, "Performance of Public Sector since 1950: A Fresh Look," *Economic and Political Weekly*, 24 June 2006.
36. Marta Harnecker, *Rebuilding the Left* (Delhi: Daanish Books, 2007).
37. Ibid.
38. K. S. Chalam, *Governance in South Asia: State of the Civil Services* (New Delhi: SAGE Publications, 2014).

10
Epilogue

India has entered a different phase in its pursuit of develop-ment. It has experimented with several models, including Western and Eastern, capitalist and socialist, etc. In the pro-cess, the country has reached what is called a 'mixed economy' model. The Planning Commission was mandated with the objective of achieving growth with justice. The idea of justice as practised by the commission was confined to economic parameters and had claimed of achieving self-sufficiency in certain areas. In the process, the policy-makers and politicians seem to have failed to recall the lived experience of the his-torically and socially marginalised groups and the dominant castes as partners in development. The dominant castes that were transformed after independence as the capitalist class, through social mobility and using MCCs, have skilfully used the State for their self-progress. Interestingly, scholars say that the marginalised are inefficient and the rent-seeking class have distorted the course of events. They did not, however, reveal the fact that the rent-seekers and the governance class or group is drawn from the same social background as the experts are. Social institutions and economic development projects have been intimately related from time immemorial. They do not explain why the traditionally marginalised and the economi-cally deprived have remained neglected. It is not far to seek to identify the contributing factors here and the foregoing discus-sion has brought out to focus some important issues for debate.

The social economy approach to development is more relevant to India than any other method of studying contemporary reality. It deeply scrutinises the philosophy, social institutions and dichotomous nature of theory and practice in India to understand the contradictions in Indian development projects. Welfare economics in the 20th century was considered as "part of social welfare that can be brought directly or indirectly, into relation with the measuring rod of money."[1] Most scholars who have excelled in new welfare economics and tried to formulate policies on the basis of abstract theories have influenced social choice theory that eventually brought down the role of the State mentioning rent-seeking behaviour of policy-makers or bureaucracy. But very few of them seem to have addressed the problem of crony capitalism as an extension of social behaviour of the privileged castes in societies like India. The application of crony capitalism in India is not just limited to social capital, but has become more complex than what the economists have assumed. The process of expansion of crony capitalism has ultimately made the State weakened to give way to the wily corporates and their cartels to manage not only giant corporations but groups of countries and their governments. The giant design of crony capitalism as part of the neo-imperialism has made 'the State' to be subservient to it making the poor deprive of the only recourse.

It appears to be trivial for scholars working on public policy to accept that rent-seeking behaviour cannot be regulated and that the State (before seizure) needs to pull out in any democratic country founded on the rule of law. Are the public servants including the elected representatives beyond accountability, or are they above the disciplinary proceedings of the laws and rules made by the legislative wings of the State? Are the rent-seekers and the fraudsters not brought to book with institutions like the Ombudsman/UPSC? Why should a traditional and time-tested political or social institution be made an adjunct to an artificial market? The assumptions and the abstract reasoning of rent-seeking experts no doubt give us an indication about the adverse influence of the unregulated power of public servants. However, that does not mean to deride institutions such as the state, family, judiciary, parliament, etc., and repose confidence only in the markets under questionable assumptions. Is the collective wisdom of humankind and its civilisation more enduring than the market and can regulate the few individuals who are labelled as rent-seekers?

The approach to study the dynamics of development in India following the Western model where there is no scope for social division such as caste becomes a painful experience. However, experts have recognised 'classes,' but failed to capture the typical Indian characters of isolation, discrimination and exploitation based on descent. In this context, we consider that the parameters of social economics developed during the 19th century are appropriate to study and understand our situation. An attempt was made to use some of the concepts in understanding the present Indian development in the traditions of social economics and philosophy of Amartya Sen, John Rawls and others. Sen's contributions to economics, particularly welfare economics, are well known throughout the world. It is relevant here to notice that in all his writings, Sen has boldly projected Indian contributions to the world of knowledge and in the process had a dig at the Anglo-Saxon attitude towards our glorious traditions. At the same time, he called in to question the fundamentalist presentation of India as a prejudiced view as it heavily relied on the Vedantic orientation rather than the universal objective presentation of facts. In *The Argumentative Indian* and *The Idea of Justice*, he recounts that there are intellectual traditions other than the Anglo-Saxon ones where questions of justice have been addressed. He has emphasised,

> [S]ome of the reasoning for example of Gautama Buddha (the agnostic champion of the path of knowledge), or of the writers in the Lokayata school (committed to relentless scrutiny of every traditional belief), in India in 6th century BC, may sound closely aligned rather than adversarial, to many of the critical writings of the leading authors of the European enlightenment.[2]

It appears that there are very few scholars of his stature who have projected the neglected glory of India as Sen did, otherwise it has always been a spiritual India from Max Muller down to the present day swamis and babas.

In a footnote to *The Idea of Justice*, Sen has lamented that Kautilya of 4th century BC is compared with the 15th century AD Machiavelli as 'the Indian Machiavelli' because of the lack of familiarity with non-Western traditions. The dominance of English education and its intellectual hegemony seem to be the contributing factors for such a trend as per another footnote in the same book. He draws heavily from the intellectual tradition of India to elaborate the concept of justice as a reasoned argument rather than trust faith and unreasoned conviction. He cites the tradition of dialogues in our epic literature between Draupadi and Yudhishtara, Krishna and Arjuna, Lokayatas, etc. and the mediaeval Mughal court of Akbar to underscore that our traditions of reasoned arguments subsisted to resolve issues of justice and they are more profane than the modern practices attributed to the West. The tradition of dialogue and argumentation in India was responsible for the sustenance of democracy and made India one of the earliest to adapt democratic norms much before the West.

In his treatise on philosophy, *The Idea of Justice*, Sen evokes two different concepts of justice in the early Indian jurisprudence. Referring to the debate between Krishna and Arjuna on *niti* and *nyaya* in the Bhagavad Gita, he has explained the concepts as part of the theory of justice. Krishna, Sen has said in the book *The Idea of Justice*, as the deontologist, was urging Arjuna to do his duty, while Arjuna worrying about the terrible consequences of war divulged his deontological morality versus consequentialism. Here *niti* relates to organisational propriety as well as behavioural correctness. *Nyaya* is concerned with what emerges and how, and in particular in terms of the lives that people are actually able to lead. *Nyaya*, Sen argues, stands for realised justice. The role of institutions, rules and organisations have to be used in the broader and more inclusive perspective of *nyaya* which is inseparably linked with what actually emerges and not the institutions or the rules. It is here that he refers to the Indian concept of *matsyanyaya* and has said that avoiding practicing it must be an essential part of justice. We must see that the justice of the 'fish world' should not be allowed in the real world of human beings.[3]

Sen has clarified that his aim was to address the inadequacies of the 20th century philosophical discourse of his friend and colleague John Rawls of Harvard. 'Justice as fairness' of Rawls[4] yields a unique set of principles through which just institutions can be set up. But, Sen says that these fair institutions will overpower and restrict freedoms that people need to experience so as to make use of their capabilities. Institutions can only play an instrumental role in the pursuit of justice and depend upon other factors such as the behaviour of people, interactions among people, etc. Therefore, democracy in terms of the public reasoning of a 'government by discussion' is essential to enable different voices to be actually heard. He has illustrated, with his flute and three kids episode, how difficult it is to arrive at a just decision as each has his/her own philosophy of justice as utilitarianism, egalitarianism and libertarianism. Thus, removing injustice by the conscious design of bringing justice through practical reasoning is intrinsic to justice, rather offering resolutions of questions about the matter of perfect justice in a roundabout manner. There are critics who have rebuked some of his formulations of the pluralistic notion of justice, shadowing the varnadharma in Gita; he could neither do justice to philosophy nor to economics, etc.[5] Yet some of his concepts seem to be relevant in addressing current challenges in a market economy.

BUDDHISM AND ECONOMIC TRANSFORMATION

There are several Indian traditions (now marginalised) that have treated human beings as born equal. Buddhism as a way of life and not as a religion evolved on the basis of a deep ingress in the traditions of India, including the philosophies that mystified the divisions among human beings. Therefore, it can be seen as a social economy approach in a rudimentary form, but obscured by rival thoughts. The noted historian Romila Thapar in her concluding chapter of her book *Early India* observed that,

> [T]he major success of Buddhism, apart from periods when they received royal patronage, were in areas of existing agrarian societies that were also developing in to centres of exchange or in areas where commerce was the primary activity. The thrust of trade carried it to distant places that in turn made attractive to those who wished to profit by this trade.[6]

The role played by Buddhism in breaking the otherworldliness of the existing traditions of India is considered as one of the greatest events in Indian history. Buddhism's economic contributions to India in terms of making it one of the richest countries of the world (with around 50 per cent of wealth) by the 11th century AD are well known to economic historians. The world is once again paying attention to Buddhism after the revival of the East Asian economies within a short period of time. In fact, all the East Asian and Far East countries including China had Buddhist traditions that seem to have promoted a model of development quite different from the so-called neo-classical model.

Though economists have studied the contributions of religion to economic transformation or development, the attention paid to eastern religions like Buddhism seems to be lukewarm. It was Vikas Mishra who studied Hinduism and found that it was not conducive for rapid economic development due to several rigidities and perhaps prepared Rajkrishna later to coin what is called the Hindu rate of growth.[7] In the case of Western or Mediterranean religions such as Christianity, Islam and others, social scientists such as Max Weber, Tawney and several others have analysed their role in the development of capitalism. Calvinism promoted values such as diligence, authority, thrift, punctuality and fulfilment of promises that led to the accumulation of capital.[8] The disregard paid to the ancient treasure of wisdom in Buddhism by scholars seemed to be due to the inability of monks' to master the English language thereby limiting the spread of their studies. It is in the recent times both in Japan and in the East Asian economies, particularly in Thailand, that some efforts are forthcoming and that might change the situation in the future.

According to Lakshmi Narasu,[9] one of the greatest Buddhist scholars from the Telugu country and who also had a profound influence on B. R. Ambedkar, Gurajada and others said that "[T]he spirit of Buddhism is essentially socialistic, that is to say, it teaches concerted action (*samanartha*) for social ends." The individual *bhikkhu* is poor, but the *sangha*, the community of aspirants for *bodhi* all over the world may be rich. Lakshmi Narasu noted that "He whose thought is only one step above the man who labours and plans solely for himself, such a man, though often an angel to his family may prove a demon to all the rest of the world." Thus, Buddhism has imparted the principles of the eightfold path (*astangamarga*) as a middle course. Lakshmi Narasu adds that, "[H]e who has merely understood the dharma but has not shaped his life and thought in accordance with its spirit is like one who having read a book on cookery imagines that he has eaten the sweets described in the book."[10] The Buddhist precepts and practice among the monks and the laity led societies in East Asia, Japan, China and other parts of the world where it had a deep influence on the people and their attitudes and world view found to have experienced rapid development.[11] I. M. D. Little,[12] the welfare economist, has critiqued that Buddhism did not contain the principles of distributive justice. But, Buddhist scholars like F. L. Pryor[13] have given a rejoinder saying that Buddhism stands for virtues such as compassion and generosity, alms giving to the poor, etc., that are to be interpreted as the principles of justice as enunciated in the Angutta Nikaya. It is further elucidated by scholars that *Agganna Sutta* talks about the functions of the king to take care of the lowly and poor as a social contract. The *Kutadana Sutta* speaks about seed corn to be given to farmers free of cost indicating how the role of a ruler is secured towards the poor. Above all, the unique welfare programmes of public works, infrastructure, alms, etc., not only for human beings but also for animals during the rule of King Ashoka, is the greatest example one could think of about justice as fairness. Then, what is its impact on the economic practices of people as some invidious critiques term Buddhism that made India a country of beggars? The uncharitable comment by some Anglo-Saxons like I. M. D. Little perhaps with the aid and advice of parochial Indian scholarship might provoke a hasty rebuke by someone saying that all the Buddhist critiques are drawn from identical ethnic arrogance.

Historical data from the studies of scholars on India has proved the above adverse comment on Buddhism as blasphemous. The history of China, Japan, Korea, Myanmar (Burma), Thailand and Bhutan, where Buddhism developed different streams of philosophical thought such as the Mahayana, Hinayana, Zen, Shinto and several other sects by the first decade of the first millennium, was expanded into eighteen out of four *Nikayas*.[14] The Meiji restoration in Japan was the turning point in achieving economic self-sufficiency and development based on Buddhist principles of "excellent work culture, industrial and management methods, culture of loyalty, whole life employment, consensus decision making, brain storming, quality control circles (QCC), total quality management (TQM), meditation and constant self-examination and self-improvement influenced by Zen Buddhism."[15] Similarly, China had accumulated capital in the form of gifts to the monks and temples that were used for giving loans, creation of infrastructure, etc. to advance the economy as well as the welfare of people. In Burma, U Nu supported land nationalisation to avoid the illusion of private property. Thailand is now practising the 'Samti Asoke Buddhist reform movement' based on the spiritual emphasis on social and environmental ethics, and has recovered from financial shocks quickly by using State power. Above all, Bhutan, the Himalayan Buddhist nation, has shown to the world what development is about and its ultimate purpose through the concept of Gross National Happiness (GNH) consisting of nine domains and 72 indicators.[16]

Buddhism as a way of life had a deep influence on the lives of people of Asia where a major chunk of the human population lives devoid of any models of development as the Anglo-Saxons. The West is a small fraction of the world but can devour the resources of others due to market-based models. This has facilitated the formulation of a new paradigm of development based on impressions of Schumacher and the Club of Rome. The interpretations of the authors are close to Buddhist principles. The paradigm of globalisation pushed through by the neoclassicals did not like it, due to the idea of their 'economic man' based on self-interest, as distinguished from Buddhist theory of conditionality and dependent origination (paticca samuppada). The self in Buddhism is connected to other entities rather than being isolated on its own and is a rational process that goes beyond the individual, society and nature. It is hoped that it will guide the future of economic transformation in India and other developing countries that follow Western models.

The emergence of Buddhism needs to be looked at as a response to the religious bigotry and institutional exploitation of an order at an early stage of *gana-sanghas* in the Sakhya and Koliya regions. The advent of Buddhist thought as a challenge to the decadence of Vedic Hinduism both in philosophy and in practice is a grave question not considered here and can be dealt with in a different context. It is instructive to note that Ajatasatru, who became a disciple of the Buddha, belonged to the *naga* clan, a native Indian tribe as the name of his grandfather Naga Sena suggests.[17] It seems the Naga state was not an advanced republic and the relations among the groups relied on ideological considerations. The conditions resemble primitive communism. This is very important to understand the so-called pre-capitalist modes of production, including primitive communism, ancient society, etc., to understand the context of the Buddhist upsurge. Primitive communism as distinguished from primitive accumulation, according to B. Hindess and P. Hrist,[18] is an articulation of a combination of economic and ideological relations between individuals. In fact, the author has revealed how Marx and Engels adopted an erroneous classification of the organisation of society in history from the writings of millionaire railway contractor-cum-missionary, Lewis Henry Morgan. The scholars who have followed the method have failed to evaluate Buddhism in its proper context. Let us not get into the debate to understand our situation now.

The enunciation and mission of the Buddha during his lifetime appears to be an integration of the downtrodden and exploited under conditions of primitive communism. After conceiving the notion of dialectics, the first intellectual breakthrough in the history of ideas, the Buddha collected his disciples. Lakshmi Narasu (apart from European scholars such as Rhys Davids, Winternitz, Oldenberg et al.) gives the list of his first batch of disciples consisting of the wretched and rejected of the earth. The list includes Anathapindaka, Alavaka, Upali, Ambapali, Jivaka, Sunita, Visakha and Angulimala (Mala, Mahar, Madigas, and Chamar claim their ancestry to him and the Mallas where Buddha breathed his last).[19] Interestingly, all of them seem to have originated from the local indigenous groups waiting for a leader to champion their cause (Visakha being a woman seems to be the exception). Earlier the Buddha had dialogues with the Ajivikas such as Poorna Kasyapa and Ajitakesa Kambal (most of them seem to have originated from the Dandaka country) and later several of them joined his order. The local princess of Kosala, Magadh, etc. joined the order, perhaps due to the expediency when a majority of the lowly subjects got admitted. The social context and the rational analysis of the existing conditions during the time of the Buddha seem to be relevant here to understand why there is a sustained attack on Buddhism in both India and elsewhere. It is more appropriate now to study the background when religious fundamentalism is being cunningly promoted by neocolonialism (for instance, the American engagement in

Afghanistan after the Soviet retreat, double standards in India allowing American market values to sustain) allowing Hindu fundamentalism to grow on American soil with more than 500 and odd temples, etc. The home-grown religious fundamentalists in India are of the same cadre. Buddhism is emerging as a countervailing force today that makes the so-called Aryan folk in the garb of cow protectors to appropriate Ambedkar (with 125 feet statutes land in Mumbai, etc.) who has revived Buddhism among the poor in India.[20]

One of the weaknesses in certain segments of Buddhist teachings and practice is alleged to be the priority given to the *Astanga Marg* and panchshila as rituals without much study and reflection on the core of Buddhism. Some of the *bhikkhus* and the laity who claimed to follow the Buddha are not aware of the greatest intellectual contributions of Buddhism to humankind, as lamented by the Dalai Lama in a seminar (I was present) at Bodh Gaya in 2009. It could be due to the split of the order into 18 groups like every other belief system. But, the distinction of Buddhism is that it did not develop as a religion (no god, no priest), but only as a way of life in the South Asian countries with a common intellectual legacy. Every Buddhist accepts the contributions of the greatest Buddhist scholars such as Dignaga and Dharmakirti[21] apart from Vasubandhu and even Rahul Sankrutyan. What seems to be extant in the Buddhist order today is a parochial approach to project a limited version or interpretations without any universal appeal to the masses. Some people appear to think that it is not intellectually challenging and may be it has emerged as a blind faith without looking at the corpus of literature of Buddhism and on Buddhism. The commentary on epistemology in *Pramanavartika* by Dharmakirti was presaged 1,200 years before what Hume propounded in the 18th century and was unfortunately out of the reach of Indians for historical reasons. Dharmakirti, who confronted the unreality of caste through his secular philosophical discourse, was thrown out of India and sheltered in Tibet.

We may now reflect on how the so-called Taliban (deriva-tive of *talib*, in Arabic meaning students) alleged to be one of the fundamentalist groups along with several other religious formations is creating social tensions. It is easy to trivialise and stereotype a community for political reasons. But, we may never get in to the roots of the rudiments without under-standing the socio-economic and historical transformation of a community. In this context, the contribution of Afghanistan to the world of knowledge and culture, particularly to the Buddhist realm, needs to be recognised. How could anyone overlook the contribution of Gandhara art (as a blend of Greek and Indian) in the Bamiyan Buddhas and the greatest ser-vice done by the Pathan brothers, Asanga and Vasubandhu, to Buddhist metaphysics.[22] As a transit of the silk route, the people of the region had enriched and were in turn profited by cross-cultural interactions. They were dragged in to the present situation due to the Arab problem. In this context, we must recognise the enlightened efforts made by Prophet Mohammed in uniting and giving an identity to the anarchic groups in the Mediterranean region. He brought peace in the region through Islam. Buddhism, scholars assert, had enriched Abrahaimic (Christianity and Islam) and Indian thought through its philosophy of logic and temple architecture as the first monastic order in history. The cross-fertilisation of ideas has contributed to the development of science and technology. It seems the discovery of crude in the region and the accu-mulation of money through exports created problems due to Sharia. Interest on lending is forbidden for obvious reasons in the Middle East and this seems to have helped in the crafting of a dubious strategy by the Saudi billionaires with the sup-port of American bankers. The region is once again torn into pieces, there seem to be no leader or Messiah like Mohammed to bring about unity and peace in the region and the poor have become prey to the wicked designs of the global powers. It is alleged that the internal and external enemies of Buddhism through Pushyamitra, Shankaracharya, Ghajani, Gori, etc. are drawn from the same Aryan ideology of expansionism. It is reported in the social media that the poor among the Muslims in Saudi constitute 20 per cent and in Afghanistan 45 per cent, and the same amount in Pakistan and India. The poor in the region irrespective of the faith to which they belong are frustrated due to poverty, unemployment and deprivations. Does faith help them to come out of it?

The transition from feudalism to international capitalism through technology seems to have complicated several social issues in non-Western societies. The conditions in India today remind us of the days of the Buddha. The leadership is in great confusion as to how to grapple with the contemporary crisis. They have been constrained to look at the historical and intellectual directions like Buddhism to find solutions to the Talibanisation of a section of the population. The oil rich have no problems as all of their investments are safe in the West and, therefore only the disadvantaged of the country are made curious. This internal socio-economic discrepancy across Asia and the Middle East is in muddles, waiting for a competent leader and ideology to take on fundamentalism (market and religious). Could the three corner stones of *anitya*, *anatma* and *nirvana* of Buddhism, with its original ideology of compassion and integration, help in addressing the contemporary upheaval in Asia?

CORPORATE SOCIAL RESPONSIBILITY AND SOCIAL IMPACT ASSESSMENT

The economic crisis in the West during 2008 and thereafter has generated a debate that the overkill greed of some corporate houses in the USA and their unethical practices were responsible for the subprime crisis that also affected other nations in Europe. The Third World countries are now brought under the orbit of neocolonialism and their scarce resources including the environment are being exploited. Therefore, the concept of corporate social responsibility (CSR), instead of the broad impact assessment, is brought as an alternative to silence the critiques of the system in India by the experts. The Ministry of Corporate Affairs has drafted the CSR guidelines and business groups seem to have agreed to implement them.[23] It seems there is broad agreement between the government and the business alliance that 2 per cent of net profit would be devoted for CSR and, naturally, the amount would be immune from taxation. Now, the social impact assessment as part of an environmental impact assessment (EIA) as a precondition for World Bank projects seem to be a washout after the introduction of CSR as an alternative.[24]

Instead of CSR, the industrialists and the policy-makers should have revived Gandhiji's idea of trusteeship in which all wealth goes to the community, the owners as trustees use the same only to the extent of their needs and the rest is left for the welfare of the community. "Earn crores ... take what you require for your legitimate needs and use the reminder for society."[25] Gandhiji said, "[I]t is compatible with nonviolence otherwise one day there will be a bloody revolution. It will practically abolish all inequity. The state will be there to carry the will of the people." The ideas appear to be utopian in the beginning, but they could have been put to practice as Gandhiji himself put them to practice in his ashram. We expected the Tatas, Bajajs, etc. who were with Gandhiji to have extended the idea further rather than succumbing to international capital. CSR or even EIA are not going to protect either the poor or the environment with the kind of unethical and dubious spiritual undercover practices like Yoga day, cow vigilantism, saffroni-sation of institutions, etc. The number of environmental clear-ances granted despite civil society protests, litigation through Green tribunal, apex court interventions, etc. during the last few years is alleged to be much higher than before.[26]

ECONOMIC AND SOCIAL COSTS OF ENVIRONMENTAL DEGRADATION

Gandhiji's precepts about parsimony and use of cottage indus-tries are interpreted as efforts to preserve the resources for the future. Gandhiji said, "[I]f I take anything that I do not need for my own immediate use, and keep it, I thieve it from somebody else."[27] This principle (trust) stops people from accumulating beyond a limit and reduces pressures on nature. This would also protect our environment. The kind of development models that the Washington consensus directly or its cohorts now indirectly have prescribed to the Third World economies have resulted in the degradation of our common future viz., the environment.

Economists have been considering the relationship between climatic change and its effect on GDP quite for some time. In this context, they seem to have remembered the 14th century thinker, Khaldum, who lamented that hot countries tended to be poorer. The recent debate on environmental issues in the country, therefore, could be reflected with reference to the publication of two important reports on environmental degradation. The IPCC report, *Climatic Change 2013*, and World Bank's *India: Diagnostic Assessment of Environmental Challenges 2013* are noteworthy here. If we read the reports and relate them to the political economy of development process and the drama in the Paryavaran Bhavan in Delhi where more than ₹10 lakh crores of pending projects are reported to have been cleared in days,[28] we would know what is in store for India. That does not mean all the projects are bad, but some are helpful to a small number and quite a few may be fatal to all in the long run.

Scholars have conducted studies and found that national income falls by 8.5 per cent on average per degree Celsius rise in temperature.[29] They have also examined whether it is a happenstance or due to any adverse effect on the productivity of agriculture, mortality, morbidity, cognitive performance, crime and so on. It is noted that this effect is severe among the poor countries and may not affect the already rich. The present global climatic change as per a report by scholars implies that global climate change would lower the median poor country's growth rate by 0.6 percentage points each year from now until 2099.[30] These calculations are based on certain assumptions and are only warning signals for our policy-makers to mend their policies. In fact, the 19th century economist W. S. Jevons, one of the founders of the neoclassical economics, wrote on the coal question in 1866 indicating how even technology was not going to solve the problem. It is said,

> [N]ow, if the quantity of coal used in a blast-furnace, for instance, be diminished in comparison with the yield, the profits of the trade will increase, new capital will be attracted, the price of pig-iron will fall, but the demand for it increase; and eventually the greater number of furnaces will more than make up for the diminished consumption of each.[31]

Modern economists have worked on the theme and developed the 'rebound' and 'backfire' concepts to indicate how technological improvements do not lead to the reduced use of a resource. For instance, K. E. Boulding has written in 1959,

> [A]ny technical improvement can only relieve misery for a while, for as long as misery is the only check on population, the improvement will enable population to grow and will soon enable more people to live in misery than before. The final result of improvement, therefore, is to increase the equilibrium population, which is to increase the sum total of human misery.[32]

Therefore, some scholars claim that the key to avoiding the Jevons paradox is to adopt the principle that neither efficiency improvements nor any other approach to reducing resource use (including voluntary conservation) can be allowed to reduce the cost of consumption. Based on empirical studies, experts have suggested that energy-efficient technologies as a solution to the world's energy and environmental problems will not work. Rather, energy-efficient technology improvements are counter-productive, promoting energy consumption. Instead of recommending an undesirable policy, we can introduce taxes, rates, concessions, etc. as incentives and penalties for circumventing the Jevons paradox. National governments should tax more energy-efficient appliances and use such revenue only for expanding natural reserves like setting aside

depletion of forest in order to prevent more human development in the long run. We can see some of these things happening in the USA, Europe and other developed countries where
forests, water courses and other natural resources are well
protected with polluting industries being dumped elsewhere.
The acquisitive and short-sighted corporate interests and their
cronies in developing countries like India might persuade governments to exchange carbon credits with the advanced countries and accept pollution, infirmities and death.

Let us examine the results of the study on environmental
damages in India and the social costs estimated by the World
Bank therein. It provides estimates of the social and financial
costs of environmental damage in India from three pollution
categories.[33] They are: (a) urban air pollution, including particulate matter and lead; (b) inadequate water supply, poor
sanitation and hygiene; and (c) indoor air pollution. The four
natural resource damage categories include: (a) agricultural
damage from soil salinity, water logging and soil erosion;
(b) rangeland degradation; (c) deforestation; and (d) natural
disasters.

The loss of life because of pollution that has shown the
strongest association with health endpoints is particulate
matter and other secondary particles with similar characteristics of less than 10 microns in diameter (PM10). The report
mentions that

> Research in the United States in the 1990s and most recently by Pope
> et al. (2002) provides strong evidence that it is particulates of less than
> 2.5 microns (PM2.5) that have the largest health effects. Other gas-
> eous pollutants (SO_2, NO_x, CO and ozone) are generally not thought
> to be as damaging as fine particulates. However, SO_2 and NO_x may
> have important health consequences because they can react with
> other substances in the atmosphere to form secondary particulates. In
> particular, the evidence implicates sulphates formed from SO_2, but is
> much less certain about nitrates, formed from NO_x. The focus of this
> report, therefore, is the health effects of all fine particulates (PM10 and
> PM2.5) since they are regarded as criteria pollutants and include com-
> ponents of other pollutants. They are an important cause of cardio-
> vascular and pulmonary disease and lung cancer in the population.

This requires data on who is exposed, the health impacts of that exposure and the value attached to those impacts. Given data limitations,
only estimate impacts for the urban populations in major cities with
TSP and PM10 monitoring data are made.[34]

Health damage estimates for PM10 were calculated based
on observations for the year 2008. The study included 96 cities
with monitoring stations and 223 cities with no monitoring
stations (254 million people in total). The population for the
cities with monitoring stations amounted to 186 million, or
about 16 per cent of the country's population. Interestingly,
the most polluted city in terms of PM1 was Meerut at 313,
Delhi ranked at 6 with a value of 214, Mumbai with a value
of 127 ranked much below Delhi, but above cities in Andhra
Pradesh. Vijayawada with 96, Ramagundam 87, Hyderabad 84
and Visakhapatnam at 81 appear to be not as polluted as Delhi.

Environmental damage means physical damages that
have their origin in the physical environment. Thus, damages
to health from air or water pollution are included as well as
damages from deforestation. The term cost means the opportunity cost to society. In summary, social costs are preferred
over financial costs because social costs capture the cost and
reduced welfare to society as a whole. All costs are estimated
as flow values (annual losses).

The report has considered six categories of damages and
estimated the costs involved. Table 10.1 provides the annual
cost of environmental damages using different assumptions.
We have taken the mid-point estimate and noted that it stands
at ₹3,751 billion per annum. In fact, the higher side of the estimate at ₹5,821 billion is more than 10 per cent of GDP and
seems to be closer to the reality and is equal to the total revenue of the union government.

The report devotes some pages for the estimation of health-
related damages. They are based on the data sets made
available by government agencies and are based on certain
assumptions. For instance, the value of statistical life (VSL) in
India as the average VSL from the available studies comes out
at about $375,000 (₹17.8 million) and this figure has been used

Table 10.1

Annual Cost of Environmental Damage—Low, High Estimates
₹ *Billion per Year*

Environmental Categories % of Total Cost of Environmental Damage	Low	Mid-point	High	Mid-point Estimate
1. Outdoor pollution	170	1,100	2,080	29%
2. Outdoor air pollution	305	870	1,425	23%
3. Crop lands degradation	480	703	910	19%
4. Water supply, sanitation and hygiene	475	540	610	14%
5. Pastures degradation	210	405	600	11%
6. Forest degradation	70	133	196	4%
Total annual cost	170	3,751	5,821	1%
Total as % of GDP 2009	2.60%	5.7%	8.8%	—

Source: The World Bank, 2013.

in the report. It can be seen that the ratio of VSL/HCA is about 16 times for children and 44 times for adults. In this report, the experts have said,

> [W]e used the average of the VSL and HCA values for adults (i.e. $192,000 or ₹9.1 million). For children we do not use the VSL value at all as none of the VSL studies are for children. Hence we take only the HCA value of $24,168 or ₹1.148 million. This conservative approach is also consistent with other costs of degradation studies that have been conducted.

The human capital approach takes in to consideration the earnings foregone or loss of income which is taken at ₹150 for urban and ₹60–75 for rural areas per day, which is lower in value and not based on facts. The baseline survey of the World Bank in its report noted above relied heavily on NFHS, NSS and other secondary sources have further reduced the values that are again adjusted for the expected value at 2010. In other words, the cost estimates of life of an Indian valued at around ₹15 million per person appear to be low and show that the advanced countries are capable of bartering their carbon consumption needs with the lives of Indians.

The IPCC *Fifth Assessment Report on Climatic Change, 2013* is complimentary to the World Bank report on India.[35] It is reported that each of the last three decades has been successively warmer on the Earth's surface than any preceding decade since 1850. The atmospheric concentrations of carbon dioxide, methane and nitrous oxide have increased to levels unprecedented in at least the last 800,000 years.

> Carbon dioxide concentrations have increased by 40 percent since pre-industrial times, primarily from fossil fuel emissions and secondarily from net land use change emissions. The ocean has absorbed about 30 percent of the emitted anthropogenic carbon dioxide, causing ocean acidification. The mean rates of increase in atmospheric concentrations over the past century are, with very high confidence, unprecedented in the last 22,000 years.[36]

The contents in both the reports are extremely useful in understanding the environmental damages and the benefits of its possible mitigation. The World Bank study shows that policy interventions such as environmental taxes could potentially be used to yield positive net environmental benefits with minimal economic costs for India. The general equilibrium model of economics shows that addressing 'public bads' via selected policy instruments need not translate into large losses in GDP growth. The environmental cost model developed in this study can, thus, be used to evaluate the benefits of similar pollution-control policies and assist in designing and selecting appropriate targeted intervention policies (such as a SO_2 tax, a CO_2 tax or emission trading schemes). Once the impact on ambient air quality of a policy to reduce particulate emissions is estimated, the tools used to calculate the health damages associated with particulate emissions can also be used to compute the welfare impacts of reducing them. The monetised value of the health benefits associated with each measure can be calculated, using the techniques developed in this study, and compared with the costs.

There are, however, several limitations in the World Bank study as indicated by the authors at the end of the report. In addition to the constraints recognised by the report, we have noticed that they have not included the costs of loss or damage to the ecosystems such as grasslands, wetlands, mangroves and coral reefs. In fact, the report has stated the value of service of this category of natural resources at ₹1.086 trillion per year. However, this excludes the damages due to the construction of major dams that affect the scarce resources in addition to the human costs. The damages done to society due to disasters, mainly as a result of the depletion or non-judicious use of natural resources mentioned previously, are not taken in to consideration either. The economists here considered resources that are tangible or scarce or that have pecuniary value for reckoning which seems to be containing a serious lag in the model. The social costs of environmental damages done to categories of disadvantaged people such as loss of livelihoods of Adivasis, the poor, fisherfolk and others that affect the identity of the group are not considered. Social costs of uprooting of communities in ecosystems such as marshlands being treated as *banjar* (fallow land) and assigned to industries or fisherfolk who are displaced due to the extinction of species with excess mechanisation, loss of indigenous knowledge systems and culture owing to displacement of communities, etc. have also not been considered here.

The growth models tested by the report and the issues raised by them are based on technology like Green Growth and models that take into consideration coal tax or green tax, etc. It is here that we get back to the earlier part where we have explained the Jevons paradox. In this context we may refer to a perceptible book, *The Jevons Paradox and the Myth of Resource Efficiency*,[37] where the authors of the book have made a very interesting observation:

Technological energy-efficient improvements such as hybrid cars may represent a crucial component of a different trajectory of evolution of the metabolism of households in developed countries. However, the adoption of hybrid cars per se will not solve the problem of the unsustainability of modern lifestyles if adopted by a world population of 9 billion people. If the energy-environment situation is to improve, consumers will need to change their behaviour patterns by including concern for the environment among the priorities determining their choices.[38]

We do feel that metabolism an attribute of living organisms seems to have been slowly influencing the technology or gadgets used by human beings as noted above by the scholars, and are slowly adversely affecting all humans. The authors have added that humans have to accept losing something in order to be able to retain something else. It sounds like the Buddhist precept that we should all be vigilant and parsimonious in the matters of the environment of a finite world with infinite greed. The neoliberal models of growth, that consider materialistic advancement measured in terms of GDP without estimating the environmental costs, are detrimental to the sustenance of not only the environment but even the survival of future generations. The GDP measured in physical terms by the above World Bank experts in terms of the use or investment of the future environment is unethical. In fact, the GDP itself would be negative if the cost of environment (as in India at 10 per cent) is taken in to consideration for reckoning. Social economics considers life sustainability and parsimonious use of natural resources as an important aspect of its deliberations which would enrich the future humankind, unlike the mainstream economics that considers only the present.

LIVING WITH NATURE

Scientists and environmental activists, including the former vice-president of the USA, Al Gore,[39] have popularised the fact that there is biodiversity only in the southern hemisphere of the globe. The northern hemisphere where all advanced countries are situated do not have the kind of resources that we, in the Third World countries of the south, have. Yet, how all the northern countries have been able to achieve economic development in just 200 years is a mystery that economists might one day address instead of singing paeans about the market. One of the important assets of the Third World is the unexplored and hidden data in the traditions of indigenous knowledge systems. We can draw from them as we progress on the road to self-sustained development. Some of the tricks that the advanced countries have been trying to play on us are through the route of GATS that protects intellectual property. They wanted to have patents on all our traditional knowledge and knowledge products such as ayurveda, siddha, herbs, grains, etc. with the connivance of some prejudiced individuals. But, they seem not to have succeeded as India has been heroically fighting against such conspiracies in international forums with the support of documentation. Sometimes government agencies also do good things, as seen in terms of the documentation of our indigenous knowledge systems project of the department of science and technology of the Government of India.

Though such efforts are limited to the mainstream and Sanskrit-based knowledge as of now, it is hoped that they would be extended to the real and historically sustained systems of the Adivasis and other indigenous populations of the country in future. Now everyone looks at our indigenous and traditionally practised unwritten structures of knowledge for insights so that they can be commoditised and marketed for economic returns. There are examples like the Patanjali products of Baba Ramdev aggressively marketed now. It is said that animals are genetically endowed to use their limbs as tools while human beings develop tools with their limbs and thinking skills. It is the accumulation of experiences of human beings as thinking animals that helped mankind develop civilisations as well as transform it at different points of time. Gordon Childe has said that "it is a practical application of remembered, compared and collected experiences of the same kind as are systematised and summarised in scientific formulae, descriptions and prescriptions"[40] as science. The application of some of the scientific principles to solve practical human problems leads to development of technology. Thus, science and technology have never remained constant. As society has progressed from one stage to another, science and technology have also undergone changes. Science has proved once again that it can unravel the secrets of nature and in that process can educate the exploiters not to harm nature since its recreation is not only expensive but impossible in the immediate future.

In fact, it has been proven beyond doubt that those people who constantly interact with nature and in that process use their physical labour to make a comfortable living alone are capable of developing technology. We can find in our society several groups of people who have remained as Adivasis, artisans, service castes, etc., but have abundant knowledge that could be codified, evaluated, systematised and finally be provided the status of modern science and technology. In fact, the native Indian philosophical school, Sankhya, is full of such concepts. Tantra, the original Indian school of thought, is considered as the epistemology of the so-called lower castes like the Dalits and OBCs while some of their ancestors/kinsfolks still live in jungles, living with nature.[41] It is the Adivasis, the fisherfolk, artisans and other indigenous people who contribute to the world of medicine, including ayurveda, even in the 21st century, amounting to billions of dollars' worth of wealth. The technology used by indigenous people is simple and relevant to the social conditions and circumstances in which they live. This peoples' oriented technology, as against the gigantic and sophisticated expertise that is generally addressed to the market and controlled by MNCs, is marginalised. Unfortunately, however, nothing that does not address the corporate market today survives.

Some of the growth and development models built on the assumptions of a European society with given institutional mechanisms do help us to come out with some results. Nevertheless, they end up in creating more divisions and discriminations that complicate contemporary society as seen today both in our legislative debates and in street fights. This muddle seems to have emerged due to lack of vigour and vision in the approach to address a socio-economic system that is India. The efforts made by scholars like Schumacher[42] in interpreting Buddhist values for socio-economic development seem to be more relevant now when the USA, Europe and other capitalist economies are in deep crisis.

Social economics that is deep in its approach as a human science with an ethical dimension of development is appropriate to understand and find solutions to our unique problems. The approach is different from the social choice or public choice theorists who claim that they are also concerned about the society, but look at issues from the prism of the market and the self-interest of individuals. However, social economics goes beyond the market and individuals to bring out the human essence and purpose in all our actions. It recognises each individual as a part of the social whole with the objective of obtaining a common good for everyone without connecting to their social or economic or some other consideration and with an eye on the future needs of humanity. The paradigm of human rights and dignity as a fundamental value in the 21st century is recognised as an essential condition for social economics and would go a long way in the social science discourse in India. It is heartening to note that the Paris Agreement in December 2015 replacing the Millennium Development Goals (MDGs) with Sustainable Development Goals (SDGs) is a great leap forward and a shot in the arm for social economics. Now the member nations have agreed to achieve 17 SDGs with 175 targets by 2030.

CONCLUSION

India as an independent nation has initiated policies for self-sufficiency in agriculture, infrastructure development for industrialisation and human capital formation to manage the giant nation from 1950. The Planning Commission was established to plan and execute policies to realise the constitutional objectives of democracy, socialism, equality of opportunity and secular inclusion of different social and religious groups. Out of seven decades of independent planned development, half the time spent has been in achieving moderate progress in self-sufficiency and attractive infrastructure to motivate foreign investments. Though the rate of growth has been moderate, the tendency to generate concentration of wealth that widens inequalities needs to be discouraged and attempts made to further the unlimited craving to accumulate and expand and control by select few need to be prevented. There were few tensions during the period. But, liberalisation and privatisation were introduced as solutions to hasten growth so as to reduce inequities at a time when social tensions had reached a crucial stage in the 1990s.

Contemporary society is witnessing one of the most uncivilised and intolerant phases in modern India where writers and intellectuals are being killed, and Dalits and non-Hindus are being lynched for their beliefs and habits. It is easy to attribute such a drift to xenophobia or Hindutva or with some other notion. But the same forces that are said to be guilty now were present in the past also. Why is it that they have taken an upper hand now? Have liberalisation and globalisation resolved our social contradictions? The answer seems to be negative. The way in which economic policies are pursued, natural resources exploited and the human element disregarded with the single objective of creating wealth and accumulation appears to be one of the reasons for the present disorder and social tensions. This is against the ethos of India and the democratic spirit of the country. Some intelligent experts try to divert the attention of people as if the social and religious intolerance is autonomous and nothing to do with the economic contradictions. In fact, they are all interrelated if one approaches the issues for understanding through either a Marxist or an indigenous approach used by some of our leaders, noted in the previous chapter. It is striking that despite several attempts of reform and restructuring of our society through the so-called social engineering, Indian society through the reforms struck at the original Four Varna quagmire.

We had indigenous thinkers in the modern period from the time of Dadabhai Naoroji, Ranade, Gokhle, Gandhi and Nehru on the one hand and M. N. Roy, Ambedkar, Lohia and the Left critiques on the other, who provided insights into our development as a social praxis. The free traders and the Marxist critiques cited lack of freedom and opportunity to experiment with innovations and to gratify self-interest as factors for the collapse of socialism. At the same time, some European dissenters in the form of schools of thought such as the Frankfurt school, post-modernism, etc. also looked at the Soviet Union critically and found that there was nothing wrong in the Marxist theory per se. Scholars such as Eric Fromm in his *Sane Society*[43] and *Marx's Concept of Man*[44] have pointed out the limitations both in socialist economies and more in the capitalist societies. Fromm and others proposed a theory called 'socialist humanism,' like M. N. Roy's 'new humanism.' Though there are some differences between the two, social economists can gain greater insights into the essentiality of human content in development by considering some of their proposals. Social democracy, as a strategy or maybe to avoid communism in Europe, seems to have not been able to solve several problems there but avoided only social tensions. Can the experiments of Europe and other countries in the 21st century with social democracy or democratic socialism be considered here as a 'transition' with Indian characters to address our immediate inequities, particularly caste, religion, colour, gender and age?

The emergence of Barack Obama in the USA and Alexis Tsipras in Greece presents a contrasting picture being similar in economic structure; they are, however, as Fromm warned (in the 1960s), subjected to "the laws of market, like gods will, are beyond the reach of your will and influence."[45] Human civilisation has accomplished incredible advances during the last two hundred years and soon might wipe out want and destitution from the earth using technology. But the human needs of man as, "relatedness, transference, rootedness, the need for a sense of identity and the need for a frame of orientation and devotion" are attainable only through a humanistic approach to development. Social economics as a growing branch of social science knowledge craves for the withering away of cruelty to fellow humans and considers discrimination and humiliation as vices with usual appeal to dignity and respect in the paradigm of development in India.

NOTES AND REFERENCES

1. A. C. Pigou, *Economics of Welfare* (London: MacMillan, 1932), 11.
2. Amartya Sen, *The Idea of Justice* (New Delhi: Oxford University Press, 2010). Amartya Sen Nobel laureate in economics is known as an indigenous scholar with deep roots in Indian systems of thought.
3. Sen, *The Idea of Justice*.
4. John Rawls, *A Theory of Justice* (New Delhi: Oxford University Press, 1993).
5. Professional jealousy and moral plunge of some of his former colleagues have gone to such an extent that he has been subjected to nasty and deplorable comments in the media, reminding the fact that he was not from the privileged caste (as noted in his book *Identity*).
6. Romila Thapar, *Early India* (New Delhi: Penguin, 2005).
7. Vikas Mishra was an economist who worked on the Economics of Religion first time in India. Mishra, *Hinduism and Economic Growth* (New Delhi: Oxford University Press, 1962). Mishra trained Raj Krishna, Agricultural economist, Member, Planning Commission, who has coined the popular term "Hindu rate of growth".
8. Max Weber, *Protestant Ethic and the Spirit of Capitalism* (London: Routledge, 1992).
9. Lakshmi Narasu, *Essence of Buddhism* (Madras: Asian Educational Services, 2005).
10. Narasu, *Essence of Buddhism*.
11. Hayami Yujiro and Yoshisha Godo, *Development Economics* (New Delhi: Oxford University Press, 2005).
12. D. Little "Ethical Analysis and Wealth in Theravada Buddhism: A Response to Frank Reynolds," in *Ethics, Wealth and Salvation: A Study*, ed. Russell F. Sizemore and Donald K. Swearer (Columbia, SC: University of South Carolina Press, 1990).
13. F. L. Pryor, "A Buddhist Economic System in Practice," *American Journal of Economics and Sociology*, Vol. 50, No. 1 (1991, January).
14. Narasu, *Essence of Buddhism*.
15. Arther Poropat and John Kellet, "Buddhism and TQM: An Alternative Explanation of Japan's Adoption of Total Quality Management," Grifith Resource online, www98.griffith.edu.au (accessed 15 August 2012).

16. A. K. Biswas, "Economic Diversification and Sustainable Development in Bhutan: The Role of Foreign Aid and International Trade" (unpublished PhD dissertation, University of North Bengal, Darjeeling 2011). GNH indicators are (a) psychological well-being, (b) health of population, (c) education, (d) time use and balance, (e) Community vitality, (f) cultural diversity, (g) geological diversity, (h) living standard and (i) good governance.
17. Thapar, *Early India*.
18. B. Hindess and P. Hrist, *Pre-capitalist Modes of Production* (London: Routledge and Kegan Paul, London, 1975); *The Asiatic Mode of Production: Science and Politics*, ed. Anne M. Bailey and Joseph R. Llobera (London: Routledge and Kegan Paul, London, 1981).
19. Narasu, *Essence of Buddhism*.
20. Ibid.
21. Dharmakirti was one of the greatest 6th–7th century Buddhist scholars of India.
22. Asanga and Vasubandhu were the Buddhist Philosophers of Yogacara school from Gandhara.
23. CII, *Handbook of Corporate Social Responsibility in India* (New Delhi: PwC, 2013).
24. Centre for Good Governance, *A Comprehensive Guide for Social Impact Assessment* (UNO, 2006).
25. M. K. Gandhi, "Enjoy Wealth by Renouncing It," *Harijan*, 1 February 1942, 20.
26. *Indian Express*, "New Govt. Old Hurdles-Checking Illegal Mining," 16 June 2015. It reported about 1374 illegal mining cases involving penalty of 5.5 lakh crores.
27. M. K. Gandhi, *Trusteeship* (Ahmedabad: Navajeevan Mudranalaya, no date).
28. *Indian Express*, "Projects Worth Rs 10 Lakh Crore Cleared: Environment Minister Prakash Javadekar," 17 May 2016.
29. Dell, B. F. Jones and B. A. Olken, "Temperature Shocks and Economic Growth: Evidence From the Last Half Century," *American Economic Journal: Macro Economics*, Vol. 4, No. 3 (2012): 66–95.
30. Ibid.
31. W. S. Jevons, *The Coal Question: An Enquiry Concerning the Progress of the Probable Exchange of our Coal to Mines* (London: Macmillan, 1866).
32. K. E. Boulding, "Foreword," in T. R. Malthus, *Population: the First Essay* (Ann Arbor, MI: University of Michigan Press, 1959), v–xii.
33. World Bank, *India: Diagnostic Assessment of Select Environmental Challenges*, Vols. I, II and III South Asia Unit (New Delhi: World Bank, 2013).
34. Ibid.
35. World Bank, *India: Diagnostic Assessment of Select Environmental Challenges*. World Bank Document, 2013.

36. Ibid.
37. John M. Polimeni, Kazo Mayumi and others, *The Jevons Paradox and the Myth of Resource Efficiency Improvements* (London: Earth Scan Publications, Routledge, 2007).
38. Ibid.
39. Al Gore, *The Earth in the Balance* (Boston: Houghton Mifflin Co, 1992).
40. Gordon Childe, *What Happened in History* (London: Penguin Books, 1952), 9.
41. K. S. Chalam, "Tantra: The Origin of Dalit Epistemology," *South India Journal of Social Sciences*, Vol. 1, No. 1 (2002, June).
42. E. F. Schumacher, *Small Is Beautiful* (London: Harper and Row, 1973).
43. Eric Fromm, *The Sane Society* (London: Routledge, 2002).
44. Eric Fromm, *Marx's Concept of Man* (New York: Frederick Unger Publishing, 1961).
45. Ibid., p. 134.

Appendix

Table A1
Assets of Top Dvija Business Groups (Bania and Brahmin) (₹ in Crores)

| Rank | Rank 1990# | Group/Family | Assets (Rs. Crores) | | | | | Capital assets |
| | | | 1989–90# | 1991–92 | 2005–06 | 2009–10 Est. | | 2014[1] |
							Assets	
1	3	Reliance (Ambani)	3,241	9,167	1,63,989	2,34,063		3,26,884
2	2	Tata	6,851	15,564	1,01,219	1,45,502		4,63,202
3	1	Birla	7,235	13,917	67,544	2,40,000*		250,000
4	26	Essar (Ruia)	437	1,898	44,949	2,55,158		$35 bn
5		Om Prakash Jindal		635	26,886	1,08,568		$10 bn
6	28	Hinduja (Ashok Leyland)	422	1,277	23,197	2,00,000*		$35 bn
7		Bharti Telcom		29	21,808	82,017		1,47,663
8		Sterlite Industries		2,480	19,457	17,869		78,403
9	7	Bajaj	1,228	1,908	16,994	54,951		61,740
10	22	Goenka	570	3,583	16,151	3,00,000*		–

11		Ispat (Mittals)		1,092	15,142	10,578	$42 bn
12	21	Mahindra & Mahindra	620	1,223	14,947	55,433	74,683
13	11	TVS Iyengar	929	1,582	14,176	40,000	1,57,968
14	SLU	Jaiprakash	484	1,164	12,845	22,443	38,808
15		Videocon		873	11,373	24,582	36,929
16		Wipro		103	9,595	30,567	1,34,111
17		Infosys Technologies Ltd.		8	9,114	36,028	1,91,877
18	4	Singhania	1,938	2,952	8,356	–	–
19	5	Thaper	1,782	2,665	8,010	–	–
20		Vedanta				1,10,029*	1,33,577
21		Adari posts					65,000

Source: For 1989–90; for the rest, CMIE, Prowess Database.
Notes: * Market Capitalisation.
1. Market cap given by *Business Today* and annual reports of companies.

Table A2
Growing Importance of Non-government Companies

End March	No. of Companies			Paid-up Capital (Rs. in Cr.)			Share of Non-Govt. Cos. in PUC
	Govt.	Non-Govt.	Total	Govt.	Non-Govt.	Total	
1989–90	1,160	2,00,968	2,02,128	47,451	17,193	64,643	26.60
1994–95	1,199	3,52,093	3,53,292	73,300	62,719	1,36,019	46.11
1999–00	1,245	5,41,189	5,42,434	1,02,850	2,15,960	3,18,810	67.74
2004–05	1,328	6,78,321	6,79,649	1,55,814	4,98,208	6,54,022	76.18
2009–10	1,642	8,34,218	8,35,860	2,52,040	7,74,563	10,26,603	75.45

Source: Annual Report on the Working & Administration of the Companies Act, 1956, March 31, 2010, Ministry of Corporate Affairs, Government of India.

Glossary

anatma	non-self or no soul as *anatta* in Buddhism
anitya	impermanent
aramas	Buddhist monastery
ati-shudra	scheduled castes or Dalits coined by Mahatma Phuley
babas	godmen
bahujan	numerous people
banias	business community
banjar	fallow land
bata	way or path
benami	anonymous, untitled
bhadralok	social class of well-educated Bengalis
bhikkhus	Buddhist monks
bodhi	awakening
bondito kailasam	everlasting physical disappearance or entering Shivas abode with body
Char Dham	the four abodes
darshan	auspicious sight
devabhumi	the land of gods
dharmashalas	Buddhist sanctuary
dharmashastras	sacred law books
dhobhi ghat	place where traditional washer men wash clothes
dukkha	Buddhist concept of suffering or pain
dvija	the twice born group in Hinduism
gana-sanghas	republic or oligarchy in early state formation

gotra	the descent from ancient sages
Gunakarma	virtuous actions of Hindus
jana	population
jati	nation or caste
jeevanmukti	realized soul
khichdi	food made from rice and lentils
korralu	a typical south Indian millet of Srikakulam district
kshatriyas	warrior class of Hindu Varna system
kuladharma	caste rule
Mahaghatbandhan	mega coalition of lower castes
maharatnas	public sector units classified on the basis of highest net worth
mathadipathis	heads of a Hindu spiritual order
matsyanyaya	the process of the big fish eating the small fish
naga	an ancient race of India
niti	ethics
nyaya	system of rules
paharias	the hill people
panchama	the fifth order in Hindu social structure
panchashila	five Buddhist principles of peaceful existence
paraganas	group of villages or subdivision
paticca samuppada	Buddhist theory of dependent origination
pattas	title deed for land
porambogs	fallow land
prabhandas	Telugu classical poetry of medieval period
prasad	substance of food in religious offerings
prasthas	social division in Iran or a level expanse in Sanskrit
puranic	ancient/old
rasa	aesthetic impression of a work of art
samanartha	having the same meaning
samata	equality
sampradaya	tradition

samtvam	equanimity
sangha	Buddhist monastic order
sangham	Buddhist association or assembly
sapta kranti	seven point revolution
sarvajan	universal or every one
satyagraha	non-violent political resistance
shudras	the fourth estate in Hindu Varna order
sulka	fees or price
swami	honorific title given in Hindu religion to a senior
Swayambhu	that which is created by its own accord
tantra	literal meaning is expand or stretch is an ancient native Indian ritual practice
thatha	grandapa
upma	thick south Indian porridge
uraikuts	castes in Sri Lanka
vaishyas	business caste
Vasudhaika Kutumbakam	the world is one family
yagna	sacrifice or offering as a ritual
yatra	journey

Bibliography

Adorno, Theodore, and Max Horkheimer. *Dialectic of Enlightenment.* Translated by John Cumming. New York: Continnum, 1982.

Althusser, Louis. *For Marx.* London: Allen Lane, 1969.

Ambedkar, B. R. *Dr. Babasaheb Ambedkar Writings and Speeches.* Vols. 1–17. New Delhi: Dr Ambedkar Foundation, Government of India, 2014.

Anderson, E. *Value and Ethics in Economics.* MA, Cambridge: Harvard University Press, 1993.

Arrighi, Giovanni. *The Long Twentieth Century: Money, Power and the Origins of Our Times.* London: Verso, 1994.

Arrow, K. *Social Choice and Individual Values.* New Haven: Yale University Press, 1951.

Bagchi, A. K. *The Political Economy of Underdevelopment.* Cambridge: Cambridge University Press, 1982.

Bailey, Anne M., and Joseph R. Llobera. *The Asiatic Mode of Production: Science and Politics.* London: Routledge and Kegan Paul, 1981.

Bailey, F. G. *Caste and the Economic Frontier: A Village in Highland Orissa.* Bombay: Oxford University Press, 1958.

Bandopadhyaya, Sekhar. "Transfer of Power and the Crisis of Dalit Politics in India 195–47." *Modern Asian Studies* 34, no. 4 (2000): 893–942.

Bardhan, P. "Green Revolution and Agricultural Labour," *Economic and Political Weekly* , Vol. 5, Nos. 29–31 (1970): 1239–46.

Baxi, Upendra. *The Future of Human Rights.* New Delhi: Oxford University Press, 2010.

Berlin, I. *Four Essays on Liberty.* Oxford: Oxford University Press, 1969.

Bhaduri, A. *The Economic Structure of Backward Agriculture.* Delhi: Macmillan, 1984.

Bhagwati, J. "The Case for Free Trade," *Scientific American* 269, (November, 1993): 42–49.

Bhikhu, Parekh. *Rethinking Multiculturalism-Cultural Diversity and Political Theory.* Harvard: Harvard University Press, 2002.

Breman, J. *Patronage and Exploitation: Changing Agrarian Relations in South Gujarat India*. Berkley: University of California Press, 1974.

Chalam, K. S. "Caste and Economic Power," *Vikalp*. Vol. VIII. (2000).

——. *Caste-based Reservations and Human Development in India*. New Delhi: SAGE Publications, 2007.

——. *Economic Reforms and Social Exclusion*. New Delhi: SAGE Publications, 2011.

——. *Education and Weaker Sections*. New Delhi: Inter-India, 1988.

——. "Inequity in the Development of Human Capital in India: Implications for a Social Policy," *South India Journal of Social Sciences*. Vol VIII, no. I (June, 2010): 291–313.

——. *Readings in Political Economy*. Hyderabad: Orient Longman, 1999.

——. "Social Science Research in India: The Social Context," *Economic and Political Weekly*. (September 28, 2002).

——. "Union Budget and Decline in Educational Effort'. *Economic and Political Weekly*. (April, 1994 Special).

Chitnis, Suma. 'Feminism: Indian Ethos and Indian Convictions." In *Feminism in India*, edited by M. Chaudhuri. New Delhi: Unlimited Women, 2004, pp. 52–68.

Das, A. *Foundations of Gandhian Economics*. New York: St. Martin's Press, 1979.

Das, Suranjan. *Communal Riots in Bengal, 1905–47*. New Delhi: Oxford University Press, 1991.

Delige, R. *The Untouchables of India*. New York: Berg, 1999.

Deniger, Wendy. *On Hinduism*. New Delhi: Aleph Book Company, 2013.

Desai, A. R. *Social Background of Indian Nationalism*. Bombay: Oxford University Press, 1947.

Dreze, Jean, and Amartya Sen. *India: Development and Participation*. New Delhi: Oxford University Press, 2002.

Foucault, Michael. *Archaeology of Knowledge*. London: Routledge, 1972.

Frankel, F., and M. S. A. Rao eds. *Dominance and State Power in Modern India: Decline of a Social Order* (in two volumes). New Delhi: Oxford University Press, 1990.

Friedman, Milton. *Capitalism and Freedom*. London: The University of Chicago Press, 1962.

Gandhi, M. *An Autobiography*. Ahmedabad: Navjivan Publishing House, 1927.

Gide, C., and Rist, C. *History of Economic Doctrines*. London: George G Harap and Co, 1948.

Gilder, George. *Wealth and Poverty*. New York: Basic Books, 1981.

Gupta, Dipankar. *Rivalry and Brotherhood: Politics in the Life of Farmers in Northern India*. New Delhi: Oxford University Press, 1997.

——, ed. *Caste in Question: Hierarchy or Identity*. New Delhi: SAGE Publications, 2004.

Habermas, Jurgen. *Between Facts and Norms: Contributions towards a Discourse Theory of Ethics*. Translated by William Rehg. Cambridge, MA: The MIT Press, 1996.

Hindess, B., and Hirst, P. *Pre-capitalist Modes of Production*. London: Routledge and Kegan Paul, 1975.

Hobson J. A, *The Economics of Unemployment*. London: George Allen and Unwin, 1922.

——. *Imperialism: A Study* (1901). Ann Arbor: University of Michigan Press, 1965.

Kuhn, T. S. *The Structure of Scientific Revolutions*. Chicago: Chicago University Press, 1962.

Lutz, Mark A. *Economics for the Common Good: Two Centuries of Social Economic Thought in the Humanistic Tradition*. London: Routledge, 1999.

——. *Social Economics: Retrospect and Prospect*. Boston MA: Kluwer Academic Publishers, 1990.

Marshall, Alfred. *Principles of Economics*. London: MacMillan and Co, 1920.

Marx, Karl. *The Grundrisse*. Mosco: Harper, 1971 and *Capital* (originally 1867–1894). Moscow: Progress Publishers, 1982.

Myrdal, G. Asian Drama: An Enquiry into Poverty of Nations. Harmondsworth: Penguin Books, 1963.

——. *The Political Element in the Development of Economic Theory*. London: Routledge and Kegan Paul, 1953.

Nathan, D. "The Future of Indigenous Peoples." Seminar 537, 2004, pp. 33–37.

Nehru, Jawaharlal. *The Discovery of India* (1992 reprint). New Delhi: Oxford University Press, 1946.

Nozick, R. *Anarchy, State and Utopia*. New York: Basic Books, 1974.

Piketty Tomas, *Capital in the Twenty-First Century*. Cambridge, Massauchusetts, London: The Belknap Press of Harvard University Press, 2014.

Ramasamy, E. V. R. (Periyar). *Collected Works of Periyar EVR*. Edited by K. Veeramani. Chennai: The Periayar Self-respect Propaganda Institution, 2005.

Rawls, John. *A Theory of Justice*. New Delhi: Oxford University Press, 1991.

Roy, M. N. *M.N. Roys' Memoirs*. New Delhi: Ajanta Publications, 1984.

——. *Selected Works of M N Roy*. Edited by Shibnarayan Ray. Vol 1–4. New Delhi: Oxford University Press, 1987.

Rudra, A. *Accumulation: The 'Mode of Production Debate in India'*. New Delhi: Oxford University Press, 1990.

——. "Class Relations in Indian Agriculture." In *Agrarian Relations and Mode of Production*, edited by U. Patnaik. New Delhi: Oxford University Press, 1990.

Samuelson, P. *Economics*. New York: McGraw Hill, 1990.

Schmookler, Andrew Bard. *The Illusion of Choice: How the Market Economy Shapes Our Destiny*. Albany: SUNY Press, 1994.

Schumacher, E. F. *Small is Beautiful*. New York: Harper and Row, 1973.

Schumpeter, J. *History of Economic Analysis*. New York: Oxford University Press, 1954.

Schumpeter, Joseph A. *Capitalism, Socialism, and Democracy*. New York: Harper & Brothers, 1942.

Sen, A. *Poverty and Famines: An Essay on Entitlement and Deprivation*. Oxford: Oxford University Press, 1981.

——. *The Idea of Justice*. New Delhi: Oxford University Press, 2011.

——. *The State, Industrialization and Class Formation in India*. London: Routledge & Kegan Paul, 1982.

Sismondi, J. C. L. *New Principles of Political Economy* (1827). Translated by R. Hyse. New Brunswick, NJ: Transaction Publishers, 1991.

——. *Political Economy and the Philosophy of Government* (1847). New York: Augustus M Kelley, 1966.

Solow, Robert M. *Growth Theory—An Exposition*. 2nd ed. New Delhi: Oxford United Press, 2000.

Stiglitz, J. *Whither Socialism?* Cambridge, MA: MIT Press, 1994.

Tawney, R. H. *The Acquisitive Society*. New York: Harcourt Brace Jevanovich, 1948 (1920).

Veblen, Thorstein. *The Theory of the Leisure Class*. New York: The MacMillan Company, 1912.

Wittfogel, K. A. *Oriental Despotism: A Comparative Study of Total Power*. New Haven and London: Yale University Press, 1964.

Xaxa, V. "Protective Discrimination: Why Scheduled Tribes Lag Behind Scheduled Castes," *Economic and Political Weekly* (21 July 2001).

——. "Tribes in India." In *Companion to Sociology and Social Anthropology*, edited by Veena Das (Volume I). New Delhi: Oxford University Press, 2003, p. 3.

Index

About the Author

K. S. Chalam is a well-known political economist and educationist, and a former member of the Union Public Service Commission (UPSC), New Delhi. He has been the Vice Chancellor of the Dravidian University in Andhra Pradesh and had taught in the Department of Economics, Andhra University, between 1976 and 2005. He is known as the founder of the Academic Staff College Scheme in the country and was its first director.

Dr Chalam was on the Planning Board of the Madhya Pradesh government during 2002–04. He was the recipient of the UGC Young Social Scientist Award in Economics in 1984. Dr Chalam has authored *Caste-Based Reservations and Human Development in India* (2007, SAGE) and *Economic Reforms and Social Exclusion* (2011, SAGE), and edited *Governance in South Asia: State of the Civil Services* (2014, SAGE). He has travelled widely and has participated in and chaired sessions at various international conferences.

Dr Chalam was associated with National Human Rights Commission, New Delhi, as a special rapporteur and is now Chairman, Institute for Economic and Social Justice.